Anthony Holden was an award-winning journalist before becoming a bestselling writer. Best-known for his biographies of figures both living and historical, as well as critical studies of the monarchy, Holden has also written several books about poker. *Big Deal*, his account of a year as a professional poker player, has been hailed as a cult classic. A frequent broadcaster, who has written for a wide range of newspapers and periodicals on both sides of the Atlantic, Holden has also published poetry, criticism and polemical pamphlets advocating constitutional reform.

Praise for *Based on a True Story*

'A writer's life told by a born writer – beautifully observed, brilliantly written, wonderfully evocative. It's a story of our time – featuring some of the most remarkable characters of our time – funny, moving and telling; a roller-coaster of a good read, at times hilarious, at times heart-breaking. My book of the year' **Gyles Brandreth**

'Unputdownable . . . Everything Holden touches, whether Arsenal or Tchaikovsky, he lights up with a fresh eye and zest. I can't think of a more enjoyable memoir, which is also a portrait of a man of remarkable talents' **Melvyn Bragg**

'An absolute page turner . . . What is truly inspiring is the way Anthony has nourished so many amazing friendships with extraordinary people. This should be read by every young person of ambition to remind them that what lasts is the love of friends and family' **Tina Brown**

'What a life! I admired and enjoyed the colossal range of Holden's interests, his energy and delight in the daily business of writing, along with his gift for friendship. And what a rich cast his life embraces, each player so vividly evoked. His prose is deftly turned, with a clear smack of authority, intelligence and wit . . . His generosity and sweetness of spirit in the face of a sudden, profound affliction touched me deeply. This is a lovely, varied, fizzy life, in which so much was achieved, so much pleasure rendered' **Ian McEwan**

BASED ON A TRUE STORY

A Writer's Life

ANTHONY HOLDEN

**SIMON &
SCHUSTER**

London · New York · Sydney · Toronto · New Delhi

First published in Great Britain by Simon & Schuster UK Ltd, 2021
This edition published in Great Britain by Simon & Schuster UK Ltd, 2023

1 3 5 7 9 10 8 6 4 2

Simon & Schuster UK Ltd
1st Floor
222 Gray's Inn Road
London WC1X 8HB

www.simonandschuster.co.uk
www.simonandschuster.com.au
www.simonandschuster.co.in

Simon & Schuster Australia, Sydney
Simon & Schuster India, New Delhi

A CIP catalogue record for this book is available from the British Library

Paperback ISBN: 978-1-4711-5469-0
eBook ISBN: 978-1-4711-5470-6

Typeset in Perpetua by M Rules
Printed and Bound in the UK using 100% Renewable
Electricity at CPI Group (UK) Ltd

MIX
Paper | Supporting
responsible forestry
FSC
www.fsc.org   FSC® C171272

To my beloved grandchildren
and their parents, along with Uncle Joe

CONTENTS

'A writer is someone for whom writing
is harder than it is for other people'

— *Thomas Mann*

I

THE GRIM REAPER

I am walking towards a cliff-top in North Wales, carrying two hefty plastic bags, a parent in each.

It is the spring of 1985. A few weeks ago my father died, without much warning, in a Liverpool hospital. After his funeral in Lancashire, I brought my mother back to my home in London – where, just a week later, she too chose to depart. On the first night I left her alone, thrilled to be babysitting the children, I came home to find her dead on the hall floor. Of heart failure, according to the post-mortem; but really, of course, of a broken heart. Margaret Holden simply didn't want to live without her John. I found a diary saying just that when I was obliged, most uneasily, to go through her belongings in our spare room.

'Anthony', I couldn't help reading, 'has been wonderful this week'. I confess I needed that. Over the subsequent three decades and more, those words have proved a source of considerable consolation. After leaving home for university in my late teens, I had been a somewhat distant if broadly dutiful son, not the most attentive or even at times amenable, telephoning them regularly but visiting rarely, even after I presented them with grandson after grandson. At the last, at least, I had been of some service. I had done my filial stuff.

Now opened simultaneously, my parents' wills expressed the wish that their ashes be scattered from this headland in Trearddur Bay on Holy Island, North Wales, beyond the far north-west end of Anglesey, where they had done their courting. This was also where they sent me away from home, at the age of eight, to a prep school I thoroughly loathed. So I have ample reason to dislike this windswept coastal outpost, where once I scrambled miserably around these very rocks, feeling so abandoned by them. But I cannot let that distract me now.

My father had been to the self-same school, and thought it best to dispatch his sons there. My older brother, who was happy enough at the school to send his own sons after him, has walked on ahead, to find the precise spot from which our parents wished to be consigned to the Irish Sea. I follow slowly, struck by the unexpected weight of these carrier bags as surely as I am unnerved by their contents. Even worse, I am now no longer sure which bag contains which parent.

When we reach the designated point of departure, we are all too aware of those macabre tales about the wind blowing the deceased back over their loved ones. That does not at all seem a fit farewell to these two very decent souls. So we adjust accordingly, and duly consign their ashes to the water beneath. Touchingly, my wife throws some wild flowers after them onto the ocean, which helps us watch their residue float away out to sea. And so, finally, they are gone. I reflect ruefully that I am unlikely to visit them much here.

Born two days apart in 1918, my parents were both sixty-six when they died – the age I am now as I recall this singular day, queasily forcing myself to remember the details of that bleak cliff-top ritual.

When will it be my turn? The shadow of their eerily early double demise hangs heavily over me, as it has since I made it to sixty. Were I a superstitious man – which (blame my mother) I am – I would also be fretting about the fact that the year is 2013.

What would my parents have made of the fact that I have recently concluded my second term in office as the (elected) president of the International Federation of Poker? That this is the fortieth of a bizarre assortment of books I have written on an unlikely range of subjects? That I now have four wonderfully happy, healthy, rejuvenating grandchildren to show for my two failed marriages?

They'd have been as appalled by the poker and the bust-ups as bemused by the books and delighted about the grandchildren. After the sacrifices they made to provide me with a first-class education, they would be proud that I have managed all these years to make a living – just – by my pen. They would not share my agonies at some of the low-rent journalism I have had to churn out, some of the cheapskate books I would rather not have written, in order to keep my ever-expanding show on the road.

My brother Robin, long a partner in the Manchester office of a big-name firm of international accountants, was much more the kind of son they had in mind, marrying for life at twenty-one, rapidly producing two upstanding sons, a keen golfer and pillar of his local community. Me, I disappeared to university – the first Holden in recorded history to do so – and thence, perhaps inevitably, down south to the 'big smoke'.

At this particular moment, in the mid-1980s, they were pleased that I had at last descended from the loftier climes of print journalism to write for a proper paper, the one they took themselves. Now I had a weekly column in the magazine of the *Sunday Express*. That was something they could boast about to their friends.

To me, it was journalistic purdah, the launch of what I thought of as 'Holden: The Wilderness Years', after a promising first decade in Fleet Street had eventually fallen foul of the monster Murdoch. Yet to come, I wish I had then known, were the books in which I could take some pride, written for reasons other than mere lucre, and a late return to 'quality' journalism.

Also in the future lay the uniquely joyous but, in retrospect, sadly fleeting delights of children growing up, going to school and university, leaving home, embarking on adult life, and the arrival of the next generation. All this I feel privileged – and, in light of the early deaths of my parents, supremely lucky – to have lived to see.

But sixty-six . . . it's not enough, is it? Given a few more years, what would my parents have made of them? They had reached the point where they had few joys in life beyond their grandchildren, whom they adored but saw all too seldom. They still played some golf; otherwise, they took sparse exercise, did little but watch TV. My soft-hearted father, in what turned out to be the last year of his life, would call London from Lancashire each morning to discuss with his five-year-old grandson Ben the finer points of that day's episode of *Postman Pat*.

At the same age myself now, the age they both died, I'm certainly not ready to pop off just yet, even if I've already crammed in enough on all fronts to have enjoyed a very rich and fortunate life, more than enough for one very mortal soul – especially one who has rarely, if ever, put his physical health above the many self-indulgences high on his list of life's priorities.

Another of life's self-evident home truths is that the older you grow, the more funerals and memorial services you attend. As more and more of your friends and acquaintances depart – some reassuringly older than you, some scarily younger – you inevitably become ever more aware of your own mortality as you try to come to terms with the grievous termination of theirs.

John Donne's celebrated Meditation XVII ('No man is an island') renders the theme unbearably resonant:

> *Each man's death diminishes me,*
> *For I am involved in mankind.*
> *Therefore, send not to know*
> *For whom the bell tolls;*
> *It tolls for thee.*

The older I grow, the more I really do feel diminished by a death, any death, of friend or stranger, while becoming increasingly reconciled to the inevitability – and comparative imminence – of my own. And yes, like you, I know quite a few people who think that penultimate line was the work of Ernest Hemingway.

Something too much of this, I can hear you thinking. But before we bid the Grim Reaper a relieved farewell, at least for now, indulge me in one last thought about the brief span on earth that leads us all towards his inevitable summons.

For me, in seasoned retrospect, life is not a cohesive story, a sequential narrative, but a series of random accidents, otherwise known as luck, or chance, though some may choose to call it fate, determinism, kismet, what you will. I have a strong sense that, for reasons I know not, I have always been a lucky person. 'You always seem to fall on your feet,' many friends have observed to me, more than once, and not without envy, as I have appeared to bounce back cheerfully from some reversal, whether trivially passing or apparently terminal. I can offer no explanation for this happy, if mysterious and undeserved syndrome; but it seemed to have proved true of my entire life, both professional and (on the whole) personal, as I shambled through my late sixties.

I have always tried to treat my fellow beings with decency, in most cases respect, without ever believing in any presiding deity, let alone accepting that there has to be some religious rather than merely civilised manifesto behind this obvious approach to daily dealings. So to have lived even this long seems to me to disprove the existence of any supreme being, as I've never believed in one, or subscribed to any religion – no, for all the magnificent works of music, art and architecture produced in its name over the centuries.

Which always makes me think of those lines of Robert Browning cited by Graham Greene as the epigraph he would have chosen for all his novels:

> Our interest's on the dangerous edge of things.
> The honest thief, the tender murderer,
> The superstitious atheist . . .

As the poet implies, it is indeed the variety of life that has spiced mine. From journalism to biographies, poetry to poker, the royals to Shakespeare, the blues to opera, football to cricket, movies to Mozart, while single to married and back again (twice), I seem to have spent my life constantly on the move from one world to another, often muddling through several at once. I calculate that I have lived in twenty different homes, and held almost as many jobs, in my fifty-year career.

Like everyone, I've had my ups and downs – more ups, I'm pleased to say, though the few downs reached depths far lower than any heights achieved by the ups. I have in my time suffered clinical depression, but for a very specific reason; my patent blend of pessimism is that of a super-cautious optimist, taking consolation from my poker motto: 'Always expect the worst'.

In the end I have failed in the marital stakes, despite many happy years in wedlock, amounting to half my adult life. I hope I may say that I have succeeded as a father; that has certainly been one of my mainstays, to the point where grandchildren have arrived in profusion, so I am now trying to be an ace grandpa.

But I was not abused in childhood, and did not get married in *Hello!* magazine, nor have I made a cameo appearance on any TV soap opera. So there is nothing in these pages for those who base their choice of reading on the Sunday bestseller lists. For the rest of you, I hope, there will at least be echoes of your own lives in the vicissitudes of mine.

Or, in the canny words of Robert Louis Stevenson, 'Life is not always a matter of holding good cards, but sometimes of playing a poor hand well.'

2

SANDGROUNDER

Born in 1889, the fifth son of a St Albans boot-maker, Ivan Sharpe was a natural right-hander – and -footer. His craftsman father made the young Ivan a football, attached it with a three-yard cord to his left ankle, and sent him out into the back yard to kick it back and forth, again and again, for hours on end.

As a result, Ivan wound up with a left foot as strong as his right, making his debut for the England football team in 1910, at the age of twenty, on the left wing. He earned a dozen caps for England and won an FA championship title with Derby County before carrying off an Olympic gold medal as outside-left of the Great Britain team that triumphed at the Olympic Games in Stockholm in 1912 – the last time the country that invented football ever won its Olympic competition.

In his day, Ivan was even to be found on a collectible player card – which, in those days, came with a packet of cigarettes.

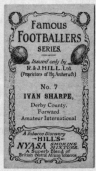

Soon after his Olympic triumph, the First World War cut short Ivan's playing career for Watford, Derby County and both Leeds teams (United and City) as well as England. He later became a prominent sports writer, editor of the *Athletic News* and its *Football Annual* before settling down as north-west football correspondent for the *Sunday Chronicle*, then the *Empire News* and finally the *Sunday Times*. In 1936 Ivan was chosen as the first reporter to provide a live radio commentary on the FA Cup Final.

In the early 1930s he was granted an interview with Mussolini – exclusively about football – and, according to one reliable source, also 'had an interview lined up with Adolf Hitler, but the Führer chickened out.' In 1947, the year I was born, he became the first chairman, then life president of the Football Writers' Association, which today awards an annual Fellowship in his name.

In the mid-1950s, when well into his sixties, Ivan Sharpe would do the same for me, another natural-born right-footer. He tied a football to my left ankle with a six-foot piece of string, and sent me out into the garden to kick it back and forth for hour upon hour while keeping benevolent watch through the window. To his delight, I would end up playing outside-left for my school – if not, alas, for England.

Ivan Sharpe was my maternal grandfather – and the closest, most supportive companion of my childhood and youth. His wife, Ada, had died in 1941, on my parents' first wedding anniversary, more than six years before I was born, so Ivan was living in the Lancashire seaside resort of Southport with my parents – or my mother, his only child, while my father was away at war – when I came along. And so he did for the rest of his life, which would not end until I was a twenty-year-old student.

My other grandfather had also died before I was born, and I barely knew his widow, who died when I was eight. Thus Ivan took on much more of a role in my life than the routine grandfather; only now, when I have become a grandfather myself, do I realise what a role model he has always been to me.

So it seems more than appropriate that my middle name is Ivan, as is that of my eldest son Sam. On 11 August 2012, the penultimate day of the London Olympic Games, Sam and I made the pilgrimage to the Olympic football final at Wembley Stadium in honour of the centenary of Grandpa Ivan's finest hour.

Ivan's England caps and Olympic gold medal hang on the wall of my London home, along with the wonderfully sepia photograph of England's triumphant 1912 Olympic team. These and his other trophies adorned the living-room wall in Southport throughout my childhood.

Ivan Sharpe, front row, far right

To me, it seemed perfectly natural that my grandfather lived with us, that he would tell me bedtime stories about Jehoshaphat the giant, later read me O. Henry and Edgar Wallace. As for my father, it did not cross my mind until many years later that he rarely spent a night alone at home with my mother – from whom, after the war, he never spent a night apart – for almost the first thirty years of his marriage.

As a result, I am sure, my parents always told my brother and me that they would never do *that* to us, never 'land on' us. But which one would be the first to go? How would the other cope? This was the vexed question that came up recurrently, especially after we had left home. At the time, of course, their deaths a week apart was a considerable trauma; but I now believe that to depart simultaneously, albeit prematurely, was exactly what they would both have wished.

But they have no grave for me to visit. Only once since that bleak day in 1985 have I been back to Trearddur Bay, when I took my three young sons there to join their cousins on a holiday with my brother and his family a few years later, between my two marriages. Naturally, I also took my boys to visit the headland sacred to their grandparents, of whom they have only sketchy memories. For a while my brother and I tried to place a bench carved with their names at the spot, still something of a Lovers' Lane for the young, romantic and wind-proof. But negotiations with Gwynedd Council dragged on to the point where we eventually abandoned the idea, opting instead for an engraved bench beside the 18th green at Royal Birkdale Golf Club, of which they and we were all active members throughout my childhood, youth and (for them) beyond.

At the turn of this century, I took great satisfaction in watching on television as spectators sat, even stood, on my parents during some major tournament at Birkdale. On my increasingly rare visits to Southport, I always make a point of going to sit down on their bench and tell them the latest family news.

My grandfather Ivan does, however, have a grave, also in Southport, which I wish I could visit more often. Presumably my other grandparents do, too, though I have no idea where. My paternal grandfather, Sir George Holden (Bart, of The Firs), died at the age of forty-seven, just before the Second World War. Like his father before him, he was Mayor of Leigh, Lancashire, where my father was born and the Holdens were such grandees there is even a road named after the family and a stained-glass window in the parish church bearing the family crest.

Had I been born a few generations earlier, I would no doubt have become a cotton trader, perhaps even a mill-owner, like my Lancashire forebears. My father was always destined for a job on the Manchester Cotton Exchange, which is why (he used to say) he did little or no work at school; when he returned from the war, however, it no longer existed. Its handsome Victorian building is now the city's Royal Exchange Theatre.

My parents married in Southport in 1940, while my father was on leave from the war. According to a local newspaper report of the occasion, the bride was 'a member of the Southport Dramatic Club, and the local Women's Unionist League Emergency Corps Luncheon Club. On many occasions she has appeared in cabaret and other shows on behalf of charity and has also acted in a play at the Southport Little Theatre.' All of which sounds fun, but it's the first I've heard of it.

When he returned home in 1945, my father started his working life at Automotors, the garage owned by Ivan's wealthy friend Harry Kirby, who was shrewdly made my godfather when I materialised on 22 May 1947, my brother's fifth birthday. Clement Attlee was the British prime minister, Harry Truman the thirty-third president of the United States; the movie of the moment was David Lean's *Great Expectations*; W. H. Auden had just published *The Age of Anxiety*, and Broadway was hosting the premieres of Arthur Miller's *All My Sons* and Eugene O'Neill's *A Moon for the Misbegotten*.

I was not, of course, the birthday present my brother sought or at all wanted. Robin immediately demanded that I be sent back to the litter of kittens at our father's garage, whence he apparently thought I had sprung. When his wish was not granted, he stuck a rusty screw up my infant nose while I lay in my pram, saying he had heard about cotton-wool 'screws' being deployed on the new baby's nose.

My mother had set her heart on calling me Angela, so my gender, too, was a disappointment. Sharing the same birthday five years apart eventually had me and my brother summoning the nerve to joke that presumably our parents 'did it' only once a year – which they took with remarkably good humour.

So my father was a Lancastrian, my mother a Yorkshirewoman, born in Leeds while her father played for the local football team. She had married well, or so she thought – into a titled family complete with crest and motto, fabled up north as Lancashire cotton millionaires.

Until the war. My father returned in 1945 to see The Firs, the mansion in Leigh in which he had grown up, being sold off; it became a maternity hospital for many years, and has since been converted into flats. His older brother George, who inherited the family baronetcy, had squandered whatever remained while his brothers went off to war. Relations were strained; at family occasions, usually weddings or funerals, we kept to the other end of the room; my brother and I were not encouraged to talk to this particular set of cousins. Sir George became a commercial traveller, reduced to living in a caravan on a farmyard in Yorkshire. Once a year, when the tabloid diaries had a slow day, we would come down to breakfast to find my mother fuming. 'John,' she'd be protesting, 'they've done it again! Look at the *Express*: "The baronet who lives in a pig sty"!'

It is a highly unlikely but amply documented fact that in 1838 the future Emperor Napoleon III, in exile as Prince Louis-Napoleon, chose to live in Southport – on its main artery; a long, straight boulevard, arcaded, canopied and tree-lined, called Lord Street. On his return to France as emperor in 1851, Napoleon summoned his chief planner Baron Haussmann and instructed him to design Paris along the lines of Southport – its parks as well as its elegant main boulevard, with which he remained much impressed. So, if Edinburgh is (for different reasons) sometimes called 'the Athens of the North', Southport should clearly be called 'the Paris of the North'. Or, in truth, Paris should be called 'the Southport of the South'.

Another unlikely resident was the American writer Nathaniel Hawthorne, who chose to live in Southport in 1856–57 (post-*The Scarlet Letter*) while serving as US consul to Liverpool; given his wife's fragile health, the sea air was 'refreshing and exhilarating'. Among his visitors was Herman Melville, with whom Hawthorne sat smoking a cigar in Southport's sand dunes discussing Hawthorne's conclusion that 'Southport is as stupid a place as ever I lived in . . . I cannot but bewail my ill-fortune to have been compelled to spend these many months on these barren sands, when almost every other square yard of England contains something that would have been historically or poetically interesting.'

Anyone born in Southport is called a 'Sandgrounder'. I have never understood why, let alone the word's derivation. But the label always gave me a proprietorial feeling about the place. In my childhood I was absurdly proud of it; and I suppose, in an expat sort of way, I still am. I am certainly a proud Lancastrian and indeed Northerner.

In Birkdale we lived up the sedate end of town, where life revolved around the golf club. Birthplace of the historian A. J. P. Taylor, the village boasted a tobacconist owned by the hangman

Albert Pierrepoint. The vicar of our local church, St James's, was Marcus Morris, founder of the *Eagle* comic, which gave the world Dan Dare, Harris Tweed and Luck of the Legion. It had improbably grown out of a parish magazine, for which Morris enlisted contributors from C. S. Lewis to Harold Macmillan; but his most important recruit, as things turned out, was the *Eagle*'s cartoonist Frank Hampson.

The *Eagle* was a bit upmarket for me; I was more of a *Beano* boy, devoted to Dennis the Menace and Roger the Dodger. Otherwise, as yet, conformity was very much the watchword. Cavalry-twilled and sports-jacketed, we youngsters would giggle at the adult etiquette but never dare breach it. To qualify as a fully-fledged grown-up, you had to be able to beat your parents at golf.

My closest childhood friend was Christopher Taylor, son of my godmother Pam, known all his life as 'Kiffy' – my infant fault, I fear – and the choice of bike rides confronting us each day was daunting. There were the sandhills, the beach, the swimming baths, the pier and the fairground to choose from, not to mention the seedy downtown coffee bar where there just might be some maiden prepared to hold hands. It rarely, as yet, came to much more than that. Southport girls – in those days, anyway – were very properly brought up.

There's many a Lancashire music-hall joke about the breadth of Southport beach, the invisibility of the shallow sea. To me, that was the glory of the place; you could get lost, be out of sight of anyone, even when a rare summer heatwave filled the foreshore with fetid cars and ice-cream vans, braces and knotted handkerchiefs. Southport's pier, with its model train carrying tourists to the café and amusement arcade at its end, was the second-longest in Britain (at 1,211 yards yielding only, and with no little northern angst, to the world's longest pier in Southend-on-Sea). Blackpool Tower was visible across the Ribble estuary, a cautionary reminder to nose-in-air locals of how low Southport might have sunk. To us youngsters, it was a symbol of our thrilling annual excursion to

Blackpool Illuminations, locally known as 'The Lights', and the quintessentially Lancashire comedian Al Read (or, later, Ken Dodd) at the Winter Gardens.

If, like me, you were sent away to boarding school at an early age, all such memories are inevitably filtered through the rose-tinted mind's eye of one perpetual holiday. In my mid-teens it was the early Beatles era, and there was an unforgettable week when the entire Brian Epstein stable packed us in every night at the Southport Odeon. En route to one of those shows, Kiffy and I even found ourselves sitting at the table next to the Beatles in a nearby diner – and, despite ourselves, staring at them to the point where John Lennon, with a friendly grin, placed his menu on the glass partition between the tables, to block our view.

We knew then, I guess, that we would later distort geography – not to mention socio-economic verities – by boasting that we'd grown up on Merseyside during those heady days. Like our contemporaries we even formed our own pop group; after a one-night stand at St James's parish hall, with Kiffy on bass being mobbed by toddlers, we broke up because we couldn't agree on a name. Neil was an expert lead guitarist, and Pete a solid drummer, while I handled rhythm guitar and vocals. At first we called ourselves The Scorpions, a pale imitation of The Beatles; but my colleagues rejected my suggestion of Us Lot – which seems to me, in retrospect, rather pleasingly ahead of its time.

On reflection, it was more because it was no use we middle class Southport kids trying to be anything other than what we really were. We still drank our gins and tonics, but some of us weren't playing golf so much; we were coming home from university rather than school, and our thoughts were already turning south.

For the first few years of my life, my father had been working at a wire-mesh factory in Manchester, whither he commuted each day by train from Southport. Even in single digits, I got the distinct impression that he was not very happy there; and I know he hated the commuting.

One of my grandfather's friends in Southport was a former foot-baller called James Fay, who had risen from the ranks of Oldham Athletic to become a co-founder, then secretary, then chairman of the Players' Union. He ran it from his thriving sports shop on Southport's Hoghton Street. In 1953, as I turned six, the shop mys-teriously passed into the ownership of my father, who soon added toys and managed it for the rest of his life. I now suspect Ivan must have bought it for him.

Ivan's involvement was certainly evident that summer, when Southport stood agog as the newly refurbished shop was formally opened by the two most famous English footballers alive, Stanley Matthews and Billy Wright. So now, only weeks after the famous 'Matthews Cup Final' of 1953, the great man was shaking my little hand and asking if I too planned to be a footballer like my grandpa. 'Oh yes, Mr Matthews,' I cooed, thrilled by the approving nod from Ivan over the great man's shoulder.

But none of this shaped my goals or aspirations in life, insofar as you think about such things before your teens. There was barely a book in the house; my parents owned a few vinyl LPs: highlights from *South Pacific*, *My Fair Lady*, *The Pajama Game*. Good choices all, for which I retain a residual fondness, but . . .

Unknown to any of us, my future was being shaped invisibly by my grandfather, who would take me with him each Saturday to the press box at Liverpool or Everton, Manchester United or City. To keep me quiet, at the age of eight, nine, ten and beyond, his kindly colleagues would feed me sweets. Many were soon to die in the 1958 Manchester United air crash in Munich, which Ivan was spared only because he had a bout of 'flu. He himself would give me pencil and paper to keep count of the game's fouls, corner-kicks and other such vital statistics. It was a wonderful afternoon out, especially the thrill of listening to him dictate his match report within minutes of the final whistle. But much more important, and even more of a thrill in football's pre-'stats' era, was seeing *my* numbers in print in the *very next day*'s edition of the *Sunday Times*.

There now seems to me no doubt, though it would take me years to realise it, that this is one of the main reasons I too eventually became a journalist.

At the time, of course, I was determined to be a professional footballer. Ivan naturally loved the idea, regardless of my (lack of) talent, but my parents somehow didn't seem so keen. This was a rather lowly ambition for the son of middle-class pillars of the *petit bourgeoisie*. Their idea of a proper job was lawyer, doctor or accountant; even the civil service, perhaps in faraway London, was occasionally mentioned with a frisson of excitement.

For now, extra-curricular treats were topped by visits to such big names as Arthur Askey or Tommy Cooper at Southport's art-deco Garrick Theatre. My hero of the moment was the cowboy actor Roy Rogers, of whom my bedroom boasted a dramatic giant cutout depicting the great man waving his Stetson astride his rearing horse Trigger.

My mother, who had trained as a secretary, acted as amanuensis to her father, who never learned to type. She was chronically asthmatic, so we couldn't have any pets. A ferocious knitter, she also made a handsome tapestry of Frans Hals' *Laughing Cavalier*, which hung framed in the hall. The sitting room was a riot of decorative horseshoes and Toby jugs. Saturday evenings spelt the treat of going 'into town' to eat out, often at the buttery bar of the Prince of Wales Hotel, then Southport's equivalent of the Ritz, for the ultimate luxury of smoked salmon.

As my brother entered his teens, our indulgent father built a log cabin behind the house for him (and later me) to host Saturday night hops. In time we even gave 'pajama parties' – which, while beyond thrilling at the time, were not quite as risqué as they might sound.

My grandfather Ivan was inexplicably devoted to budgerigars – president, no less, of the Southport Budgerigar Society – and fondly appointed me honorary secretary of the aviary my father built him behind the garage. Once a year, at the least, this same Hon. Sec.

would carelessly leave the entrance door open, with the result that a neighbour would soon be phoning to say that all the street's trees were swarming with budgies – which my father and brother, and to a lesser extent my young, mortified self, were obliged to risk life and limb to recapture.

Ivan also loved fly-fishing, heading north every summer to the Perthshire estate of my godfather, his pal Harry Kirby, where they would pull many a plump salmon or trout from the Tay. Back in Southport he also developed a soft spot for the theatrical art of wrestling, after its arrival on TV, and would often take me with him to super-hammy bouts in the Town Hall. Most afternoons, near the pub where he would sink his lunchtime pint or two, he would go Crown Green bowling with pals his own age, and regularly took me along.

At home, to my mother's chagrin, Ivan's chronic indigestion obliged her to cook him a separate meal, which he would eat on a tray in front of the TV, where the non-sporting fare was not always to his liking. 'They're being paid for this, you know,' he would complain just as you were beginning to warm to some new act on *Sunday Night at the London Palladium*. His supper-tray lived in that corner of the sitting room, so it would often go flying when football was on TV, as his left leg instinctively lurched out for a shot on goal.

Ivan's corner of the room, where he was always half-listening to whatever else was going on, was a perpetual source of memorable one-liners. There was, for instance, the day my mother was inspecting my teenage appearance before I went out on a date with a girl of whom she didn't altogether approve.

'So are you in love with this girl, or what?' she asked with some irritation.

'I'm not sure yet,' was all I could think of to reply.

'You'll know when you fall in love, lad,' came the voice from the corner. 'It's worse than arthritis.'

Then there was the day my mother was smartening me up to send me off to tea with a girl she *did* approve of, whose father was the chairman of the Manchester Ship Canal – much more in line with her aspirations for me. As she straightened my tie, and tut-tutted about the length of my hair, the voice from the corner proclaimed: 'Don't let her mother get your knees under the table, lad, or you're doomed!'

Every morning at breakfast, my mother would read out the horoscope from the daily paper, which soon proved utterly pointless when I realised that it applied to everyone at the table. My brother and I were both born on 22 May, our grandfather on 15 June, my mother 16 June, my father 18 June – all Gemini.

Besides, my horoscope gave me no warning of the domestic drama which was to unfold in the summer of 1953, soon after my sixth birthday, while we were on a fortnight's holiday in the North Wales seaside resort of Aberdovey (these days, Aberdyfi) – most of it, of course, in driving rain.

The caravan park was in the sand dunes beside the ample beach, whence my brother and I would rarely stray throughout the trip. Each afternoon we would head off to the nearby jetty for what became, for me, the most exciting daily feature of the holiday: fishing for crabs. We would walk halfway down the jetty, to where the accessible water was deepest, tie a worm on a weighted piece of string, lower it into the sea, and compete to see who could haul up the fattest, juiciest crab – purely for the excitement of the challenge.

Whether it was the weight of an especially fat crab I rather doubt, but one evening I was pulling so hard on my trusty piece of string that the wooden barrier on which I was leaning gave way, pitching me straight into the choppy ocean, fully clothed and barely able to swim. Only later did I discover that Aberdovey was known for its treacherous riptides, particularly at that time of year. As my brother watched helplessly, I was being swept out to sea, to a certain death by drowning.

Robin set off over the dunes to the caravan where our parents were preparing our nightly campfire meal, oblivious to the off-shore drama engulfing their younger son. Back on the jetty, a middle-aged man at its end must have noticed my head bobbing helplessly up and down, for he abandoned his companion to dive straight in – also, of course, fully-clothed – and swim to the rescue of this forlorn little tyke.

After he reached me, this noble stranger dragged me back to shore in expert style; we were both floundering on the sand exhausted, like a pair of beached whales, by the time my distraught parents arrived, panting, on the scene. An ambulance was summoned, and I was taken off to hospital to have the seawater pumped out of my stomach. After lengthy deliberation, my parents then went out to buy a box of Cadbury's Milk Tray, sought out this same stranger on the beach and presented it to him as a reward for saving the life of their beloved younger son – who never even learned his name.

So that's it, I have thought ever since: my life is valued at a box of Milk Tray. A sanguine lesson, indeed. If it had been my decision, or one of my own sons whose life had been at stake, I like to think I'd have stretched to a bottle of champagne at the very least.

By now I had already fixed on my career path – not, after all, to my grandfather's dismay, life as a footballer, but something of much more signal service to the world at large. Literally 'signal'; one had to be in one's car to benefit from this worthy's services. Driving *en famille* around the north-west — usually in rainy North Wales, scene of the next, all too grim few years of my life — we often encountered these stylish figures who filled little me with awe, counting the miles until we saw another one, and I could blissfully return his greeting.

In those days, members of the Automobile Association had an AA badge affixed to the radiator grille on the front of their car. When an AA patrolman rode towards you, your badge was the signal for him to offer a respectful salute as he sped by on his trusty steed, a yellow motorbike plus sidecar packed with his essentials. From my vantage point in the back, I would dutifully return his salute. How I coveted the dashing, open-air, peripatetic life of the gallant man with the yellow trimmings! All too early, I had no doubt what I wanted to be when I grew up. I was going to be an AA man.

3

PRIVILEGED ABANDONMENT

In my early fifties, when my second wife ambushed me with a demand for a separation, I was sufficiently traumatised to seek out a shrink for the first (and, as yet, only) time in my life. For five days a week I was really paying him to be my friend, banging on about all the things I was acutely aware that my real friends had long since tired of hearing.

'But I've never been dumped before!' I wailed yet again, at some point in our third or fourth session, once I had given him my own version of my life so far.

'Oh yes, you have,' he replied coolly. 'Your mother dumped you when you were eight.'

He was right, of course. My junior self couldn't believe it then, and my senior self can barely believe it now. But my doting mother somehow gave in to my kindly but conservative father's edict that I be sent away to school at the age of eight – to that same bleak outpost in remotest North Wales where I would wind up scattering their ashes, which he had himself attended as a boy, and which my brother was now leaving just as I arrived.

They wanted the best for me, of course, but at what price? 'Smile, though your heart is breaking,' sang Robin, as my father reversed the car out of the drive to convey me to my doom. My grandfather waved, then turned away from his upstairs window, unable to watch. I was in floods of tears, as was my mother, which soon set off my father at the wheel of the car. The same tear-stained ritual was to be performed three times a year for the next five years – and, alas, beyond.

In February 2011 Trearddur Bay earned its fifteen minutes of fame as the unlikely setting for Prince William's first public appearance with his fiancée Kate Middleton after the announcement of their engagement. Two summers later, after the birth of their son George, William bid farewell to his three years of RAF duties in Anglesey – 'the Mother of Wales' – by avowing that he would miss the place 'terribly'. As the world lapped this up, I found myself slumped beneath a deluge of miserable memories, not just upset but *angered* that anyone could be so complimentary about the place. Yes, Anglesey is a beautiful island, peopled by unpretentious working souls; but Trearddur Bay once played host to a boys-only boarding school that blighted the lives of countless sons of aspirational north-western parents.

'Privileged abandonment' has become the vogue phrase for the plight of those children whose parents choose to send them away from home, into the care of stern-faced strangers, at the age of seven or eight – the age at which my own grandchildren were so touchingly innocent, and blissfully reliant on their parents, as to render the idea unthinkable. These days there are even self-help organisations such as Boarding School Survivors, founded by the psychotherapist Nick Duffel, whose book *The Making of Them* goes into toe-curling detail about the lifelong damage these places can inflict upon their hapless inmates.

You can tell a lot about Trearddur House from its school motto, 'They Can Because They Think They Can' – the Victorian scholar John Conington's translation of a line from Book V of Virgil's *Aeneid*, '*Possunt, quia posse videntur*'. I can quite see why its corny aspiration of self-fulfilment appealed to the school's ferocious and undoubtedly sadistic headmaster, George Cartwright.

Thoroughly wretched throughout my five years in this bleak outpost on the edge of nowhere, I missed home acutely. I was repeatedly caned, which at that age may or may not be a form of sexual abuse; but I was not directly subjected to sexual interference. I like to think that those who know me would say I have not been left emotionally damaged to any significant degree. But there are certainly scars, less fundamental scars, of which I am only too aware.

All my life I have had an aversion to cheese. More than an aversion; I cannot stand the stuff, especially if cooked. When ordering pizzas for my teenage sons, I had to hand them over at arm's length, as the smell of cooked cheese still makes me heave. It is not so much an allergy as a mental scar, the kind of scar these Dickensian prep schools have left on so many middle-class boys of my generation.

Trearddur House was very strict about table manners. If you spilt food down your front, you had to wear a bib for a week – humiliating, at an age as advanced as eight or nine, in front of your sniggering peers. If you didn't sit up straight and tuck in your elbows, a rod of wood was placed across your back, so the only way you could eat was to wrap your elbows around it and desperately stretch your forearms towards the food, with back ramrod-vertical.

Every Wednesday lunch was macaroni cheese. The very look of its sludgy viscosity made me queasy; the smell made me heave. One mouthful, and I was on the point of vomiting; one swallow and I did, all over the table – the ultimate breach, as you might suspect, of table manners. Cartwright certainly thought so. The humiliating punishment was to be seized by the earlobe and dragged across the flagstone floor in front of my peers to the cat mat, where I was made to squat on the floor beside the cat and eat my plate clean, vomit and all – yes, *vomit and all* – every Wednesday for five years.

Throughout my life I have been obliged to explain politely to society hostesses, or jocularly to friends offering expensive cheese plates, why I cannot under any circumstances eat cheese of any kind, cooked or uncooked.

Then there was the evening in February 1959, when my neighbour at dinner told me he had heard that our hero Buddy Holly had died in a plane crash; I just had to get up and cross the dining-room in mid-meal — strictly, of course, against school rules — to pass on this traumatic news to a fellow-fan at another of the long refectory tables. Another caning offence.

Parents were allowed to visit their sons, and take them out for the weekend, once a term. These were the highlights of the school year — anticipated with day-charts that soon became hour-charts. But before you were permitted to go out with them, you had to pass an ear and fingernail inspection; the slightest speck, and the weekend was off.

The tension palpably mounted as we stood in line, desperately checking and re-checking our fingernails, poking and gouging our ears. There was just one occasion when an illicit speck beneath one of my nails somehow survived to be subjected to matron's steely gaze. I could see my parents through the window, fresh from their three-hour drive from Southport, excitedly awaiting my emergence. Then I saw Cartwright going out to tell them I had failed the fingernail test, and so would not be forthcoming. There was much protestation, as you might expect — they were, after all, paying for this dubious privilege — before they got into their car and drove forlornly back home again. All I could do was stand watching through the window in floods of helpless tears.

Cartwright was also very keen on regular bowel movements, first thing every morning. Outside the school lavatories was a chart with every pupil's name on it, and a space for each day of the month. Once you had performed your morning ablutions, you were obliged to put a cross against your name. Failing that, for whatever reason, you were force-fed milk of magnesia. So disgusting did I find this slimy stuff, and so humiliating the entire ritual, that I found it easier to lie. Well, how were they going to find me out?

In the mid-1950s there was a worldwide pandemic of Asian

'flu estimated to have killed at least two million people. It even reached Anglesey, where I contracted a case so acute that, after a week or two in my sickbed, I returned to the classroom to find that I couldn't read the blackboard. The virulent infection had rendered me short-sighted for life. Condemned to wearing specs since the age of eight, I have ever since blamed that, too, on Cartwright and his wretched school.

So the summer holidays of 1956, just after I turned nine, were especially happy days for me – not least, yet again, thanks to my grandfather Ivan. When the Surrey spin bowler Jim Laker set a record that still stands, taking 19 wickets for 90 runs in England's defeat of Australia at Old Trafford, the *Daily Express* ran a competition for congratulatory telegrams, the prize being a match ball signed by Laker himself. Ivan submitted an entry in my name, deploying all his journalist's telegrammatic dexterity: 'Laker + K for Kennington, O for Oval + KO for Australia, OK for England!' It won, naturally, and the prize ball was soon mounted in a handsome trophy beside my bed.

When the dread day came for my return to school, the thrice-yearly tear-stained farewell ritual in our driveway preceded the all too familiar drive in sombre silence to Manchester, where my father would take me to a morning cartoon show – in the forlorn hope of cheering me up – before proceeding inexorably to the city's Central Station, where countless other boys stood around in their uniforms and caps awaiting the train ride to Holyhead.

There came one such end of school hols when my parents were away, as my mother recuperated from an operation, so Ivan himself had to undertake the grim mission of putting me on the train at Manchester. Having always avoided the forlorn farewell-from-home ritual, he now had to see for himself the even worse spectacle of all those small boys in floods of tears, as indeed were many of their parents, as the wretched Holyhead train steamed in. Ivan couldn't bear it – to the point where, at the last moment, he jumped onto the train with me. All the way past Chester and on across the Menai Bridge to Anglesey, he regaled my friends with stories of his buccaneering days travelling the world with the England football team as player and journalist. I had heard them all before, of course, but what did that matter when my fellow pupils were so impressed that they too forgot the misery of the moment? When we reached Holyhead Ivan gave me a hug, saw me fondly onto the school bus and, with a wave, smiled and shrugged before getting back on the train for the long ride back to Manchester, followed by the drive home to Southport, alone.

My stock at school soared; no one else could boast such a cool grandpa. And just occasionally, amid the ritual beatings, the brutal boxing, the wretched rugby and accursed crap-charts, there were better moments. It was exciting, for instance, to be selected to sing in the school choir in the Welsh Eisteddfod in Llangollen. Later, waltzing with my mother, I won the school dancing competition – only to mislay the winner's medal, which was eventually found rusting on the school rubbish tip. Another caning.

And I made some good friends, especially a boy called Alan Ravenscroft, whose older brother John was doing his national service nearby. Occasionally a uniformed John would come and take us out, a decade or so before becoming a radio DJ and changing his name to John Peel.

Their mother, Harriet Ravenscroft, was the weekday partner (he had another for weekends) of the classical actor Sebastian Shaw. This kindly, handsome old-school gentleman had been my mother's pin-up during the Second World War, when he played a series of suave heroes in morale-boosting movies. So she was excited beyond words – and, I suspect, rather jealous – when I was invited to spend a summer holiday with Alan at Sebastian's home in rural Ireland.

Also a playwright, novelist and poet, Sebastian would remain a much-cherished friend until his death in 1994, in his nineti-eth year. Only ten years earlier, to his own bewilderment, this veteran RSC stalwart had finally achieved global fame as Anakin Skywalker, alias the original Darth Vader in *Star Wars: Return of the Jedi*.

Back at school, I was not the only one who had discovered the unspeakable excitement of naked female breasts lurking in the *National Geographic* magazine in the school library. This was also where the unprecedented sight of a television set appeared briefly in 1960, so we could all watch the wedding of the Queen's sister, Princess Margaret – which abruptly ended as the couple processed back down the aisle, when Cartwright snapped off the TV with a sniffy: 'Very well, boys, the princess has married her photographer. Now back to work!'

And so it dragged on, from terrifying doses of orienteering on Holyhead Mountain to the delights of school strawberry feasts on other boys' birthdays – highly embarrassing on my own, as my parents could not afford to lay one on. From the scary presence of venomous adders beside the playing fields, to the magical day my father somehow managed the impressive feat, in the annual cricket match against a Fathers XI, of edging a catch to his wicket-keeper son.

The one major plus in these grim years featured in my last, 1960, when my twelve-year-old self was somehow proclaimed the winner of a national essay competition for which some of us had been entered, on the theme of 'My Favourite Street'. I had extolled the beauties of the wide, grass-fringed main street of the Cotswolds village of Broadway, where my parents had taken us for a weekend at their favourite 'treat hotel', the Lygon Arms. The prize involved the impossible excitement of a visit to London, staying with my mother at a hotel near Marble Arch while I received my award from the artist Hugh Casson.

It was around this time that the little swot in me expressed a wish for one of those exotic new Anglepoise lamps. Perhaps sensing that I might one day become a writer, Ivan set out to smoke enough Embassy cigarettes to get me one via the gift coupons inside each pack. And so eventually he did, musing the while that he was smoking himself to death for the sake of world literature. The lamp would ornament my desks at school, university and beyond, but eventually expired, long after he did, to be replaced by another – a sleek new stainless-steel version, which represents him above me now as I write.

My parents bequeathed me my lovingly preserved school reports, in one of which I find Cartwright inexplicably speaking of me as having 'an eye for the ladies'. What can he have been talking about? There weren't any women in sight – apart, perhaps, from one or two elderly cleaners – and I was still some way short of puberty, which momentous event was now scheduled to overtake me some 300 miles to the south. As I turned thirteen, it was taken for granted that I would proceed from Trearddur House to Oundle School, another all-male institution in Northamptonshire – where my brother, father and indeed paternal grandfather had been before me. Again, Robin left just before I fetched up in this second bout of exile, even further from home, in a stately little market town built around the school since its foundation in 1556.

Broken in by Trearddur House, I was not quite as miserable here, if a bit of a misfit. Thanks to its most celebrated headmaster, F. W. Sanderson, Oundle has long been known as a science school; one of its best-known old boys is the biologist Richard Dawkins. But in the twentieth century it also produced a handful who would make their mark in the arts: the poet and critic Al Alvarez; the sometime CEO of Sony, Howard Stringer; and my own contemporary, the playwright David Edgar. The answer to that extra-curricular riddle lies, as it should, in inspirational teaching.

But all that as yet lay somewhere in the distinctly uncertain future. For the first year or more, there was the 'fagging' – functioning as the servant (or 'fag') of a house prefect, who had the right to beat you if you failed to perform to his satisfaction all those antique *Tom Brown's Schooldays* tasks, from getting up early to build his fire of a morning, toasting his bread on it to perfection, and cleaning up afterwards, to the same and more in the evenings. There was the rugby, which I hated from day one; small for my age, and cast against type as a supposedly plucky scrum-half, all rugger meant to me was constantly being jumped on by much bigger wing-forwards. Where my first school had put me off cheese for life, this new one performed the same service for rugby.

And then there was Corps. Where Wednesdays at Trearddur had meant macaroni cheese and all its consequences, at Oundle they held the horrors of dressing up in military uniform to square-bash in the Combined Cadet Force. Countless off-duty hours had to be spent polishing boots, webbing and cap-badges to absurd degrees of gleam before ferocious inspection on parade. 'Monty' himself, a.k.a. Field-Marshal Viscount Montgomery of Alamein, was somehow persuaded to perform this ritual on one of the grand annual Inspection Days – which meant standing to attention in uniform for hours in whatever weather, waiting for the great man to pass by and cast a cursory eye over you.

Later that day the whole school was back on parade in civvies, arrayed in the school's Great Hall to hear the visiting hero deliver a lecture. Apart from Monty's views on apartheid (pro) and homo-sexuality (against), this consisted of a vainglorious plug for his recently published memoirs, which he held aloft with a rallying cry I have often recalled but somehow never been tempted to use myself: 'Some books are good books. Some books are bad books. This is a good book. I wrote it.'

I cannot now believe that my young self managed to pass a quasi-military exam – its name was Certificate A – which involved taking a Bren gun to pieces and putting it back together again. But eventually I came up with a solution. Newly installed running the school bookshop was a friendly ex-army officer named Major Tod, who was obsessed with horses. So I persuaded him that he was just the man to start a school cavalry, the Equitation Cadre, with me as his first recruit. To my delight, the authorities approved the idea – with the result that, as I had hoped, we went riding instead of rifle-ranging each Wednesday, and pony-trekking in the Lake District instead of the Corps camp everyone else had to endure at least twice during their five years at the school. One of these, square-bashing at some beyond-bleak, rain-drenched army base in Northumberland, had been more than enough for me.

In an attempt to escape rugby, I soon volunteered to become cox of my house rowing crew. Still small for my age, I appeared to be the ideal candidate, for all my short-sightedness. On my first outing all seemed to be going well until we approached a bridge. Intent on steering through it, I forgot to tell the backward-facing crew to 'ship oars' and so steered them beneath the bridge to the crash-crash-crash of shattering blades. Back to the rugby field.

In the classroom I found myself specialising in Latin and Greek, winding up as one of just three, then two pupils in the Classical VI (the other being Robin Soans, later a gifted actor-playwright). In my third year, as I was absorbed in the wonders of Horace, Catullus and Propertius, there arrived from Gresham's School in Norfolk a classics master named John Harrison, newly married to the headmaster's au pair, a blonde German beauty named Amrei. This impossibly glamorous union was to prove central to my young life, and has remained an important part of it ever since; I am godfather to the Harrisons' daughter Lisa – the second of my six godchildren – and have for years paid summer visits to their rural cottage in north Norfolk.

Harrison also taught me Russian, which he had learned in the navy, and in which I managed to squeak an 'O' level. Another inspirational teacher – one of a handful who treated you as an adult, invited you to dinner and in time even offered the occasional glass of wine – was one of my housemasters. A musician called Andrew Milne, he had once played trombone in the legendary jazz band of Humphrey Lyttelton. Thanks to Andy, 'Humph' would occasionally bring some variant of his band to play Saturday-night 'Coke-n-crisp' concerts in the Great Hall. Life at Oundle rarely got much more vivid than that.

I remember exactly where I was standing in November 1963, dressed in a fetching frock and wig, about to go onstage in the house play as Mrs Dubedat in Shaw's *The Doctor's Dilemma*, when I was told that the sole performance had been cancelled because of the assassination of the young president of the United States. Thus was the stage deprived of its next Laurence Olivier.

Across town, on the very same evening, my pal David Edgar was about to go onstage as Miss Prism in *The Importance of Being Earnest*. This performance – unfortunately, as it turned out – was *not* cancelled. Intent on a dashing career as a Donald Wolfit-style actor-manager, David could not wait to hear the post-show verdict of his parents, a distinguished TV producer and actress respectively. As he greeted them excitedly, his mother's first words were: 'Well, it's not going to be acting, then, is it, darling?' To this day, a mortified David blames it all on the high-heeled shoes he had borrowed from a teacher's wife. Soon thereafter, however, so manifest already were his other theatrical talents, Edgar was chosen as the first pupil in the school's 400-plus-year history to direct the school play. He made the boldest of choices, not least for an all-male school: Bertolt Brecht's *Mother Courage and Her Children*. We all auditioned for the title role, and all but one (named Roland Jack) failed to secure it. I was put in charge of props – a key role in this particular play, with its crucially large wagon. The same fate befell me the following year, when we all auditioned for leading roles in John Harrison's school production of *Henry IV, Part 2*; I was again put in charge of props, while my pal Soans played a dashing Hotspur.

By now I'd managed to escape rugby again by becoming a gymnast, spending hours in the school's well-equipped gym under the expert tutelage of a barrel-chested master named Jack Hogg.

I was especially intrepid on the high bar, swiftly graduating from half-swings to full-swings that look most impressive if you can get them right. Usually I could, despite high anxiety as I swirled round and around; then, inevitably perhaps, came the day when my hand slipped and I came off the bar, crashing feet-first into the mat beneath with a painful crunch. Mercifully, nothing was broken, but it turned out that I had done severe damage to my left patella tendon – in which I occasionally still feel a twinge to this day, like some superannuated war wound.

Few believe me these days when I tell this story, but my family can testify that even in middle age I used to impress them on vacation with a few nifty handsprings around the beach. Not, alas, anymore.

When you became a sixth-former, you could apply to become a school librarian, which meant nothing apart from jealous looks from your peers as you disappeared into the Tower Room, a small retreat atop the school Cloisters reserved for School Librarians only. It was cleaned by a chronic diabetic called Jack; we would avert our eyes as he injected himself with insulin before – for a percentage – taking our bets to the local bookies. On the day before our 'A' levels, when we were granted a day off, Robin Soans and I took ourselves off to Lingfield Park, where I won the Tote Treble for the first and last time in my life.

But the primary purpose of the Tower Room was, naturally, illicit smoking. So smug did we grow about this flagrant abuse of school rules that we cockily invited the headmaster for morning coffee once a week, making sure there were plenty of fag-ends stuffed down the armchair in which he would sit. To our surprise he was always very genial, never seeming to notice the stench of smoke in the room or the mess of ash in which he was sitting. In hindsight, of course, he knew perfectly well what was going on. We were the boys most likely to win entrance, maybe even scholarships to university, especially to Oxbridge. We were the pupils whose results would justify the school's ever-rising fees.

Not least because of the smoking, no doubt, I never achieved the supreme accolade of being made a school prefect, whose main perk was to march in proud single file down the aisle of the chapel to signal the start of each day's service. Restricted to the rank of house prefect, I declined to exercise my right to inflict corporal punishment, no doubt with Trearddur House in mind – to the point where I was shunned by my peers and lost such little authority as I ever managed to muster.

My *amour propre* was soon restored by my appointment as editor of the house magazine, in which role I found myself impressed by a poem submitted by a boy who subsequently became a renowned entrepreneur. It began:

> *Do you remember an inn, Miranda,*
> *Do you remember an inn?*
> *And the tedding and the spreading*
>   *Of the straw for a bedding,*
> *And the fleas that tease in the high Pyrenees*
> *And the wine that tasted of tar?*

That's good, I thought. Really good. So much so that – phew! – my teenage self mustered the good sense to look it up in a dictionary of quotations. It is, of course, the work of Hilaire Belloc.

In his 2013 autobiography, *An Appetite for Wonder*, Richard Dawkins looks back fondly enough on his days at Oundle, but speaks of having to 'fight off other boys' after dark. I suffered no such trauma, not least because the girls back home in Southport were finally growing up. 1965–66 became a personal *annus mirabilis*, during which I was relieved of my virginity by an indulgent local lass and became the first player to score a hole-in-one at the new short 14th hole at Royal Birkdale. My playing partner, and so the witness who signed my historic card, was none other than Peter Unsworth, once Pete the drummer in our rock band, later president of the club and eventually chairman of the Royal

& Ancient's championship committee – whom I last saw on TV presenting the winner of that year's Open tournament with his trophy.

At Oundle I also won the school golf tournament in the year that to my delight saw Harold Wilson become prime minister in Labour's overdue election victory after thirteen years of Tory rule. At Oundle, I was in a significant minority. The derisory sneers about HP Sauce at No. 10, from the future bankers and hedge-fund managers who comprised most of my contemporaries, confirmed me as Labour for life.

Already I had heard Kenneth Tynan use the dread f-word on television, when my housemaster invited the prefects to join him in watching the risqué new TV show, *That Was the Week That Was*. The Swinging Sixties were well under way, though I would not really realise it – or indeed live my own version – until the 1970s. By now I had forsaken rugby, science and square-bashing for the rarefied realms of fine art, under another inspirational teacher named Arthur Mackenzie.

Himself a gifted sculptor, 'Arty' Mackenzie was another of the handful of benevolent masters who would invite you home to talk about the outside world, that tantalising realm awaiting us all when these grim years of strictly policed incarceration were at last over. He didn't bother to deny that his own work was his priority, that teaching was a chore required to finance it; but it came naturally to him to treat his pupils with respect, rather than as a lower order of inmates in the asylum.

On each term's Expedition Day, when the aspirant City boys would head off for a thrilling day out at the nearby London Brick Factory, Mackenzie would lead a charabanc-full of us arty types to London, to his beloved Tate Gallery, for a salutary fix of Turner and co. A tall, shaggy-haired figure, he would stride up the steps ahead of us, waving his arms as he extolled the delights of the Post-Impressionists, arriving at the top *tout seul* as his charges quietly slipped away to jump on the Tube to Soho, and the thrills of its strip clubs. As long as we were back at the Tate in time for the bus back to Oundle, preferably having glanced at a canvas or two, nothing was ever said. I suspect most artists we can think of – especially my own hero of the moment, Pablo Picasso – would have thoroughly approved.

Another such enlightened teacher was the head of English, Roy Haygarth, who played what turned out to be a pivotal role in my life when I decided I could not face four years of Latin and Greek at Oxford – rather pompously, I thought, dubbed 'Greats' – and would rather spend those precious few years wallowing in English literature. After a year's crash course from Haygarth – often in his spare time, even in the school holidays at his cottage in rural Wales – I travelled to Oxford in December 1965 for my post-exam entrance interview at the ancient college of Merton, shrewdly chosen for me by persons unknown. As I climbed a spiral staircase in one of its stately towers, escorted by the relevant tutors, I felt obliged to break the tense silence with some remark, any remark, however banal. 'Oh, what a wonderful view!' I proclaimed feebly, as we reached one of its arrow-slit windows. 'Yes,' said the English tutor, John Jones, 'on a clear day you can see Marlow.'

'And on an even clearer day,' harrumphed the terrifying head of Classics, R. G. C. Levens, 'you can see Beaumont and Fletcher!'

At the top of the staircase was a visibly nervous gaggle of fellow interviewees, for many of whom it was the first time they had left home alone. For me, it was the first time in my life I had been called 'Mr' Holden – on notices detailing the day's events, by the unexpectedly respectful college porters. When Levens emerged from his study for the next victim, I was sitting alone. 'And you are . . .?' he enquired.

'Mr Holden,' I replied.

'Ah!' said he with a malicious grin, 'come in, *MIS-TER* Holden.'

It was a tense tussle, but English eventually won the day, the only remaining hurdle being my interview with the college

Warden, an Ancient History don named Robin Harrison. As fate would have it, that day's papers carried the news of the death of W. Somerset Maugham, whose novel *Of Human Bondage* I just happened to have been reading, at the suggestion of Roy Haygarth.

'Ah, Mr Holden,' began the Warden, consulting his notes. 'I see that you are a Classics scholar intent on reading English.' There was a mischievous look on his face as he looked up at me and asked: 'So tell me your views on the late, lamented Mr Maugham.' I was able to answer him with new-minted expertise, thus settling my immediate future for sure.

In my last year at Oundle, I failed my 'A' level in dreary Ancient History, while chalking up straight As in Latin, Greek and English. But my heart was really in Arthur Mackenzie's art school, where I had now become an enthusiastic disciple of Cubism. In my London apartment still hang a lurid quasi-Picasso and a brash faux-Braque which, if you take them off the wall, are inscribed on the back: 'A. Holden, 1965'.

As the time finally came for me to leave Oundle, and at last escape the long wilderness of my schooldays, I now knew exactly what I wanted to do. The phrase 'gap year' had not yet taken root, but I had made plans for the year ahead before Oxford. Back in Southport I would get a temporary job (with the building firm of my parents' friend Noel le Mare, later to become the owner of the steeplechaser Red Rum) to finance a few months in Paris, where I had applied for – and, to my amazed delight, been granted – a summer place at an art school on *la rive gauche*, L'Académie de la Grande Chaumière, where Gauguin himself had been a pupil.

Yes, I was going to be a painter.

4

1968 AND ALL THAT

I enjoyed a wonderful six months in Paris – where, at the height of my teenage obsession with existentialism, I glimpsed my hero Jean-Paul Sartre through the windows of Les Deux Magots, his regular haunt in Saint-Germain-des-Prés. From a photograph in a new biography, I even worked out where he lived in the Place Saint-Germain, and managed to bluff my way past the concierge to ring his doorbell in the absurdly optimistic hope of an in-depth existentialist chat. There was no reply, of course, but I left a bottle of his favourite beer on his doorstep, with a note inscribed 'D'un admirateur'. Next day, when I returned to try again – *en vain encore, naturellement* – the empty bottle stood outside his door with a handwritten note saying: 'Merci! J-P.S'

Meanwhile, I loved my daily sessions at the Académie, not least the many hours spent staring at, sometimes even drawing, naked female models. But the crude charcoal sketches I brought home persuaded even me that I was not really cut out for fine art. Instead, I now determined, I was going to be a novelist. I already had the title (from *Hamlet*, of course) for my debut, *The Interim is Mine* – if not much else.

So maybe a poet. Poetry seemed to be everywhere when I arrived in Oxford. There were countless student magazines offering aspirants a chance to give their work a wider airing. There were weekly readings by celebrated literati at meetings of the O.U. Poetry Society. And Merton of all colleges was renowned for its poets: T. S. Eliot, Louis MacNeice, Keith Douglas and Edmund Blunden, among many others.

Surely this was some sort of omen – rendered more propitious by the fact that Blunden was still there, available to be bought drinks in the bar of the Junior Common Room. His advice? In essence: go for it. Sartre, I felt sure, would have approved.

In the early autumn of 1966, my father had driven me down (or was it 'up'?) to Oxford from Southport. I was smartly dressed in a suit and tie in the sure expectation that the Warden of Merton College, or my tutor, or indeed both would be standing outside the college entrance, waiting to greet the new arrival. Neither of us had the slightest inkling of the protocol; there was no precedent for this in the hallowed annals of Holden-dom. As we had left home some five hours earlier, I was abuzz with excited anticipation; now, as we inched down the ancient cobbles of Merton Street, I grew ever more apprehensive.

The college's ivy-clad walls bespoke a history, a high seriousness, way beyond my then ken. As we drew to a nervous halt outside the Porter's Lodge, I wanted nothing so much as my father to come in with me, to help me find the room I could only assume would be waiting for me somewhere behind the college's forbidding ramparts. But one look at his face, staring up at those ancient spires, showed me that he too was way out of his comfort zone, even more unnerved than I was. A fond hug and he was gone – on his way back to the safety of Southport, leaving me and my school trunk out on the street to face our fate alone.

The next day, this well-brought-up young product of the north-western *petit bourgeoisie* thought it prudent to re-don his suit and tie for his first meeting with his tutor, John Jones, author of distinguished books on Aristotle and Wordsworth. For the first year, he explained, at the end of which awaited 'Prelims' (the Preliminary Examinations which would determine all our futures), I would see him one-on-one to talk Literature, while I would have a tutorial partner for the Language (or

Anglo-Saxon) side of things, for which we would be 'farmed out' to a specialist.

This tutorial partner, in fact, should be here by now, murmured the engaging, mercurial Jones, wondering what had become of him. We were both about to give up hope when in wandered a sombre, earnest figure with long dark hair and extensive 'mutton-chop' sideburns, wearing what looked like an embroidered smock (which I later learned to be a Bavarian 'kittel'). His speech was very precise, his manner rather remote, with a twang of the patrician. Who was this aloof aesthete, with whom I was destined to share the scary-sounding sessions ahead? I had no chance to find out as, once Jones wrapped up the meeting, this mysterious stranger wandered off in an intense reverie without so much as a farewell.

Abreast the tidal wave of the post-war 'baby-boom' genera-tion, I was one of almost a million nineteen-year-old Britons in 1966, only 4 per cent of whom went to university – and just 15 per cent of that 4 per cent to Oxbridge, where a parental means-test decreed that my college maintenance be paid in full from the public purse. Did I realise at the time how lucky I was? Of course not. Not until my own sons went to university – tuition fees still paid by the state pre-the betrayals of Blair and Cameron, but weighed down by Thatcher's iniquitous student loans – did I realise how enlightened was that 1962 legislation.

As I gradually settled in it was pleasing to discover that the food in the college hall was renowned as Oxford's finest, Merton being one of the richest colleges as well as one of the smallest. Seating at college meals was random, first-come-first-served, which also meant that one made some welcome new friends. As I arrived a tad late one evening, the only gap available was next to my distant tutorial partner, his kittel still visible beneath his Exhibitioner's gown. So, at last, we had no alternative but to talk to each other. Slowly but surely I managed to penetrate his natural reserve, and soon we seemed to have struck up some sort of kinship. That first conversation turned out to last forty-eight hours, without a break, and was still continuing as intensely more than fifty years later — even though those three years at Oxford proved the only time in his adult life that he spent even part of the year in his supposed homeland of England.

His name, I discovered, was John David Morley, but he asked me to call him simply 'J'. Born in Singapore, six months after me, he had spent his childhood in Malaysia and Africa, wherever his father's Colonial Office duties happened to take the Morley family. As was the way of such patriarchs, Morley *pere* had sent his only *fils* to a British boarding school, namely Clifton College in Bristol (where one of his contemporaries was Roger Alton, later to be my editor at *The Observer*).

Poetry-wise, I had discovered a kindred spirit. In that first term at Oxford Morley impressed me not only by playing Bach chaconnes on his guitar, but writing elegant, sharp-eyed poetry which had already won the admiration of the future poet laureate Cecil Day-Lewis, then a director of the publishers Chatto & Windus. Even at that age, however, J was mature enough to decline publication; his 'stuff' wasn't up to much, he shrugged, and he wasn't sure he would persist with it. My wide-eyed protestations were firmly swept aside.

I myself, by contrast, was busily publishing ornate youthful stanzas in sundry student magazines — all of them, mercifully, long since lost to posterity. Perhaps I should try acting instead? At the end of our first term, Morley and I were cast respectively as the swaggering Irish hero Cuchulain and his ditzy Fool in W. B. Yeats' brief two-man drama, *On Baile's Strand*. It was Merton's entry to the freshman drama competition, which imposed a half-hour time limit. Come the big night, after weeks of intense rehearsal, J and I gave it all we'd got — he bestriding the stage like a Shakespearean colossus, me trailing loyally in his wake, singing my silly song and, at the climax, scattering my bag of feathers with such histrionic abandon that it took the crew longer than usual to clear up – with the result that Merton was disqualified for over-running its time.

Twenty years later, I would dedicate my biography of Laurence Olivier to that same John David Morley, by then a distinguished novelist, 'in memory of Cuchulain'. In the thirty years since that book was published, no one has ever asked me what that means.

John Jones, to my delight, was a football fanatic who had written regular match reports for *The Observer* in the 1950s. He was an ardent admirer, he told me, of my grandfather Ivan, whom he knew only by repute; so I was delighted to get them together when Ivan came to visit during my first term. That evening Ivan took me off to dinner with his friend Harold Thompson, a chemistry don at St John's. I was amazed that Grandpa knew *any* Oxford dons, let alone a professor who, as I later learned, had taught the student Margaret Thatcher, née Roberts, in the 1940s. But the conversation that evening was primarily of football, and especially Alf Ramsey, the World Cup-winning England manager. Thompson was another football obsessive, by now on the board of the Football Association, later to become its president, instrumental in the abrupt firing of Ramsey when England failed to qualify for the 1974 World Cup.

During that evening, amid much musing about Ramsey, we

were able to relive with Thompson Ivan's own 'near-death' experience of England's triumphant World Cup final just three months before. Entitled to a press seat at Wembley, he had decided he couldn't face it. By then seventy-seven, he was so desperate for England to win – it would be their first international victory since his own for Great Britain more than half a century earlier – that he feared he 'might have a bloody heart attack'. Instead he had watched it on TV at home in Southport with me; my brother was married by then, and our parents were away somewhere. When West Germany scored in the twelfth minute, Ivan slumped in his seat, muttering his thanks that he hadn't gone to Wembley; when Geoff Hurst equalised seven minutes later, he revived again, and asked me to fetch him another stiff drink. 1-1 at half-time was a moment for cautious optimism, bolstered in the seventy-seventh minute when Martin Peters' opportunist goal for England saw us both leap from our chairs.

During the long countdown to the final whistle, the tension became ever more acute. In the eighty-ninth minute, when Jack Charlton conceded a free kick from which Germany equalised, Ivan slumped back in his chair as if he really had suffered that heart attack. But no, by the time the referee's whistle signalled extra time, he was leaning forward again, only to announce: 'I can't take any more of this. I'm going out into the garden. Keep me posted.'

For the first five minutes of the extra thirty, England pressed to the point where through the window I gave Ivan a cheery thumbs-up. But I was so worried about his heart that I decided not to tell him when a Bobby Charlton shot hit the post. When Hurst scored off the crossbar after eleven minutes, I ran to the window to beckon him in; there ensued the Swiss referee's deliberations with the Russian linesman – not speaking each other's tongues, they communicated in sign language – which ended with the ref pointing back to the halfway line: YES, it was an England goal (although latter-day technology has shown that it wasn't). Again, all this proved too much for Ivan; clutching his chest, as if in pain, he went back out into the garden. There were still, after all, twenty minutes to go.

So he missed the celebrated moment when, with one minute left to play, Hurst took what he later admitted was a 'blistering' kick intended to send the ball 'as far as possible into the stands . . . to kill as much time as possible' – which instead found its way into the top corner of the net. At the time, the commentator Kenneth Wolstenholme – not one of Ivan's favourite colleagues; they had argued on radio and TV about the quality of English football then and now – was in the middle of a sentence which has since passed into sporting folklore: 'And here comes Hurst. He's got . . . some people are on the pitch . . . they think it's all over. It is now! It's four!'

I hammered on the window hard enough to smash it. Ivan came running back from the garden. We yelled and hugged each other as if we were part of that crowd swarming onto the pitch at Wembley. Now, he said, he could die happy.

During that brief visit to Oxford Ivan presented me with a vinyl LP of Tchaikovsky's first piano concerto, one of his favourite works, which duly became one of my own. He was also delighted that I had just had my first piece published in *Isis*, the student magazine. A review of a new book about Ernest Hemingway, it was a welcome diversion for a freshman supposed to be studying *Beowulf* for his Prelims.

It was little more than a year later that I returned from an illegal night out of college, chez an early *inamorata*, to find that my mother had telephoned the previous evening, leaving a message for me to call home. This was unprecedented. I was suddenly guilt-stricken about my overnight absence as I sensed the only news that would move her to call. Ivan had died the previous day, 9 February 1968, aged seventy-eight.

My grandfather spent what proved to be his final few weeks in the same Southport hospital where I had been born twenty years earlier. 'I see you didn't get the poet laureateship, then!' had been his greeting to me the previous month, on what proved to be the last time I saw him; with a grin, he was holding up a paper carrying that day's news of Day-Lewis's appointment. So we parted, appropriately enough, with much laughter and the longest, most devoted of hugs.

Ivan had even approved of my publishing poetry, about which he teased me gleefully in front of my baffled parents. So his last words to me were typical of the man: gently joshing but ever supportive, generous and witty. Having himself risen from humble origins to the happiest of careers in his chosen field, perhaps he could see – even before I did – that Oxford would prove my escape hatch from Southport out into a wider world. If only he'd still been around to share it.

By then J Morley and I had become firm friends. Together we slogged through our induction into Anglo-Saxon and Middle English, which in fact we rather enjoyed, under the stewardship of a Mrs Wallace-Hadrill, the dour wife of a Merton history don. It was not long before J christened her Mrs Lobster-Quadrille.

We both managed to pass our Prelims, after which I felt I could take my foot off the academic pedal for a while. I became editor of the college magazine, *Postmaster*, and started making trips to the theatre in London with J. On the train ride back that evening – as on all such day trips, he complained – I quoted some favourite lines from Louis MacNeice's *Autumn Journal*:

> *I take the train*
> *Through Biscuit Town and Didcot to the seat*
> *Of learning, which I sat in half in vain . . .*

Now, with the supreme self-confidence of youth, I wrote to the classicist E. R. Dodds, custodian of the MacNeice estate, proposing my twenty-year-old, far-from-published self as the poet's official biographer. I received a courteous, kindly reply, to the effect that I would no doubt make an admirable candidate, but the job was already assigned to an Irish poet. How differently my life might have turned out, I have occasionally reflected, had I somehow managed to land that gig; I might have become a literary biographer of the order of the Richards Ellmann or Holmes, instead of the jack-of-all-trades I turned out to be.

Oxford was agog that year at the arrival in town of Richard Burton and Elizabeth Taylor for an otherwise all-student production of Marlowe's *Doctor Faustus*, directed by Nevill Coghill, who had been Burton's tutor at Exeter College in the mid-1940s. Burton himself played the title role, with Taylor in the non-speaking role of Helen of Troy, 'the face that launched a thousand ships'. Several of my friends were in the cast at the Oxford Playhouse, and in the subsequent film version produced by Burton himself.

By then film critic of *Isis*, I later attended the world premiere of the movie in Oxford, to be followed by a dinner with the Burtons at the Randolph Hotel. At a briefing that afternoon we had all been firmly told to behave ourselves – to act like grown-ups, not students, i.e. not to get drunk, not to smoke pot and above all not to badger either of the Burtons for their autographs. My friend Ivor Roberts, one of the cast, nevertheless joined most of us in having a few free drinks too many, then broke the golden rule by wandering over to the top table with his commemorative menu and asking La Taylor to autograph it for him. Which she did very charmingly, signing herself Elizabeth Taylor-Burton.

'Why do you sign it like that?' asked a swaying Ivor.

'Because,' she replied sweetly, 'that is how I like to be known.'

'In that case,' he continued, 'why don't you sign it Elizabeth Taylor-Hilton-Wilding-Todd-Fisher-Burton?'

At which point Ivor was strong-armed away from her presence and escorted off the premises. I am obliged to report that this same Ivor Roberts subsequently enjoyed a distinguished career as – what else? – a diplomat, winding up as British ambassador to Yugoslavia,

Ireland and Italy, before retiring in 2006, as Sir Ivor, to become president of Trinity College, Oxford. When we remember that happy evening these days, we update his fatal reply to: 'Why don't you sign yourself Elizabeth Taylor-Hilton-Wilding-Todd-Fisher-Burton-Burton-Warner-Fortensky?' – taking particular relish in that double Burton.

The Yeats play which had so disastrously marked the end of my first term had been directed by an ambitious young Mertonian named Ray Miles, who was now angling to direct the annual summer production of the Oxford University Drama Society (OUDS). He had offered them one of the most powerful of ancient Greek tragedies, Aeschylus' *Agamemnon*, in a specially-written new verse translation.

Knowing of my classical schooling, Ray asked me to under-take the task, and between us we secured the commission from OUDS. So I spent much more of my first year absorbed in Greek literature than in English. John Jones, as always, was under-standing, nay delighted that I was taking on so daunting a literary challenge. The resulting production in a college garden – with Ivor Roberts among the cast, along with such others as the future TV historian Michael Wood – proved a triumph. So much so that we were invited to take the production to a summer festival in the ancient theatre of Delphi, where Greek drama began, and it was agreed that I could tag along as a spear-carrier. Even more excitingly, Cambridge University Press offered me the princely sum of £20 to publish my translation.

We travelled across Europe by train to Athens, and thence to Delphi, where we arrived to discover that we were one of the very few companies to have turned up at a festival boycotted by most invitees because of the international notoriety of Greece's ruling 'colonels', who had seized power in a military coup that April. The thought of *not* going, even for that reason, had not occurred to any of us. Indeed, so pleased were the colonels that we had shown up that they did, too, sitting through the performance in the front row and coming up onstage to shake our hands. As you might imagine, we were roundly denounced on all sides – quite rightly, of course – when we arrived back in Oxford.

Before that, however, lay the rest of an eventful summer vacation for my twenty-year-old self. The leading role of Clytemnestra in our production of *Agamemnon* was played by Oxford's Zuleika Dobson of the moment, an extremely beautiful and talented actress with the equally dazzling name of Petronella Pulsford. She had played Gluttony in the Burton–Taylor *Faustus*. In Delphi, to my amazed delight, she seduced my still boyish self into a summer romance. But she was not planning to return from Greece with the rest of us; she had other plans for the remainder of the summer. So distraught was I that, back in Athens, I let the others leave without me, still hoping Clytemnestra might change her mind. After minimal hesitation, she did not – and, with some placatory, even tear-stained mutterings of regret, duly went on her way.

Now I was in a fix. I had no money and no ticket home. I took advantage of a state offer to give some blood for the equivalent of a few quid, and made my sorry way to the British Airways office in Athens. I wasn't feeling too well, I complained; could they please get an urgent message to my parents back in England, asking them to pay for a one-way flight home? Of course, said the charming and very pretty BA clerk; what's your address in Athens? 'Ah', said I, 'I don't have one. Or any money. Just put "street", and I'll come back tomorrow.'

'You have nowhere to stay?' she asked sympathetically, capping my summer of Greek tragi-comedy with the unforgettable invitation, in her attractively Greek-hued English: 'Would you like to come and stay with me? My name is Iphigenia, but you can call me Fifi . . .'

And so I dallied with Fifi for the next few days, until my ticket arrived. Yet again my poor parents had come up trumps. When the plane taxied in, I could see them waiting anxiously on the tarmac with an ambulance. Just as well; it reminded me that I was supposed to be sick, in time to grimace with pain, clutching my stomach as I descended the aircraft steps to greet them. Weirdly, the pain seemed to have vanished by the time we got home to Southport.

I went straight back to Oxford early, ten days before the new term began. Taking a walk beside the Parks, I saw a familiar car – a vintage Riley – parked in the road leading to Lady Margaret Hall. I knew that car – it was Morley's! I left a note beneath the windscreen wiper, saying: 'What are you doing back here early? Me, too!'

The next day J ambled into my rooms to say that he had been wandering the Welsh countryside with a friend, who had just gone back to Germany. Her name was Armgard. She was the matriarch of the family with whom he lived in Munich.

At the age of fourteen, J now confided in me, when he had been studying for German 'O' level at Clifton, his parents had responded to a classified advert in *The Times* offering an exchange with a German coeval studying English. The boy had been to the Morley home in Surrey before taking young J with him to Munich. When Morley senior went to meet his son at Heathrow, to drive him back to Clifton for the new term, he was not on the plane. He had fallen in love with his friend's mother, and she with him. In the ensuing fifty-plus years, Morley never returned to the UK, except for those nine terms at Oxford.

There was a husband, a charming and gifted sculptor called Alfred, who welcomed the *ménage à trois* as a way of saving his failing marriage. Over the years both he and Armgard told me that it would not have survived, were it not for the intervention of this third party young enough to be their son. For decades they all lived in unlikely domestic bliss, to which I was a regular visitor. Alfred died some years ago; both sons have long since left home. But Morley was still living in the same house in a Munich suburb with Armgard as she entered her nineties. In his tenth novel, published in 2014, he wrote a fictionalised account of her life story, amounting to a history of post-war Europe, under the title *Ella Morris*.

John David Morley with his Armgard

The long, hot summer term of 1968 saw the Che Guevara of the hour, Christopher Hitchens, leading Oxford's version of student revolt, including the occupation of sundry university buildings. In a Broad Street pub one evening, we decided to go for the holy of holies, the Christopher Wren-designed Sheldonian, home of Oxford's grandest ceremonies. To our own amazement, we actually got in, before realising we had no idea what to do next. So we looked to our leader for orders. I could see Christopher going through his mental Che Guevara manual, before eventually commanding: 'Seize the filing cabinets!' We all rushed off obediently, only to return somewhat sheepishly ten minutes later to inform him: 'There aren't any filing cabinets. It's a theatre.' There ensued a few more minutes of earnest deliberation, before he shrugged and said: 'Oh hell, let's go back to the pub.'

There my protests that we should be picketing with the car workers at Cowley were shouted down, before it was decided that the next-door Clarendon Building would make a much better target. There ensued a far more successful occupation, which lasted rather longer.

That term I was elected editor of *Isis*, then owned by one Robert Maxwell, Labour MP for Buckingham. Normally the job was held for a term, and fitted in around the editor's supposed studies. Himself living in Oxford at Headington Hill Hall, headquarters of his Pergamon Press, Maxwell had instituted a system whereby the student editor took a year off from his work, doing the job on a full-time, semi-professional basis. Maxwell replaced your student grant for the year, with the result that you got an extra year at Oxford before deciding what to do with the rest of your life. This seemed to me like a very good deal. The ever-obliging John Jones negotiated the agreement of the Merton authorities, and I had a whole summer vacation to contemplate how best to become the voice of the feisty student left of 1968 and all that.

The young editor of *Isis* with Cyrano de Bergerac

'What are you doing for the summer?' I asked Hitchens in the pub one evening. 'I'm going off to Cuba,' he replied with a huge grin, 'to one of Fidel's terrorist training camps.'

'Wow, that would make a great piece for *Isis* next term!'

'*Journalism*,' he sneered. "Running-dog, lickspittle, capitalist-lackey, yellow trade . . .'

'Look, Christopher,' said I. 'You know that picture of Che we've all got on our walls? You write me that piece, and I'll print it with your face on it instead of Che's.' Which proved enough to persuade him. So I can proudly lay claim to having been the first editor to publish a piece of journalism by Christopher Hitchens, who would remain a lifelong friend.

Later that term, in *Isis'* 'Horoscopes' column, with which I had replaced the overly gushy 'Isis Idols' to predict the future of young Oxford whizz-kids, we prophesied that Hitchens would meet his end in the Fleet Street bar El Vino, after falling into a glass of gin and tonic while admiring his own reflection. He was gratifyingly amused – and told me more than forty years later, only a few months before his cruelly premature death in 2011, how much he regretted forgetting to include it in his own recently published memoirs, *Hitch 22*.

That year's *Isis* was also to prove the launch pad for a diverse array of subsequent luminaries from Gyles Brandreth to Patrick Cockburn, who recently reminded me that I had personally taken down a piece he dictated from embattled Northern Ireland. In Brandreth's 2009 'diary of a lifetime', *Something Sensational to Read in the Train*, the entry for 8 December 1968 reads: 'With M [his wife Michèle] watch *Pride and Prejudice* (1940 version) on TV at Tony Holden's in the afternoon. *P&P* still my favourite film. And Tony Holden one of my favourite people – except he smokes and drinks all the time.'

'Still do, Gyles, still do!' I was pleased to remind him some four decades later.

There had been an ugly precursor to all this, in the last week of that summer term of 1968. The rival student newspaper *Cherwell* splashed with a lurid front-page story to the effect that Maxwell had made me editor of *Isis* only because I had agreed to appoint his son, Philip, the magazine's business manager. The byline surprised me as much as the wholly inaccurate article; it was that of *Cherwell's* star investigative reporter, Denis Matyjaszek, a buddy of mine at Merton who was later (at the request of his first employers, the BBC) to change his name to MacShane and went on to become a Labour MP, Minister for Europe under Tony Blair and belatedly fell foul of the 2009 parliamentary expenses scandal.

It was true that after my election as editor I had asked Philip Maxwell to stay on as the business manager of *Isis*; he had already performed the role for my predecessor and, with no head for business myself, I was delighted that he had agreed to continue. But at that point I had not even met his subsequently notorious father. The evening the paper appeared, as it happened, I was undertaking the highly unlikely task of proposing the health of my old school, Oundle, at an old boys' dinner at next-door Corpus Christi college. It was the perfect alibi – which I was going to need in view of what happened in my absence and, as I would repeatedly have to insist, without my prior knowledge, let alone consent.

Outraged by his calumnies in *Cherwell*, a handful of *Isis* staff had stormed over to Merton, lured Denis out of the college, bundled him into a car and driven him to a village some twenty miles out of town. There ensued a punch-up before the staff photographer, who moonlighted as a security guard, unleashed his Securicor spray all over poor Denis, whom they proceeded to abandon by the roadside, dishevelled and indelibly pink. What else could he do but awkwardly hitch a ride back into Oxford and retreat into his rooms, at the foot of the same staircase where I lived at the top, and sit there fuming? It took quite some time for Denis to accept that I knew nothing of the plot against him – and would never, of course, have approved it.

Such was the ensuing brouhaha that, for the first of only two occasions in my life, I was required to issue a statement to the Press Association. While grateful for the touching loyalty of my staff, said I, I could not possibly condone such an outrageous, nay illegal act.

Before *Agamemnon* appeared in print that spring, Cambridge University Press had commissioned me to translate another Greek tragedy of my choice; I had opted for Euripides' thrilling *The Bacchae* – the dissolute, uproarious tale of the enmity between Pentheus, King of Thebes, and his cousin Dionysus, god of wine, women and wholesale debauchery. Once I had knocked it off, the 'Syndics' of CUP, its academic governing body, decided that my version was a bit too steamy for their taste and declined to publish it, after all. This outraged not just me but one of the many firm friends I had made via Oxford theatre, an American Rhodes Scholar with the memorable name of Richmond Crinkley, who vowed to stage it at his alma mater, the University of Chapel Hill, North Carolina. So that summer saw me making, in high excitement, my first visit to the United States.

It was the summer of student protest which had spread all over the world from the Sorbonne in Paris; in Oxford, moreover, the Hart Report on student discipline was imminent, which had the campus in restless mood. So I headed west with a big state-of-the-nation piece for *Isis* in mind as much as my own fevered curiosity about the New World.

After a very happy ten days in North Carolina, savouring Richmond's stylish staging of my version of Euripides, I considered Greyhound buses the ultimate luxury as I paid my first visits to New York and Washington DC before travelling cross-country to Los Angeles and San Francisco. On Manhattan's west side I was housed by Richmond's college roommate, Everett Fahy, then curator of European paintings at the Metropolitan Museum, later to become director of the Frick Collection. This proved the beginning of another cherished long-term friendship, the nearest

I would ever get to the rarefied world of fine art. After-hours tours of the Met in such expert company were an especial thrill.

I did not meet that many protesters – it was to prove two years before America's own real summer of student protest, sparked by the shootings at Kent State, Ohio – but I did manage the soon-to-be-familiar task of spinning it all into a lengthy in-depth analysis in the first edition of the following term's *Isis*. Alongside it was the first in a radical series of campaigning articles denouncing the Oxford Union as an effete, elitist debating society and calling for a democratically elected student union in Oxford. After a few weeks of this campaign, I received a summons to see the proprietor at Headington Hill Hall.

While waiting apprehensively in Maxwell's grand library I could not help but notice that he chose to line his walls with fake books – leather-bound spines of classics with resonant titles glued onto mahogany panelling. Soon I was ushered into his substantial presence, with no idea what to expect.

'This campaign of yours about a student union . . .' he began without so much as a hello or a do-sit-down.

'Er, yes,' I replied uncertainly.

'Splendid!' he beamed. 'Is there anything I can do to help?'

Taken aback, I found myself bereft of all rational thought. 'That's a very kind offer, Mr Maxwell, but I can't actually think of anything . . .'

'Would it help if I bought the Oxford Union?'

Aghast, I stammered: 'Well, yes, I suppose it would. We could even convert it into a . . .'

'Excellent,' he cut me short. 'See to it.'

With which he waved me out again.

Back at the *Isis* office, the threadbare handful of staff were eagerly awaiting news of my audience with the great man, while it was dawning on me that I barely knew how to buy a pair of shoes, let alone a building, in this case of unknown ownership. After telling my awe-struck colleagues of the boss's plan, I said briskly

to them: 'See to it!', in grandly Maxwellian manner, before
sweeping off to interview Ken Dodd, then playing Oxford's New
Theatre, about the finer Freudian aspects of comedy. Nothing,
I need hardly add, ever came of Maxwell's masterplan, though I
did get a good line out of Ken Dodd: 'The trouble with Freud is
that he never had to play Saturday night at the Glasgow Empire!'
Half a century later, I heard him on the radio still recycling that
same old gag.

I subsequently caught a glimpse of *le vrai* Maxwell during one
of his summer garden parties – with his six-year-old daughter
Ghislaine running happily around amid the throng – when he
encouraged me to try out the delights of his new sauna. Once
I was installed, unsure what I was supposed to do in so fetid
an environment beyond taking off all my clothes, he took great
pleasure in locking me in and peering through the porthole in the
door, grinning gleefully. It was a sweaty hour or more before his
bedraggled editor was finally granted his freedom.

As if I were not already busy enough, I also rose that year to the
dizzy heights of president of the O.U. Poetry Society, in charge
of inviting eminent poets to come and give the society a reading
each week, and entertaining them before and afterwards. Before
was a case of drinks at a local pub; afterwards, some even stayed
the night on my sofa.

The most significant visit for me personally turned out to be
that of A. Alvarez, a fine poet himself but also the editor of an
influential Penguin anthology, *The New Poetry*, which had shaped
the taste of my generation. At the end of his reading, when he
returned to join me at my chairman's desk before taking questions, I was obliged to tell Al that his flies appeared to have been
undone throughout the proceedings; sitting behind him, I had
not noticed until now. He thought this hilarious, and took me off
for a dinner at which the conversation swiftly moved on – inevitably, in hindsight – from poetry to poker, as did countless such
meals together over the subsequent half-century of laughter-filled

friendship, from Hampstead to Las Vegas and back many times. In his 1999 memoirs, *Where Did It All Go Right?*, Al touchingly called me 'the kid brother I never had'.

1968 saw the latest in a near-300-year line of quinquennial contests to elect a new Professor of Poetry at Oxford, which had in recent years turned into a series of no-holds-barred bunfights. All it then took to nominate a candidate – with or without the nominee's knowledge, let alone consent – was two votes from Oxford MAs. A sure-fire chance to make some mischief, this had recently resulted in contestants from Muhammad Ali to the prime minister's poetry-loving wife, Mary Wilson. As editor of *Isis*, I launched a campaign for Alvarez. When a flurry of other candidates emerged, I wrote a desperate letter to *The Times*, announcing that I was organising a student ballot – quoting Auden to the effect that 'they're the ones who have to listen to the bloody lectures' – and urged its then editor, William Rees-Mogg, to announce the result while urging Oxford MAs to vote for the student choice. To my wide-eyed delight, Mogg printed it as the lead letter.

Then, on the eve of the student ballot, a comely undergraduette rode all but naked through the city streets in support of Yevgeny Yevtushenko, who duly romped to victory in the next day's vote. But would he be allowed to leave Russia to give the lectures? A student journalist's phone call to Brezhnev at the Kremlin raised only an office cleaner, who thought he 'probably would'. The more pressing problem was that he couldn't speak English.

The eventual victor turned out to be Roy Fuller, also solicitor for the Woolwich Building Society, over ten other candidates, with Alvarez in fifth place behind the still *incommunicado* Yevtushenko. Al summed it all up with an apposite quote from his beloved metaphysical poet George Herbert:

After so foul a journey, death is fair
And but a chair.

The same year saw me represent Merton on TV's *University Challenge*, in which we appeared several times, losing in the semi-final. The best thing about appearing on the show, I soon discovered, was the number of letters you received from young female 'admirers', not a few of which I followed up. Then came the day the programme's host, Bamber Gascoigne, announced 'the picture question', for which I donned my spectacles, in those days rather heavy-duty, so hitherto concealed from the camera behind my name-plate. 'Oh no, I'm sorry,' Gascoigne went on, 'it's the music question.' There followed the familiar strains of a French horn balefully introducing . . .

'Merton – Holden.'

'Brahms' second piano concerto.'

'Correct,' said Gascoigne. But, fatally as it transpired, I was still wearing my unbecoming specs. The letters from girls stopped arriving.

Following publication of my *Agamemnon*, Penguin Classics boldly commissioned me to translate a collection of *Greek Pastoral Poetry* for one of those black-backed paperbacks which sat authoritatively on our bookshelves. I cannot say that I was overly familiar with the poems of Theocritus, let alone Moschus and Bion, but I naturally accepted the challenge with alacrity. Amid all else – not least my final exams – this daunting task would take me the next couple of years.

It began during my final year at Oxford – my fourth, thanks to Maxwell – for which I moved north to stately Park Town, where I shared digs with a postgraduate friend, the poet Craig Raine.

With 'finals' looming at the end of the summer term, I took to earning useful money on the side by appearing as a £5-a-day extra in various movies shot at nearby Blenheim Palace; you can see my youthful self, for instance, in sundry crowd scenes behind Marcello Mastroianni in a beyond-dreadful 1969 heist movie called *Diamonds for Breakfast*.

Meanwhile, a student composer named Richard Morris had approached me with the idea of turning my version of *Agamemnon* into an opera. I was intrigued, to say the least. After winning the commission from the O.U. Opera Club, he had asked me to condense my translation into a libretto.

And so it came to pass that the first term of my final, bonus fourth year saw the *Sunday Telegraph* of 30 November 1969 declaring: 'It is all starting to whizz for Tony Holden', in a page lead headlined 'Money for old Greeks', justified only by a photo of a fetching choreographer, my friend Ros Erskine, with this pushy, curly-haired young man lurking with faux modesty behind her. 'At 22, his opera *Agamemnon* was performed all last week at the Oxford Playhouse. Penguin Classics have commissioned him to re-translate Theocritus. He goes to Washington next year to see his translation of Euripides' *Bacchae* performed. All of which is not bad for an undergraduate at Merton College, Oxford, whose subject turns out to be English.'

Highly gratifying, of course, for a supposedly ambitious young student, but in which of these apparent accomplishments was there a living to be earned?

During my last term at Oxford, in the summer of 1970, when I should really have been catching up with all the academic work

I hadn't been doing these past four years, I couldn't resist an invitation to become assistant director to the theatrical man-of-the-moment Clifford Williams on an OUDS production of Thomas Middleton's *A Chaste Maid in Cheapside*. In 1967 Williams had directed a celebrated all-male production of *As You Like It* at Laurence Olivier's nascent National Theatre, then still based at the Old Vic, which I had so admired that I'd been to see it all of three times. He had since been in the news for directing Kenneth Tynan's wilfully outrageous revue, *Oh! Calcutta!*, which capitalised on the abolition of the office of the theatrical censor, the Lord Chamberlain, by featuring nudity, both male and female, amid daringly sexual material written by a host of voguish names from Samuel Beckett to John Lennon.

While simultaneously working in London on the world premiere of Anthony Shaffer's two-man thriller, *Sleuth*, Williams needed an assistant in Oxford to take rehearsals in his absence. How could I refuse? No wonder my then girlfriend, Maggie Gee, caught me reading *Great Books of the World in Digest Form* in the university library on the eve of my finals. As it turned out, I managed to scrape a second-class degree. Morley, like other such contemporaries as Martin Amis, achieved a nonpareil First.

In those days, the Oxford exam results were printed in *The Times* later that summer, by which time I was on a sybaritic vacation with my Oundle friends the Harrisons and my latest beloved on the Balearic island of Formentera. Each day for a week I bicycled into the tiny island's capital city, the incongruously named San Francisco, to invest more than I could afford in an export copy of that paper, until the morning I finally discovered my fate. On the beach that afternoon, I wrote a bitter little ditty to the chairman of the Board of Examiners, Helen Gardner, whose first quatrain still lingers:

> *I thank Dame Helen, Providence and me*
> *That I have won a second-class degree.*

My mind is second-class, I've always known,
And this the Board has now most kindly shown . . .

That put a certain end to any further thoughts of a career in poetry. Now, perhaps, after my joint triumph with Clifford Williams, I could become a theatre director? Or an actor? Or . . .

The end of my final term at Oxford had already determined my fate. Still embarrassingly unsure what I wanted to make of myself, I had applied for a graduate traineeship at the BBC. For a young man of my assorted interests, that could lead anywhere! But I failed the interview. 'What is your source of news?' asked the chairman of the intimidating panel before me in Broadcasting House.

'Er, I watch the BBC news,' was my duly diplomatic reply.

'What is your source of news?' he repeated with some emphasis.

'I read *The Guardian*.'

'What is your source of news?' he repeated yet again.

I can't remember what I said to that. If my first two answers had been unsatisfactory, I still don't understand his question.

Meanwhile, I had heard that in the last few weeks of your final term at Oxbridge, the anonymous men from MI5 materialised to tap the shoulder of a chosen few. This now became my dream assignment. Yes, I would be a spy! The illusion was shattered one day when the captain of our *University Challenge* team came crashing into the college bar to announce to all and sundry: 'I've just been asked to be a spy!'

'Well, if you're telling all of us,' we responded in unison, 'you won't make a very good one, Mr Bond!' Nor did he. For whatever reason, he wound up in quite another, more humdrum line of business.

But my own shoulder, to my intense dismay, was never thus tapped. After the similar disappointment of the BBC, the only other potential employer to whom I had applied was Thomson Newspapers, owners of *The Times* and the *Sunday Times*, and a chain of provincial newspapers on which they offered a handful of graduate traineeships. Now there arrived a letter from Thomson's offering me a job. I had already had two pieces published in national newspapers; but was this, I have always wondered, because Ivan had had a word in someone's ear?

At last, it was settled. I wasn't going to be a poet or a painter, after all, let alone a novelist, an actor, a director, a playwright, a scholar of Ancient Greek, a spy or even, dammit, an AA man.

After all that, I was going to be a journalist.

5

'WON'T MAKE A WRITER'

In the autumn of 1968, at the ripe old age of twenty-one, and still midway through my time at Oxford, I had found myself sitting in the Bloomsbury offices of A. P. Watt, one of Britain's leading literary agencies, being offered a cigarillo by its *eminence grise*, Hilary Rubinstein. As I took my first drag, and beamed at the genial proprietor of this book-lined room wrapping me in its embrace, I permitted myself to think: *Yes! This is it! I've made it!*

A tad premature, perhaps, but nonetheless a memorable moment. This was certainly, at the very least, a long way from Southport.

It was also to prove the beginning of a forty-year professional and personal friendship with Hilary, a benevolent man with impressive literary credentials. His brother Michael had represented Penguin Books in 1960 in its celebrated defence against obscenity charges of D. H. Lawrence's *Lady Chatterley's Lover*. Post-Oxford, Hilary had started out as an editor at the eponymous publishing house of his uncle, Victor Gollancz, whom he had persuaded to publish *Lucky Jim*, the first novel by his Oxford chum Kingsley Amis, as well as J. G. Ballard, among many others. Now, having turned literary agent, he represented the likes of P. G. Wodehouse, Robert Graves and Nadine Gordimer, as well as estates such as those of H. G. Wells, Rudyard Kipling, G. K. Chesterton, W. B. Yeats and Somerset Maugham. Heady company indeed!

I could scarcely call myself 'connected', like many of my

London-bred contemporaries, but it was my supremely good fortune that Hilary had been an undergraduate at Merton with my tutor there, John Jones. Now he introduced me to another of his Oxford pals, Godfrey Smith, who just happened to be editor of the oh-so-glamorous *Sunday Times* magazine. On the evidence of my journalistic output so far, not to mention my supposed expertise as a classicist, the supremely generous Godfrey offered me a staff job on the magazine straight out of university while hiring me to tutor his daughter Deborah for Latin 'O' level.

Godfrey remained undeterred even when Debbie failed her Latin 'O' level (we spent more time, she later reminded me, discussing life than Livy). But the portcullis of 'restrictive practices' had just been lowered by the National Union of Journalists, and all direct routes to Fleet Street were now firmly blocked. While my Oxford pals Hitchens, Amis, James Fenton and others negotiated their way towards literary glory via the *New Statesman* or the *Times Literary Supplement*, I was banished to that Thomson traineeship, and so to a two-and-a-half-year stint in provincial journalism, specifically at the *Evening Echo*, Hemel Hempstead.

In my last year at Oxford I had written a review of some Gore Vidal essays for the *Sunday Telegraph* and a piece about Oxford's plans for a Samuel Beckett Theatre for the *Financial Times*. Hilary Rubinstein was already enfolding me in his extensive professional network. Now, instead, I would be chasing car crashes, minor crime and local council stories in Watford at a time when, like all graduate trainees, I thought I should be writing leading articles for *The Times*.

Somehow, I had even managed to get myself an interview with *The Times*'s then editor, William Rees-Mogg. 'Thinks he wants to write. Won't make a writer,' was his verdict. 'May have administrative abilities.' All I knew at the time was that I heard nothing further from Rees-Mogg; this verdict was revealed to me from internal files a dozen years later when I fetched up at *The Times* as heir apparent to its editorial chair.

But for now, it was up the M1 to Hemel Hempstead. Before what felt like a lengthy apprenticeship at the *Evening Echo*, however, there would be a four-month training course in Cardiff, then the British mecca of journalistic aspiration. While *Picture Post*'s long-time editor Tom Hopkinson ran the UK's first university degree course in journalism, Thomson Regional Newspapers hosted fifteen hand-picked graduates a year. We were taught newspaper practice and law, shorthand and touch-typing. The latter I could never quite manage; so, despite supplementary lessons from my expertly trained mother, I still type – many millions of words later – with only two fingers.

Roy Thomson himself came to visit us in Cardiff, launching into a speech hailing the glories of advertising – until an aide whispered in his ear and he paused, looked puzzled and proclaimed: 'You guys *are* marketing, aren't you?' We were very jealous when the editor of the moment, Harold Evans of the *Sunday Times*, for whom we all aspired to work, went to talk to his pal Hopkinson's students instead of us.

Otherwise, it was a matter of mastering a brand of shorthand called T-line, which some of us still use to this day, and the minutiae of such essentials as the Public Bodies (Admission to Meetings) Act 1960. The key questions to ask of any interviewee on any story were, we were taught: 'Who what where when why?' Much of this classroom fare has lodged with me ever since; our chief tutor, the amiable Clive Pulman, was for instance insistent that no one (i.e. everyone) dies 'suddenly', and so banned this quotidian journalistic coinage, at which I still flinch most days.

In the evenings, in our suburban digs, we would play cards – not poker, as yet (none of us had any money), but hearts – and every night one of us would say as he shuffled the deck: 'One day I'm going to be rich and famous as a novelist.'

'Oh, shut up and deal,' we'd reply, 'we're *all* going to be rich and famous novelists!'

The dealer in question was Ken Follett, who (after a brief career on the *South Wales Echo* and London *Evening News*) has since sold some 200 million copies of his globally celebrated fiction. I was one of the very few of the fifteen who actually did become a long-term newspaper journalist, let alone at Thomson (now Times, i.e. Murdoch) Newspapers. This unlikely crew still meets up for annual reunions, the fiftieth by Zoom during the 2020 Covid pandemic.

All destined for local papers around the country, we were remorselessly drilled in their idiosyncratic news values. The supreme test came in an exercise to write for the Cardiff-based *South Wales Echo* the 'intro' of a news story involving a supposed multiple-death crash in Cardiff at one of those new-fangled 'continental-style' level crossings, as British newspapers then chose to call them with an anti-European sneer. The victims were the prime minister, the archbishop of Canterbury and the lord mayor of Cardiff – all dead. Yes, it was a tricky one. The winner, of course, was: 'Traffic was delayed for up to three hours yesterday on the main Cardiff-to-Swansea road after . . .'

The Holy Grail to which we aspired was to pass the proficiency test of the NCTJ, the National Council for the Training of Journalists. Beyond knowing what such initials as IRA and TUC stood for, this involved conducting an interview with some stooge representing the prime minister of the day. I soon got the hang of the procedure required.

Knock on door before entering. Five points.

Say: 'May I come in?' Five points.

Upon entering: 'May I sit down?' Five points.

'May I take notes?' Five points. Take out notebook.

'You are the prime minister?' Yes. Five points.

'Of the United Kingdom of Great Britain and Northern Ireland?' Yes. Five points.

'And your name is Edward Heath?' Yes. Five points.

'That's spelt H-E-A-T-H?' Yes. Five points.

'Are you going to resign?' No. But five points for bold question.

I could go on, but I had already earned enough points for a pass – quite possibly a distinction.

Towards the end of this seminal period in our lives, our thoughts were redirected towards the refined arts of feature writing – then a lofty ambition indeed. I was sent off to interview a Cardiff hypnotherapist named Arnall Bloxham, a devout believer in reincarnation. No shortage of material there, I thought; the obvious ploy was to get him to hypnotise me so as to find out who I had been in a previous life. After succumbing promptly to fingers being waved in front of my eyes, I turned out – to my delight – to have been the celebrated Georgian actor Edmund Kean. *Wow! I'd really rather be him than me,* I thought with a thespian thrill while cobbling together a few hundred words, an expanded version of which would later find its way into Godfrey Smith's *Sunday Times* magazine.

By then, however, an even more momentous turn of events would see me sharing a flat in north London with a young woman for whom I had fallen big-time. I have fallen in love with countless women during my life, and been lucky enough to have married two of them. The first, to my delight, was a musician.

According to a journal discovered forty years after his death, W. H. Auden wrote in his diary after his first night in bed with the love of his life, Chester Kallman: 'It is impossible to listen to music and get an erection at the same time.' This, I now discovered, was not true of me.

I had first met Amanda Warren in the summer of 1969, when she came to visit Richard Morris in the rented cottage near Ross-on-Wye where he and I were working on the opera of *Agamemnon*. That very morning, I had posted a letter to my Oxford girlfriend, Maggie Gee, idly wondering if she thought it would be a good idea for us to get married. It wasn't, of course, as Maggie was not slow to let me know, which has never dulled my memory of posting that letter as a supremely

authentic act of existentialist Sartrean *engagement*. Immediately
I had slipped it nervously into the letterbox, I was down on my
hands and knees, scrabbling around in an absurd attempt to get
it out again. Forlornly I walked back to the cottage to find that
Amanda had arrived to check on our progress, in her capacity as
president of the O.U. Opera Club. I took an immediate shine to
her, and pursued her to Edinburgh at Festival time that summer.

Since then my pursuit had become ardent, and I had often
had occasion to listen to her playing the piano. So effortless
did her playing seem, her lovely face so serene the while, that
I suffered quite the opposite of Auden's problem, and was
ungallantly obliged to remain seated whenever her formidable
mother entered the room. This was the eminent gynaecologist
Dame Josephine Barnes, the first female president of the British
Medical Association. Amanda's father was Sir Brian Warren,
personal physician to the prime minister, Edward Heath, as well
as half his Tory cabinet. Was this upstart Lancashire lad out of
his depth here? Perhaps so – and Amanda's sister Penny certainly
seemed to think so. Married to Martin Neary, organist of St
Margaret's, Westminster, later of Westminster Abbey, Penny
stationed me outside the entrance to sell programmes for one
of his recitals.

And she was probably right. But I was young and in love. I
danced attendance on Amanda all the way through my extra
year at Oxford, then my three months in Cardiff, and eventually managed to persuade her to share a flat with me in West
Hampstead when I started work in Hemel. Thus it was that,
when her highly traditional father enquired as to my prospects,
I could reply only: 'Well, I'm the deputy Watford correspondent
of the Hemel Hempstead *Evening Echo*.' He was unimpressed but
indulgent, and a generous dowry from her parents enabled us to
buy a tiny country cottage in the rural village of Bricket Wood,
Hertfordshire, as close to my grandfather's birthplace in St
Albans as to the *Echo*'s office on an industrial estate up the M1.

Now, when Penny stationed me outside St Margaret's to sell programmes, I realised that she was touchingly recognising me as a member of the family. Amanda and I were married in Kensington Register Office on 1 May 1971. We were both twenty-three. A reception followed at Chandos House off Harley Street, the headquarters of the British Medical Association. It was a truly Lancashire-meets-London occasion; my Uncle George, the farmyard-dwelling commercial traveller for L&G fire appliances, stood in the reception line clutching a fire extinguisher, which he handed over as our wedding present. My Uncle Jimmy snapped to attention and saluted upon bumping into his commanding officer in the Egyptian desert during the Second World War, who turned out to be Amanda's godfather.

Also among the guests was Godfrey Smith, who had worked in this very building as personal assistant to Lord Kemsley, the former owner of Times Newspapers – and whose own wedding present was to publish my first piece in the *Sunday Times* magazine, that scoop about my previous life as Edmund Kean, the following day. An incurable romantic, and himself the father of three daughters, longing for the day he would walk them down the aisle, Godfrey asked where we were going for our honeymoon.

'No honeymoon for us, I'm afraid, Godfrey,' I replied. 'It's back to work in Watford for me, first thing Monday morning.'

'No honeymoon?' he spluttered. 'That's ridiculous!' Turning to the bride, he asked her: 'Where would you like to go?'

Immediately I sussed what he had in mind. Sundry exotic dreams began taking shape in my imagination as she demurely replied, 'Well, I've always wanted to go to Amsterdam.'

She could have said Bali, Bora Bora, the Seychelles, the Caribbean. But ... 'Amsterdam it is!' replied a beaming Godfrey, at whose expense we soon jetted off for me to write an 'Amsterdam Notebook' for his magazine.

Back in Hemel Hempstead, my proudest moment as a local journalist came when I ordered fish and chips in a local chippy one evening, only to see them slapped down on my very own *Evening Echo* byline.

By then we had three cats – one blond, one ginger, one dark – uncannily presaging the three sons we were soon to have: one blond, one ginger, one dark-haired. The ginger one was called Oedipuss, the youngest Buster Kitten – which Christopher Hitchens thought so droll that he took to calling me 'Buster' for the rest of his life.

One weekend the black cat (named, embarrassingly enough, Pussy) went missing after the local hunt had swept through the fields beside our cottage. Amanda was distraught. When I casually mentioned this to someone at the office, I could not have anticipated that the news editor would commission a heated piece which wound up as a front-page splash: LOCAL HUNT SAVAGES PET CAT. So I told no one when, a few nights later, I was awoken in the middle of the night by an all too familiar cat – yes, black – tiptoeing across our bed.

Better by far was the day the paper splashed on ECHO MAN SEEKS FAME IN STATES, hailing my trip back to New York for Richmond Crinkley's off-Broadway production of my translation of *The Bacchae*, now transformed into a rock musical called *Dionysus Wants You!* Richmond had opened it in Washington DC, at no less a venue than the theatre of the Folger Shakespeare Library, where it had caused enough of a stir for the Broadway impresario Joseph Papp to bring it up to his famed Public Theater on Manhattan's Lafayette Street.

It was a thrilling adventure for me – if less so, it seems, for audiences; the show lasted barely a fortnight. So that same *Echo* man was soon back from Broadway to the lesser thrills of Watford council meetings, and death crashes on the M1's two-lane 'killer stretch', right at the bottom of our little country garden. Promoted to leader writer, I enjoyed a daily conference with the editor, Ivor Lewis, who would launch into an in-depth discussion of the Rhodesian crisis, saying, 'I want you to get Ian Smith by the balls today!' before conceding, as he saw me musing about the extent of the *Echo*'s influence in southern Africa, 'Okay, maybe we'd better do the Watford ring road again.'

Early one morning, when I was on the unenviable all-night 'graveyard shift', it fell to me to write a picture story involving a local who had built a yacht in his back garden, only to realise that he couldn't get it out without the help of a crane to lift it over his house. Soon after dawn, an *Echo* photographer and I found ourselves intrepidly stationed outside a terraced house in the Hemel Hempstead suburbs, knowing how much better the story would be if the crane were to drop the yacht, smashing it to smithereens on the roof of its owner's house. At the critical moment, as the vessel was at the highest point of its airborne maiden voyage, there was a distinct wobble, then a sway in the lightest of breezes, to the point where our hopes soared. But the moment passed; the yacht made a safe landing on the

trailer behind its owner's truck; and now the crane operator
was making his way over to me.

'Terrific, huh?' he ventured.

I just smiled.

'You didn't see that little wobble at the top, did you?'

I said nothing.

'Because there wasn't one, was there, eh?'

He held out his hand to shake a cheery farewell, and turned
to depart, leaving something crinkly in my palm. A £10 note. It
was the first bribe I'd been offered as a journalist. But it wouldn't
be the last.

Given that we'd agreed on a 'modern' marriage, Amanda and I
were cheerfully committed to separate holidays that summer. She
was going on a Turkish cruise with her mother, I to the *corridas*
of Spain with J Morley. At the last minute we began regretting
this decision so much that I arranged a magical mystery tour of a
weekend away together.

'Where are we going?' asked Amanda as I edged us up our
Hertfordshire country lane in my zippy Triumph Spitfire
convertible.

'That's a surprise!' said I gleefully, heading the car north-east.
All too soon she worked out that we were headed for Suffolk,
specifically Aldeburgh. 'And we're going to a Britten concert at
the Maltings?' Now she was getting excited.

'Yes,' I replied, 'and no.'

I had indeed booked a beachfront hotel in Aldeburgh, and inves-
tigated the possibility of a Benjamin Britten concert at his home
concert hall, the Maltings in Snape, only to discover that none was
on offer that weekend. On arrival, it turned out that a Jacques Tati
film was showing at the local fleapit, so we went there instead.

The cinema was empty. We were its only customers until,
soon after the lights had gone down, one other couple entered:
none other than – yes – Benjamin Britten and his partner Peter
Pears. Mission (sort of) accomplished.

The following week, the night before we were to set off in our separate directions, we drove to an address in Hampstead where Morley had asked me to pick up some books for him.

The door was answered by Elizabeth Taylor.

'Ah yes,' she said, 'you must be Anthony and Amanda. Why don't you come in for a drink?' Typical Morley, I thought, still in a state of shock, to warn her but not me.

Thanks to Burton's pal Nevill Coghill, also an admirer of the young Morley's poetry, J had gone straight from Oxford to the Burton–Taylor ranch at Puerto Vallarta, Mexico, as tutor to her sons by Michael Wilding. He had just finished a year's stint there before taking the boys back with him to Munich.

So in we went, and she couldn't have been more charming. The sometime child star of *National Velvet* was watching the Horse of the Year Show, which she kept on while fetching the drinks. 'So,' she said, 'you're off to Paris tomorrow, I hear?' That was indeed where I had agreed to meet up with Morley the next day en route to Spain in my Spitfire. 'You must have dinner at our favourite restaurant!'

She must have noticed me trying to work out the polite phraseology for 'We couldn't possibly afford it . . .' before adding: 'as our guests, of course.'

The following evening, I had arranged to stay overnight with my Oxford chum Ivor Roberts, that same proto-diplomat who had so fatefully asked Taylor for her autograph, by now second secretary at the British Embassy in Paris. So I got Ivor to book us a table – in the name of Burton and Taylor, of course – at said restaurant. Whose *patron* was duly disappointed, given that he had set up an elevated table for all to see, when we turned up in our scruffy jeans and T-shirts in place of the expected Burtons in all their glory.

We were already ordering our first drinks while Ivor patiently explained things with his suave diplomatic charm. We then proceeded to get completely plastered, running up the most spectacular of bills, to the point where an exasperated Ivor was obliged to surrender his diplomatic passport as a guarantor of eventual payment.

During the night, as can happen to the young and inexperienced after too much grape-and-grain, I awoke in Ivor's spare room knowing that I was on the verge of throwing up. Like the polite houseguest I have always aspired to be, I swiftly got out of bed, crossed the room and opened the window to deliver my load out onto the street below, rather than Ivor's rug. When I finally awoke again the next morning, I looked down to see my handiwork by the light of day. It had all landed on the balcony a floor beneath.

'That's the official residence of the Italian consul!' barked an enraged Ivor, who has never really forgiven me. Even though he, Morley and I formed a human water-passing chain to wash (most of) it off, it took months for Ivor to dig himself out of that diplomatic hole – as he still enjoyed reminding me decades later over the occasional dinner on the high table of Trinity College.

J and I had a terrific summer pursuing the *toreros* all over Spain, often driving all night from one *fiesta* to another, learning enough about the *corrida de toros* to discriminate between the truly brave matadors and their more showy but shifty brethren. That autumn I wrote an enthusiastic, sub-Hemingway account of it all for Anthony Howard's *New Statesman*, which Tony later told me brought in several years' worth of lucrative *anti*-bullfight advertising.

Back on the *Evening Echo*, I was assigned to cover the trial in St Albans of the serial killer Graham Young, charged with poisoning several of his workmates, some fatally, at the photographic laboratory where he was employed as a storeman in the village of Bovingdon, near Hemel Hempstead. Not until he was convicted could the nation (let alone the jury) be told the truth I had been investigating for months: that he had done it all before.

Born in 1947, Young had been convicted at the age of fourteen of poisoning several family members and schoolfriends – one, again, fatally – in the north London district of Neasden, where he was born and raised. At his tender age he was sent to Broadmoor, the hospital for the 'criminally insane' in Berkshire, whence he was released eight years later after persuading its chief psychiatrist that he was reformed. Within months he had embarked on another murderous spree, again choosing as his victims those closest and, in many cases, kindest to him.

Graham Young was a deranged psychopath, highly intelligent but acutely narcissistic and wholly lacking in any moral sense. Fascinated by poisons, and expertly self-taught about their use, his life changed when his father gave him a chemistry set for passing his 11-plus. He began to conduct experiments on his own family, slipping poison into their cups of tea and calmly noting the effect on them of various dosages until his stepmother died in agony and his father and sister were permanently maimed. Even in Broadmoor he managed to extract cyanide from some laurel bushes, again with fatal results, while quietly slipping Harpic and sugar-soap into the itinerant tea-urn.

Young's poisons of choice were antimony potassium tartrate and the deadly heavy-metal poison thallium, about which he learned from an Agatha Christie novel, *The Pale Horse*. When his workmates at Hadland's laboratory in Bovingdon began developing acute stomach pains, vomiting, even losing their hair – usually after drinking cups of tea kindly brought them by their friend Graham – the management put it down to a passing virus they christened 'the Bovingdon bug'. When the local GP visited to give staff a supposedly reassuring talk, Young publicly asked such technically expert questions that he gave himself away – just as he had in his teens. This time he was sent for life to a high-security prison, Parkhurst.

Naturally his conviction provoked a national outcry under such headlines as RELEASED TO KILL AGAIN. Before covering Young's trial, I had conducted so much research on his life story that I had more than enough material for a book, which now I duly wrote under the title *The St Albans Poisoner*. By then, Young had achieved his ambition of going down in criminal history as one of Britain's most notorious poisoners. During his trial, he sent me a note across the courtroom, via his solicitor, expressing the hope that my coverage would see him installed in the Chamber of Horrors at Madame Tussaud's. That wish, too, has long since been granted.

With Graham Young's waxwork at Madame Tussauds

In August 1990, two weeks before his forty-third birthday, Graham Young was reported to have died in Parkhurst 'of a heart attack'. I didn't believe it then, and I don't believe it now. I had long expected to read that he had died by 'falling' (in the old lags' cliché) 'down the prison stairs'; both his fellow inmates and indeed the guards had good reason to dispose of a companion who could extract poison from a stone, or perhaps even metal bars. Some later hinted as much to me.

That was certainly one reason I was reluctant to accept the constant invitations to visit Young in Parkhurst which regularly reached me via Lord Longford and other habitual prison visitors.

'Graham was so pleased with your book,' Longford told me. 'He'd love you to go and have a cup of tea with him.'

I'll bet he would. Somehow, the idea never appealed.

All this time I was also translating *Greek Pastoral Poetry* while covering Watford council meetings and knocking on the doors of families who had lost loved ones overnight in yet another M1 death crash. In later years, Harold Evans would write that I was 'more modest and more canny' than the 'aspiring young journalists fresh from Oxford' who 'look with disdain on the scuffed rungs of the ladder from provincial journalism, shorthand and local government lessons, to Fleet Street.' In truth, as I saw it, I had little alternative.

Was this unwonted 'modesty' on my part, I wondered, something to do with my father's genteel conservatism? I wondered even more when I occasionally drove down the M1 for drinks in Barnet with Martin Amis and his father, Kingsley. They revelled in such zestful repartee, cleverly playing with words while gleefully trashing other writers, that I felt intensely jealous of such a lively, animating father–son relationship. It was a revelation to me.

One evening I met up in London with Christopher Hitchens and James Fenton for one of our regular drinking sessions at the Bung Hole off High Holborn, then the favoured watering-place of the nearby *New Statesman*, where they were both staff writers. That week's *Statesman* competition had been set by Tom Driberg, the maverick Labour MP, whose fiendish challenge was to write a limerick about Stoke Poges, with a double rhyme on both 'Stoke' and 'Poges'.

Lifelong lovers of limericks, the three of us set about it over a bottle or three of claret. We soon came up with a terrific punchline; the difficulty was the interim double-rhyme at the end of line two. Our hard-wrought solution was less than perfect, so much so that it required an advance footnote: the reader needed to know that there was a US air force base near Stoke Poges.

> *There was a young Yank from Stoke Poges*
> *Who when touring abroad would croak 'Oh, Jeez!*
> *It's an absolute menace:*
> *Whenever I'm in Venice,*
> *I'm always being asked to poke doges!'*

It turned out to prove the only entry, but Driberg declared it a worthy winner, the sole problem being that *New Statesman* staff were not allowed to enter. So instead he took the three of us out to dinner at a Soho restaurant, where the conversation was so liberally sprinkled with limericks that we proceeded back to his Barbican apartment, where he took out a cherished file of unpublished limericks by W. H. Auden.

One example has always stuck in my memory:

> *The Bishop-Elect of Hong Kong*
> *Has a cock which is ten inches long;*
> *He thinks that the spectators*
> *Are admiring his gaiters*
> *When he goes to the Gents – he is wrong.*

Not until years later did it strike me that, whatever the date of this witty ditty, it deserves the most honourable of niches in the hallowed firmament of Auden studies. That punchline – 'He was wrong' – finds a resonant echo towards the end of his 1938 poem 'Funeral Blues', rendered even more famous (as 'Stop all the clocks') by the movie *Four Weddings and a Funeral*.

> *I thought that love would last forever;*
> *I was wrong.*

By now the limited journalistic challenges of Hemel Hempstead were, frankly, beginning to pall. There was more fun to be had in the paper's caravan, which toured its rural catchment area supposedly touting for news, but could often be seen swaying as staff locked the door to enjoy some consensual high jinks inside.

Apart from the delights of translating Ancient Greek poetry, I was also writing more regular pieces for Tony Howard's *New Statesman* and Godfrey Smith's *Sunday Times* magazine. A profile for the latter of Al Alvarez, on the publication in 1972 of his literary study of suicide, *The Savage God*, was incongruously followed by a study of motorway rescue teams when Amanda and I had our own near-death crash, rolling over on the M1 when there was a sudden pile-up ahead of us. In between came a party at the British Film Institute on the South Bank to celebrate the magazine's tenth birthday party. It was an all-nighter, of course, with two films voted for by the staff – *Citizen Kane*, naturally, along with *Singin' in the Rain* – shown before breakfast was sent across the Thames by boat from the Savoy. Yes, those were indeed the budget-busting days!

The time finally came to take the exam that these two and a half years, from Cardiff to Hemel, had been all about: the proficiency test of the National Council for the Training of Journalists, which I sat alongside other graduate trainee colleagues in the nearby 'new' town of Harlow. When the results were announced, it transpired that my marks were somehow the highest in the land, winning me the title of Young Journalist of the Year along with a handsome prize financed by the pharmaceutical company Pfizer. This entitled me to spend a few months travelling anywhere in the world at their expense, with the stipulation that whatever I wrote had to be concerned with matters medical.

So, with the encouragement of Godfrey Smith, now editor of the *Sunday Times* Review Section, I decided to head back to the States, to investigate the inequalities thrown up by its private medical system. From coast to coast I watched physicians performing high-risk surgery with half an eye on a TV screen in the operating theatre showing the changing values of their stocks and shares. In California I interviewed a prominent opponent of affordable health care, dismissed by its adversaries as 'socialised' medicine, the state governor Ronald Reagan; in Washington I interviewed its leading proponent, Senator Edward Kennedy. I even managed to make it into the Nixon White House.

At the end of the previous year, 1971, Prime Minister Edward Heath's first summit with Nixon had taken place in Bermuda. Heath had naturally taken along his personal physician, my father-in-law Brian Warren, who returned with a witty anecdote about the presidential physician turning up with bullet extractors, blood plasma machines and resuscitation devices while all he had brought from Blighty was his stethoscope and prescription pad. Somehow this vignette found its way into *Private Eye*, which did not amuse Brian; but he forgave me long enough to offer an introduction to Nixon's own personal physician, Major-General Walter R. Tkach, who treated me to an off-the-record visit to the Oval Office. With the Watergate scandal bubbling up, I was allowed to shake the presidential hand, but not to ask Nixon any questions about the US medical system or indeed anything else of substance. Tkach told me in Nixon's presence, however, that he had got the president jogging on the spot 300 times each morning, with the result that he weighed a constant 172 pounds – 'just right' for a man of six feet who had recently turned sixty. That, I thought, had the makings of a pretty good intro.

Good enough, thought Godfrey Smith, for a *Sunday Times* Review Front, complete with cartoon of American surgeons counting their money while performing operations with huge cigars dangling out of their mouths. It appeared on Sunday 11 March 1973, and the following Thursday – the Ides of March, as we would both have cause to remember – I was granted an interview with the editor, Harold Evans. Complimentary about my piece, and impressed that I had been editor of Oxford's student magazine, he promptly offered me a job on the *Sunday Times*.

If only my dear grandfather Ivan had still been alive to share this moment, the realisation of both our dreams. Harold Evans's *Sunday Times* was the outstanding newspaper of its day, a paragon of campaigning and investigative journalism since unmatched, with its exposures of Kim Philby as the 'third man' in the Burgess–Maclean spy scandal, the crimes of British troops in Northern Ireland on Bloody Sunday, publication of Richard Crossman's diaries in the face of government opposition and, above all, its campaign to win rightful compensation for the victims of the birth-defect drug Thalidomide from its shameless manufacturers, the now defunct Distillers Company.

Graduate trainees are not the most popular people on provincial newspapers; they are regarded, often with some justice, as arrogant dilettantes reluctantly passing through en route to greater heights elsewhere. But everyone at Hemel was delighted for me – and not a little jealous, as most freely admitted, of my good fortune. They even gave me a farewell party, at which they presented me with a snooker cue – handsome recognition of one of my favourite off-duty pastimes.

I've left a lot more places since, but this was to prove the first and last time I would ever receive a leaving present.

6

RAT-LIKE CUNNING

Tuesday 1 May 1973: my second wedding anniversary. In a suit and tie, I present myself at the *Sunday Times* office promptly at 10 a.m., and ride the lift to the fifth floor, as instructed – to find no one there but the newsroom secretary, Ruth Easter. She shows me to my pre-assigned desk, in prime position right outside the news editor's office.

I have a desk! I am only twenty-five and already I have arrived – metaphorically, at least – in Fleet Street! And I have a phone! Suddenly, amid the eerie calm, it rings. My phone! My phone is ringing! This is Harold Evans's *Sunday Times*, the newspaper of the moment, and there's no one else here yet. It must be . . . it must be the beleaguered prime minister calling to leak his resignation!

The switchboard tells me there is a gentleman downstairs waiting to see me. Can Heath have come in person to grant me an exclusive farewell interview? My father-in-law, after all, is his doctor and close friend. And no one outside the family even knows I'm here.

I head back down in the lift to find a portly middle-aged man striding back and forth across the lobby, muttering to himself. In the process he is attracting giggles from the adjacent tele-ad girls, who are peering over the glass partitions to get a better look at him. It isn't Heath, dammit. No, it can't be . . .?

'They've got bloody Minimax here,' he is saying in a broad Lancashire accent, 'bloody Minimax!'

He turns to confront me. 'Ah, Anthony,' he begins brusquely. It takes me a moment to recognise him. This is my Uncle George – Sir George Holden Bt, no less, the 'toff who lives in a pig-sty', paterfamilias of the branch of the family we rarely spoke to while I was growing up. The last time I saw him was at my wedding to Amanda, two years ago to the day, when he stood in the receiving line carrying that fire extinguisher. And this unique visitation, it turned out, was also on behalf of L&G Fire Appliances.

At the time, Thomson Newspapers' security officer was none other than the semi-retired Robert Fabian, a household name as the inspiration for *Fabian of the Yard*, the TV series based on his dazzling Scotland Yard career. He was played by the dashing and very English Bruce Seton, for whom my mother had a bit of a thing.

Uncle George didn't even say hello. 'Anthony,' he rasped, 'they've got bloody Minimax in this place. I want you to use your influence around here to get Fabian – *Fabian of the Yard* – to switch to L&G. Here's my card. Get in touch when you've managed it.' With which he turned on his heel and strode out of the building. I never saw him again.

Back upstairs, I had plenty of time to mull the full extent of my 'influence around here', as there was still no one else in the newsroom. I soon learned that, on this first day of the working week, people would gradually drift into the office just in time to drift out again for a long, boozy lunch on expenses. Luckily, I had a pre-arranged rendezvous with Godfrey Smith, who was insisting on welcoming me to the paper over lunch in the pub across the road, the Blue Lion. It was typically generous of this senior figure to take a rookie to lunch on his first day.

When I eventually got back to the office, only slightly the worse for wear, there were still few signs of life. Everyone seemed still to be otherwise engaged. I sat at my desk, absurdly wondering if I was allowed to make personal calls.

The news desk phone rang; Ruth took the call, then summoned me over. After all, I was the only person in the room.

'You're going to Warsaw.'

'*Warsaw*? But I haven't got my passport with . . .'

'No, not Warsaw. *Walsall*.'

'Oh, Walsall. Right, yes, okay, fine, great!'

I rang Amanda to let her know that I would not, alas, be able to take her out for our anniversary dinner tonight, as planned, and jumped into a taxi to Euston to travel at someone else's expense for the first time in my adult life – and in first class, too. It may only have been to Walsall, but it sure felt good.

When I got there, and took another cab to my pre-booked hotel, I soon got a call from the office telling me the assignment had been cancelled. I was to come straight back, and I would be given another task the next day. As I checked out and boarded the train back to London, I couldn't help musing what a thrilling first day this had been on Fleet Street.

Next morning I was summoned into the office of my immediate boss, Derrick ('Del') Mercer, the paper's news editor. Del had been the *Sunday Times*' education correspondent before his recent promotion; now he needed a replacement, and he had decided to give me the chance – a big opportunity, he emphasised, to make my mark. I waxed suitably enthusiastic, while in truth somewhat dismayed; education sounded like rather a dull beat.

This was immediately remedied when he told me that my first assignment would take me to Oxford, where they were in the throes of electing a new Professor of Poetry. I was able to tell Del that, yes, I knew all about the quirks of the Oxford poetry professorship, having myself run a campaign during the last election five years before, and covered it for the student magazine.

So now it was a taxi ride to Paddington and little more than an hour on the train – first class again, naturally – to a room in my own right at the Randolph Hotel, where all the bigwigs stayed, scene of that eventful Burton–Taylor dinner five years before. My few days back at my alma mater included my first taste of the journalist's mixed blessing of getting to meet his heroes – not always, proverbially, a success. On this occasion it certainly was, when I was thrilled to spend a few hours with a chain-smoking W. H. Auden, who had himself been elected Poetry Professor twenty years before. As Auden grew older he had finally left his beloved New York for fear of being mugged, seeking sanctuary at his old college, Christ Church. On his first day back in Oxford, he had been mugged while crossing the High Street.

I was too polite, of course, to mention that. But Auden seemed to enjoy a long, discursive chat about the job of Poetry Prof. Then he dispensed a vodka martini or three, and our chat ranged far and wide. Only four months later, Auden would die in Vienna.

So the record shows that my first piece as a staff member of the *Sunday Times*, atop the Spectrum page (with the 'h' missing from my first name in the byline), was an in-depth analysis of the latest candidates for the Professorship of Poetry at Oxford University. I was thrilled; but this arty-farty stuff didn't go down too well with the tall, gangly, unkempt reporter with whom I was now sharing a desk, in the sense that we sat facing each other on opposite sides of two contiguous desks, his voluminous mess invariably spilling over onto mine.

His name was David Blundy, and he turned out to be a deceptive figure. A tall, dashing and wonderfully witty man, serially attractive to women, he was brutally contemptuous of all things pretentious – among which, in conversation, he would include the 'high' arts – proudly pronouncing himself a philistine while in fact quietly reading Dostoevsky and listening to Beethoven. A dogged and very brave reporter, he also prided himself on his snappy prose style, regarding adjectives as 'an admission of defeat'. David had a daughter, Anna, by a delightful woman he had left (by mutual agreement) on the steps of the Register Office after legitimising their offspring. I know all this – and more, much more – because he was to become my closest friend for the next decade and beyond.

Over the previous year I had reviewed books and written several pieces for the *New Statesman* and indeed for the *Sunday Times* magazine. But Blundy's real problem, which he was not slow to share with the rest of the newsroom – was my *Sunday Times* Review Front, which had appeared (complete with turn to next page) six weeks before I arrived at the paper.

A Review Front – then the Holy Grail of all reporters' aspirations – before I had even joined the staff! Blundy soon took to calling me Erskine, after Erskine Morris, the graduate trainee in Michael Frayn's wonderful Fleet Street novel *Towards the End of the Morning*. Straight out of Oxbridge, Erskine arrives at the desk of the recently deceased compiler of the Rural Notes and 'Years Gone By' column, but is soon writing features, diary items, even leaders, and proposing new sections to the editor. Before long, he's just about taken the place over.

My own version of 'Erskine' boasted no fewer than three pieces – two page-lead news stories as well as that feature on the Oxford poetry wars, in his first Sunday's issue of the paper. Across the desk from him, Blundy slumped into mock-suicidal gloom before shrugging and taking me across the road to the Blue Lion pub, where we all went every evening – especially Saturdays, while waiting for that week's paper to 'come up' from the printing presses, then in the bowels of the building.

All too soon he was delighted to see me reduced to the same weekly diet as all rookie reporters: the axle-weight of 'juggernaut' lorries (one of Harold Evans's less well-remembered campaigns); continuing student unrest all over the country; by-elections; proposals for yet another new London airport, etc. I was a hopeless education correspondent, floundering feebly in my attempts to understand dense circulars about comprehensive schools while laboriously producing lists of college vacancies for The *Sunday Times* Degree Service. And no one discerned anything of particular interest in my getting to know Heath's secretary of state for education, the only woman in his Cabinet, one Margaret

Thatcher – who, while notoriously abolishing free school milk, personally poured taxpayer-financed gin at her Christmas party with, dare I say, liberal abandon.

As I strained to appear hard-nosed enough to graduate to the paper's renowned investigative team, Insight – the supreme objective of every rank-and-file reporter – my arty credentials were further enriched one day, to ruinous effect, when Cyril Connolly wandered into the newsroom and started spouting Greek poetry at me, clearly expecting me to reply in kind. He had just delivered his (generous) review of my *Greek Pastoral Poetry* to Godfrey Smith, who had directed him down the corridor in my direction. Blundy was gobsmacked. The entire newsroom looked incredulous. Now, as word spread around the building, I was *never* going to make it onto the Insight team. It was tough enough to show my face in the Blue Lion.

During the Cameron–Clegg coalition negotiations of 2010, the TV news showed archive footage of the last equivalent moment in British politics: February 1974, when an inconclusive general election result saw Edward Heath refusing to concede defeat to Harold Wilson's Labour Party, staying on in Downing Street all weekend in a vain attempt to cling to power by striking a similar deal with the Liberal leader, Jeremy Thorpe. Amid the throng of hacks besieging the front door of No. 10, as Thorpe and others came and went, was a long-haired young man with a face I found strikingly familiar. After struggling awhile for his name, I finally realised it was me.

Hanging around outside Downing Street on a cold, wet Saturday in February was one of the more exciting assignments given a rookie reporter – if, alas, relatively pointless. The paper's venerable political editor, James Margach, would have had a much better idea than me of what was going on inside; and, even if I did have something to report, these were the days before any form of communication beyond the public telephone. Every so often that day I had to join the queue for one of the few nearby phone boxes to call the office and tell them I had nothing to report. While dreading their dismay, I also fretted about what I might have missed while standing in line.

Other delights of that first year on the *ST* also saw me making a lifelong new friend in the inveterate campaigner Des Wilson, founder of Shelter and Friends of the Earth, while covering the by-election in Hove at which he stood (in vain) for the Liberal Party. There was a nerve-racking trip by helicopter to a North Sea oil rig, and a brief but pleasant sojourn on the remote isle of Lundy. When the MP William Deedes was appointed editor of the *Daily Telegraph*, I enjoyed a long lunch with him trying to establish that he really was the original of Evelyn Waugh's intrepid William Boot in his immortal Fleet Street novel, *Scoop*. No, no, Bill protested modestly, while pointing out with a sly, proprietorial grin that 'I cannot deny that the first name is the same . . .'

I had been on the paper barely a year when I was thrilled to be sent abroad on my first foreign assignment: all the way to exotic St Malo on the north coast of France, to cover some ineffably tedious Euro-conference on agriculture. The big news of the week was yet another Tory sex scandal, this one involving the under-secretary for defence, Lord (Tony) Lambton. Granted an interview with the French minister for agriculture, I started trying to ask questions in my far-from-adequate French about Euro-agri-policy, of which I knew less than nothing. His answers came in a version of French that seemed to me indecipherably fast while strangely deadpan, exuding his own personal air of ennui. After barely five minutes of this, he suddenly said in perfect English: 'Look, you clearly know nothing at all about this, and aren't even the slightest bit interested. Why don't you tell me instead about your latest Tory sex scandal – Lord Lambton and all zat?'

I filled him in on the details of Lambton's cannabis-stained sessions with the high-end hooker Norma Levy.

'Oh, you E-e-e-nglish!' he exclaimed. 'We French don't understand such prudery about the private lives of your politicians. 'Ere een France, we get worried if our politicians are *not* having affairs. All zat *energy*! We don't want it to go into *governing . . .*!'

After Lambton's resignation that summer, I was sent to cover the by-election in Northumberland that resulted in victory for the Liberal candidate, Alan Beith. The constituency contained the historic island of Lindisfarne, also known as Holy Island, where in the mid-1960s Roman Polanski had made his haunting film *Cul-de-Sac*. But the news desk was more interested in my finding out how the mead-producing monks were proposing to vote. So across the causeway I struggled at low tide to pursue my enquiries at the journalist's habitual first port of call, the local pub. Where, I asked the landlord, could I find some monks to interview?

'Monks?' he laughed. 'There haven't been any monks here for five hundred years – not since the Middle Ages!'

With high tide now stranding me on the island for the rest of the day, I had no alternative but to spend all afternoon conducting increasingly boozy in-depth interviews with the regulars.

Back on the mainland, there was an early encounter with the militant leader of the Yorkshire miners, one Arthur Scargill, not to mention contrasting others with the Soho pornographer Paul Raymond and globetrotting evangelist Billy Graham, amid more run-of-the-mill stuff before – to Blundy's horror – I was given my first big break. Somehow I had caught the eye of the paper's all-powerful managing editor (features), Ron Hall, known to *Private Eye* readers as 'Badger' Hall (supposedly because his favourite activities were all nocturnal). I was summoned upstairs to see the great man – who had decided, he said in so many words, to make me a star.

After its yachting triumphs with Francis Chichester and Donald Crowhurst, the *Sunday Times* was sponsoring a British boat in the Whitbread Round-the-World Yacht Race, skippered by a pugnacious Scotsman named Chay Blyth. I was to interview Blyth for a big pre-race feature, and report his progress week by week via regular ship-to-shore phone calls.

During our Saturday evening sessions in the Blue Lion, Blundy and I had taken to competing with yarns of the absurd things that happened to us that week on our routine beats around the nation. So surreal were some of the situations in which we found our-selves that we developed a competitive WATFAD – or 'What The Fuck Am I Doing Here?' – index. He couldn't match my Chay Blyth story: going to meet the master-mariner in Portsmouth, taking an immediate dislike to each other, and then being ferried out to his yacht in the harbour to eat a disgusting homemade curry with his surly crew of fellow Paras. On a yacht, in the middle of Portsmouth harbour – I couldn't even make an excuse and leave. It was the ultimate in WATFADs.

But it gave me a front-page lead as the race set off in September 1973, with continuing weekly reports via ship-to-shore phone calls for nine months until Blyth and his men returned to Portsmouth in triumph, equalling the record time for a round-the-world voyage: 292 days. By then I had been to Israel as the Yom Kippur War brewed, causing chaos in a coachload of journalists as it drove through Bethlehem by announcing: 'Wow – did you see that newspaper placard?'

No, they all cried in panic. What did it say?

'Local boy makes God.'

I had also been on an education-themed trip to Japan, in truth a chance to catch up with J Morley, then living there on a scholarship from the Japanese Ministry of Culture to study the language at Waseda University in Tokyo. J's three years in Tokyo would form the basis of his first published novel, the fictionalised memoir *Pictures from the Water Trade*. Back in Munich, it would later earn him employment with the Japanese Broadcasting Company NHK, for whom he worked all over Europe for twenty years while continuing to write accomplished novels — to the point where the *New York Times* would eventually call him a writer of 'protean, creative intelligence'.

At the time, it earned us a dinner with some sinister members of Japan's Red Army. J and I vividly recalled their chosen method of testing my mettle; when a raw fish was brought to our table, and sliced up alive in front of us, its tail was still twitching and its eye looking at me reproachfully as they invited me to taste the first slice. That encounter yet further irritated Blundy in the shape of another daredevil feature for Tony Howard's *New Statesman*.

Every Saturday Blundy and I, along with most of our newsroom colleagues, would go out for a long lunch at a nearby restaurant known to us simply as 'the Greek'. Our week's work was done, after all; on Saturdays the paper hired 'casual' reporters, mostly from *The Sun*, to cover any live stories that might arise.

1 June 1974 turned out to be one of those rare Saturdays when a major story broke, requiring all hacks on deck. There had been an explosion at a chemical plant in Flixborough, Lincolnshire, and a fire was now raging through what was left of the building. The result, in the words of one safety campaigner, was to send out 'shock waves that rattled the confidence of every chemical engineer in the land'.

We rushed back to the office, where Blundy and I keyed in the dialling code for nearby Scunthorpe, followed by random numbers, and between us found all of a dozen eyewitnesses with vivid tales to tell — whom we then had to ask politely to give us the very phone numbers we had just dialled. As it turned out, twenty-eight lives were lost that day, out of only seventy-two people on the site at the time; the disaster would clearly have been even worse, as a subsequent government inquiry pointed out, had it happened on a weekday.

Saturday lunches out at 'the Greek', or indeed anywhere else, were promptly banned indefinitely. By then, however, I was spending most of my Saturdays in Northern Ireland, which was to become my home from home for the next three years – at the height of the absurdly euphemised 'Troubles' in Belfast and environs, then characterised by car bombs, pub bombings and brutal assassinations.

My first Saturday there happened to coincide with the biggest art theft in history – at Russborough House in County Wicklow, the stately home of the elderly millionaire Sir Alfred Beit, a former Tory MP, and his wife Clementine. I raced down there from Belfast to find that both had been pistol-whipped, bound and gagged by a gang led by an apparently cultured woman with a French accent, who made off with twenty paintings then worth some £8 million, including a Goya, a Vermeer and a Gainsborough.

It turned out to be an otherwise quiet Saturday elsewhere, so this dramatic story filled the whole of the front page of the *Sunday Times*, in which I took the legal risk of reporting that police suspected the gang's leader to be one Bridget Rose Dugdale, whom they were also accusing of hijacking a helicopter to bomb an RUC station in Strabane. Barely a week later the paintings were indeed found in the boot of a car outside a house in County Cork rented by Dugdale, who was promptly arrested. An Oxford-educated PhD, she turned out to be a sometime debutante-turned-self-styled 'freedom fighter' for the IRA, who was planning to use the paintings as ransom for two sisters convicted of bombings, then on hunger strike in Brixton jail. After pleading 'proudly and incorruptibly guilty', Dugdale gave a clenched-fist salute as she was sentenced (albeit pregnant) to nine years in Limerick prison.

This was colourful stuff by Ulster standards, where events otherwise remained unremittingly bleak and depressing. No less an authority than the Ulster-born poet Seamus Heaney, the future Nobel Laureate then teaching in Belfast, later specified 1974 as 'the worst year' of the Troubles. 'There was a sense of an utterly wasteful, cancerous stalemate, and that the violence was

unproductive. It was villainous, but you were living with it . . ..
day by day, week by week . . .'

So much so that Blundy and I, who often worked there in
tandem, would idly find ourselves wondering during our weekly
flight over to Belfast whether we would rather the plane landed
safely or crashed en route ('just a *little* crash', he used to say).
Merely getting around town was hair-raising, given the road-
blocks improvised by armed paramilitaries on both sides of the
dispute. We couldn't tell them we were en route to our weekly
briefing from the subsequently notorious Colin Wallace, then a
senior member of British Intelligence in Ulster, or the leadership of the Provisional IRA in the Falls Road social club – where
Blundy grew so nervous of the terrorists that, when it came his
turn to buy a round, his nervously shaking hands would make
things worse by spilling beer all over them.

Amid the perpetual tension, we had a desperate need for
laughs – of which, between us, we managed to keep up a steady
flow. During the Ulster Workers Council strike in 1974, which
eventually brought down the Northern Ireland Assembly, we
toiled all night by gaslight in the bomb-shaken Europa Hotel.
At Blundy's insistence – quite rightly, he never left people's
appearance unchronicled – we filed a vivid description of the
'bulges' beneath the armpits of some Protestant thugs we had
encountered, not least to show the newsroom how bravely we
were representing the paper. 'Bulges' came out in the next
day's paper as 'bugles' – doubly risible in that season of loyalist
Orange marches.

Eating together most nights in the dining room of the Europa,
we had even been sitting there when most of a car bomb was
blown through its first-floor window, miraculously injuring no
diners. In the process, we also grew friendly with the resident
pianist, whom I quietly told one March night that it was David's
birthday. As bidden, he came over to ask Dave if he had a request.

'Yeah,' he grinned. 'How about shutting up for half an hour?'

Back in London I inadvertently gave David – not to mention the rest of the newsroom – premium value for money when the travel editor, Jean Robertson, unexpectedly approached me one day to ask if I would like to go to Jamaica.

'Oh, I'd love to!' I told her. 'But I couldn't possibly afford it . . .'

She looked puzzled, and Blundy led the entire reporting staff in a tidal wave of hysterical laughter.

Thus did my naïve young self first become acquainted with the crucial journalistic concept of the free trip – or 'freeby' – which was to pay significant dividends in the years ahead. A glowing report of ten days with Amanda in the fleshpots of Montego Bay duly appeared in the travel pages that winter. I regarded it as due reward for my continuing exertions in the grim civil war-scape of Northern Ireland.

Later in 1974 the journalistic narrative in Ulster was temporarily diverted by the unexpected arrival of Enoch Powell, the Tory MP and former minister who had become a divisive national figure since his notorious 'Rivers of Blood' speech of 1968 – which, according to pollsters, had helped Edward Heath's Tories win the 1970 general election. Powell had recently alienated his own party by urging the country to vote Labour in the snap general election of February 1974, because of what he saw as Heath's 'betrayal' in taking Britain into the European Common Market by signing the Treaty of Rome. Many blamed Powell for Labour's slender victory, and by the next election that October he had defected to the Ulster Unionists.

That autumn, as I covered Powell's campaign in South Down, I received an unexpected message from the candidate saying that he would grant me the only interview he would give anyone during the campaign – potentially a major scoop, given that his defection was one of its main themes – in return for a copy of my translation of *Greek Pastoral Poetry*. Powell had long been an ardent Greek scholar – a professor, indeed, while still in his mid-twenties.

So the next time I made the flight to Belfast I took a copy of the black-backed Penguin paperback with me, along with the *Sunday Times*'s picture editor, Kelvin ('Steve') Brodie, who rated this assignment momentous enough to require his personal expertise. The in-depth interview, it turned out, would come later in the campaign, in its final, climactic week. This was to be an informal get-to-know-you meeting, in which – yes – Powell would be willing, most unusually for him, to do whatever my photographer wanted. But first I must sign my book for him – complete, he was insistent, with Greek inscription.

This last injunction I wasn't ready for. I dithered awhile between two ancient maxims still in my head from my schooldays a decade earlier, the only ones I could be confident of writing accurately in Greek: the celebrated Delphic oracle γνῶθι σεαυτόν (*gnothi seauton*, or 'know thyself') and/or the inscription on the temple of Apollo at Delphi: μηδὲν ἄγαν (*meden agan*, or 'nothing to excess', sometimes rendered as 'all things in moderation'). Each seemed, in Powell's case, potentially rather insolent from a young supplicant seeking a career-enhancing favour, so I opted for the latter as marginally less offensive. He looked at it, and appeared pleased; I later explained my relief to myself by musing that Powell would commend the latter truism to others, while lacking the self-knowledge to apply the first to himself.

Throughout this unlikely, nay unprecedented ritual, Steve Brodie watched dumbstruck – even more so when Powell then turned to him and enquired: 'So, Mr Brodie, what would you like me to do for you?' The exterior of the hotel was being painted at the time, and Brodie had for some reason decided it would be fun to get Enoch to pose halfway up a painter's ladder. The candidate duly obliged.

As we drove away, Brodie turned to me and said: 'My God, that was a clever trick of yours.' Henceforth I could do no wrong in the eyes of my paper's all-powerful picture editor. It was unthinkable that I could actually have translated some Greek poetry; Brodie genuinely believed I had mocked up a fake book to take in my interviewee. In his long experience, this veteran of many a smart journalistic manoeuvre had never known quite so daring a journalistic stunt.

A couple of weeks later, towards the end of the campaign, Powell gave me my exclusive interview, which took place on a train to London from some political pit-stop in south-west England. After managing to sidetrack him from an in-depth discussion of Greek literature, I placed on the table between us a new-fangled Sony Walkman tape recorder, which he surveyed with evident distaste.

For years I kept the tape that begins with Powell's distinctive Midlands accent declaring: 'I'll bet that nasty little Japanese machine isn't recording a word I'm saying!' It then runs for best part of an hour before I summon the nerve to ask him the question to which the entire country wanted to know the answer: 'Mr Powell, do you still seriously entertain hopes of one day returning to your party as its leader and so becoming prime minister of the United Kingdom?'

After Powell begins 'Well, of course, that would depend on . . .' the tape continues 'Ladies and gentlemen, we are now nearing Paddington, our final destination. Please be sure to take all your hand baggage and personal belongings with you as you leave the train . . .' before returning to Enoch's unmistakable voice concluding: ' . . . so that is what I mean!'

After transcribing the tape, sure enough, I had to telephone Powell and say, yes, he was right, that nasty little Japanese machine had petered out just as we got to the climax of our interview. What was it again he had said in answer to that last question? With grim satisfaction in his own powers of prophecy, he trotted it out a second time.

Early the next year I was again to follow Powell all over the country when assigned to cover the 'anti' side in Harold Wilson's 1975 referendum on Europe, during which Powell became unlikely political bedfellows with Labour's Tony Benn, Barbara Castle and Michael Foot. In the meantime, he had duly been elected an Ulster Unionist MP. While back in London, where the IRA had embarked on a campaign of lethal bombings, I suddenly found myself a minor star on local radio, when asked about the likely targets in London next week. Probably a department store, I ventured, or perhaps a Tube station? When one of each was bombed the following week, I found myself under interrogation by MI5 as to my sources. Nonetheless, I was as surprised as delighted to find myself commended, for my work in Northern Ireland, as News Reporter of the Year in the 1976 British Press Awards.

By then I had become a father. Samuel Ivan Holden was born in December 1975, and named as much after Humphrey Bogart's pianist in *Casablanca*, Dashiel Hammett's detective Sam Spade, the great lexicographer Dr Johnson and indeed 'Sam, pick up thy musket' of Stanley Holloway's monologue about the Duke of Wellington's foot-soldiers, as after my much-missed grandfather.

That same year Amanda and I had moved to Islington, north London, to save me the daily commute from Hertfordshire. A lucrative, week-long serial deal with *The Sun* for my Graham Young book had assisted with the finances. It also gave me something to talk about that week to the *Sunday Times*'s proprietor, Lord (Roy) Thomson, when I bumped into him one day when leaving the office.

'Where are you going, young man?' he asked as I hailed a taxi.

'Covent Garden,' I replied, omitting that I was meeting a pal there for lunch at his expense.

'So am I!' he beamed. 'We can walk together!'

So much for my cab ride – which would also, of course, have been at his expense. I was half an hour late for my lunch, but I had to hand it to Thomson, one of those with so many millions that he still made every penny earn its keep. Where John Paul Getty famously installed a payphone in the guest room of his country house, Thomson used his penny-pinching to benefit the vast corporate interests under his control – not least the newspapers with huge budgets for investigative and campaigning journalism, in which he would never interfere – no, not if they cost him advertising, or even assailed his own companies.

If this was the golden age of the expense account – you could take your wife out to dinner, and put her down as a government minister – life on Harold Evans's *Sunday Times*, unencumbered by an interfering proprietor, was also a platinum age of British journalism. The apparent indolence on Tuesdays and Saturdays concealed 24-hour activity the rest of the week, often by teams as much as individuals all over the world. It remained the newspaper of the moment, with an *esprit de corps* among the editorial staff – a sense of community, of pride in the product, of working together for the common good – on a scale I have never known elsewhere. This was certainly due to the inspirational leadership of Evans, but Harry himself was always the first to concede how heavily he relied on the talents of such senior executives as Bruce Page and Ron Hall, John Barry and Godfrey Hodgson as well as stellar writer-investigators from Nicholas Tomalin and Philip Knightley to Murray Sayle and Lewis Chester.

While covering *Private Eye*'s momentous legal battle with the entrepreneur James Goldsmith, who had sued its editor, Richard Ingrams, for criminal libel, I decided I needed a witness for one particularly sensitive interview – and asked the nearest person on hand in the office, Philip Knightley, if he would be good enough to accompany me. Although a far more senior figure than myself, Phil graciously agreed; and found himself, after my report appeared, the victim of a libellous attack by Goldsmith in fact directed at me. 'Goldenballs' had got his journalists confused. Knightley sued Goldsmith for libel – successfully, not least thanks to one of his lawyers, Edward Adeane QC, who was soon to loom large in my life in quite another guise.

To my mind it was the features supremo Ron Hall who coined

the memorable *Sunday Times* phrase of the moment: 'There are only two types of journalism: "We Name The Guilty Man" and "Arrow Points To Defective Part"' (this last minted after Insight's investigation into the fatal DC10 crash of March 1974). To this day contemporaries choose to dispute who first came up with this pithy dictum. But there was no disputing Nicholas Tomalin's authority for the maxim even more symbolic of the 1970s *Sunday Times*, which began a 1969 magazine article Nick wrote under the title 'Stop the press, I want to get on': 'The only qualities essential for real success in journalism are rat-like cunning, a plausible manner and a little literary ability.'

Until, that is, as recently as 2016, when our colleague Lew Chester astonished my journalistic generation by re-attributing this legendary adage to the roguish Australian reporter Murray Sayle, still fondly remembered for (amid much else) his way with words. No, wrote Lew, in his introduction to an anthology of Sayle's journalism entitled *Making Waves*. 'Prior to this [Tomalin's 1969 article], on becoming a junior feature writer on the paper, I happened to be sharing an office with both of them and well remember Murray coming up with this formulation. And the alert Nick was, as ever, all ears . . .'

Another senior figure from 'upstairs', Magnus Linklater, had been editor of the paper's feature section Spectrum when he had led it with my very first piece for the paper two years earlier, the meditation on Auden and the Oxford poetry professorship. Linklater had subsequently been editor of the colour magazine. Now, in mid-1975, he descended to the newsroom as news editor, i.e. my boss.

This was potentially tricky, as Magnus and I were already close friends (to the point where he would soon become godfather to my second son, Joe, born in 1977). His first move was to broaden my journalistic horizons, or maybe test my unknown mettle, by sending me to join the forces of King Hassan of Morocco invading Spanish Sahara, ranged against hostile Spanish tanks as well as the menacing forces of the Polisario, the Popular Front for ridding the Western Sahara of what they saw as its Moroccan interlopers.

Back in London, Magnus soon felt the need to demonstrate that his authority as my new boss overrode our friendship. My desk was still right outside the news editor's office, into which he summoned me one day to muse about the elusive East Ender George Davis, whose name was then plastered all over the capital and beyond in graffiti declaring GEORGE DAVIS IS INNOCENT OK, which also featured on T-shirts worn by sundry rock stars on *Top of the Pops*. That summer the Test match pitch at Headingley had been dug up in support of the campaign for Davis's release for a wrongful conviction, which Home Secretary Roy Jenkins was now said to be considering.

'This guy Davis,' mused Magnus. 'I think we need to know more about him, Tony. Get round to his house this evening, huh?'

'But Magnus,' I protested, assuming my pal would sympathise, 'I've got tickets for the opera tonight. *La Bohème* at Covent Garden!'

'Well, I'm afraid you're going to have to skip Puccini to go and find Mr Davis.' As indeed I dutifully did. That is to say, I found Mrs Davis, his wife Rose, who was leading the (eventually successful) campaign for George's release.

Inadvertently, I soon got proxy revenge on Magnus for hijacking my night out at the opera. Most Saturday evenings, when I was in London, I used to share a taxi home to Islington with him after the ritual review of that week's paper in the Blue Lion. One Sunday morning he was just realising that he had left his briefcase behind in the pub when he got a call from Holborn police, saying that it was now in their possession and he should come at once to collect it. Magnus arrived to be handed a bag containing the charred remains of what had once been his worldly goods. At closing time, in this era of London bombings, the landlord had called in the cops about this apparently abandoned briefcase, which had duly been blown up by the very latest in robotic remote-control devices. When said landlord apologised to us about the resulting scorch-mark in the Blue Lion's ceiling, promising that he would have it cleaned up in a few days, we all protested: *NO*, it must be kept just as it is: a.k.a. the Linklater memorial scorch-mark. And so it remained for the next few years.

By now I had learned always to carry my passport in my pocket, as you never knew where you were going to be sent when. One Friday in May 1976 I arrived at the office to find there had been a major earthquake overnight in northern Italy. I was to meet up at Heathrow with Bryan Wharton, one of the more colourful of the staff photographers, to head at once to the scene.

As I got back into the lift, the editor was just coming out of it to begin his working day. 'Where are you off to?' Evans asked me.

'To Italy,' I told him. 'There's been a big earthquake.'

'Do you speak Italian?' he enquired.

'Not much, I'm afraid.'

Harry pressed the ground-floor button and came back down with me. '*Quanti sono morti*?' he spelt out in slow motion. '*Quanti sono morti*?'

This was to come in handy. By the time I met up with Wharton at Heathrow, he had booked us both on a flight to Milan, the nearest place available at such short notice. So it was evening before we'd driven the 300-plus miles to the earthquake zone around Friuli, 100 miles north of Venice. Almost 1,000 people had been killed, we gradually discovered, 2,500 injured and some 200,000 left homeless. But how to capture the whole story within less than twenty-four hours, now that night had fallen? We drove around the devastated area, at one point braving a little road bridge that collapsed as soon as we had crossed it, eventually agreeing that the best plan would be to stop and stay in one place, waiting and watching in the hope that some symbolic human story would develop.

The author covers the 1976 Italian earthquake

In the mountain village of Osoppo we soon came across yet another group of men clearing a heap of rubble. This time, I noticed, there was a human arm protruding from the ruins of a family house, so we agreed to stop and see what transpired. Standing beside the scene was an elderly man clearly hoping against hope (and indeed all logic) that these human remains were not those of his son, whose house this had been. As the body was gradually uncovered, it eventually became clear that his hopes were in vain. Looking completely out of place, in his habitually flamboyant Chelsea Arts Club gear, Wharton captured the precise moment at which the old man's face collapsed in grief.

The picture, which subsequently won awards, dominated the next day's front page, adorned by my emotive text. But it so nearly wasn't. So excited was Bryan by what he knew to be an outstanding news photo, beyond poignant, that he leapt into our hire car and raced back to Milan, to fly himself and his film home to London in time for the first edition – leaving me alone and helpless in the middle of an earthquake-ravaged nowhere. Somehow I managed to hitchhike my way down to Venice, checked into the Gritti Palace hotel (where else?), called the newsroom with my whereabouts and promptly fell asleep. Well, I had been up all night. Were it not for a call from Blundy, who couldn't resist reading me the latest instalment of the long-running Jeremy Thorpe–Norman Scott saga in that night's paper ('Bunnies can and will go to France'), I would have remained comatose long past my deadline. As it was, I got David to transfer me to the copytakers and I hastily ad-libbed what proved to be the next day's front-page splash.

© The Times/News Licensing

This classic episode soon took pride of place among our pub anecdotes – right up there with the weeks I spent beside the pool of the Rabat Hilton waiting for an interview that never came with King Hassan of Morocco. Since invading Spanish Sahara, I seemed to have become the paper's makeshift Morocco correspondent. Hassan had offered me the interview, and was indeed paying my hotel bill, before evidently changing his mind; all I was granted, by way of special access, was to watch from a distance as the king played a round of golf. But I even managed to make a feature out of that, thanks in part to the retainer who walked alongside him, at a respectful distance, wielding a six-foot-long pair of tweezers to remove the permanent cigarette dangling from the royal lips as Hassan squared up to each shot.

There were many more such vivid adventures all over the place, amid many more deadly downbeat days in Ulster, before my life was radically altered – not for the first or the last time – by Harold Evans. That year I was relishing a gilded-youth moment evoked by my friends Hitchens, Amis and Fenton, who had initiated a sparkling, all-day Friday 'lunch-athon' with the likes of Salman Rushdie and Ian McEwan, Clive James and Mark Boxer, whose witty, word-playing revels are vividly recalled in Hitchens' memoirs, *Hitch 22*. Among other visitors were Kingsley Amis and his friend Robert Conquest, who one day came up with the best non-dirty limerick I know:

> *There was an old bolshy called Lenin,*
> *Who did one or two million men in.*
> *That's a lot to have done in;*
> *But where he did one in,*
> *That old bolshy Stalin did ten in.*

But my treasured place at this glitzy table was not, alas, to last long, for the most banal of reasons. The one day of the week my otherwise irresistible new job would henceforth require my presence *all day* in the *Sunday Times* office, preferably sober, was – yes, dammit – Friday.

7

'WHAT ARE *YOU* DOING HERE?'

Since 1929 the *Sunday Times* has carried a column called Atticus – named after the garrulous Roman publisher Titus Pomponius Atticus, close friend of Cicero. Over the decades since its launch, the column's anonymous writers have proved an unlikely crew, ranging in its early days from Margot Asquith to Sacheverell Sitwell, John Buchan to Ian Fleming.

During Harold Evans's editorship Atticus was deemed important enough to fill the whole of the back page of the *Sunday Times*'s main section. Amounting to the paper's diary column, it was a name-dropping survey of the lesser issues of the moment – a far cry from the back-biting political chitchat to which it has since been shrivelled.

Few reporters, Harry told me, possessed the requisite personality for such a task. So I had taken it as quite a compliment when he had asked me to stand in occasionally over the past couple of years. Now Evans offered me the job full-time, ruling that I also deserved to have my name at the top. The cartoonists engaged to embellish my scribblings would include Mark Boxer (a.k.a. Marc), Ralph Steadman and Barry Fantoni. I would have a part-time assistant named Julian Barnes, then a humble drudge on the *Oxford English Dictionary*. Among my holiday stand-ins would be the journalist-turned-TV chat-show host Michael Parkinson.

Over a celebratory drink with Blundy in the Blue Lion, I won his eager support for my notion of adopting what we had long called the 'pub principle' – the painful truth that most of our colleagues were much more entertaining in the pub about what-ever they had been covering that week than they were in the newspaper. And then, of course, there were those mini-scoops too offbeat for the news pages.

I secured one such in my very first week in the job, in January 1977, with some internal memos leaked by John Boyden, man-aging director of the London Symphony Orchestra, suggesting that the LSO board wanted to divest itself of its chief conductor, André Previn. Sure, Previn's glamour was making them plenty of money in TV specials and suchlike; but it was generally felt that musical standards were slipping under his stewardship. Not long after the appearance of my piece, Previn duly departed. That week I also published a previously unseen Picasso drawing, passed on by a literary friend, and noted some top situations-vacant which had not yet been advertised elsewhere.

It felt like a decent start, continued with interviews with stellar names from Brigitte Bardot to Bob Hope, Jimmy Carter's brother Billy to Spiro T. Agnew. Lunch in Paris with Diana Mosley (née Mitford) moved her husband, Sir Oswald, to get in on the act by revealing that he was a 'huge' fan of Diana Dors – which gave me an entrée to her, too. From Rita Hayworth to Zero Mostel (in his capacity as painter more than actor), Rudolf Nureyev to Henry Moore, there were gratifyingly few who would turn down a chance to appear in Atticus. Harold Wilson gave me his word-perfect version of my beloved Stanley Holloway monologues. Edward Heath took me with him around the country on his private book-signing train; after lunch I sat and polished off his favourite Gewürztraminer while he snored gently in the corner.

Some even became friends, as can happen with the occasional interviewee, from the actor Joss Ackland to the guitarist John Williams and the writer Jan Morris – to whom I was introduced by my colleague David Holden (no relation), the eminent for-eign correspondent, who had known her in her previous life as James Morris.

Others could teach you valuable lessons, as was the case at the 1977 Edinburgh Festival. A decade earlier, in my student days, I had dragged J Morley to see John Mortimer's version of Feydeau's farce *A Flea in Her Ear* at Laurence Olivier's fledgling National Theatre, then still at the Old Vic. I had loved Olivier's show-stealing performance as Etienne the butler, mincing about at the back in a lesser role with such panache as to upstage the entire cast. The night I went with J, however, the hapless man-in-black-tie came on to announce that 'Owing to the indisposition of . . .' (*oh, no, not Olivier!*) ' . . . Sir Laurence Olivier . . .' Half the audience was already leaving as he continued ' . . . his part tonight will be taken by Mr Derek Jacobi.' As the theatre all but emptied, such sympathy did I feel for Jacobi, then an unknown spear-carrier, and so much did I admire his own distinctive version of the butler, that afterwards I wrote him a congratulatory postcard. Ten years later, when I told this story to the Hamlet of 1977 over lunch at Edinburgh's Café Royal, Jacobi took my hand and gasped: 'It was *you*!' Lesson learned: if you *really* admire some performance, some recital, some book, *always* send that postcard.

Then there was my fellow Northerner Melvyn Bragg. Fresh from the BBC's *Monitor* and *Read All About It*, Melvyn had defected to ITV to launch a new arts programme; over lunch one day, however, he told me that he could not think of a name for it. 'Don't worry, Melvyn,' said I. 'I'll hold one of my regular readers' competitions' – bottle of champagne for the winner – 'so let's meet here again next week, same time same place, and I'll come armed with a list of goodies for you to choose from.'

So dire did my readers' suggestions turn out to be that I was mightily relieved when a week later Melvyn sat down again with the words: 'I'm really sorry, Tony, but I've just come from a committee meeting where we've actually come up with a name we all like.'

'What's that, Melvyn?' I asked, secretly thrilled that I did not have to recite my list of dud suggestions.

'The South Bank Show.'

'The *South Bank* Show?' I repeated, aghast. 'Did you say you'd come from a *committee* meeting, Melvyn? What's our friend Mrs Grimsdyke in Rochdale going to say about that? Bloody arty-farty southerners mincing about on their own private version of *la rive gauche* . . . It won't last a week!'

Forty-plus years later, needless to say, *The South Bank Show* is still going strong, its name having passed seamlessly – and with great distinction – into the language.

It so happens that I was born on Laurence Olivier's fortieth birthday, with the result that his seventieth in May 1977 coincided with my thirtieth. I wrote to the foremost actor-director of the twentieth century, by now the founder-director of the new-ish National Theatre, pointing out this charming coincidence, and requesting an interview to mark the occasion. The great man promptly wrote back, basically saying no, but doing so at such length, and with such candour, that his agonies amounted to a long session in the confessional. At the time I would naturally respect his wishes that the contents not be published until after his death, but use of them I would certainly one day make.

Meanwhile, I shamelessly used Atticus to assist my Oxford tutor, John Jones, in being elected the latest Oxford Professor of Poetry. I started presenting ITV's weekly newspaper review *What the Papers Say*, while conducting a fearless investigation into the fate of *The Journalists*, a play written in 1972 by Arnold Wesker after Harry Evans agreed to let him spend some months at the *Sunday Times*. Some of my colleagues, as well as most of the RSC cast, took exception to his conclusions, with the result that Wesker's play has still never received a professional production in this country.

On Friday afternoons I saw Atticus 'off stone', i.e. into print via the wonderfully tactile process of hard metal, where you had to learn to be able to read upside-down, and if necessary make last-minute adjustments – without *ever* touching the metal itself, at the risk of provoking the printers to down tools (as they were soon to do all too often, with disastrous consequences). This usually took place under the expertly beady eye of the editor, who was as pleased as I was when the Queen herself was pictured reading Atticus in a portrait for the Silver Jubilee of 1977. That is to say, it was the *Sunday Times*'s turn in the royal rota, so the staff photographer naturally got H.M. to pose reading his own paper, concentrating on the back page so that the title on the front was visible for all to see.

Evans was also as delighted as I was when my Atticus saw me voted Columnist of the Year in the 1977 British Press Awards – not least, perhaps, because of what Harry, who had warmly endorsed my notion of the 'pub principle', took to calling my 'VIP trips'. I would travel abroad with national figures and write about the offstage events overlooked by everyone else. I was not the only one to be stunned, for instance, when Evans chose Atticus to travel to China that April with Margaret Thatcher, then leader of the Opposition, and later to the Indian subcontinent with the prime minister, James Callaghan.

So, at the time, was Thatcher herself. It now seems a shameful period piece to recall that, to Thatcher's vocal annoyance, the BBC sent Sue MacGregor of *Woman's Hour* and most papers their diarists (such as myself) or sketch writers (such as the famously bibulous George Gale of the *Express*) rather than their political correspondents. We each had our own car in Thatcher's twenty-five-vehicle motorcade in Peking – Maggie up front, of course, with her daughter Carol, whom she had brought along instead of husband Denis, who had apparently misbehaved with the travelling hacks in sundry hotel bars during her tour of India the previous summer.

The Times had imported its Hong Kong-based correspondent, David Bonavia, who asked Carol one evening if she would like him to show her Peking after dark. 'Oh, that sounds fun,' said Carol, 'but I'd better ask Mummy.' We all watched expectantly as she crossed the bar to whisper into Mummy's ear, thus bypassing the dour advisers surrounding her, only to return looking glum, with the memorable line: 'Mummy says there's *no such thing* as Peking after dark.'

When it came to walking the Great Wall of China – harder up-and-downhill work than photos might suggest – photographers lugging heavy equipment, let alone we out-of-shape hacks, were soon gasping for breath as Thatcher became audibly determined to venture further than previous visitors from Edward Heath to Richard Nixon.

A.H. on the Great Wall of China with Margaret Thatcher
and her daughter, Carol

In a gesture towards informality, Thatcher later took me with her on a shopping expedition in the provincial city of Soochow. With my Islington décor in mind, I asked her opinion of a jade figure within my price range but maybe up to her exacting standards – with, as I put it, 'a hint of the Michelangelo about it'.

'Put it back at once, dear boy,' she barked. 'It's fright-fully ugly.'

Upon my return to Blighty, I discovered that *in absentia* I had made my debut at Prime Minister's Questions in the House of Commons, when James Callaghan was called upon to explain some recent remarks he had made about the 'cynicism' of the press. 'Was he referring,' asked the Labour MP Dennis Canavan, to 'the wandering wizard of the *Sunday Times*, Anthony Holden, who flies all over the Eastern hemisphere and reaches the heights of journalistic magic by managing to turn the cast-iron maiden into a rather black china doll?' Laughter, according to Hansard, ensued.

Nine months later, in January 1978, I was again among a group of travelling journalists – this time more heavyweight politicos – who accompanied Prime Minister Callaghan to Bangladesh, India and Pakistan. A couple of days after our arrival in New Delhi, I woke up one morning feeling distinctly off-colour, and naturally assumed that I'd fallen prey to 'Delhi belly'. But a visit from no less a figure than the prime minis-ter's personal physician, the handlebar-moustachioed Dr Monty Levine, led to a cautious diagnosis of mumps – which, he added, we must keep secret, as the PM had not had the disease. Next day, in the air between Ahmedabad and Bombay, en route to President Sadat in Aswan, Levine saw that my face was swelling up, giving him no option but to make the diagnosis there and then, in mid-air. The gentlemanly Callaghan immediately came down the aisle to commiserate, so I got up to move away from him; thinking that I was moving closer, he recoiled across the aisle into the galley, whence ensued a loud crash.

I now glumly assumed that, when we reached Bombay, I would be left behind in some scary hospital a long, long way from home. But an airborne meeting of Callaghan's kitchen cabinet, also attended by his kindly wife Audrey, resolved that I should remain aboard the prime ministerial VC10, which would be reconfigured to allow me my own isolation area at the back. Levine told the PM that if I was going to infect him, I would probably have done so already. I had been incubating the disease for a fortnight, since before leaving London, and my victims would not reveal themselves for perhaps another ten days.

This made Callaghan blench, and set me to thinking. In the past week I had not only spent my entire time around the prime minister and his most senior staff (not to mention the political cream of Fleet Street), I had shaken hands and conversed with General Zia-ur-Rahman, president of Bangladesh, and 82-year-old Morarji Desai, prime minister of India, as well as the likes of Indira Gandhi and countless diplomats and senior politicians of all three countries. What might I have done to the newfound stability of South Asia?

In my *cordon sanitaire* at the back of the jet, Callaghan paid me occasional visits, keeping a safe distance while lending me histories of Indian independence to while away the hours. The cream of Fleet Street meanwhile abandoned me to my fate, while filing stories about me to their papers. I even made the front page of the *Daily Express* under the headline PM IN MEDICAL ALERT. When we reached Aswan, I naturally kept my own company, not wishing to foul up Jim's Middle East peace initiative; in Islamabad, I was allowed to meet the president, General Zia-ul-Haq, but not the visiting England cricket team. Heaven forfend that I should give mumps to Geoffrey Boycott.

Back home, still confined to my bed for a while, I was delighted to receive a crate of oranges from Downing Street, delivered on the personal instructions of the prime minister. I also received a hand-delivered memo from my editor, Harold Evans, suggesting that I should now bring Atticus back to London, where it belonged. Another reason for this may well have been that, in between China with Thatcher and India with Callaghan, I had taken another VIP trip to Canada – an even more, as it turned out, fateful one – with Prince Charles.

'What are *you* doing here?' were the first words addressed to me by Charles, Prince of Wales, at a cocktail party in Calgary, Alberta, in July 1977. They were also to prove the last, more than twenty years later – in a significantly different tone of voice, rather less kindly meant – when he rounded a bush in some far-flung corner of the Commonwealth to find me lurking behind it.

Had I known how profoundly this jaunt to Canada would turn out to affect my mid-term professional future, I doubt I would have taken it. Yet it all started as a bit of a joke – just another far-flung trip for the ever-inquisitive Atticus.

In those days, the mid- to late 1970s, the so-called 'quality' British press rose above coverage of the royal family, the implicit assumption being that these Saxe-Coburg-Gothas-turned-Windsors were *petit bourgeois* arrivistes beneath the interest, let alone concern, of the intelligent middle classes. So when a press release reached the *Sunday Times* news desk proclaiming that the heir to the throne was off to visit one of his future dominions – to be installed as an honorary Indian chieftain one day, and open the annual Calgary Stampede the next – it was naturally passed on to the mischievous Atticus.

Hence the prince's opening gambit: what *was* I doing there? He was not used to the 'posh' papers trailing around after him on these kinds of royal jollies. 'Cowboys and Indians with Charles in Canada', was what I did not reply. The whole jaunt seemed just too tacky to resist. So I had popped aboard the same plane as HRH – for once in his life, he was travelling on a scheduled flight – to find myself cruising over Prince Charles Island, off the coast of Greenland, in the company of the man himself.

Except that he was naturally up front in first class, with his private secretary, his press secretary, his private secretary's private secretary, his equerry, his air attaché, his security officers and his valet – these were the days before he took along a personal chef or three – while I was crammed in the back with 300 tourists and a headache. This turned out to be a portent for the weeks, months and, alas, years ahead.

In conversation later, Charles and I discovered that we were both bored enough to watch the tedious in-flight movie, *Logan's Run*. 'Frightful' was his verdict, confessing that he stuck it out only because he was an admirer of Jenny Agutter. Knowing of the princely penchant for other film stars, such as Susan George, and the increasingly hot topic that he was approaching the age of thirty unmarried, this seemed a somewhat rash confession on his part to a hungry hack like myself.

When his brother Andrew arrived in Calgary to help him declare the rodeo open, I pronounced Andrew 'taller, more relaxed and much more of a dash-cutter' than Charles. My major scoop of the trip was to reveal to the world that the heir to the throne was nursing an incipient bald patch. The whole-page piece was adorned by two Barry Fantoni caricatures of the prince in Cowboy and Indian mode, which still hang among the memorabilia on my study wall.

The following week, as it happened, Charles was paying an official visit to the *Sunday Times* back in London, including its Tuesday morning editorial conference, while I moved on to New York in pursuit of more big names. Thanks to a Manhattan cop I had befriended, who was in charge of movie shoots around the city, I managed to get myself onto the set of a film in which Frank Sinatra was starring as a cop on the trail of (ironically enough) sinister Mafia bosses. As the cast and crew of *Contract on Cherry Street* stood around waiting for the great man to make his entrance – belatedly, of course – I found myself chatting amiably to his co-star Martin Balsam. Suddenly, the door behind me was thrown open, hitting me hard in the back. As I doubled up with pain, the guy coming through the door smirked at me, whacked me over the head with a rolled-up copy of *Playboy*, and moved blithely on. Yes, Sinatra. 'Hey,' grinned Balsam, 'he likes you!'

That evening, a power failure plunged Manhattan into the

worst 'blackout' in the city's history. As I stayed on to help cover the orgy of arson and looting, I sent a message to London asking Mark Boxer, alias Marc, to draw Sinatra for my column. Mark did so with his customary panache, after sending back to the *Sunday Times* New York office a note saying: 'You know, Tony, you should really try to *talk to* the people you interview . . .'

When I got back to London, Mark also told me that the *Sunday Times* editorial conference had grilled Charles for his response to my waspish column about him from Canada. 'I don't read back pages,' the prince had quipped, an evasive suggestion that mine might be the sports page. When some of his staff invited me for a reunion drink, however, they said they had enjoyed my piece so much that they insisted on his reading it, too – and proceeded to astonish me by saying how much His Nibs had also liked it. 'It really made him laugh,' declared his press secretary. Apparently, even the Queen had liked it. 'My mother cut it out and kept it for me,' Charles was quoted as saying in the *Times* diary.

Events then, alas, moved fast. When I next saw Hilary Rubinstein, who had also liked the column, I naturally told him I had heard that Charles too had found it amusing. The next thing I knew, Hilary's friend John Curtis of Weidenfeld & Nicolson was suggesting I write a biography of the young heir to the throne. I demurred; I had a full-time job I enjoyed, and I wasn't sure I was interested enough in Charles to write a whole book about him. Besides, was there enough to say? He hadn't even turned thirty yet.

But a book is a book is a book – as all journalists intone in their cups, ill-disguising their desire to write one as proof that they are serious-minded grown-ups, at least more than mere hacks. One evening I was sitting at home at my desk when a phone call from Hilary announced that Weidenfeld was offering me an advance against royalties of £15,000. In 1977 that was the equivalent today of six figures. I had never in my life had as much as four figures in my bank account – and I would be receiving one-third of it up front, on signing the contract. I was so stunned that I involuntarily smashed the glass bell of a treasured lamp on my desk as – perish the day – I accepted.

All I had to do now was find out if there was really anything worth saying about His Royal Highness The Prince Charles Philip Arthur George, Prince of Wales, Duke of Cornwall, Duke of Rothesay, Earl of Carrick, Earl of Chester, Baron of Renfrew, Lord of the Isles, Prince and Great Steward of Scotland, Royal Knight Companion of the Most Noble Order of the Garter, Extra Knight of the Most Ancient and Most Noble Order of the Thistle, Grand Master and Principal Knight Grand Cross of the Most Honourable Order of the Bath, Member of the Order of Merit, Knight of the Order of Australia, Companion of the Queen's Service Order, Member of Her Majesty's Most Honourable Privy Council and Aide-de-Camp to Her Majesty.

The only interesting thing he had said to me as yet was: 'Married, aren't you? Fun, is it?'

People seem to think that you need permission to write a royal biography. Far from it. But it does help, as I was later to discover with other living subjects, to have his or her knowledge and at least tacit consent, ideally permission to talk to colleagues and friends.

So my logical first port of call was Buckingham Palace, to see what they thought of the idea. Charles's press secretary at the time was an Australian named John Dauth, the latest in a long line of junior Commonwealth diplomats seconded to London to get some supposedly useful experience serving as deputy press secretary to the Queen, and so part-time press secretary to her heir.

My Canada piece had got me off to a good start. But there is no such thing, I was firmly told, as an authorised biography of a monarch or future monarch in his or her lifetime. After a third-degree grilling about my intentions (unknown, as yet, even to me) it was agreed that I could get some informal access to the prince – travel with him, chat to him off the record – so long as I did not make out that the book was in any way official or authorised. He would also give his staff, his friends and others in his circle permission to talk to me. What the heck, I decided; if only for purely pecuniary reasons, let's do it.

Nine months later, I am delighted to say, it was Charles himself who gave the assembled British press quite the opposite impression. After I had started travelling around the world with him, most recently through South America – staying in the same hotels, often dining together in the evening – it happened to fall to him to present me with my Columnist of the Year award at the 1978 British Press Awards luncheon at the Savoy. In those days there were no speeches on these occasions. Your name was read out, you went up onstage to accept the gong from that year's dignitary, smile for the cameras, and that was it.

In this instance, however, perhaps because we had just spent three weeks together travelling through Brazil and Venezuela, including a much-photographed princely rumba at Rio's Mardi Gras festival, Charles chose to tell the assembled *crème de la crème* of Fleet Street: 'Anthony Holden's style is most enjoyable: witty, amusing, slightly sardonic. And his English is a real pleasure to read.'

So I too felt obliged to improvise a few words of thanks for this compliment – which, to Charles's annoyance, would naturally appear on the dust jackets of my next few books – as the prince was photographed grinning with approval behind me. From that moment, the entire British press was persuaded that I was writing an authorised biography.

My work-in-progress now became such a hot property that there was to be an auction in New York for the US publication rights. I duly flew Atticus back for another bite of the Big Apple, while doing the rounds of Manhattan publishers to flog my wares-in-the-making. When I got back to the *Sunday Times*'s 42nd Street office one day, after my umpteenth potentially lucrative literary lunch, there was a letter awaiting me from the BPC Publishing Company of Sepulveda Boulevard, Los Angeles, offering no less than a million dollars for the US rights.

In high excitement I rushed to tell the news to my pals Peter Pringle, the *ST*'s NY correspondent, and US manager Bob Ducas, who were so thrilled for me that they insisted on closing the office early so I could buy them a few drinks. Not until we were all sitting comfortably in a nearby bar, admiring the handsome vellum on which the letter was printed, did they reveal how expensive it had been – ditto to have it specially inscribed with that fictional LA address so they could forge the contents. So what did BPC stand for? Bonnie Prince Charlie.

I'd been well and truly had. Whatever their jolly jape says about my cocky young self using their office as a mere base in search of big bucks, I'm pleased to recall that I thought it a spectacular con, and bought them a few more drinks and then a handsome dinner (on expenses, of course) to salute their ingenuity.

As it turned out, the American auction was won – for a rather smaller if still handsome sum – by Alfred Knopf Jr of Atheneum Press. Known to his friends as Pat, Knopf had boldly turned down the chance of inheriting his father's celebrated eponymous imprint to start his own. A devout Anglophile, he would publish several more of my books, even a collection of my journalism a few years later.

Harold Evans gave me six months off to write the book, on full pay, in return for the serial rights. The *Sunday Times* would also fund my travels with Charles, all over the world, in return for the occasional dispatch. Harry always seemed to have a way of making me offers I couldn't refuse; hence my farewell to Atticus readers, which I chose to make in a whole page of heroic couplets, beginning (with apologies to J. Keats):

> *Much have I travell'd in Bodoni bold*
> *And many guilty men and doorsteps seen;*
> *Round many sweaty newsdesks have I been*
> *Which hacks in fealty to Lord Copper hold . . .*

The prince's permission to talk to major figures in his life proved crucial. Lord Snowdon, for instance, who had choreographed his investiture as Prince of Wales in Caernarvon Castle in 1969, gave me vivid new detail that made this one of the more entertaining chapters in the book.

Perhaps its biggest scoop came from an interview with the retired politician R. A. ('Rab') Butler, Master of Trinity College, Cambridge, when Charles was an undergraduate there in the late 1960s – and still there, on the verge of retirement, when I went along to see him. Butler talked candidly about the young Charles, describing him as 'talented – which is a different word from clever, and a different word from bright . . . When he arrived, he was boyish, rather immature, and perhaps too susceptible to the influence of his family.' To remedy this, he told me, Butler cleared forty-five minutes before dinner each evening for man-to-boyish-man chats with Charles, to whom he gave a key to a side entrance to the Master's Lodge, whence a 'secret staircase' led to the private apartments.

Among Butler's Cambridge household at the time was a young history graduate named Lucia Santa Cruz, daughter of the then Chilean ambassador to London, whom Butler had hired as his research assistant on his memoirs, *The Art of the Possible*. Charles, he explained to me in some detail, would never again enjoy such privacy as he had in Cambridge; though young for his age, the prince seemed to have taken something of a shine to Lucia. She was three years older than Charles and much more sophisticated. Nevertheless, the Master decided to encourage a romance. His only problem was the Trinity curfew, which then locked the gate at night between the college's all-male students and their girlfriends. Very much aware of his role *in loco parentis*, and the especial resonance of the phrase in this context, Butler decided – as he put it to me with a grin – to 'slip her a key'.

The wily old politician seemed rather keen for the world to know via my book that it was he who had thus arranged for the twenty-year-old Prince of Wales to lose his virginity. Three years later Lucia was to perform another signal service to Charles by introducing him at a polo match to her friend Camilla Shand, soon to become Parker Bowles.

Among overseas notables who actually replied to my enquiries was the actor David Niven, who confirmed a rumour that he had been in the happy throng outside Buckingham Palace when Charles's birth was announced in November 1948. Another was ex-President Richard Nixon, who admitted he had not taken notes during Charles's 1970 visit to the White House – of which he then proceeded to give a glowing account – because 'his visit came during a very busy period shortly after I had ordered the attacks on Communist sanctuaries in Cambodia.'

Among useful home-grown sources were Charles's school-masters at Cheam and Gordonstoun, his tutors and friends at Cambridge – all of whom also, at my request, read the manuscript for accuracy.

Just one potentially awkward ritual remained before I could hand in the finished manuscript. On the strict understanding that I was not surrendering editorial control, I had taken the highly calculated risk of inviting Charles to read my final draft; he was welcome, I said, to make any comments, point out what he considered inaccuracies, but the final decisions would remain mine. Despite these insolent terms, he agreed.

In January 1979 I made my way back into Buckingham Palace, by now for the umpteenth time, scrunching across the forecourt with the wide eyes of countless tourists boring into my back, wondering who the heck I could be.

As I sat across the desk from John Dauth, there was still just one more request I had made of him and his boss, purely for descriptive purposes: a ride in an aircraft with the Prince of Wales at the controls. So I was really hoping this meeting would go well.

But it certainly did not start well. As I reached across the desk for my precious manuscript, on which I could see copious scribblings in the margins, Dauth pulled it away from my anxious grasp, saying: 'I'm afraid I can't let you have your manuscript back, Mr Holden. The thing is, he took it to Sandringham over Christmas and New Year – and they've all read it. The Queen, the Duke of Edinburgh, Princess Anne . . . and they've written comments all over it.

'As you know, we don't allow the royal handwriting out of the Palace. So your manuscript will now go straight to the royal archive at Windsor, where future biographers and historians will be privileged to pore over it after the deaths of all relevant parties.'

He was grinning as he spelt out this last sentence – but I, clearly, was not. 'I can't have my manuscript back?' I gasped.

In this pre-word processor era, all I had at home was one rather scruffy carbon copy.

'Don't panic, Tony,' John continued, reaching into a drawer to pull out a hefty sheet of vellum, covered in comments in those large type-face letters then favoured by royal typewriters.

'Here is a list of the comments made on your book by those members of the royal family. Take a look and see what you think. But I must warn you: any dissent, and we will be obliged to withdraw all future co-operation.' By that, we both knew, he meant my aeroplane ride with Charles at the controls.

I started scanning the document. 'The Queen has no memory of the incident involving the rabbit, the canary and the corgi.'

'Prince Charles has no memory of encouraging Barbary apes to jump on Princess Anne in Gibraltar.'

But the real problem came on page 52. 'For the first few weeks of his life, the then Princess Elizabeth breastfed the infant prince.'

'What's wrong with that, John?'

'If you insist on keeping that in, Mr Holden, we will have to withdraw all future co-operation.'

'But it's a fact! Are you saying that it's inaccurate? Or that it's in dubious taste? Or simply that one does not mention the royal, er, breasts?' In my imagination, the ceiling of Buckingham Palace started to crack, and the chandelier to sway.

'I think you could say the latter, Mr Holden.'

There was a pregnant, you might say, pause. John smiled and shrugged: 'Let's go and have a drink, Tony.' With which we went off to a nearby pub, and together laughed off this absurd royal coyness. I am pleased to report that this particular detail stayed in the book, and that its opening line is: 'It is a blizzardy Friday in February, and we are a thousand feet above snow-clad Hampshire, in a tiny twin-engined de Havilland Otter, the Prince of Wales at the controls.'

That airborne excursion, all the way from Basingstoke to

Farnborough, in fact proved a right royal bonus, as the prince decided to seize the occasion to show off his aeronautical skills by landing on the icy runway and immediately taking off again – not just once, but twice, to the astonishment of the assembled dignitaries down below, and the ill-concealed discomfort of his private secretary, Squadron-Leader David Checketts, himself a veteran RAF officer. Because of the conditions, I later learned, Charles had been urged before take-off by the captain of the Queen's Flight to take the co-pilot's seat, leaving the potentially treacherous take-off and landing to the Otter's regular pilot. 'There was a curl of the royal lip,' I wrote, 'rather like that of the spoilt child deprived of a cherished toy. There was a look of mingled frustration and annoyance, then a few sharp words too staccato to overhear. Wing Commander the Prince of Wales had pulled rank.'

Now he was taking six icy risks – with some dozen lives at stake, including my own – for the price of two. When eventually we landed for the last time, he emerged from the cockpit to say, with a distinctly sadistic note in his voice, that he hoped we had enjoyed our flight.

It was moments like this that first moved me to write in my Preface that there were times the prince got 'ideas above his station'. Apart from rendering his private secretary a quivering wreck, it was almost as if he were showing off just to earn a few awestruck sentences in my book. I fear I found myself unable to oblige.

The episode rather seemed to prove my point that the prince as yet preferred to take physical risks at the cost of intellectual ones. With no one in his life to challenge him, to question his received attitudes, several of Charles's staff referred to their boss as 'the cushion'. When I asked what they meant by that, they explained that he tended to bear the imprint of the last person he had spoken to – particularly, at this early stage of his life, the South African-born writer Laurens van der Post, who had first introduced Charles to the philosophy of his own mentor, Carl Jung. After taking the prince on a safari to Kenya in 1977, van der Post cast a spell over him for the next two decades. So it was somewhat embarrassing that, after his death in 1996, van der Post was revealed to have embellished many details of his life, his official biographer labelling him 'a fraud, a fantasist, a liar and a serial adulterer' who had 'inflated his own importance at every opportunity'.

The rest of that day in Farnborough amounted to a routine royal visit to the British Transglobe Expedition, led by Charles's chum Sir Ranulph Twistleton-Wykeham-Fiennes – and the journey back was, mercifully, by car. It turned out to be one of the highlights of a pretty humdrum year, the other being a visit (by me, not the prince) to the Great Train Robber Ronnie Biggs when the royal party passed through Rio de Janeiro. To my amazement, Biggs quoted Shakespeare at me, namely *Measure for Measure*: 'They say, best men are moulded out of faults / And, for the most, become much the better / For being a little bad . . .'

The essential picture of the prince that emerged from the book was that of a rather solitary, often lonely young man still living at home with his parents in his thirties, eating TV suppers alone, if off trays delivered by liveried butlers. It soon became a commonplace perception of pre-Diana Charles – the 'Action Man' sewing plenty of wild oats, at the behest of his beloved 'honorary grandfather' Lord Mountbatten, but otherwise prone to acute self-pity as he contemplated a long life waiting in the wings to inherit the job to which he was born.

At the time Charles himself told me that he was broadly pleased with my portrait; I had demonstrated that the life of the Prince of Wales was 'not' (as he put it) 'all wine and roses'. I had been the first writer to draw this personal a profile, warts and all – and indeed, as he pointed out, the first of his biographers much his own age. Royal biographers before me tended to be

Fleet Street types using female pseudonyms like Helen Cathcart, a serial royal writer in fact named Harold Albert.

There were, of course, aspects of the book Charles did not like, as one of his then speechwriters, Byron Rogers, testifies in his 2009 autobiography. At that Press Awards lunch Rogers had wanted Charles 'to poke fun at Anthony Holden, known at the time to be writing the Prince's biography and thus accompanying him on every royal tour, by saying that his own job was "bad enough without my Boswell padding behind me in the Economy section."' Instead, to Rogers' evident dismay, Charles 'chose to be nice to Holden'. But the prince's attitude apparently 'changed dramatically when the book appeared'.

No doubt he was less than pleased (as indeed I later heard) with Lord Butler, for his revelations about the lovely Lucia. When the book came out, in fact, Butler felt moved to protest all over the front page of a national newspaper, which I was easily able to deal with. To the relief of my publishers' lawyers, His Lordship seemed to have forgotten that he had signed his approval to a pre-publication copy of the manuscript I had sent him with precisely that in mind.

Intent on limiting Charles's scope for protest, I was also careful to list in my Preface the many names of all the others who had read my manuscript for veracity. The book was to become a No. 1 bestseller on both sides of the Atlantic – more because of its subject's name, I readily concede, than its author's. Yes, the proceeds gave a new and very welcome double meaning to the word 'royalties'.

I dedicated it to all three of my sons – Sam, Joe and Ben, then aged four, two and zero respectively. Well, I didn't know if I would ever write another book.

Proud parents look on as A.H. signs books in Southport

8

3435 34TH PLACE

The front page of the *Sunday Times* of 12 November 1978 was adorned by a photo of five members of my poker game — all, absurdly, standing up and facing front while looking at their cards with conspiratorial grins beneath the green eye-shades real poker players never wear. The caption referred readers to my report on page 3 of Britain's first national poker tournament, held that weekend in Birmingham.

In the home straight of writing my Charles book, I had given myself the weekend off to travel with assorted pals to this unmissable event, in which I wound up in the money — and so buying all the drinks — by coming ninth out of seventy-five starters. But the true personal significance of this piece is that it would turn out to be the last I would write as a staff member of the *Sunday Times*. This was indeed the last issue of the paper for quite some time, as Thomson Newspapers abruptly closed it down indefinitely because of a long-running dispute with the print unions, which had for months been disrupting production.

Even so, I hesitated at first when Donald Trelford, editor of the paper's main rival, *The Observer*, seized the moment to offer me one of the most coveted postings in British journalism: Washington DC. On the *Sunday Times*, to the consternation of many more-than-qualified candidates, this was the one job that remained permanently unavailable, thanks to an immovable object named Henry Brandon, its correspondent there since 1949 (who would not retire until 1983).

As much as I relished the prospect of Washington, I was still constrained by my loyalty to Evans and his peerless paper – which would surely reopen eventually? Consultations with family and friends, however, soon confirmed my own instinct that this was an irresistible chance to function as a more upscale journalist, to graduate from the lightweight prattle of Atticus to the heavy-duty issues of the day, while exploring the unparalleled mysteries of the United States.

Naturally enough, Harry tried to dissuade me over a drink at his club, and in retrospect even I am surprised that he didn't succeed. I must indeed have been an ambitious young tyke, at barely thirty, to resist such blandishments as specialist positions with impressive-sounding titles to a 'key role' on the Insight team.

The cons and pros of *The Observer*, meanwhile, were that it had just been sold to an American oil company, Atlantic Richfield (ARCO), but that it boasted a new editor-in-chief in Conor Cruise O'Brien, the fiery Irish politician and writer, whom I much admired. I had already met Conor a few times at the home of his son Donal, who happened to be our next-door neighbour in Islington. Conor persuaded me not to worry about the American oilmen – they had offered persuasive guarantees of editorial independence – and added that he would be coming over to DC regularly to pursue various causes on his many agendas; he would introduce me to high-ups of his acquaintance in the administration and on Capitol Hill.

Besides, I *really* did not want to become known as a royal-watcher. That could surely be avoided by establishing myself in the States as a foreign correspondent six months before the Charles book appeared? Quitting Harold Evans's *Sunday Times* still feels to me like heresy, like leaving my spiritual home. But that settled it. Not for the first or the last time, the New World beckoned.

My priority on arrival in DC was to wallow in an all-day lunch beside the pool of the Washington Hilton with David Blundy, now the *Sunday Times*'s New York-based US correspondent. It was only six years since David and I had started sharing that tumultuous desk in the *Sunday Times* newsroom; on this bright spring day in 1979 we clinked glasses to celebrate the fact that now, between us, we seemed to have taken over the United States. The only problem was that Blundy's newspaper had ceased publication indefinitely; he grimaced as I mused that I now had Britain's upmarket Sunday readership to myself. But David, characteristically, kept on working regardless. Many were the WATFAD adventures we were to share all over the States on the 1980 US campaign trail.

My next port of call was the imposing British Embassy on Massachusetts Avenue, where my erstwhile colleague Peter Jay was installed as British ambassador. Eighteen months earlier, it had fallen to me to write the *Sunday Times*'s main feature on the pros and cons of Prime Minister Callaghan appointing his forty-year-old journalist son-in-law to a post of such consequence via their mutual friend David Owen, then foreign secretary. As charges of nepotism hogged the headlines, I felt impelled to observe that the only man I knew to be as expert a bridge player as poker player seemed to me eminently qualified for the calculated risks of diplomacy.

That was long before I had any inkling that I would be joining him in DC. Peter now gave me an appreciative critique of my piece, so we were off to a good start; I was to be granted regular audiences. The only dissident voice came from the most senior career diplomat among the embassy staff, John Robinson, whom I knew already as the brother-in-law of my Oxford tutor, John Jones. Robinson regularly took me aside to tell me that Jay was getting it all wrong, to the point where he was writing his own dispatches to London behind his back. I was far from convinced that Robinson was right, and quietly disapproved of his professional disloyalty; but these opposing points of view certainly made my early *Observer* columns unusually well informed.

This inside access, however, was not, alas, to last long. On the evening of 3 May 1979, barely a month after arriving in Washington, I was invited to a party at the Embassy to watch the results of the British general election coming in. With the US East Coast five hours behind the UK, it was good timing to catch the wee-small-hours developments over mid-evening drinks funded by the voters. With mounting angst, I watched the nose-in-air career diplomats nudging each other as it soon became all too clear that, after a mere five years of Labour in power, Margaret Thatcher's Tories had ousted the Callaghan government – which would surely mean the hasty repatriation of its US ambassador.

Callaghan himself soon came to Washington with his wife to lick his wounds in private chez his daughter Margaret and her husband. Knowing of my adventures with them in the Indian subcontinent, the Jays invited me and Amanda to dinner with Jim and Audrey at the ambassador's handsome Lutyens residence. Already drilled in the American protocol of calling all former presidents 'President', throughout the evening I kept addressing Callaghan as 'Prime Minister' – to the point where he desperately pleaded, 'Stop calling me that!' When I told him how delighted I was that, in his farewell honours list, he had knighted his doctor, Monty Levine, he replied: 'Yes, largely for services to you, I think!'

Not long after, when Thatcher did indeed relieve Jay of his duties at the Embassy, he chose to stay on in Washington – perhaps a mistake, as I was advised by Laurence Stern of the *Washington Post*, a warm soulmate who was perennially kind to newly arrived fellow journalists, particularly Brits. Once deprived of even a quasi-political post in the capital, declared Larry, 'the waters close over your head very fast'.

Peter Jay took a post at the Brookings Institution, the economics think tank, while Margaret embarked on the affair with Carl Bernstein of Watergate renown subsequently made famous by Bernstein's wife, Nora Ephron, in her novel-turned-movie *Heartburn*. Peter proceeded to enjoy a dalliance with the family's nanny, rendering her with child. So it is hardly surprising that the marriage didn't last much longer, with Peter moving back to London to co-start a breakfast TV station before bizarrely becoming Robert Maxwell's chief of staff, while Margaret followed her father into politics, rising to the leadership of the House of Lords.

Thirty years later, after several further encounters along the way, I would bump into Peter Jay again when he had risen to the dizzy heights of Mayor of Woodstock, Oxfordshire, where he had settled with his second wife. This was a much more knotty assignment, he told me with a grin, than representing British interests in the United States.

One of the first topics addressed in *The Observer* by ANTHONY HOLDEN'S AMERICA, complete with gritty picture byline, was a Jimmy Carter press conference at which the president became exercised about the allocation of parking spaces at the Bureau of Indian Affairs, soon followed by a denial that he exercised personal control over the schedule for the White House tennis courts. Already Carter was forging a reputation as a details man lacking a grand vision. As 'gas lines' formed outside petrol stations all over the country, reflecting the global oil crisis, the president told the voters in an impromptu national TV address that it was pretty much their own fault; Carter's so-called 'malaise' speech drove the first nail into his own political coffin.

With an election looming the following year, Senator Edward Kennedy decided to capitalise on the backlash against Carter by challenging him for the presidential nomination. At first even he did not seem able to explain his reasoning, beyond divine-right hereditary ambition; asked why he wanted to be president, in his first big television interview, Ted could only mumble incoherently.

It was Kennedy's great good fortune – and, longer-term, Ronald Reagan's – that this was wiped off the front pages the next morning, a year to the day before the election, by the dramatic news that fifty-two American diplomats had been seized and were being held hostage in the US Embassy in Tehran. Its proximate cause being that the US had given sanctuary to the deposed Shah, this stand-off would persist for 444 days. After countless missteps, which would prove corrosive to Carter's campaign, and a disastrously abortive rescue attempt, the hostages would eventually return home on 20 January 1981, Reagan's inauguration day.

For an overseas journalist, there were rich pickings to be had from all this. Whereas the US papers naturally assigned a senior reporter to each campaign, where they tended to develop 'localitis', foreign correspondents like myself were granted a day or two on each, a much more objective way of sampling the action. With Carter I flew over Mount St Helens a few days after it erupted in May 1980; aboard Air Force One I came across a pack of presidential playing cards, which I confess I pocketed, and still proudly possess. Well, Carter wasn't going to miss them. Where poker had once been part of the job description, there would be no poker-playing president between Nixon and Obama.

On each campaign plane, every reporter on board would get ten minutes alone with the candidate. Alone with Reagan – then, at sixty-nine, the oldest candidate in the history of the presidency – I seized the moment to ask, amid more consequential enquiries, the topical questions as to whether he dyed his hair, or had indulged in a facelift. Reagan plunged his head into my lap. 'Run your hand through my hair for the clues in the roots!' he invited. 'Look behind my ears! See if you can find any tell-tale scars!'

By the time I boarded Ted Kennedy's plane, for a chic dinner of crab and champagne with the candidate, I had already got to know him and was indeed writing his biography – at his own request. On one of Conor Cruise O'Brien's frequent visits to Washington, where he loved staying at the Watergate Hotel and sinking several bottles of his ancestral (or so he claimed) Château Haut-Brion, he had taken me along with him to visit Kennedy, whom he was trying to dissuade from supporting Noraid, the Irish-American organisation raising funds for the IRA. From his experience as an Irish cabinet minister, the only one publicly to have opposed the IRA, Conor was able to tell Kennedy in confidence the daunting scale of the Irish government's secret plans to accommodate refugees from across the border in the event of civil war.

I must have chipped in once or twice, as a *soi-disant* veteran of 'the Troubles', but Kennedy had evidently been briefed that I was also the biographer of the Prince of Wales. 'How long are you here in the States?' he asked me. Open-endedly. 'Covering the election campaign?' Of course. 'How would you like to write a book about me and my progress to the White House?' Wow, I'd love to!

Thus it was that, with my subject's enthusiastic endorsement, I embarked on an ambitious, warts-and-all, insider's biography of Ted Kennedy. Which would soon wind up biting the dust along with his fortunes in the presidential race – where Carter would, in his own atypical words, 'whip Kennedy's ass'.

As for the fortunes of the Holden family, the first thing to have happened in our absence from London was that Terry Neill's Arsenal won the FA Cup for the first time in a decade – and we hadn't been there to see it. After a few months living on rather bland Dexter Street NW, where the boys have always remembered too-tall Blundy crashing into the chandelier in the hallway, we moved to Washington's high-end Cleveland Park, where most of the powerbrokers lived, and an address I have always cherished: 3435 34th Place. The two older children went to a nearby school called the National Child Research Center, which had me worried that they would one day come home in specimen jars.

That spring I travelled to Martha's Vineyard, the chic vacation island off the south coast of Cape Cod, to interview William Styron about his imminent novel *Sophie's Choice*. Bill and I quickly warmed to each other; and so wide grew my eyes at the elegance of his ocean-side home that he offered to find me a Vineyard rental for that summer. So just months later the Holden family duly travelled north for a few weeks beside the beaches made famous by *Jaws*, receiving a stream of visitors including Peter Jay on his transatlantic yacht.

Another afternoon that summer saw me driving to the tiny airfield of Martha's Vineyard, so small as to put me in mind of the immortal closing scene of *Casablanca*, to pick up yet another houseguest heading over from New York (who just happened to be the Prince of Wales's press secretary, John Dauth, which later prompted much tabloid mischief in the gossip columns back home). The flight from La Guardia, announced a disembodied voice, was delayed – at least an hour, maybe more. There was just one other person waiting, whom I recognised as the composer-conductor André Previn, who had a house on the island with his then wife Mia Farrow, for whom he was waiting to arrive on the same flight.

I had long been an admirer of the sheer range of Previn's work, so I thought I would go over and say hello. We both had unexpected time to kill, and no one else to kill it with. I had a handy memory of a lecture he had given at the US Embassy in London a dozen or so years before, when he had said something I had never forgotten about how 'obscene' it was that these days we can listen to, say, Bach's B Minor Mass at the mere flick of a switch.

'Hello, Mr Previn,' I began, 'I'm Anthony Holden, the US editor of *The Observer*.'

'No, you're not,' he replied. 'You're the bastard who wrote all that shit about me in the *Sunday Times*.'

The maestro and I then proceeded to sit fifty yards apart for an hour and a half, the only people at the airport, awaiting our respective arrivals.

Yes, some things sure do come back to haunt you.

Before our vacation, soon after Carter's counter-productive 'malaise' speech, I had been in the White House press office when the president's spokesman, Jody Powell, put his feet up on the desk to announce that Carter had fired four of his cabinet members, saying he wanted 'a new start'. With inflation roaring and gasoline lines still enraging voters, Powell's faux-nonchalance was a vain attempt to reassure Americans that Carter was 'changing the terms' of his administration. Predictably enough, it backfired completely. The incumbent's polls nosedived. The popular perception was that Carter was going down in flames.

But there was still much fun to be had on the campaign trail, not least a week following the president's progress down the Mississippi aboard an ancient paddle-steamer called the *Delta Queen*. It was billed as a vacation, but Carter spent each day ashore shaking countless hands, kissing numerous babies and making interminable speeches at public meetings through what just happened to be the three states holding early primaries the following year.

Other collectors' items included a visit with Carter to the Grand Ole Opry in Nashville, Tennessee, and a New Hampshire picnic with Jane Fonda, Jesse Jackson and other notables on the 'leftie fringe' when California's governor Jerry Brown launched his abortive campaign for the Democratic nomination. Ted Kennedy was always good value, though I noticed that even the most assiduous journalists kept their distance from the candidate, expecting an assassin's bullet at any minute.

Among lasting friends I made in Washington was the maverick British journalist Henry Fairlie, renowned for coining the phrase 'The Establishment' for the people who really run Britain. I remained seriously impressed by this – and enjoyed many a memorable lunch with Henry at our favourite Washington restaurant, the Palm.

Through Henry I also came to know the radical American journalist I. F. ('Izzy') Stone; a wonderfully entertaining companion, offering the sharpest insights into the political scene, Izzy had been an influential figure since the 1950s via his dazzling investigative journal *I. F. Stone's Weekly*. Throw in our mutual friend Marcus Cunliffe, the engaging scholar of American studies by then in semi-retirement in Washington, and our neighbour Jim Lehrer, of PBS's nightly *MacNeil/Lehrer Newshour*, and I had a bottomless pit of past and current expertise at my disposal.

No wonder Clive James, who also dropped by while writing one of his occasional 'Postcards from . . .' for *The Observer*, told me I had the best job in Fleet Street. 'To Tony, with thanks and affection after having a nice day,' wrote Clive in the handsome volume of Edmund Wilson with which he presented me as a parting gift over yet another lunch at the Palm.

Most of the other British journalists, I noticed, seemed to enjoy their own inbred company. I became all the more determined that my circle of Washington friends would remain predominantly American, and resolved that the regular dinner parties I gave with Amanda (thanks to her expertise as cook, hostess and indeed pianist) would always have more indigenous than European guests.

One of the first Washington veterans to take me under his wing was Jack Valenti, a former aide to Lyndon Johnson – his press liaison in the Dallas motorcade on the day John F. Kennedy was assassinated – who went on to become an influential president of the Motion Picture Association of America. Among useful chums in the administration, with whom I would go drinking in the fashionable DC bar the Class Reunion, was Carter's chief speechwriter Hendrik ('Rik') Hertzberg, subsequently editor of the *New Republic* and long-term senior editor at the *New Yorker*. One evening Rik told me that Carter, contemplating a trip to Germany, had asked him to come up with a presidential line as memorable as JFK's 'Ich bin ein Berliner'.

'Where's he going?' I asked.

'Hamburg and Frankfurt.'

'Hmm,' was all I could think of saying. 'I see your problem.'

Another regular in the Class Reunion was the State Department spokesman Hodding Carter, who conducted the daily State Department briefings at which convention required the questioner to identify himself before speaking. Knowing Hodding well, I forgot to do so on the day in 1979 that I stood up to ask, on the resumption of the election campaign after Labor Day, why the president had not publicly denounced the IRA for its recent murder of Lord Mountbatten. Could it be that he didn't want to risk alienating the Irish-American vote?

'Who's asking?' he replied.

'Oh, sorry. Anthony Holden, *The Observer* of London.'

'Quite,' said Carter. 'Next question.'

Which in translation again means: no votes to deliver. Or, to my mind: so much for the so-called 'special relationship'. For decades this anecdote remained Exhibit A in my standard derision of the 'special relationship' that Britain likes to claim with the US – until, nearly forty years later, I saw a supplicant British prime minister, who just happened to be female, holding hands with the self-confessed serial groper Donald Trump barely a week after he took office.

That autumn publication of my Charles book came and went as a mercifully incidental detail in my now blissfully US-based life. A brief trip back to Britain for a publicity tour was launched with a lavish party chez Weidenfeld, where I learned a handy lifelong lesson from John Mortimer: 'A copy signed is a copy sold.' When the same ritual was repeated in the States, travelling coast to coast in company from Tom Wolfe to the young Hilary Mantel, Americans kept coming up to me to coo how much they loved the British monarchy; to which I replied by telling them, in public as in private, how much it cost the British taxpayer, and how happy I'd be to have the whole hereditary pantomime shipped over for them. This seemed to give them pause – and later earned me an apposite dedication in Mantel's early novel *A Place of Greater Safety*, set in the French Revolution: 'Anthony – love and good wishes, you rabid republican, you!' Tom Wolfe signed my copy of *The Right Stuff* 'with a deep bow in the square in Cleveland'.

In the autumn of 1979 Pope John Paul II came to tour the United States – which saw me earn a papal in-flight blessing over the public address system of his plane, codenamed Angel 1. With my parents also visiting at the time, I was walking them over from their bargain hotel in New York to my smart one for dinner just as the Holy Father was entering St Patrick's Cathedral to take mass. Fifth Avenue was a sea of cops as far as the eye could see in both directions. 'Yes,' said my mother thoughtfully, 'they said New York was like this.'

Otherwise the election proceeded predictably enough, with the children loving Reagan's movie *Bedtime for Bonzo* (in which he co-starred with a chimpanzee) as the former governor of California moved inexorably towards the Republican nomination. Not noted for his excess of grey cells, Reagan was proving a skilled and genial communicator, who would leave the hard work of actually running the country to others more qualified than himself.

That July I flew to Detroit for the Republican convention in the company of Anthony Howard, who was fast becoming the grand old man of British journalism. Chair of the judges for that year's British press awards, Tony said to me on the plane: 'You think you're going to win Foreign Correspondent of the Year, don't you?' The thought had not even crossed my mind, as I told him with hand on heart, while adding that I would naturally be delighted to do so. 'Well, you're not,' he replied. 'You've written off Carter far too soon.'

Tony was far from alone in believing it inconceivable that the incumbent president could be defeated by a sometime Hollywood cowboy with minimal experience of national, let alone international, affairs. But the Iran hostages were still in captivity, with the venerable Walter Cronkite counting up the days night after night on CBS news.

Thanks to Alan Coren, I could leaven my *Observer* gravitas with much-needed frivolity in a fortnightly column for *Punch* called Transatlantic Cables. It had become a regular item after Alan commissioned a piece enumerating what I missed most about Britain. This double-barrelled approach to the election campaign – responsibly straight-faced for *The Observer*, irresponsibly frolicsome for *Punch* – suited my built-in leanings towards both ends of the journalistic spectrum. My habitually casual dress sense came in handy, for instance, when Margaret Thatcher rounded the Christmas tree at a White House reception to find me lurking behind it in a rather crumpled green corduroy suit, of which she volubly disapproved.

One of Georgetown's legendary hostesses, Evangeline Bruce, who had been especially welcoming to me, came to our house for dinner with Conor Cruise O'Brien on the arm of the senior ARCO-Observer executive Douglass Cater. Given the grandeur of the occasion, I had also laid on such glitzy guests as the *New York Times* columnist James ('Scotty') Reston, ex-ambassador Peter Jay and the Irish ambassador, Seán Donlon. The conversation ranged far and wide, with an especially vivid debate on still embattled Ireland. A somewhat inebriated Conor told both Donlon and Jay that they didn't know what they were talking about, before Reston embarked on what was clearly going to be a long paragraph with the words 'Well, I come from Calvinist stock . . .'

'Reston,' interrupted Conor, 'you're full of shit!' – at which point America's most celebrated journalist got up and walked out mid-meal, promptly followed by Cater and Mrs Bruce, then the Irish ambassador. Assuming that Cater would have us both fired the next morning, Conor and I decided that the only solution was to drink even more while singing traditional Irish songs, in which we were joined by Peter Jay, with Amanda at the piano. Amazingly, despite a few nights of lost sleep, we both survived to tell the tale – and indeed many more.

To get our small sons interested in the election, which was taking Daddy away from home so much, we played a game with them called: 'Who do you want to live in the White House?' Four-year-old Sam opted for the dashing Mr Kennedy. Three-year-old Joe, who had already developed an eye for a winner, chose Mr Reagan. Which left baby Ben, much to his brothers' amusement, with a sure loser in Mr Carter. Between them, they were eventually to meet all three.

If you are Brits vacationing on Martha's Vineyard – which, in the summer of 1980, we were for the second year running – you get a steady stream of British houseguests, all of whom demand a visit to Chappaquiddick Island, scene of Ted Kennedy's disgrace in July 1969. You show them how he had to fight the camber to leave the road at that point; that the Dike Bridge is a tiny wooden footbridge, not designed for motor traffic; and that the water beneath it is barely six feet deep, for all Kennedy's protestations that he had 'dived repeatedly' in his attempts to save his companion when he drove the car off the bridge, a 28-year-old RFK 'boiler-room girl' named Mary Jo Kopechne.

A decade later, Bill Styron had been saying all summer that his friend Ted would be sailing over from Hyannis for lunch one day, and that I must join them. The call eventually came with unfortunate timing; the previous night our nanny had abruptly walked out. So I had to tell Bill that of course we'd love to come to lunch, but we'd have to bring the children.

'Oh, that's fine,' he said immediately. 'Ted loves children.'

As we drove over, four-year-old Sam was especially excited about meeting his hero, Senator Kennedy. 'Oh, this is great!'

he piped up from the back. 'Now I can ask Mr Kennedy what *really* happened at Chappaquiddick!'

I stopped the car. 'Now look, Sam,' I said, leaning round to him. 'This is not a great day to ask Mr Kennedy that question. He's feeling very sad today, because he's just lost the nomination to Mr Carter. And he's still *really* sad about poor Mary Jo being drowned. Coming to this island always reminds him of it. Today's *really* not the best day to bring it up . . .'

I carried on in this vein to the point where Amanda told me I was mad, just planting the idea more firmly in the child's head.

Half an hour later I was standing in one of the most galactical circles I have ever graced – the Styrons, Katharine Graham, Art Buchwald, Lillian Hellman and others – as Kennedy strolled up the lawn towards us from his yacht. Clad in only his swim-trunks, and the back brace he wore following his 1964 plane crash, Ted was a visibly deep shade of red, puce all over, the result of far too many daiquiris on the voyage over from Hyannis.

And these were his friends, his *real* friends, on the day he most needed them. They were in the middle of commiserating with him about Carter, and I was awaiting my turn to say hello again, when this four-year-old blond boy burst into the middle of the circle, and yelled at him: 'Hey, Mr Kennedy. Mis-ter Ken-nedy! There's something I want to say to you!'

The conversation abruptly ceased. Everyone looked down at this sweet little boy as Kennedy said, 'Hi there!' and asked him: 'What's your name?'

'Sam.'

'Well, Sam, what is it you want to say to me?'

I started backing out of the circle, motioning to Amanda to start the getaway car.

'Mr Kennedy,' said Sam, 'I want you to live in the White House!'

'Well, Sam, so do I!' said Kennedy, who promptly picked him up and would not be parted from him for the rest of the day. He sat Sam on his knee throughout lunch, apparently engaging him in earnest conversation.

Later that afternoon, as the party broke up, a post-drunk Kennedy was being taken by Styron to his private beach for a quiet chat. Bill invited me along. Still with Sam on his lap, feeding him pretzels, Kennedy finally got serious, talking in the most candid detail about Carter, the SALT talks and more.

As the light started to fade, we wandered back to our two cars and finally bid each other farewell. I had already started the engine when Kennedy got out of Styron's car, walked over and tapped on the back window of ours. Sam excitedly rolled down the window.

'Hey, Sam,' said Kennedy, 'do you still want me to live in the White House?'

'Ooooh yes, Mr Kennedy.'

'So d'you think I should run again in '84?'

'Ooooh yes, Mr Kennedy.'

'Well, tell you what, Sam, if I run again in '84, will you be my running-mate?'

'Ooooh yes, Mr Kennedy.'

'It's a deal,' said Kennedy. 'Stay in touch, kiddo.'

Four years later, there was indeed talk of Kennedy running again, despite Chappaquiddick and countless other blots on his record. 'Hey, Dad,' said Sam, now an intelligent, TV news-watching eight-year-old, all summer. 'Get him on the phone! He said I'd be his running-mate!' So it came as a mighty relief to me when, at the last, Kennedy decided not to run and threw his support behind Walter Mondale.

'Say what you like about Ted Kennedy,' I observed when the senator died in 2009. 'He was really good with children.'

That autumn, to make the election even more exciting for our boys, we took them to see both candidates going to church in Washington a few Sundays before the vote. Carter, as I hoped, could not resist coming over to be photographed with the only

baby in the crowd, who just happened to be his unwitting supporter Ben Holden, now all of eight months old, before shaking
hands with his brother Sam. When Reagan later walked straight
past us, Sam called him back: 'Hey, Reagan, come and shake
hands with my brother Joe. He voted for you!' The candidate
duly obeyed orders.

The election-eve picture of Carter shaking hands with an
excited little four-year-old boy went around the world as the
agency photo of the day. Later that week, as Carter embarked
on the long, painful transition period following his defeat, our
neighbour in 34th Place, who happened to be a White House
staffer, offered to take a print into work for the outgoing president to sign. When he surprised me by bringing it back that
same evening, duly signed to Sam by the outgoing president, he
explained: 'Well, he's got damn-all else to do right now!'

Watched by his daughter Amy, President Jimmy Carter
shakes hands with four-year-old Sam Holden

A week before Christmas, in what was a very cold winter, I was
obliged to get out of bed in the middle of the night to answer the
phone, only to be told I had a person-to-person collect call from

the South Pole. Assuming this must be some prank by drunken revellers at *The Observer*'s Christmas party in London, I hung up and went back to bed. It was ineffably cold in my study, next to our bedroom. But two minutes later, the phone rang again. Like any conscientious journalist, if on this occasion wearing only a T-shirt, I dragged myself reluctantly back out of bed and into my sub-zero study.

'No, please don't hang up again!' pleaded the caller, who explained that he was a radio ham in New Mexico genuinely relaying a person-to-person call from the South Pole for the Washington correspondent of the London *Observer*. After much clicking and scratching, a voice finally proclaimed: 'Holden?'

'Yes, I replied, mystified.

'Holden, this is Ranulph Fiennes. We met with the Prince of Wales a couple of years ago. You will know that I have an arrangement with *The Observer* to relay the progress of my Transglobe Expedition. I can't raise anyone in London; they must be having their Christmas party or something. But this is very important. We have finally reached the South Pole by an unprecedented route, and I'm calling to dictate my detailed report to you.'

'Well, it's rather cold here . . .' I began, intent on asking if he could call London the next day.

'Rather cold *there*!' he exclaimed. 'What the hell do you think it's like here at the *South fucking Pole*!'

For an hour and more, I was thus obliged to take down Fiennes' dictation, punctuated by 'Over!'s like my ship-to-shore calls from Chay Blyth, with my extremities freezing off to the point where I let the details of a broken limb or two pass without comment. Fiennes seemed at last to be reaching the end when the link was suddenly broken by static. I lay awake all night, expecting the damn phone to ring again any minute – but, as the *Observer* diary reported that Sunday, Fiennes was obliged to finish his report direct to London the next day, as I went straight to my office to file the rest and report the latest hitch in the Iran hostage saga, before sleeping it all off over the weekend.

All this time my relations with the veteran *Sunday Times* correspondent Henry Brandon – until recently, of course, a colleague – were at best frosty. As his newspaper resumed publication that autumn, I paid Brandon a courtesy call in the National Press Building, where we were both housed, to introduce the visiting Conor Cruise O'Brien – who promptly ensured that *The Observer* got itself (i.e. me) an even bigger and better office on a higher floor, which proved a great vantage point for the children to watch Reagan's inauguration parade in January 1981.

One of the first appointments made by Reagan, evidently quite as important to him as any cabinet post, was that of social secretary to the First Lady, his wife Nancy. She chose Brandon's wife Mabel, known as 'Muffie'. Having met her socially – and fearful, as the representative of her husband's rival newspaper, for my cherished invitations to White House events – I deemed it politic to write Muffie a polite letter of congratulations. Next thing I knew, old *Sunday Times* chums were calling to say that a copy of it had wound up on the noticeboard in the paper's London newsroom. Don't fret, they said, the entire paper was on my side about Brandon's tawdry betrayal of confidence.

The irrepressible Henry Fairlie was especially incensed by this, calling it 'the first diplomatic incident of the new administration' in a *Spectator* meditation on the dubious ethics of a newspaper correspondent permitting his wife to take sides publicly in Washington party politics. Henry went much further when Prime Minister Thatcher paid her first visit to the new president that February. Did Muffie's new position not place her husband in an 'uncomfortable' position? Would Brandon not face 'severe' conflicts of interest? 'His job is to report fearlessly the doings of President Reagan while his wife holds an influential post on the staff of Mrs. Reagan.' There was 'speculation' in

Washington that Brandon's 'dastardly deed' in sending a copy of his rival's letter to his paper in London might well have been 'to quieten the rumblings of discontent on his own newspaper following his wife's appointment'.

The remedy open to Mrs Thatcher was clear. She should 'scrap' the hospitality on offer at the White House and instead go to dinner 'at the home of Mr. and Mrs. Holden, where she will, I can assure her, be wined and dined as befits her station, and probably be entertained after dinner by a rendering by her hostess of the Goldberg Variations.'

Remarkably, Thatcher did not show up for dinner. Later that week, however, I found myself dancing with her daughter Carol, alongside her prime minister mother and President Reagan, during a dinner at the British Embassy.

At the end of the following month, March 1981, I was lunching with a friend from *Newsweek* near the Washington Hilton when the waiter asked us if we had heard that the president had been shot. She and I both ran to the scene, whence Reagan had already been rushed to hospital. My vivid account in *The Observer* that Sunday earned me an even more vivid message from one of my predecessors in Washington, Gavin Young: 'You lucky bastard: you've had an election, a change of president and now an assassination attempt!' That's one way of looking at the busy job of a Washington correspondent. Gavin was not to know it, however, but by then my professional life was already heading, yet again, in another completely different direction.

After two years based in Washington, I had visited forty-nine of the fifty states – all except South Dakota, a painful omission as I had always longed to gaze in wonder upon Mount Rushmore. So fascinated had I become by this vast nation's huge range of particularities – its sheer scale and diversity, history and culture (high and low) – that I was contemplating a magisterial book attempting to capture all this under the crafty if vainglorious title of *Holden, USA*. This I could justify by finding typical towns and cities in pretty much every state, from coast to coast, with Holden or some version of the word in their names. From Maine and Massachusetts to Missouri and Utah there are towns or villages named Holden; add variants from the city of Holdenville, Oklahoma, to the Holden Chapel at Harvard University, and I could visit a wide range of emblematic destinations, from the Ivy League east to the mid-west rustbelt, assembling a jigsaw of Americana via my family name.

I had just managed to get George Weidenfeld interested in the idea when a phone call from Harold Evans was again to re-route my life. I was in the throes of negotiating a long-term contract with *The Observer*, after discussing with Amanda the notion of raising our sons in DC, when suddenly much of unforeseen relevance began happening back in Blighty. It all kicked off with Thomson announcing the sale of Times Newspapers to Rupert Murdoch – whom, for reasons credible only to conspiracy theorists, the government had spared a referral to the Monopolies Commission in return for solemn, legally binding undertakings that Murdoch would respect the papers' editorial freedom, appointing a board of independent directors as guarantors.

On the morning of 24 February 1981, as I prepared for Prime Minister Thatcher's arrival in Washington the next day to pay her first visit to the newly inaugurated President Reagan, Murdoch announced the appointment of Harold Evans to the editorship of *The Times* in all but the same breath that Buckingham Palace announced the engagement of the Prince of Wales to Lady Diana Spencer.

Within hours I was writing an impromptu royal Review Front for *The Observer*, and gearing up to finish in three weeks a lucrative little hardback to mark the wedding, while trying to clear the decks to cover Thatcher's visit. In the midst of all this I received a phone call from Evans inviting me to become features editor – and one of the select band of his assistant editors – back in London at *The Times*.

Harry could not know that the night before I had taken

another transatlantic call – from Ron Hall, editor of the *Sunday Times* magazine, who had been promoted to deputy editor. Would I be interested in returning to edit the magazine?

It wasn't long before Harry had got wind of this, and was phoning three times a day before meals, pressing for an answer. I was still hesitating. 'Are you saying you'd rather be editor of the *Sunday Times* magazine than assistant editor of *THE Times*?'

'No, Harry, I'm saying I'd rather be US editor of *The Observer*.'

'How old are you now?' He had always underestimated my age.

'Thirty-two, Harry.'

'Well, I'm fifty-two. I've told Rupert I'll do this job for eight years. Then you can take over. Think of it, lad – editor of *The Times* at forty! I'll groom you.'

That clinched it. This was yet another Evans offer I couldn't refuse.

9

A-CHANGING

'No,' she said, her eyes confirming that she meant it.

'Let's see you practise your curtsey,' I persisted – playfully, as I thought.

'NO!' repeated Amanda, unamused. 'You have just spent a fortnight in Australia with that man. I have no interest in meeting him. Tomorrow is our tenth wedding anniversary. You should be taking me out to lunch.'

'I am,' said I. 'At the British Embassy, with a few hundred of our closest friends.'

'*NO!*' she said again. 'Alone – just the two of us!'

We went, of course.

Having largely stood by his promise not to make me write about the royals, at the last Donald Trelford combined my unexpected resignation with the offer of a first-class air ticket to twist my arm into working out my notice in Australia, whither the Prince of Wales had vanished surprisingly soon after announcing his engagement to Lady Diana Spencer. No one read any ominous portents into the tears streaming down Diana's cheeks as she was pictured waving him off at Heathrow. Nor, I suspect, did she herself know that her fiancé was intent on securing himself the post of governor-general – the nearest he was going to get for many years to any quasi-monarchical role – which would mean embarking on their married life down under, whether she liked it or not.

Thanks to my Oxford friend Ivor Roberts, by then a senior

diplomat in Canberra, I secured an interview with the high commissioner himself, Sir John Mason, at his summer residence in Sydney. I dived straight in, gleaning his off-the-record views on the pros and cons of Charles becoming governor-general, then turned to broader questions about Australia.

'Your first time here, is it?' he asked somewhat sardonically. Yes.

'And you're here for, what, a week or two?' Er, yes.

'And this Sunday I assume you are proposing to write the definitive piece about Australia?' Well, I guess that's the general idea.

'Look, I'll tell you the only thing you need to know about Australia. What's the population?'

Luckily, I had mugged that up. 'Fifteen million?'

'Correct. So that's how many potentially cut fingers and toes?'

'Er, three hundred million.'

'Correct. And yet, you know, last year Elastoplast went out of business in Australia. Because half those people are crammed down here in the bottom right-hand corner of the country, and the other half are stranded 2,500 miles away over on the left. And there's damn-all in between. So, even with three hundred million potentially cut digits across the nation, Elastoplast couldn't hold its own here commercially. There you have it, young man.'

I thanked him profusely, and gratefully accepted his offer of a farewell drink outside on the terrace of his stylish villa. The sun was shining benevolently, and beneath us countless little boats bobbed on the outer reaches of a shimmering Sydney harbour. When the time came for me to take my leave, I politely said I hoped we might meet again one day back in London, where I was soon to return.

'Back in London?' he exclaimed with incredulity, gesturing at the magnificent vista beneath us. 'Back in London? You must be joking!' After retiring three years later, Mason chose to become an Australian citizen and did indeed stay there for the rest of his life.

The report I filed that weekend quoted notables from the Nobel Prize-winning novelist Patrick White to Australia's six-volume historian, Professor Manning Clark, to the effect that the country should mark its forthcoming bicentenary by declaring itself a republic independent of Britain and the crown. This was the view I heard from Australians of all ages and backgrounds around the country. Less than half of Australians were now of British descent, with a quarter of the population of Asian origin, and a third Catholic. After Athens and New York, Melbourne was the third-largest Greek city in the world, Sydney the fourth; ex-King Constantine of Greece, I was told more than once, would make as logical a choice for governor-general. 'How many other countries in the world,' as Clark put it, 'have a foreign head of state who chooses to live as far away as possible?' No, it was time for an indigenous governor-general to pave the way for an independent republic of Australia within the decade.

My farewell piece to *Observer* readers, this heartfelt harangue ended with the news that while Charles was moving on to Venezuela, I would be returning to Washington, where I would see him again the following week, before heading 'most reluctantly' back to London. 'From two countries looking alive to their future,' I concluded, 'to one which, from both vantage points, seems able only to take a decaying satisfaction in its past.'

This remark was to earn me the ire of my arch enemy (as it would turn out) at *The Times*, its deputy editor Charles Douglas-Home. First, I had to endure the ire of my wife, as I took her to lunch at the British Embassy with the Prince of Wales on our tenth wedding anniversary. Her Majesty's post-Jay ambassador, Nicholas ('Nico') Henderson, had somehow been persuaded that the prince and I were best buddies; so it was as much of a surprise to me as to my Fleet Street colleagues when I found myself grinning from the other side of the rope holding them back, and waving in regal style to my photographer pals, as I escorted Amanda up the red carpet into the imposing Lutyens residence.

Charles, too, seemed a bit surprised to see me on the guest list – alongside dignitaries from Vice-President George H. W. Bush to Douglas Fairbanks Jr – but, to be fair, he took it in good part. He was interested, he said, in what I had written the previous Sunday, urging him to abandon his plans to become quasi-monarch of Australia. He sat me down for an intense conversation about it all while Mrs H stood grumpily beside us, understandably irritated to be so ignored.

'Sir,' said I, when I could get a word in, 'may I introduce my wife, Amanda?'

'Charmed to meet you,' said Charles. 'What do you do?'

'I'm a pianist,' she replied (without the curtsey).

'Oh, how interesting,' he went on, with a finger-strumming gesture. 'Does that mean you type out his articles?'

'*NO!*' she gasped, with wide-eyed incredulity.

Even Charles could see what a gaffe he had made. 'Oh,' he said, trying to mend his regal fence. 'So you know about music, do you? Well, you know, I'm getting married soon . . .'

'Yes, I *had* heard . . .'

'Perhaps you could give me some advice about the music for the service?' He took Amanda by the arm and led her down the imposing ballroom for an extended conversation. All I could lip-read were words like 'Handel' and 'Mendelssohn' before he finally returned her to my side. 'What a charming man!' she declared.

The luncheon proceeded without further incident before at length I bid farewell to the prince, to the ambassador – and a few days later, with the greatest regret, to DC itself.

Our London home was unavailable when I flew back ahead of the family the following week, in early May, so I checked into a hotel and collapsed to sleep off the overnight flight. All too soon my slumbers were interrupted by a call from *The Times*; apparently the editor wanted to speak to me.

Harry said I was urgently needed in the office. It transpired that a rogue journalist had managed to get hold of transcripts of phone calls between Charles and Diana during the prince's absence in Australia; they had been tapped by republican-inclined Aussies during Charles's stay at the ranch of his polo coach, and were about to be published by a German magazine immune from the inevitable royal injunction. As well as the couple's supposed intimacies, they quoted Charles making less than polite remarks about Malcolm Fraser and indeed Australians generally.

And so it came to pass that my name adorned the front-page lead of *The Times* on my very first day at the paper, 5 May 1981. For me, it was irksome that it was yet another royal story; for the majority of *Times* journalists who pre-dated Evans, whom they regarded with some suspicion, it was an even more irksome symbol of the bumptious new regime. I had returned from Australia with a bumper sticker advertising the country's favourite automobile: YOU CAN TRUST HOLDEN. It was perhaps overly cocky of me to stick it on the door of my office as features editor; mercifully, however, *Times* veterans were above petty graffiti. But they took to calling the features department 'the kindergarten'; I was thirty-three and my deputy, Peter Stothard, thirty; our No. 3, Nicholas Wapshott, was twenty-nine.

So I soon started making my presence felt, with the eager support of my editor. At the daily editorial conference I imported the American term 'op-ed' for the flagship page of my features empire; Charles Douglas-Home led the old guard by treating it with the utmost disdain, spitting it out with contempt whenever required to refer to what had traditionally been called the 'opinion' page. Symbolic of many other such anachronisms, this served only to confirm my mental portrait of all these veteran *Times* journalists attached to their desks by cobwebs in urgent need of sweeping away. One such was a feature writer newly but reluctantly under my sway named Roger Berthoud, who had himself (I later learned) hoped to be made features editor – 'a senior but actually rather horrible, nerve-racking job.' In his 2009 memoirs, Berthoud would also write: 'Tony Holden was all charm as features editor, but it soon became obvious that his loyalty was to Harry Evans, rather than to some relic of the Rees-Mogg era, as he doubtless saw me.'

Indeed it was, and so I did. When that month saw an assassination attempt on Pope John Paul II, in only my second week in the job, I hastily re-jigged that day's op-ed page to reflect this momentous event. I vividly remember persuading the Archbishop of Canterbury, Robert Runcie, to cancel his lunch to write a tribute for *The Times*, and deliver it before I got back from mine. When the proofs appeared that evening, Berthoud came into my office to complain that his scheduled feature about the artist Graham Sutherland (whose biography he had just written) had not appeared, as expected. I explained that I had been obliged to postpone it; there were other global events that day of rather more significance.

'But this is *The Times*,' protested Berthoud. 'We don't do things that way here. We *think* about them for a few days before pronounci . . .'

'Not any more, we don't,' I replied. '*The Times*, it is a-changing.'

The Times had indeed begun a-changing before my arrival, at the end of March, when Harold Evans responded to the attempt on Reagan's life with a dramatic front page of three rapid-succession photographs, signalling extended and carefully calibrated coverage inside. It was typical of an editor as intent on (and skilled at) layout and display as on the quality of the reporting. In his first month in the job, Harry was showing them how he proposed to continue. Already, in other words, he was alienating what he and I came to call 'the old guard'.

There soon followed another bold initiative he entrusted to me: editing a colour magazine – the first produced by a daily British newspaper – to mark the forthcoming wedding of the heir to the throne. It appeared the day before the event on 29 July 1981, which was marked by a piece from the groom himself. Its headline, 'Why I Feel So Close to the Commonwealth', suggested that the prince was taking advantage of my editorial hospitality to stake a long-term claim to a role that, contrary to popular belief, is not necessarily hereditary – as indeed I had recently reminded him over that lunch in Washington.

I myself spent the day as a commentator for America's ABC News channel, perched precariously high on a platform improvised amid scaffolding opposite St Paul's Cathedral with Peter Jennings, ABC's London anchor, and the network's star interviewer, Barbara Walters, who had flown over specially for the occasion. Peter and I had both worked our way thoroughly through the voluminous briefing book supplied by ABC. When the bride took longer than expected to process down the aisle, on the frail arm of her post-stroke father, Peter grinned mischievously as he lobbed me an unexpected question: 'Anthony, tell us about the veil Diana is wearing.' I extemporised desperately until a disembodied hand reached up towards me through the floor, proffering a briefing paper about the veil's long history. Now I droned on in interminable detail, boring even myself as I sensed La Walters beside me growing agitated at her lack of airtime. When another such hand eventually reached up towards her, with another such briefing paper, she cut me short with a ferocious 'Lemme tell y'all about the boo-kay!'

Once we had watched Diana head off from her 'fairy-tale' wedding into royal life – 'like a lamb', in her own (we now know) words, 'to the slaughter' – I rushed back to the office to help Harry see into print a special edition of the paper, its front page adorned by a celebratory colour photograph of the occasion. This was another first for British journalism, thanks to the use of a hired helicopter and special printing arrangements that had between them been shredding our nerves all day. The next day's circulation figures broke all records – which just might, you'd have thought, have pleased its new proprietor.

Thereafter, mercifully, daily life resumed its normal pattern of a slow morning burn growing ever more frenzied as the day wore on. I was used to this pattern on a weekly basis; this was the first time I had worked for a daily national paper rather than a Sunday. It seemed to me like much harder work, and you didn't get paid any more for doing it. As an executive, it was certainly easier to get other people to write things than to do so yourself; but, in this case, placating the rampant egos of Britain's most pompous journalists, and refereeing their *prima donna* squabbles, was not my idea of fun, nor indeed of journalism.

'Producing a newspaper is a serious business,' Harry wrote me in a private note that year, 'but it should also be fun.' Henceforth he kept a close eye on what he called my fun index. 'Let me know when it stops being fun.' It often did.

At the same time, after two years working in the US, I was painfully remembering what it was like to be a British journalist in Britain. In Washington, even as an overseas correspondent with no votes to deliver, I had enjoyed frequent visits to the White House, where the president gave a monthly press conference and regular banquets and balls. If I phoned an American cabinet member, he or she would actually return my call. Perhaps the supreme example was Cyrus Vance; when he had resigned as secretary of state amid the hostage crisis the previous year, he chose to give his only interview to me for the London *Observer*.

Returning to London as an assistant editor of *The Times*, and its putative next editor, I enjoyed no such privileges: no direct access to No. 10, or cabinet ministers, let alone the PM. I was struck by the contrast in openness and accountability. The other glaring disparity was the scale of the daily issues: in DC I had last been investigating the MX missiles that could change the face of the earth. Back in Blighty, the most pressing topic of the moment was the battle for the deputy leadership of the Labour Party between Denis Healey and Tony Benn.

That would not climax until the early autumn. In the meantime, there was blessed relief that August, after the exertions of the royal wedding, when the Holden family again summered on Martha's Vineyard – in a house booked the previous year, when I had assumed I would still be living and working in Washington.

I heard from the office that the editor and his young girlfriend, Tina Brown, then editor of *The Tatler*, were vacationing around the eastern seaboard, and would like to drop in the following weekend. So I organised a lunch befitting the editor of the London *Times*, inviting Katharine Graham, Art Buchwald, Walter Cronkite and the Styrons, among other Vineyard notables. Over the pre-prandial drinks, Tina motioned me aside and steered me by the arm for a little walk in the grounds, beside the ocean. 'Tony,' she said, 'you know this man as well as anyone. Is he ever going to marry me? I *do* hope he proposes soon . . .'

Lunch proceeded smoothly enough, only the host being aware of any tension between the guests of honour, before Harry too steered me outside for a little walk in exactly the same place.

'What are you doing', he enquired, 'next Thursday?'

'I'll still be here, Harry, still on vacation. David Blundy's coming to stay, with his daughter Anna.'

'Well, I'm going to marry Tina on Thursday, and I really want you to be there. Bring David and Anna, too.'

'Er, does Tina know about this, Harry?'

'No, not yet – it's all a big surprise!'

'Well, if I were you, Harry, I'd tell her as soon as possible.'

'Sure. We're doing it at Grey Gardens, Ben Bradlee's home on Long Island. Ben's going to be best man. There won't be time to get Tina's parents over from Spain, so I'd like you to give away the bride.'

'That will be a real honour, Harry, but I still think it would be wise to fill Tina in ASAP . . .'

'Don't worry. I'll tell her tomorrow. Not a word in the meantime. See you Thursday!'

Five days later, for the first and only time in my life, I rented a private plane to whisk myself, David and Anna Blundy from Martha's Vineyard to Long Island. The complexities of scheduled travel via La Guardia in time for the nuptials had proved insurmountable. David and I agreed to split the cost; it was only a few hundred bucks for the day, but left us both feeling like millionaires.

Nervous millionaires, in truth, as this was one of those tiny, held-together-by-bits-of-string twin-props in which David and I had already endured far too many bumpy flights in our journalistic lives. What's more, industrial action by US air traffic controllers meant that the pilot, with eleven-year-old Anna in the co-pilot's seat in front of her nervous dad and me, kept asking questions like: 'I need to turn east soon – can you keep an eye out for any other aircraft on our left?'

We made it intact, in time for me to congratulate the delighted bride and leave her in peace to render herself suitably stunning for the occasion. Given a lull before the arrival of the other guests, let alone the main event, Ben Bradlee invited me out onto the stoop for a much-needed noon-time whisky. Still executive editor of the *Washington Post*, he agreed with me that Jason Robards had done him proud in the film version of his paper's Watergate coup, *All the President's Men*. As we went on to shoot the breeze of the moment, a diminutive figure dashed out of the front door between us and ran off up the dirt-track driveway at high speed.

'Hey, wasn't that Harry?' asked an alarmed Bradlee, looking anxiously after the disappearing runner, and knowing perfectly well the answer to his own question. 'He can't be running out on us, can he? You'd better get after him!'

Though all of twenty years younger, I knew I'd never be able to catch up with Harry, a fanatical jogger much fitter than myself. Besides, as I told Ben, I was in charge of the bride – who, as far as I knew, was still getting ready upstairs. 'No, you're the best man, Ben. He's your responsibility . . .'

After the briefest of pauses, Bradlee shrugged, 'Oh, fuck it,' and recharged our glasses.

Whatever we talked about for the next half-hour or more, there was an exponential increase in unspoken apprehension for every minute Harry remained missing. Eventually, like a mirage in a desert western, a grinning figure carrying a dry-cleaning bag appeared over the horizon, trotting towards us like a one-man US cavalry. 'Had you there for a moment, didn't I?' grinned Harry. 'Just went to pick up my suit.'

The Blundys were meanwhile hiding a giant boom-box in the bushes to play, when the moment came, a tape of Harry's favourite Handel. Which added enormously to the sense of occasion as I escorted Tina down the staircase of Grey Gardens and out into the oceanside garden where the young Jacqueline Kennedy had once played, when this was the home of her Bouvier cousins. 'Who's that guy in the hideous outfit?' Tina whispered to me while smiling to the handful of friends who had made the day trip from Manhattan. 'That,' I replied, 'is the judge, who's come straight from the golf course to make an honest woman of you.'

Once the joyous deed had been done, I found myself sitting between two wonderfully entertaining writers, Nora Ephron and Joan Juliet Buck, at the pool-side wedding lunch. 'So what are the happy couple's plans for this evening?' Nora asked me. 'Oh, Harry's very excited,' I told her. 'Tina doesn't know yet, but he's got tickets for *The Pirates of Penzance* in Central Park.'

'*The Pirates of Penzance*?' exclaimed Nora, the incredulous italics clear in her voice.

'It's Gilbert and Sullivan,' I replied. 'Harry's a great G&S . . .'

'I *know* it's Gilbert and fucking Sullivan. I . . .'

Apparently speechless, she threw down her napkin, got up and stormed off into the house. Joan and I were still speculating as to what she could be up to, when Nora reappeared with some emphatic instructions. 'Now you go and tell your friend Harry that he's *not* taking his bride to Gilbert and – *pause* – Sullivan in the Park this evening. He's taking her to Lena Horne's one-woman show, and they're having dinner with Lena afterwards.'

And so they did. Duly embarrassed by the old tin cans Blundy attached to the fender of their limo, and the JUST MARRIED in shaving cream on the boot, Harry and Tina drove off into domestic bliss, which snide commentators back home gave three weeks max, but was still going strong almost forty years later.

Back in London, the month ended with a review under my name of two new books about Reagan adorning the front page of the *Washington Post*'s Book World. A couple of book reviews were also the only pieces I wrote for my own paper, amid mounting hostility towards Evans and his lieutenants from a group calling itself JOTT (Journalists of The Times). To my colleagues in the kindergarten I quipped that I'd rather be a member of JOOT – or Journalism on One's Own Terms.

Among the weekly columnists I had inherited, to my delight, was Anthony Burgess. I never knew what would be coming next from Monte Carlo, where he then lived; he was the only *Times* columnist immune to any staff briefing, even a telephone chat over the issues of the day. But it was always worthwhile. When Burgess unexpectedly came up with a column about being colour-blind, I remember being especially chuffed with my saucy headline: 'Perhaps I wrote *A Clockwork Lemon*?' On a rare visit to London, my fellow Lancastrian forgave me such frivolity over a very happy lunch at Claridge's. For some reason, there were no complaints about Burgess from JOTT.

Among the weekly columnists I had introduced, meanwhile, was Henry Fairlie from Washington. Harry was particularly pleased to have Henry's eminent name on his pages. But one day he came downstairs from a meeting with Murdoch to tell me that an anti-Reagan column from Fairlie had moved the proprietor to complain to the editor about his 'pinko-Trot friend Holden'.

There was worse, much worse, to come. Pre-Fox, Murdoch had little else to do but sit atop the building keeping an eye on his latest acquisition while monitoring its advertising and circulation figures. Ignoring the so-called independent directors, he would fire orders on all fronts – including editorial, in defiance of his solemn undertakings to the government, which turned out to be (in his own words to the news editor, Fred Emery) 'not worth the paper they're written on'. Given his debt to Prime Minister Thatcher, to whom he owed his ownership of the *Times* titles, Murdoch grew increasingly infuriated at our attacks on her government, especially its policy of monetarism.

There was a brief moment of light relief that September, when my duties required me to attend the Labour Party conference in Brighton at which Denis Healey finally saw off Tony Benn's attempt to oust him as deputy leader. Christopher Hitchens cadged a lift with me; en route we picked up our mutual friend Ian McEwan – whom I had known since the mid-1970s, at the start of his illustrious career, when he had spent weekends at our Islington home as our lodger's boyfriend. When we arrived, Hitchens and I had press passes, but Ian didn't; so we advised him that the real plotting was to be overheard in the bar of the Grand Hotel, where we would join him later.

That conversation in a multi-storey car park, plus the details of the drive down and sundry subsequent events that day, would all feature the following year in McEwan's first movie script, *The Ploughman's Lunch*, a tangled love story doubling as a satire on Thatcher's Britain during the Falklands War for Channel 4's series Film on Four. While Hitchens was clearly the model for the earnest journalist played by Jonathan Pryce, I fear that I must have been the original of the Flash Harry embodied by Tim Curry.

While in Washington I had bought myself a Pontiac Firebird, known in DC as a 'pimp-mobile', a flash American sports car (complete with personalised licence plate) so vulgar to British eyes that many visitors were shocked into saying, 'You're not planning to bring that back to England, are you?' So many, in fact, as to persuade me that I must, which no doubt contributed to the McEwan version of jaunty me en route to Brighton and back that day. Driving home from my poker game one Tuesday night, my winnings in cash on the passenger seat, I was stopped in central London by police, pulled out of the car and aggressively pushed up against it before being frisked; unbelievably, they were looking for the same model of blue Pontiac, which had just been involved in a nearby armed robbery.

A.H. in DC aboard his beloved Pontiac Firebird

My beloved Firebird would also add lustre to another treat that month, when I found myself sitting next to Lauren Bacall at a dinner party chez Harry and Tina. In those days you could smoke anywhere, so I didn't feel the need to ask her permission before lighting up over the coffee. 'What's a charming young man like you doing smoking?' she asked, to my surprise. My improvised reply somehow didn't seem to please her. 'You know how to smoke, don't you?' I smiled. 'You just put your lips together and blow . . .'

Chilly though her response to this was, it fell to me to drive Bacall home that evening – or, in fact, back to her Park Lane hotel. After pulling up at the kerb, I leapt out of the left-hand-drive Firebird to go round and open her door into the midst of the dark and busy highway, before seeing her safely onto the wide pavement across which I escorted her to the hotel entrance, where she turned around, held aloft a gloved palm, and proclaimed: 'Thus far, but no further!' That she even thought I might have any such intentions I found immensely flattering.

By the following month the internal warfare at *The Times* was becoming alarmingly public. The ruder we were about Thatcher, the more Murdoch was whipping up internal opposition to Harry Evans and his senior appointees; adopting a characteristic divide-and-rule policy, he had deputed Douglas-Home to incite rebellion. A nephew of the sometime prime minister, Charles Douglas-Home had arrived at *The Times* some fifteen years earlier via Eton and the Guards; Harry had made him deputy editor in a conscious gesture towards the paper's 'old guard'. Little had he known that he was appointing his own personal Judas among his otherwise loyal disciples.

A classic example of Murdoch's violation of his editorial vows came that October, with the late-breaking news that President Sadat of Egypt had been assassinated. I had swiftly secured a tribute from former prime minister Jim Callaghan, but was still awaiting the illustration from our resident American cartoonist, Ranan Lurie. It arrived so late in the day that my first glimpse of it was on the stone, upside-down in hot metal; in classic Lurie style, it showed a capstan marked SADAT being torn apart by two vast ships respectively named ISRAEL and EGYPT. I hesitated awhile; to me, it looked like it might be suggesting that Israel had a hand in Sadat's murder. I called Harry over for a ruling; as we discussed it, Murdoch materialised beside us, wondering what the problem was.

When I explained, Murdoch asked whether it was really a matter of fact or taste. Potentially both, I replied. 'Oh, fuck it, print it' came the proprietor's elegant response, usurping the editor's prerogative to his very face.

For years Harry got me to tell that story whenever we were both involved in discussions of those increasingly dark days. Another of his running complaints was that Murdoch was denying him an editorial budget – an undertaking solemnly guaranteed in those promises to Parliament. Without a budget, an editor has paradoxically restricted freedom of movement, and a proprietor carte blanche to complain about his spending. The instrument of Murdoch's will in this instance was the managing director he had recruited from Reuters, Gerald Long.

A devout Francophile, and *haute cuisine* gourmet, the self-regarding Long decreed universal application of his own exacting standards. At a board-room lunch for the Chancellor of the Exchequer, Geoffrey Howe, for instance, the guest of honour requested mint sauce with his roast lamb. 'Mr Long', Howe was haughtily told by the head waiter, 'does not allow mint sauce anywhere near the fifth floor.'

One evening Harry called me into his office to show me a protracted correspondence between Long and the eminent chef Albert Roux about the quality of the French cheese on offer at his Michelin-starred London restaurant Le Gavroche. The selection was not up to scratch, complained Long at some length, and in over-wrought detail, to which Roux predictably took exception. Swiftly rather bored, I asked Harry how these documents had come into his possession. 'Long showing off,' he said. 'He gave it me to read, thinking I'd admire his expert knowledge of *le fromage* as much as his exquisite prose style.'

'Very droll,' said I, stifling a yawn, not to mention my lifelong aversion to cheese. 'But why are you making *me* read it?'

'Because you're going to print it on Saturday. On the *Times* Review Front.'

I was incredulous. Long had spelt nothing but trouble for Harry, especially in recent weeks, and now he was willing to boost his giant ego? I said as much, but my editor persisted. Only from his mischievous grin did I finally grasp what he was up to.

On the Friday evening, when the proofs were ready, I invited Long into my office to read them. As he did so, even he appeared to begin to have his doubts.

'How do you think I emerge from this, Anthony?'

'Oh, you know, Gerry, the grand old British tradition of eccentricity' was all I could think of saying.

'Eccentric?' he snorted. 'What's eccentric about it?'

The following day, when the piece appeared, Harry's ploy worked like a charm. As Long took his weekly turn around the *Sunday Times* office with Murdoch, he was as horrified as his boss to find the *Business News* staff – with their feet up on their desks, their day's work largely done – heaving with laughter over the vehemence and pomposity of their managing director's indignant protests over London's finest cheese board. The following week Murdoch fired Long from *The Times*, moving him into some sinecure at News International.

The *Times'* fashion editor, Suzy Menkes, happened to be married to a member of my Tuesday night poker game, David Spanier, the paper's diplomatic correspondent. She was one of the handful of the 'old guard' supportive of the new regime, telling all comers that I was the best editor she had ever had. This was in truth because, knowing nothing at all about fashion, I just left her to get on with it, allowing plenty of space for photographic spreads. But my travails with the likes of Roger Berthoud were steadily growing worse.

Early that December, after thirty-five years with Times

Newspapers, Sir Denis Hamilton stepped down as its chairman; he had been editor of the *Sunday Times* before recruiting Evans as his successor, and then editor-in-chief of both titles during the transition from Thomson to Murdoch. By Berthoud's account, Douglas-Home had asked him to do a farewell interview with Hamilton: 'I knew Sir Denis quite well, and went happily up to his eyrie.' Some fifteen minutes into their chat, however, 'in burst Tony Holden, explaining a trifle sheepishly that Harry had wanted him to be in on the exercise. Such touching faith, I thought.'

So 'disgusted' was Berthoud 'that I left Tony to write the piece . . . and rejected his suggestion of a joint by-line'. This enabled me to add a distinctive personal touch. When explaining that his father had been an engineer, like his own father and grandfather before him, Hamilton said: 'So I had no journalism in my blood – unlike others I could name!' Upon saying which, he 'screwed up a piece of paper and threw it at the present writer, whose grandfather was one of many *Sunday Times* journalists Hamilton was to cherish and befriend.'

Soon thereafter, as Berthoud reports via a rare compliment, 'Tony, a man whose subsequent career as a versatile biographer I admire, invited me for a drink – rarely a good sign.' He was right. Under pressure from Murdoch to reduce the staff journalists on his payroll, Harry had told me to 'let go' three of my feature writers. 'If you're going to be editor of this paper after me,' were his very words, 'you've got to learn how to fire people. It's not pleasant, but sometimes it's necessary.' He suggested three names, one of whom was Berthoud.

In the pub I told Roger that there were generous redundancy terms on offer, based on length of service, and I would strongly urge him to accept them while they were still available. He would be pleased to do so, he said, given the 'rough ride' he had suffered under Evans and Holden. This awkward ritual was all the more excruciating in the cases of the other two specialists with whose services I had to dispense – Marcel Berlins and David Spanier, respectively legal and diplomatic correspondents – because both had become friends of mine, all too rare among *Times* veterans. In the case of Spanier, I softened the blow by agreeing to his plea to gain him re-entry to our Tuesday night poker game, from which he had been barred for playing too tight. Thus did I also incur the wrath of the Tuesday Night boys.

Early in 1982 Des Wilson, by now leading a national campaign for lead-free petrol, leaked me an internal letter from Sir Henry Yellowlees, chief medical officer at the Department of Health, confirming the need for urgent government legislation. This, I thought, could spur some campaigning journalism of the kind of which Harry was the undisputed master. When I raised the matter at the editorial conference that Sunday, with Douglas-Home editing the paper in Evans' weekend absence, he contemptuously spat out the phrase 'campaigning journalism' and refused to print the story. I telephoned Harry at home, but still the piece did not appear. When it did after his return the next day, along with a persistent series of follow-ups which are the essence of such campaigns, it caused as much of an upstairs furore as features I had commissioned from the ASLEF leader Ray Buckton, arguing his union's case during a rail strike, and the historian and nuclear disarmament campaigner E. P. Thompson in support of Lech Wałęsa's embattled Polish trade union Solidarity.

Along with extensive economic coverage of a recession denied by Thatcher's government, these were but the latest weapons amassed by Murdoch in his covert conspiracy with Douglas-Home. Tuesday 9 March 1982 was Budget Day, the busiest day in any newspaper's year. Harry, who had just been named Editor of the Year, had the previous day returned from his beloved father's funeral in Wales. This was also the day that Murdoch chose to summon Evans upstairs and demand his resignation. After a heated discussion, Harry declined, turned on his heel and returned to edit the Budget Day edition of *The Times*, intent on producing 'the most extensive coverage in the paper's history'.

Into his office wandered Douglas-Home, who jerked his thumb upwards and enquired: 'Been upstairs, have you? Seen him? Too bad . . . He had me up before you. He offered me the editorship of *The Times* and I have accepted.'

'But I have not resigned the editorship,' replied Harry, before turning away to get on with his work. Douglas-Home was 'less cheerful when he left the room,' according to Evans, 'than when he came in.'

True to form, Murdoch leaked the news that he wanted rid of Evans, and Harry arrived at work the next day with a quote from Mark Twain for the scrum of reporters besieging the office: 'Reports of my death are greatly exaggerated.' Now *The Times* became front-page news in all other national papers, with its assistant editor (features) only too happy to go on the record. In *The Guardian* I was quoted as saying: 'Murdoch wants a poodle as editor, and I'm not going to work for a poodle. If Harold Evans goes, so will the *Times*'s proud record of editorial independence.' Murdoch wanted to sack Evans, said Holden, 'for resisting his pressure for a right-wing editorial line supporting Reagan, Thatcher and monetarism.' Evans, by contrast, had 'held out for editorial diversity, reflecting intelligent opinion'.

To London's *Evening Standard* I declared: 'Murdoch's public justification for wanting to remove Harry is that he has lost the confidence of his senior staff, but this is not the case.' The real reason Murdoch wanted to dispose of Evans was 'his insistence on his right to editorial independence . . . Murdoch has attempted to impose his own views.' I made similar remarks elsewhere, not least on the BBC's *Newsnight*. Such was the national furore that my mother had the TV set removed from my father's hospital room in Liverpool, as she thought it might all prove too much for the heart into which the NHS was about to insert a pacemaker.

By Saturday 13 March *The Times* itself carried front-page coverage under the headline THE TIMES AND ITS EDITORSHIP, quoting one of the independent directors as saying that Murdoch had got things 'a bit confused'. The weekend papers were full of detailed analyses, which advanced the drama not one inch. On the Sunday evening, Douglas-Home took me aside into the darkened diary area and deployed some elaborate bridge metaphor to say: 'You'd have done what I have, wouldn't you? Anything to edit *The Times*!'

'No, I would not,' I replied and walked away.

On the Monday, 15 March, Harry came back in to edit the paper as usual. That evening, after seeing the final pages off-stone, he called ITN into the office and quit his now impossible job, live on camera, in front of the entire nation. Then, taking me with him, he went home to Pimlico, where Tina had laid on a star-studded party of supporters. En route, I pointed out something neither of us had yet realised: today was the Ides of March. As we exchanged pained quips about Shakespeare's soothsayer, we also recalled that it was nine years to the day since he had first hired me as a cub reporter on the *Sunday Times*.

The next morning, I went into the office so I could walk straight out again for the last time. Having tendered my resignation to Douglas-Home, I slipped back into his office while he was chairing the editorial conference, and left a note on his desk: a xerox of a page from *Macbeth*, with a couple of lines highlighted:

> *Thou hast it now . . . and I fear*
> *Thou played'st most foully for 't.*

The following morning saw front-page coverage of my resignation in the *Daily Telegraph*, *The Guardian*, even the *Financial Times*. 'I've always wanted to write a Fleet Street novel,' the *Daily Mail* quoted me as saying, 'but until now I didn't have a plot.' In his detailed account of it all in his 1983 book *Good Times, Bad Times*, Harry himself put it this way:

> Nothing surprised me as much as the emergence of Anthony Holden as my champion. I would never have thought that the companionable Holden, an excellent but apolitical features editor, would throw himself into a fight of this sort. But when the press and radio sought someone to go on the record and say something, Holden did it boldly. In view of later events it has to be said that his exercise of the right of free speech consisted in taking pride in what had been achieved in the year, rejecting the story that the senior staff were up in arms, and critically reciting the Murdoch complaints against giving a place for dissent on the features pages. Holden spoke for himself. It was none the less rapidly put about by Murdoch's men that Holden was only my mouthpiece, an understandable error since the only principles they were acquainted with were those of ventriloquism.

The following evening, by way of diversion, I was looking forward to the Hatchards Authors of the Year party, a congenial annual event held on this occasion, for some reason, in the gracious presence of HM The Queen and HRH The Duke of Edinburgh. Soon after I arrived, I was talking to John Mortimer and Alan Whicker, who were both peppering me with questions about the story of the moment, when John grabbed my arm and confided: 'He's just come in.'

I assumed he meant Philip, but turned round to see that it was Murdoch. He was the last person I had expected to see there; in my innocence, I hadn't worked out that Murdoch owned Collins, which then owned Hatchards. Instinctively, I set off in his direction at some speed; seeing me coming, he started heading the other way. The result was that I wound up brushing shoulders with the Queen, almost knocking her over when she made her stately entrance just as I was pursuing Murdoch into the opposite corner.

There followed a fierce exchange, which ended with him saying, 'You'll never work for me again!' and my replying, 'I do not choose to, thank you very much', before turning on my heel to see that *le tout* literary London was agog at this spectacle – to the point of ignoring the monarch, who stood alone with her husband and a handful of acolytes at the other end of the room. Suddenly Murdoch cut a lonely figure as fellow writers rushed over to congratulate me, a literary peer embracing me and a knight of the realm proclaiming in a deliberately loud voice: 'Well done! I thought you were going to hit him! Glad you managed not to!' I looked back at Murdoch to take satisfaction in the solitary, isolated figure to which he had been reduced as he watched me basking in the acclaim of the British literary establishment.

As the event resumed some vestige of normality, the Queen herself even granted me a few non-controversial words, despite my history with her eldest son. But Philip seemed genuinely intrigued by what had been going on at *The Times*, and showered me with questions in front of a crowd of interested parties before grimacing, 'So he's here, is he? Well, I knew his father . . .' It was a crafty royal way of expressing an opinion without appearing to do so.

'Yes, he's over there,' I replied, pointing towards the isolated figure still lurking in the corner. In the next day's *Daily Mail*, via some literary leak to Nigel Dempster's diary column, this came out as 'The ogre's there' – soon a running gag in sundry published accounts of, even books about, the entire *Times* saga.

That same day had seen Harry Evans shadowed around London by the tabloids as, for the first time in twenty years, he went about his daily business as a non-newspaper editor. Among the shops he was reported to have visited was Asprey, the Bond Street jewellers – presumably, I supposed, to buy something special for Tina, who had proved so supportive throughout his prolonged Murdoch ordeal.

A few days later a delivery from Asprey arrived at our home, bearing a package from Harry which turned out to be a handsome silver salver, engraved with his signature beneath the words:

'For Anthony Holden, to salute his constancy and courage on the Ides of March.'

The following year Harry also wrote a generous preface to a collection of my journalism published by George Weidenfeld to mark my first, albeit turbulent, decade in Fleet Street under the title *Of Presidents, Prime Ministers and Princes*. The articles therein, he wrote, 'represent good reporting by someone you feel you can like'. It came as 'no surprise' to him, for instance, that when Holden was admitted to Reagan's Oval Office for a short ceremonial, 'he made a note of the President's private telephone number. Just in case.'

Of my public support during the *Times* crisis, he observed: 'Though he felt passionately about the issues, he did it with coolness and good temper' – which enabled him to conclude: '"Smile when you call me that", said Owen Wister's *Virginian*, when faced with a lethal insult at the poker table. That is very much the Holden ethic.'

I would still like to think that he was right about that. But British journalists were certainly right when, twenty years later, in 2002, they voted Harold Evans the 'greatest newspaper editor of all time'. Not for another decade, however, was he finally able to prove his case about the Murdoch takeover of Times Newspapers.

Murdoch had even told the official historian of Times Newspapers, Graham Stewart, that he and Thatcher had 'no communication whatsoever during the period in which the Times bid and referral was up for discussion'. On 16 March 2012, however, the Churchill Archives Centre in Cambridge released

two documents from the Margaret Thatcher Foundation proving the precise opposite: that Murdoch had in fact, at his own
request, enjoyed a secret meeting with the then prime minister
at Chequers on 4 January 1981. According to Thatcher's press
secretary, Bernard Ingham, he was under instructions from the
PM not to allow his report of the meeting outside No. 10, which
is to say that ministers would not have been briefed that it had
taken place, let alone what had been said. 'Had this secret meeting come out at the time,' wrote Evans in 2012, 'it would have
destroyed Murdoch's chances of acquiring Times Newspapers.'
Ingham's 'note for the record', he added, 'reeks of cover-up'.

Ostensibly, Thatcher met Murdoch to be advised on the current state of the bidding for Times Newspapers; in other words,
she was receiving such a briefing from one of the interested
parties, who naturally made no mention of rival bidders from
Lord Rothermere to the *Sunday Times* management team led
by Evans, who had themselves put together a bid at exactly the
same financial level.

It was 'ludicrous', Evans continued, to suggest that there
was 'no mention at the lunch of the clear legal requirement for
Murdoch's bid to be referred to the Monopolies and Mergers
Commission.' The prime minister had a duty to remind
Murdoch of the laws she had sworn to honour and enforce.
'Did she not emit at least a polite cough? If she did not, she was
uncharacteristically negligent.' At the cabinet meeting three
weeks later endorsing Murdoch's takeover, it was Thatcher who
claimed that 'the fine print of the act would exempt Murdoch
from its provisions on the grounds that both papers were
unprofitable.' This, as Evans demonstrated in *Good Times, Bad
Times*, was manifestly untrue.

Thus did Margaret Thatcher assist a man who already owned
an unusually large slice of the British media to acquire even
more without due legal process. The quid pro quo, one can only
assume, was a guarantee from Murdoch of positive coverage

for her and her government. Which was why he fired Harold Evans, changing the course of his life as much as, in the process, my own.

Asked about his meeting with Thatcher when he appeared before the 2011–12 Leveson Inquiry into the culture, practices and ethics of the press, precipitated by the criminal conduct of journalists in his employ, Murdoch replied that he had no memory of it. In his subsequent report, even the scrupulously objective Lord Justice Leveson drily observed that it was 'a little surprising' that Murdoch did not remember a visit to 'a place as memorable as Chequers', in the context of 'a bid as important as that which he made for Times Newspapers'.

'Perhaps,' he added, 'that is all I need to say.'

THE WILDERNESS YEARS

So deep, even then, ran the universal loathing of Murdoch, especially within the trade of journalism, that there ensued a shower of private and public plaudits for my 'principled' resignation. The truth was that I had walked out on Murdoch in the white heat of the moment, disgusted by his squalid treatment of Harry, not to mention his abjuration of those editorial vows – and so not even, like other Evans appointees, hanging around to be sacked and thus paid handsome compensation. Now, all too suddenly, I was broke and unemployed. So, in truth, my abrupt exit earned me more credit than I deserved; there have since been times I have thought what a chump I was not to have taken a slice of the Murdoch millions with me. Harry himself had certainly done so, as had several other loyalists. Why not me?

At moments like these, you find out who your true friends are. One of the first to call me to commiserate was George Weidenfeld, who invited me round to his stately apartment on the Embankment; he had an idea for a book I could write for him. It turned out that George had come into possession of some secret documents – manna from heaven for any journalist – suggesting that the French entertainer Maurice Chevalier had been a Nazi collaborator during the German occupation of France. So how about a revisionist biography of Chevalier?

It was a typically generous gesture by George – but, as much as I needed the money, the dirty old man from *Gigi* ('Sank 'eaven for leetel gels') was really not my kind of guy. I was burning to write a Fleet Street novel, I told George, whose face promptly fell. It would be about a British newspaper with a dastardly foreign proprietor where events on the paper itself would overshadow those it was covering. I would call it *Splash*, a cunning pun, as it would end with the boss drowning in the Mediterranean after being pushed off his own yacht by a dissident hack who would make it look like suicide.

Reluctantly, George commissioned the book – another act of supreme generosity, as I knew it was the last thing he wanted – and advertised it in his next annual catalogue as 'an explosive novel about Fleet Street by the award-winning journalist'. And I would spend the next couple of years trying to write it, eventually giving up before the demise of Robert Maxwell rendered its denouement wildly implausible.

I was commissioned to write pieces by the sympathetic editors of *Punch*, Alan Coren, and the *Times Literary Supplement*, John Gross (in his case, another poke in the eye for Murdoch, his proprietor), and, of course, Tina Brown for *The Tatler*. But this was not enough to keep the Holden show on the road. As I tried to think of a congenial but commercial book to write, I also found over the following week or three that true friends feel moved at such life-stopping moments to buy you a meal and talk it all over. One such was Ron Hall, another victim of what we called the Murdoch diaspora, now in exile as editor of the *Sunday Express* magazine. A friend of the notoriously rackety restaurateur Peter Langan, Ron took me for lunch at his eponymous Langan's Brasserie in Mayfair, then the most fashionable place in town.

Whenever I have since visited Langan's, I have always had reason to be grateful for the fact that it then used paper tablecloths. Once they were replaced by linen under new ownership in 2013, I lost interest in going there, even though I frequented an office nearby. Had linen been the order of the day in the early 1980s, my life might have turned out quite differently.

As we chomped on our Norfolk duck, and swigged fine

expense-account claret, I naturally wondered aloud if Ron might be able to give me any work? People thought I was well off because of the Charles book, I explained, but Amanda and I were committed to pouring all those (ho ho) royalties into a family house in Highbury. We'd already invested six figures in a large, decrepit shell; by the time we'd spent as much again doing it up, there would be precious little left.

'Let's see,' said Ron, who began to muse on the kind of articles I could write for him. As he took a tug on his pipe and put his mind to the matter, it was my great good fortune that he loved designing and laying out pages. He got out his pen, cleared aside the crockery and started scribbling on Langan's paper tablecloth. A rectangle designated a page . . . two vertical lines its three columns . . . horizontal squiggles my immortal prose . . . a couple of boxes signified small pictures . . . and then, at the top left, a large hole into which, after some thought, he wrote the word HOLDEN in hefty capital letters – paused another minute, tugged again on his pipe, and then AT LARGE.

Ron looked upon his handiwork, and found it pleasing. 'That's it,' he said. '*Holden At Large.* Yes, I know, it's basically "What I Have Done This Week", but you can make that interesting. It can be the opening section of the mag. I'll pay you £500 a week.'

'Done!' said I, raising my glass to clink his, so grateful for his philanthropy as to hide my disappointment that the *Sunday Express* was not really the dream destination for a hack who until recently was going to be the next editor of *The Times*.

But my parents were thrilled; at last I was writing for a proper paper, the one they took themselves. My weekly column for Ron's *Sunday Express* magazine started that June, by which time I was also theatre critic of *The Tatler*. When Tina offered me the job, I fretted that I was too fond of the theatre (and actors, not to mention playwrights and directors) to become a critic. On the other hand, it would be fun to celebrate what the great *Observer* critic Kenneth Tynan memorably called 'high-definition performance'.

The solution, I suggested to Tina, was that I would go to all openings but write only positive reviews about shows or performances I admired; the rest could go unmentioned. To my delight, she agreed, and the monthly rave-fest began with the original production of Michael Frayn's ingenious farce-within-a-farce *Noises Off*, continuing with Joss Ackland's magisterial *Falstaff* for the RSC. The only problem was the lavish glossy's advance lead time for my copy; some of the shows about which I enthused had closed by the time my accolade appeared.

On BBC Radio 4, meanwhile, I had embarked on a weekly chat show rather limply called *In the Air*; the producer, Julian Hale, had liked my Atticus, and together we fashioned a formula for a verbal version. Of the few highlights that linger, I recall the war correspondent Martha Gellhorn walking out on me when I inevitably started to grill her on the forbidden topic of her marriage to Ernest Hemingway; the present Duke of Gloucester defending his namesake, King Richard III; and a hilarious interview with Denis Thatcher in the shape of John Wells, during the 1983 general election, being pulled by the director-general, Alasdair Milne, for reasons of political impartiality.

At the same time I was commissioned by the BBC to make a TV documentary about exiled European royalty, under the title *The Men Who Would Be King*. This involved travels all over Europe to interview a dozen such thwarted monarchs, including the kings *manqués* of Germany (Prince Louis Ferdinand Hohenzollern, an amateur composer), Portugal (the duke of Braganca, a conservationist), even Russia (Prince Nicholas Romanoff, a passionate boar hunter) and the would-be queen of Romania (Princess Margareta, a sociologist).

Among the most interesting were the exiled king of Italy, Umberto II, who reigned for barely a month in 1946, only to spend the rest of his life in forlorn exile; and Archduke Otto von Habsburg, the putative ruler of the Austro-Hungarian Empire, whom I interviewed in Strasbourg in his capacity as a member of the European Parliament. Asked which team he would be supporting in a football match between Austria and Hungary, Otto replied: 'Who are we playing?'

'They say that monarchy is like virginity: once gone, lost forever' was my slogan for the film. In Seville, however, at the christening of the twin sons of the exiled king of Yugoslavia, Crown Prince Alexander (an insurance executive), I got to meet the man who disproved it: King Juan Carlos of Spain, present that day as a godparent. The Spanish monarchy had been driven into exile in 1931 on the establishment of the Second Spanish Republic; in 1969, however, it had suited the dictator Franco to bring it back.

As HM and I chewed all this over, it struck me that I had unthinkingly lit a cigarette while conversing with the king. When I mumbled a belated enquiry as to whether he minded, and apologised for not offering him one, he replied with a smile: 'Not at all, Mr Holden. But today is perhaps the day when *I* should be offering *you* a cigarette?'

I looked puzzled.

Juan Carlos explained that he had just been on the phone to Elizabeth II in London to sympathise, as one monarch to another, with what she had been through the previous day: 9 July 1982, when a 33-year-old unemployed decorator named Michael Fagan had scaled the walls of Buckingham Palace at 7 a.m. and shinned up a drainpipe before wandering into the Queen's bedroom. He had sat on the end of her bed and asked her for a cigarette, a pack of which was duly brought him by a maid. Said Fagan's mother: 'He thinks so much of the Queen. I can imagine him just wanting to discuss his problems.' Said Fagan himself: 'Her nightie was one of those Liberty prints, down to her knees.'

Those first few freelance years also saw me reviewing (non-royal) books not just for the *Sunday Times*, *The Observer* and the *Times Literary Supplement* but for the *New York Times* and the *Washington Post* as well as writing from Britain for the Washington-based *New*

Republic, not least a passionate piece deploring the Falklands War. In March 1982 several newspapers said I had been offered the editorship of the *New Statesman*, which was news to me. Having long been a contributor, however, I duly applied for the post on the departure of my erstwhile *Sunday Times* colleague Bruce Page, but it went to Hugh Stephenson, who subsequently became Professor of Journalism at London's City University.

Nothing so grand for me. Within months I was applying for the editorship of – can this be a unique combination in the history of British journalism? – *The Tatler*, on the urging of its outgoing editor, that same Tina Brown, who was off to New York to edit *Vanity Fair*, and still touchingly concerned about my career prospects after my conspicuous display of loyalty to her husband. The louche goings-on in London SW3 were really not my beat, so I turned up for the interview armed with what seemed to me an impossibly upscale manifesto. I thought *The Tatler* should be much more highbrow, I told the panel, more political than gossipy, visiting overseas landmarks from the Elysée Palace to the White House. To my alarm, they seemed intrigued. But they decided on a far more suitable candidate, Libby Purves. My immediate resignation as theatre critic was blamed in some quarters for the fact that Purves lasted only a few months in the job; the *Express* even reported that she was threatening to throw a glass of red wine over me, as Anna Ford famously had over Jonathan Aitken after being sacked from *TV-am*.

A series of books based on my articles was the signal for Holden at Large to go monthly, with long, lavish interviews in exotic locations, ranging from Steven Spielberg on the Universal Studios lot in Hollywood to the world's richest man, the sultan of Brunei, in his Xanadu of a palace. I also made the shrewd, methought, decision to be the first journalist into the Falkland Islands *after* the war. Following an interminable flight via Ascension Island in an RAF Hercules, I helicoptered my way around the still-mined battlefields before playing snooker in Port Stanley with the genial governor, Sir Rex Hunt, who proudly showed me the bullet-holes dotted around his walls.

First journalist into the Falklands *after* the war

Another serendipitous quirk of timing came in late 1983, when Ron tried finally to shut me up about my beloved Arsenal by sending me to spend a week there for a feature supposedly entitled 'An average week in the life of a football club'. It turned out to be anything but.

A season-ticket holder at Arsenal since we'd settled in Highbury a decade earlier, I thrilled to the unprecedented treats of sitting in the dugout with the manager, Terry Neill, during a home match, watching another from the directors' box and then travelling with the players on the club coach to an away game. The real problem that week was that Arsenal lost all three of those games, including a Cup tie against third-division Millwall. After eighteen years at Arsenal, eleven as a player and seven as manager, Terry Neill was fired a week before Christmas. As he prepared to drive home forlornly in his club Mercedes, his old friend Ken

Friar, the managing director, walked over apologetically, holding out his hand for Neill to return the keys.

Neill subsequently became a lasting friend, who much excited my sons – passionate Gooners all – by watching an Arsenal game with us on TV post-Sunday lunch, and telling us at half-time what he would have yelled at his hapless players in the dressing room.

There were interviews with Hollywood stars from William Hurt (whom I liked and admired) to Charles Bronson (whom I didn't). But I was especially pleased to pay homage to the heroic American actor-director Sam Wanamaker, then still bogged down in his long-drawn-out battle with Southwark Council to replace their road-sweepers' hut on Bankside with a working replica of Shakespeare's Globe Theatre on its original site, rather than yet another office block. It would be another decade and more before Sam's fifty-year dream would finally be realised – if not, alas, until four years after his death.

But perhaps the most memorable encounter was a week spent in the Brazilian rainforest with Mick Jagger (and his then partner, Jerry Hall, plus baby Scarlett) to mark his first solo album, itself to be immortalised with one of the first music videos, directed by the fashionable Julien Temple. Jagger granted me exclusive journalistic access to this week-long jungle frolic, which was due to end with a formal interview back in Rio, where he was installed in the Presidential Suite at the Copacabana Hotel. In a humbler room down below, I waited for several days as he was besieged by agents, publicists and financial advisers, before booking a flight to London. Christmas was coming, and I wanted to be back home with my family.

I had just fixed myself an overnight flight when the phone in my room finally rang. 'Hello, Tone, it's Mick. Wanna come on up?'

Of course I did; I had a few hours before heading to the airport.

'Whatcha doin' tonight?' he asked.

'Heading home.'

'Aw, but it's the Brazilian Cup Final,' protested my fellow

Arsenal fan. 'The president just rang me and offered a couple of seats in his box. Thought you might like to come wiv?'

'It's not in the Maracanã, is it?'

'Course it is. Two hundred thousan' fans!'

This – the world's largest soccer stadium – was the only major world football venue my grandfather Ivan had never visited. There was a wide-eyed fold-out picture of it, then brand new, in his memoirs. I need exaggerate only a jot to say that on his deathbed Ivan had urged me to go there one day on his behalf. So I naturally said yes to Mick and delayed my flight home.

Riding to the stadium beside Jagger in the back of his limo, I couldn't help noticing that, for all its tinted rear windows, he was nervously flinching, hiding his face with his hands, as we picked our way through the crowds flocking to the game. 'You okay, Mick?' I asked.

'Not really, Tone. I'm thinking of poor John . . .'

John, of course, was his friend John Lennon, shot dead by a crazed fan in New York only four years before.

But we made it intact, to be greeted by the president of Brazil himself, not to mention most of his cabinet, before joining them in the presidential box. At half-time, I opted to hang back discreetly as they toasted Mick in vintage champagne – to the point where he eventually left them and came over to join me.

'Look at that!' he said indignantly, pointing at the beaming politicians.

'What?' I asked, baffled.

'Well, they're all wearing jeans and T-shirts. Last time we were here, they were wearing suits and ties, like they oughta be.'

This from the man who *invented* jeans and T-shirts? It took me a while to realise that this alumnus of the London School of Economics was making a macro-economic point about the geo-politics of South America.

Mick was pleased with the resulting piece, to the point where he asked me to ghost-write his autobiography. In a meeting in his suite at the Savoy, he told me he couldn't remember a thing about the '60s, or indeed much before or since, so I'd have to do an awful lot of research. Despite his $2 million advance from Weidenfeld, of which the writer would enjoy a healthy slice, I decided against – not least because I had already embarked on another project. The task of chronicling Mick's life and times eventually fizzled out; no book has ever appeared.

I was meanwhile rejuvenated by the purchase of an early computer, one of the first from Apple, which enabled me to write my weekly column to word-perfect length in three narrow blocks of text, exactly as it would appear on the page. Himself a gizmo-freak, Ron Hall was hugely impressed. But he got it wrong about the future of the compact disc, nonchalantly handing over to me a prototype Hitachi CD player he had received for judging some awards with a dismissive 'These things won't last.' At the time, there was indeed very little of the classical repertoire we both favoured available on CD – which soon started expanding rapidly to the point where I wrote a piece, complete with photos, proving you could do exactly what its pioneer advertisers claimed: eat your breakfast off a disc with a knife and fork before inserting it into the machine to listen to its flawless outpourings.

Sunday lunches at Ron's sleek modernist house in Hampstead were by now a regular event, which would begin with guests from Fleet Street luminaries to the harmonica player Larry Adler (who would boast about playing tennis with Charlie Chaplin) listening to Amanda playing duets with Ron's harpsichordist wife Ruth. After Ruth's early death, Ron asked me in 1982 to be best man at his wedding to a *Sunday Times* colleague, Christine Walker. Earlier that year I had given away another Christine, who left our friend Christopher Booker to marry the historian Norman Stone; so, despite having no daughters, I had found myself giving away the second of two brides in a year. The natural order of things was being pleasantly upheaved.

Until the following summer, when I inadvertently learned an

elemental lesson about myself as we took our three small boys on a villa holiday to a Greek island with David Blundy and his daughter Anna. We were all on the beach one day when suddenly there was a huge explosion in the distance, soon followed by a dramatic fireball climbing into the sky. What could this have been? A terrorist incident, even a coup? I rounded up the kids and rushed them in the opposite direction, away from the ominous sight, back to the house, while David started running towards it, leaving Anna behind with us. That night over dinner – the explosion having turned out to be some random gas incident, no one hurt – Dave and I decided amid much cackling that this symbolised the fundamental difference between us as journalists. I thought of the moment again almost two decades later, when my colleague and friend in New York, Ed Vulliamy of *The Guardian*, found himself the only person running towards the Twin Towers on 11 September 2001 just as the rest of the world was running the other way.

A year later, again thanks to Ron Hall's magazine, we enjoyed another 'freebie' of a summer holiday in Northern Cyprus. A decade after the Turkish invasion, I confess I was already there before starting to feel as guilty as I should about visiting the northern coastline so recently seized from its native Greek inhabitants. It was undeniably very beautiful; the restaurants were pleasantly empty, and the boys enjoyed climbing all over the odd tank still rusting on the beach. But a tour of the countless abandoned houses, being done up on the cheap by unscrupulous developers for rent or sale to unwitting tourists, made me ever more regretful that I had agreed to come. I was thinking especially of my esteemed friend Christopher Hitchens, then married to a Greek Cypriot whose family had been displaced from their home.

One day an imposing limo arrived at our villa with the unexpected news that the president wanted to see me. I had little choice but to smarten up and take the chauffeur-driven ride into Nicosia for what I assumed would be a routine journalist's audience with Rauf Denktaş.

'You are enjoying your holiday?' he began by asking me.

'Oh yes, Cyprus is very beautiful.'

'And you have been looking at houses?'

What was this? Had he had people following me around? After some hesitation, I said simply, 'Yes.'

'You would like a house?'

It took a moment for this to sink in. As I paused, Denktaş kept nodding and grinning in encouragement. Yes, I realised he was offering me a hefty bribe to ensure positive coverage of his tourist paradise, despite its then ropey streets and pockmarked buildings, not to mention its distinctly dubious political pedigree. I went through my mental Rolodex of all my friends, notably Hitchens, who would never speak to me again if I repeated my mistake, albeit inadvertent, of trousering that crane operator's bribe in Hemel Hempstead some fifteen years earlier. My career may now be on the slide, but I had since had some journalistic integrity drilled into me by Harold Evans and his proudly incorruptible lieutenants.

'That is a very interesting offer,' I said, trying hard to sound as cool as a character in a le Carré novel, 'but I cannot possibly accept it.'

Denktaş stopped smiling, and I was promptly dismissed.

Later, having sworn I would never dare, I inevitably found myself telling this tale to Hitchens, who turned out to be furious with me. 'You idiot!' he exclaimed. 'Every Sunday evening, Eleni's family walks to the border on the mountains, and looks down wistfully at what used to be her father's orange groves. They are not allowed to walk a step further. The only way they can regain access to their homeland is by written invitation from someone owning a house there . . .'

As it happens, Hitchens was wrong about that – Denktaş would not open his artificial 'border' until 2004 – but at least I got it right that autumn when I was called one day by Jim Callaghan's former press secretary, Tom McCaffrey, whom I had known since our mumps-ridden adventures around India. Now one of Peter Jay's ever more unlikely successors as chief of staff to Robert Maxwell, Tom had evidently been told by his boss that he had launched my journalistic career at Oxford. 'Captain Maxwell has told me, Tony,' said McCaffrey, 'that he would like you to ghost-write his memoirs.'

I was stunned – and unwontedly speechless. While I wondered what to say, Tom added: 'He has also asked me to assure you that you would, of course, be handsomely rewarded for your services.'

'Tom,' I replied after a moment's thought, 'that is an offer I cannot possibly accept.'

'Good for you, Tony,' said McCaffrey. 'If you had, I would never have spoken to you again.'

Tom apologised that he had even had to ask me; it was typical of the unwelcome chores he had to perform every day for his unspeakable master. It was not long now till his pension kicked in; he couldn't wait to get out of there. The task was eventually undertaken by another of Maxwell's acolytes, Joe Haines, once press secretary to Harold Wilson.

Soon after the deaths of both my parents that March, Amanda and I were at dinner with Mark Elder and David Pountney, then music director and head of productions at English National Opera. They were talking excitedly about a new staging by Jonathan Miller that autumn of Mozart's *Don Giovanni*, and I started teasing them about the company's policy of performing all operas in English, going so far as to say: 'Why don't you commission a translation from us?' No, they replied, they would be using the standard translation by Edward J. Dent. 'It's not as easy as you think,' remarked David, who had already himself translated his first few operas of many. 'We'll see about that!' said I.

Over Easter we went off for a break in Dorset, ostensibly to help me get over my double bereavement, about which I was still in some understandable shock. Once the boys were tucked away each evening, we had a crack at translating some of *Don*

Giovanni's most celebrated arias, and I began to see David's point. While roaming Dent's pretty dated 1921 translation, however, I made a crucial discovery. The Don's cocksure rallying cry in the final scene, '*Viva la libertà!*', he translated as: 'Oh for a life that's gay!' That must surely seal Dent's doom; if there's one thing Don Giovanni certainly is not, it's gay.

By midsummer, after sending them some sample arias, we were sitting around Amanda's piano with Elder, Pountney and Miller, going over various key moments in this most majestic of operas, before being given the commission – just six weeks before the start of rehearsals. In the frantic days that followed, I fondly remember a eureka moment in the bath one evening when I finally cracked an especially tricky couplet in Leporello's celebrated 'catalogue' aria detailing his lascivious master's thousand-and-three Spanish conquests:

> *But the highest common factor*
> *Is the girl who's still intacta.*

In the interval of the first night, already intoxicated by hearing a superb cast singing *my* words to Mozart's music, I was approached by Tom Rosenthal of André Deutsch to ask if the publication rights of the translation were available. A parallel-text version appeared soon thereafter.

Translating opera into English really is *not* easy, at least to one's own satisfaction as much as that of some very fussy if eminent singers. At the time I used to say that it was like completing a 3D crossword puzzle, but in truth it's much more complicated than that. Among other fiendish challenges, you have to match most vowel sounds of the original language in English (for the singers), and you also have to match the rhymes of the original in English, a tongue much less easy to rhyme. Mark Elder was also insistent that the word order of the original be reflected in that of the translation. I could not even have begun to think about it all, of course, without Amanda's musical expertise. But together we managed another two, Rossini's *The Barber of Seville* and Puccini's *La Bohème*, before I was diverted in other directions. Amanda herself has since translated many more, as well as writing original award-winning libretti and co-editing *The Penguin Opera Guide*.

While working on *Don Giovanni* I had been invited to lunch by my old colleague Brian MacArthur, who had by now also parted company with Murdoch to become editor of the *Western Morning News*. Brian had recently been approached by the entrepreneur Eddy Shah, with a view to launching a new national newspaper: Britain's first computerised seven-day-a-week paper, complete with colour photographs. Would I be interested in joining him in this exciting venture as editor of the weekend (i.e. Saturday and Sunday) editions?

After my failure to become editor of *The Times*, I would have said yes to editing pretty much *any* newspaper. And this one sounded interesting. My first hurdle was an interview with Shah himself in his imposing suite at a Hyde Park hotel. I knew a fair amount about him – who didn't? He was nationally known to be Prime Minister Thatcher's favourite self-made business-man – from his days as a floor manager on *Coronation Street* to the millions he had made after mortgaging his home in Warrington to launch Britain's first wildly successful 'freesheet' newspaper. But I didn't know that he had been at Gordonstoun at the same time as Prince Charles.

'Were you expelled from school?' was his first question, after a cursory amount of the customary small talk. It was an unusual, to say the least, opening salvo in a job interview.

'No,' I said, sensing he hoped otherwise. 'Were you?'

'Oh yes,' he replied with a grin.

'What for?'

'Stealing other kids' sweets, of course!'

Shah outlined his plans for the first daily newspaper in the UK to use the 'new technology' so resisted by the print unions, and spoke with pride of breaking their grip on Fleet Street. We laughed at the suggestions both of us kept hearing that colour pictures in a newspaper would look like cartoons; people would never take them seriously. A mid-market tabloid (or 'qualipop', as we called it), the paper would be the only one to give you the news straight – without the prejudices, even bigotry that then as now contaminates so much of the British press. Shah rather fancied himself as Citizen Kane, he endearingly admitted, but he wouldn't interfere in editorial policy. He even produced a Kane-like 'Declaration of Principles' to guarantee editorial freedom. He had yet to find a title for the paper, but himself fancied *Today* (as in the then new *USA Today*). That's the name of an influential Radio 4 programme, I objected. I myself favoured *The Inquirer*, as in *Citizen Kane*. But Shah naturally won the day.

I took an immediate liking to Eddy, and we were soon nattering away like old friends. 'My only problem with editing the weekend papers,' I told him, 'is that I'm an Arsenal fan. I have season tickets . . .'

'Well, I'm a Spurs fan,' he declared. 'Weekend editor it is!'

So I bid farewell to *Express* readers in November 1985 with an in-depth study of the latest vintage of Beaujolais Nouveau. Once I'd sobered up, I went off to join MacArthur in the arduous task of interviewing potential recruits for this great adventure.

And we assembled a top team. I hired Alastair Campbell from the *Mirror* as my weekend news editor and gave his first job on a national paper to Geordie Greig, later editor of the *Daily Mail* (after *The Tatler*, the London *Evening Standard* and the *Mail on Sunday*). Other recruits ranged from Colin Myler, eventually the last editor of Murdoch's *News of the World*, to a recent arrival from Australia, Amanda Platell, later spin doctor to the Tory leader William Hague. There were Sunday columns by Christopher Booker and (in pictures) the cartoonist Michael Heath. Our weekend sports correspondents were all stellar names: racing by Peter O'Sullevan, cricket by Phil Edmonds, football by John

Motson, then the voice of *Match of the Day*, and Patrick Barclay, later chairman of the Football Writers' Association. My immediate boss in my Atticus days at the *Sunday Times*, a supreme 'shirt-sleeve' journalist (i.e. technician and editor rather than writer) named George Darby, was meanwhile gracious enough to accept my invitation to become my deputy weekend editor.

To this day I meet people who say, 'You interviewed me for *Today* – and you didn't give me a job!' To which I reply: 'You were one of the lucky ones . . .' After the installation of very expensive giant computers in the basement, and months of keyboard and layout training for all concerned, the launch of *Today* in March 1986 went famously wrong, as rival national newspapers had gleefully been predicting. The journalism was top-notch, and at a cover price of 20p the paper soon reached a daily circulation of a million; but there swiftly emerged flaws in electronic transmission, production, distribution and more.

A self-professed tech-head, Eddy not only possessed the first fax machine I had ever seen, but gave all his senior executives pagers, then the latest thing, so that he could contact us at any time of day or night. So dire did I find this thought that I 'accidentally' dropped mine into the Thames. But I was delighted by the new-fangled phone in my company car; I still remember how weird it felt to talk on the phone while moving, and to be asked the unprecedented telephonic question: 'Where are you?'

Events leading up to the launch were chronicled for a BBC documentary, in which Brian at one point spilled coffee all over himself (which they kept in, of course, as some sort of omen), and we were all filmed for a TV commercial chanting our advertising slogan: 'We're ready, Eddy!'

Except we weren't. My *Sunday Today* included a colour magazine called *Extra*, the first issue of which contained a rare interview with John le Carré by Melvyn Bragg. Around noon that Sunday, Melvyn called me at home to say that he was walking up and down Hampstead High Street with le Carré, and they couldn't find a

copy of it anywhere. When I raised this at the next day's morning conference, Eddy declared: 'Great! I don't want your poncey
liberal friends in Hampstead reading it!' But it was a portent of
worse to come.

That month saw Cambridge win the Boat Race for the first time
in ten years, and I was absurdly pleased with being able to give a
light-blue tint to my front-page headline CAMBRIDGE MAKE
IT ONE IN A ROW. But the colour picture beneath came out
rather blurred, as did most such photos every day of the week.
One rare exception was the result of my sending Geordie Greig
to Paris to interview Samuel Beckett on the occasion of his eightieth birthday, 13 April 1986, which just happened to be a Sunday.
Geordie tracked him down and rang his bell, which Beckett
himself answered. '*Bonjour, Monsieur Beckett. Je suis George Greig du
journal anglais* Aujourd'hui. *Puis-je parler avec vous?*'

'*Non*,' replied Beckett, and firmly closed the door. But the
photographer had seized the moment to capture a picture of both
men's noses during this brief conversation. It duly dominated the
front page that Sunday, clear as crystal, to accompany the lengthy
profile Geordie contrived to make out of this exchange.

We were still doing dummy runs and pilot editions when I sent
Alastair Campbell off to write a profile of his pal Neil Kinnock,
then leader of the Opposition. These were Alastair's pre-teetotal
years, as he has himself recalled, and there followed an incident
in Her Majesty's Dockyards which saw him arrested and placed
in a medical care unit. Eddy wanted to fire him, as did Brian,
but I fought successfully to save the job of a journalist I liked and
admired. So I have always considered myself able to boast that,
whether you like it or not, I saved Alastair Campbell for (Tony
Blair and) the nation.

But perhaps the definitive moment of my time on *Today* was
actually a couple of weeks before the launch, when Eddy came
into my office and said, 'Tony, make me laugh.' This was one of
my various roles; whenever something was getting him down,

which was often, Eddy knew I could cheer him up. As I launched into my latest wisecrack, I leaned nonchalantly against the plain white wall of my office, only to find it red hot.

'Hey, Eddy, come and feel this. Something's not right here.'

'Too true,' said he. 'I'll go and see what's happening.'

Twenty minutes later, he returned to announce that he had good news and bad news.

'The bad news is I've discovered the basement isn't earthed, and the computers are on fire.'

'Shit!' I exclaimed. 'What the hell's the good news?'

'It's raining and the roof leaks.'

In retrospect, *Today* was a brave experiment doomed to fail, through a combination of bad planning and worse luck, but to pave the way for others to succeed. Some twenty years later Sue McGregor brought a few of us back together for an edition of her BBC Radio 4 programme *The Reunion*. At the end, as usual, she went round the table with the question, 'So why did it all go so wrong?' Eddy, Brian and the others ran through all the technical problems that had beset us – to the point where, last in line, there was nothing left for me to say. On the spur of the moment, I proclaimed that I didn't think it had been a failure at all. '*Today* pioneered the new technology, introduced the colour pictures we now take for granted, broke the print unions and paved the way for Murdoch to move to Wapping . . .' On I went, to the point where Eddy sighed to me afterwards: 'Oh, I wish I'd thought of saying all that!'

Mercifully, there was no mention that day of my own departure, after all of ten weeks as a national newspaper editor. The job had been the usual nightmare of clashing egos, and people wanting more expenses, a secretary, their own column, whatever. But the Saturday nights writing the front-page headline often put me in mind of my favourite Peggy Lee song 'Is that all there is?' One week our front-page lead was about a spat between Prime Minister Thatcher and her Chancellor of the Exchequer, Nigel

Lawson. In the tabloid format, there was room only for TIFF AT
THE TOP. Which was, in its way, deft enough, but . . . well, was
that all there was to this job?

With sales figures still thin, my growing doubts were unexpectedly resolved one Monday after just two months, when an
embattled Eddy called me into his office and said: 'I think I've got
to take the Sunday paper downmarket.'

'I can understand that, Eddy,' I replied, 'but I really don't think
I'm the person to do it.'

'Nor do I.'

'So what exactly are you saying to me?'

'I'm saying that I want to fire you.'

'But,' I spluttered, 'I might want to edit another newspaper
one day. Couldn't it be one of those "by mutual consent" things?
Or I could resign . . .'

'No, Tony,' he said, 'I've only fired two people in my life, and
I really liked both of them. And I really like you. So I want to
fire you.'

I kept on protesting.

'Look,' he said, glancing at his watch. 'It's 11 a.m. Don't tell
anyone – it's going to be announced this afternoon – but I sold
the paper last night to Tiny Rowland. Let me fire you, and I'll
show you how to get lots of Tiny's money for wrongful dismissal.'

So that's exactly what happened. I worked two more weeks
before departing with a year's salary, my company car (including
phone), and even a well-paid weekly column in the paper. It was
portrayed as a resignation – to finish a biography I was known to
be writing – amid much eyebrow-raising in the trade press, where
I was even quoted as saying that being part of 'the media event
of 1986' was 'boring'. In his own account of it all, published two
years later, Brian MacArthur repeated this unlikely fib, adding
that Eddy had me in mind to edit a centre-left upmarket daily he
was planning under the title *The Tribune*. 'So it's really a promotion!' I bragged to the *UK Press Gazette*.

No, it wasn't. Needless to say, no *Tribune* ever materialised. My role with *Today* was at best a minor footnote in UK media history, given that the following year Murdoch bought the paper from Rowland simply to close it down and recapture the readers it was stealing from his own tabloids. Many of the journalists with whom I shared the ride went on to great things, while I myself finally realised that it was time for a much more radical change in my life.

That summer we took an Italian villa holiday with the boys, during which I reflected that my marriage was falling apart. I had been a devoted father, I hoped, despite my frequent absences, but an ever less happy husband. Working together on *Don Giovanni*, I now registered, as well as hatching the idea for the opera guide Amanda would go on to edit, had been my attempts to save a marriage I could feel terminally floundering. Over fifteen years Amanda and I had slowly but inexorably grown apart; married in our early twenties, we had both become very different people by our late thirties. Despite my devotion to our three small sons, for me our relationship had become untenable. Vowing to remain an ever-present father to my children, I walked out of the marital home, to embark on an unknown *vita nuova*.

It remains by far the most difficult thing I have done in my life.

'Of course, you had to wait for your parents to die,' said a sympathetic friend soon afterwards. The thought had not even crossed my mind; but it immediately carried an unquestionable ring of truth.

IS ANYBODY THERE?

One May day in the mid-1980s I found myself in the rear end of a long-haul flight to Las Vegas, translating some arias from Puccini's *La Bohème* en route to the World Series of Poker. At the time, I had just rendered '*Che gelida manina*' as 'How cold your little hand is', and was congratulating myself on a marked improvement – more faithful to the Italian, too – on the time-honoured 'Your tiny hand is frozen'.

The plane being half-full, I was spread out across a whole row at the back – armed with large score, Italian dictionary, cassette tape plus Sony Walkman with headphones, pencil, paper, rubber. So when a huge guy in a Stetson hat, slumming it down the back while stretching his legs, stopped to stare, clearly wondering what the heck I was up to, I could come up with no top-of-the-head answer other than the truth to his direct question: 'What's that you're doing there?'

'Er, translating an opera . . . from Italian into English.'

He paused for quite a while, apparently struck dumb.

Eventually, after deep thought, he enquired: 'Any money in that?'

'More than you might think!'

Another, shorter pause.

Then an enthusiastic '*O-K*' as he smiled and reached out to shake my hand. 'O-K!' he repeated with a wave, before wandering back off to first class.

Despite our separation (and, eventually, divorce) I was still collaborating with Amanda on the translations to which we were jointly committed – and rewarded by 2 per cent of the box-office gross at London's biggest theatre – while already embarked on another project: the biography diplomatically cited by Brian MacArthur as my real reason for leaving *Today*.

Towards the end of my time in Washington, I had been invited for an audience with George Weidenfeld – staying at the British Embassy, as the guest of the ambassador, whose study he nonchalantly commandeered for a few days of meetings.

'Well,' he began, 'you've written us a No. 1 bestseller. Now you must write us another. Who would you like to "do"? Whom do you most admire?'

Clever old George phrased it well. All my post-poisoner, post-Charles life I have written biographies only of people I admire, dead or alive. We may all be fascinated by studies of evil, by reading lives of historical monsters from Attila the Hun via Genghis Khan to Stalin and Hitler, but I had long since decided that I could never devote several years of my own life to getting inside the skin of someone for whom I felt no empathy at all.

And I had readied myself for this moment.

'I'm a great admirer', I told him, 'of Laurence Olivier.'

George grimaced. 'Ah, dear boy, what a sorry coincidence. He's a very good choice, but that's the one person you cannot "do" for us at present. Don't tell anyone – we haven't announced it yet – but Larry is writing his own memoirs for me at this very moment.'

This was not, of course, what I wanted to hear. But I should have anticipated it; a commission of this pedigree was typical of the supremely well-connected Lord Weidenfeld. Yet I had a full-time job, which then showed no sign of changing. I was living open-endedly in the United States, which would somewhat hamper research on a British actor. But then, to my delight, George added: 'Don't give up on Olivier. Keep it between ourselves for now, but when we have published his book, which will be very personal, I will suggest you to Larry as the right man to erect a monument to him.'

Those were his very words. If there were such a thing as a warts-and-all monument, I replied, I was his man. In the meantime, I'd get on with my own life, and await Olivier's account of his with high anticipation.

And so it came to pass that in the summer of 1983, a decent interval after the publication (to decidedly mixed reviews) of his *Confessions of an Actor*, I found myself having a drink with Laurence Olivier at London's Garrick Club.

He even remembered – or so he said – that I was born on his fortieth birthday, and his candid response to the letter I had written him six years before, suggesting a round-figure interview. His reply at the time had begun by confessing to a profound dislike of himself, a self-hatred so powerful as to make him reluctant to contemplate the effort of memory involved in any account of his life or career. To dredge into his past would be too painful; there was too much of which to be ashamed.

After a wearisome series of professional disappointments, and a debilitating series of major illnesses, Olivier could no more bear to look forward than to look back. His working life was already confined to the depressing artificiality of film and television studios, rather than the inspiriting exertions of live theatre. Now he began to wonder if even camera work was beyond him. Would he ever act again?

Nonetheless, he had eventually been persuaded by Weidenfeld to 'concoct' some account of his life, which had cost him extreme effort, even with the help of a ghost-writer (with whose services he eventually dispensed). The result was a maudlin dramatisation of events, both private and professional, typical of a supreme performer. Said his son Tarquin: 'It says absolutely nothing, and gives everything away.'

After reading Olivier's book, I naturally had a few specific questions prepared, which he answered patiently, if somewhat evasively. But this was the first and last time he would do so. It was really more of a get-to-know-you (to a pretty limited extent) session, a kindly pat on the head, an almost papal blessing from His Nibs on the work that lay ahead of me. He would not speak to me while I was researching my book, would not answer any specific questions that might arise, but he would give others his clearance to talk to me.

This was what I had really wanted – the key to writing a decent biography of anyone still living. Without it, I'm not sure I would have proceeded. As with royalty, which in theatrical terms he surely was, friends and colleagues would naturally check with Olivier, for fear of incurring his displeasure, before agreeing to see me. Many of those who did so seemed rather impressed that I had won him over to that degree.

So, while continuing my Sunday magazine column, before that brief interlude on *Today*, I relished interviewing a wish-list of people I was eager to meet. I have always had an especial fascination with actors, and have been lucky enough over the years to befriend quite a few. To me there is a tantalising mystery involved in taking to the stage night after night as a person other than oneself, placing great trust in others also so inclined, even if there is some truth in the old cliché that many actors are most themselves only when they turn into other people. Especially, by his own confession, Laurence Olivier.

Or, as Al Pacino has put it, 'If I knew who I was, I wouldn't be an actor. Acting is lying.' Olivier himself seems to have embraced this notion when warned by Christopher Plummer that it was 'impossible to lie' on the arena stage of the new Shakespeare Theatre at Stratford, Ontario. 'My God,' he replied, 'what are we going to do?' He was far from sure, said Olivier, when he was acting and when he was not. 'For what is good acting but convincing lying?'

Two very different actors took an especial delight in all this, and were extremely helpful with my work: Nigel Hawthorne, who lived on the same street in Islington, and became godfather to our third son Ben, born in 1979; and Kenneth Griffith, who lived back-to-back with us, and was one of the most ebullient, mischievous people I have known. When Nigel came down the street to meet the newborn Ben, Ken came with him to place a Welsh rugby scarf around the baby's neck. In November 1981, at the height of my troubles on *The Times*, Ken had been in New York when the death was announced of the screen actor William Holden (né Beedle); Griffith mailed me the front page of a New York tabloid declaring HOLDEN DIES IN DRUNKEN FALL, with the handwritten annotation: 'Trust reports greatly exaggerated!'

In recent years Simon Russell Beale has talked of an actor's classic combination of 'low self-esteem and huge ego'. Asked why he thinks actors choose to appear onstage, he mused that it's 'not always to do with self-confidence; often to do with the opposite.' For Olivier, by contrast, acting was no more than reliving 'the childhood game of let's pretend'. He had never been conscious of any motivation beyond 'a deep-seated need to show off'.

One evening in 1965, in the middle of his run as Othello at the Old Vic, Olivier's performance transcended even its usual heights, to the point where his fellow actors, as the audience still cheered, formed a backstage arcade to applaud him all the way to his dressing room. The Moor swept past in grim silence, slamming the door behind him. Anxious they might have offended their boss, the company delegated Iago (in the shape of Frank Finlay) to make sure all was well. Through the keyhole Finlay called: 'What's the matter, Larry? It was great!'

'I know it was great, dammit,' came the reply, 'but I don't know how I did it. So how can I be sure of doing it again?'

A perennial lover of stage disguises – in this (now outmoded) case, black stain from head to toe beneath greasy black make-up polished with chiffon, his lips thickened, drops adding a penetrating sheen to the whites of his eyes and even his tongue dyed with incarnadine – all of which took three hours every night – he would have no idea when he removed it all of what he had just done, even less of who he really was.

This was what most fascinated me about Olivier. 'Is anybody there?' was the opening sentence of my book. He himself once said: 'I am not sure what I'm like, and I'm not sure I want to know.' Although one of the most looked-at faces of the twentieth century, Olivier was able all his life to walk down a street, travel on public transport, even stroll around his London club, quite unrecognised. In his memoirs he quoted his third and last wife, Joan Plowright, as saying: 'Larry? Oh, he's acting all the time.' She was never sure from day to day, she said, with whom she'd be living.

Even the writer who helped ghost his memoirs, Mark Amory, failed to recognise him when first they met: 'The man who came through the right door at the correct time was too short for Henry V, too urbane for Archie Rice, too ordinary for Richard III.' The same fate befell another of his biographers, Melvyn Bragg, who invited him to dinner at the Garrick Club with the composer William Walton: 'When the man in the over-large pin-striped suit trudged into the room I had no idea who he was. The spectacles were City-clerkish-heavy; the clothes correct but a little crumpled; the air deeply diffident; in all a brilliant disguise for one of the most famous faces in the theatre this century.'

What if his Huguenot ancestors had not preserved the French combination of Laurence with a 'u' and O-liv-i-er *à la française*, whose innate ring of its own bequeathed him the early alter ego he needed? In later life, already the youngest actor ever to be knighted and the first in history to be made a peer, he himself proved as much with zany impersonations of Larry *Oliver*, an outrageous vulgarian midway between Bottom and Archie Rice, who had haunted his early years in the shape of many a misprint. 'It was hilarious,' said his lifelong friend Ralph Richardson. 'Had Larry been born Lawrence-with-a-w *Oliver*, he might never have grown up to be the actor he was. An actor, perhaps, but not one with his dash and sweep.'

Most of my 200-plus interviewees were up for intense debate

of these absorbing topics, which naturally made all the difference to the finished product. Again at the Garrick Club, for
instance, John Gielgud mused to me that 'Larry and I are opposite sides of the same coin . . . Larry is a great impersonator; I
am always myself.'

This theme recurred with Michael Caine, his co-star in Joe
Mankiewicz's film of Anthony Shaffer's two-hander *Sleuth*: 'I'm
not like you,' Olivier told his awestruck young colleague. 'You
can act as yourself; I can never act as myself. I have to have a
pillow up my jumper, a false nose, or a moustache or a wig . . .
I cannot come on looking like me and be someone else, like
you can.' In a later conversation with Caine, he did not demur
when I mused what dream casting his Iago would have been to
Olivier's Othello.

As for his private life, two married actresses failed to tell me
over lunch of their dalliances with the great man, later revealed
on their own terms. No such coyness inhibited the luminous
Claire Bloom, whom I first met with her then husband, Philip
Roth, and who has remained my much-loved theatre-and-opera-
going companion ever since.

One of my most memorable interviewees, as it turned out, was
Anthony Hopkins, whom Olivier had given his first theatrical
break in his nascent NT company, and soon made his understudy,
mock-moaning about the panache with which Hopkins took over
(when Olivier was laid low with appendicitis) his commanding
role as the vicious Edgar in Strindberg's *Dance of Death*. Having
agreed to see me at the Old Vic after a performance, Hopkins
apologised profusely that he had to go off to a party – 'but that's
not a problem. You can come with me!' When we arrived at the
Dorchester, it turned out that our hostess was none other than
Elizabeth Taylor, giving her annual bash for the Burton/Jenkins
clan from Wales – an especially memorable one on this occasion,
the first since Burton's death.

Amid this mounting wealth of material, my most delicate

problem was the question of Olivier's sexuality. During all three of his volatile marriages – to the actresses Jill Esmond, Vivien Leigh and Joan Plowright – there were hints, dropped not least by himself, of sexual 'experiments' with men from Noël Coward to Kenneth Tynan. Throughout my extensive travels, moreover, showbiz people kept telling me that Olivier had enjoyed a long and passionate affair with Danny Kaye. Both were still alive, and married, while I was writing; so it would have been libellous to spell this out. But I sewed in a hint while describing Olivier's rush to Hollywood to bring home his second wife, Vivien Leigh, who had suffered a nervous breakdown after an affair with Peter Finch; when the couple changed planes in New York, they were met by Kaye, 'whose reunion with Olivier grew so intense that Vivien had a jealous relapse'. Gratifyingly, actors who read the book registered this, and grasped its veiled significance; no one else did, not even reviewers.

When I visited him in 1988 on the set of his final film, Derek Jarman's *War Requiem*, Olivier himself told me that my book had 'pleased' him. I had certainly given it my all, over five turbulent years of my own life, so was mightily relieved when the reviews were equally positive. To my especial delight, actors themselves still tell me they admire the book, that they feel it managed to get beneath an actor's skin to an extent unusual for a layman.

In July 1989, six months after our last meeting, Laurence Olivier died in the month my book appeared in paperback. That October I attended his memorial service in Westminster Abbey. At that event, revealed Olivier's official biographer (with his widow's blessing), the Prince of Wales had chosen to repre-sent him 28-year-old Kenneth Branagh – then a rising star who appeared to be modelling his career on Olivier's; he had already directed himself in the title-role of a film of *Henry V*, and soon would as *Hamlet*. In this quasi-regal role, Branagh would have been the final figure to make his grand entrance into the abbey, while the congregation stood in his honour, thus upstaging long-standing Olivier friends from Alec Guinness and Richard Attenborough to Peggy Ashcroft – any or all of whom, feared Olivier's younger son Richard, might have 'died on the spot'. That Branagh would thus appear to have Olivier's blessing as his theatrical heir so horrified his family that they reportedly went to the lengths of barring him from the service. The executor of Olivier's will, his lawyer Laurence Harbottle, opined that the Prince of Wales's nomination had shown 'real poverty of imagination'.

Which was to prove a sorry coincidence, for the poverty of the prince's imagination was again about to haunt my own life.

Since leaving the marital home in Highbury, I had been renting a riverside apartment atop a corner house in Chiswick Mall, where my young sons and I would delight in looking down from the balcony as each day's high tide slowly flooded the cars parked below by unwitting visitors. I have a particularly fond memory of throwing down bread on the day an insolent duck started pecking at the windscreen of some smart Alec stuck in his half-submerged Porsche.

As I adjusted to life as a single man, work occasionally got in its way; I had no alternative but to take all three boys along with me after school one day, for instance, to interview the latest Arsenal manager, George Graham, for a Sunday colour magazine. Unprofessional of me, to say the least, but they of course loved it. The same Sunday magazine commissioned me to write a piece for that year's Father's Day, in which I wrote with the utmost sincerity that my sons were my best friends – as indeed, several decades on, they still are.

In Chiswick Mall bachelor pad in 1986 with my sons
and 'best friends' Ben, Sam and Joe

By now I had started seeing other women, not least a smart
and sassy American novelist named Cindy Blake, whom I had
first met when she organised a parody newspaper called *Not The
Times* during the real *Times*'s closure in 1979–80; I had contributed
a lampoon of the Saturday Review Front. At *Today* my deputy
George Darby had encouraged me to hire Cindy, whom he knew
and admired as a regular contributor to the *Sunday Times*, to write
a weekly column for our Sunday magazine. She and I had developed a lively friendship, which we now resumed.

Before long it had blossomed into a full-blown romance.
Although we both had children from our marriages – five in all,
including her own Benj and Siena – we soon swapped my bachelor
penthouse for the whole house beneath, and moved in together.

When Cindy and I had first, tentatively, talked about this radical move, I was alarmed to hear myself sounding distinctly like Prince Charles as I warned her: 'You've really no idea what life with me will be like.' What I meant – beyond the obvious – was that Charles still haunted my life to such an extent, from endless phone calls and media requests to interminable 'what's-he-really-like?' questions at dinner parties, that I feared she might swiftly become as sick of it all as I was.

And all too soon she was to find out precisely what I meant. The second book I wound up publishing that year provoked prolonged trial by tabloid, mysterious robberies and burglaries, even death threats.

As Charles (and I) approached forty, I had been offered an absurdly large sum to update my ten-year-old biography – plus a handsome four-part *Sunday Times* serial deal (so now I *was* taking six figures of Murdoch's money!) – as well as fronting an ITV documentary, *Charles at Forty*. These were the last things I wanted to do, especially now that *Olivier* could have led me in other directions; but my divorce was proving expensive and I had three children to educate.

When we returned from Washington in 1981, I had signed up as a member of the Islington Labour Party (incensed at the defection of the 'Gang of Four' to found the short-lived SDP) while inspecting state schools throughout the borough. There was one at the end of our street, to which our sons could have walked without crossing the road. That year it boasted not one 'A' level. Like so many others who cannot but put the interests of their children ahead of their political principles, I felt obliged to swallow my pride and send all three to fee-paying schools – strictly day-schools in London, not the boarding schools to which I had been subjected – to pay for which, I reluctantly persuaded myself, I must also sabotage my career so that the royals could foot the bill.

The only way I could begin to justify a second Charles volume to myself was that he had become a completely different person in the decade since my first biography. Apart from all else, he had married and fathered two sons. But already the marriage appeared to be in trouble. And he had meanwhile developed a habit of shooting off cheap one-liners about 'modern' architecture that were subverting statutory planning procedures and putting British architects out of business.

Peter Ahrends, architect of the proposed National Gallery extension notoriously denounced by Charles as 'a monstrous carbuncle', was, he told me, just one of several architects who lost commissions and began to struggle financially as a result of the prince's interference. If the Prince of Wales attacks an architect's work, developers are no longer going to invite them to enter the competitions that are their lifeblood.

As a rank-and-file citizen, I considered it unacceptable that the prince should use his unelected office to cause such damage. And I thought it was more than time that someone stepped forward to say so.

One of our neighbours in Chiswick Mall just happened to be the eminent architect Michael Manser, who had been president of the Royal Institute of British Architects (RIBA) in 1984. So he was chairing the celebratory 150th anniversary dinner at Hampton Court Palace where the prince chose to make his distinctly uncelebratory remarks.

At the time, Manser told me, he had been 'outraged'. He had contemplated a counterattack there and then, but restrained himself for fear of turning what was supposed to be a celebratory evening into an acrimonious 'bunfight'. Later he came increasingly to regret this decision, as Charles – evidently gratified by the headlines generated by his 'monstrous carbuncle' quip – started scattering with heedless abandon increasingly destructive one-liners that caused yet more damage to yet more architects.

The prince did so against the advice of his private secretary, Edward Adeane, who would resign within the year. Adeane later told me that he had tried to talk Charles out of the 'monstrous carbuncle' jibe, even drafting a different version of the speech, which he offered the prince in the royal limo as they were driven together to Hampton Court. This was, after all, a dinner marking the RIBA's 150th anniversary, and so the least appropriate moment for the launch of a wholesale royal assault on the profession, not least the passing insult: 'For far too long, it seems to me, some planners and architects have consistently ignored the feelings and wishes of the mass of ordinary people in this country.'

Charles appeared to heed his advice, thought Adeane in the car, as he watched him read through the alternative draft; but he later proceeded regardless with his own original text. The RIBA website still refers to the speech as 'a discourtesy to architectural history'. Not for twenty-five years did the prince apologise, in his way, saying he had never intended to 'kick-start some kind of "style war"' between classicists and modernists'. At the time, he was only just warming to his task.

His next target was a modernist design intended to replace a Victorian building in the City of London. 'It would be a tragedy,' said the prince, 'if the character and skyline of our capital city were to be further ruined and St Paul's dwarfed by yet another giant glass stump, better suited to downtown Chicago than the City of London.' Again his remarks prevailed, and the Mies van der Rohe building was replaced by a James Stirling design that Charles then described as looking 'rather like an old 1930s wireless'. Said his polo chum Peter Palumbo, who had commissioned the original design: 'I can only say God bless the Prince of Wales, and God save us from his architectural judgment.'

Next on the princely agenda was Paternoster Square, the historic area beside St Paul's Cathedral, destroyed in the Blitz but now scheduled for long-overdue regeneration by a consortium led by Richard Rogers. 'You have to give this much to the Luftwaffe,' Charles told the annual dinner of the Corporation of London's Planning and Communication Committee in 1987. 'When it knocked down our buildings, it didn't replace them with anything more offensive than rubble.' The effect of this princely jest was to scupper the consortium's plans and delay the square's restoration another decade and more.

There followed the prince's 1988 TV documentary, *A Vision of Britain*, in which Charles boated down the Thames past Canary Wharf, saying 'I personally would go mad if I had to work in a place like that, because I would feel how the hell would you get out in the event of a fire apart from anything else.' A risibly careless hostage to fortune, this remark inevitably enabled me to point out that the prince had never had a proper job anywhere, let alone commuting to 'a place like that', while salt was poured in his wound as the tower at One Canada Square became symbolic of the hugely successful regeneration of London's Docklands, and many of the buildings around it won design awards.

Several demolition jobs later, Charles described the Reading Room of the British Library, designed by Colin St John Wilson, as looking 'more like the assembly hall of an academy for secret police'. One wonders if the prince has ever worked there, like myself and countless other writers who cherish its elegant surroundings. 'Those of us who have never been privileged to see inside an assembly hall in an academy for spooks were left baffled,' the *Guardian*'s architectural correspondent, Jonathan Glancey, taunted Charles. 'The Reading Room of the British Library, a comfortable, generous and much-liked space, looks uncannily like a reading room in a great library.' In 2015 the British Library became the youngest UK building ever to be awarded Grade 1 listed status. How that must have piqued HRH.

I could go on; fifteen years after Hampton Court, Charles was still telling planners that 'We should build legacies, not blots, on our landscape', and a 2009 row with Richard Rogers, after the prince's interference with his plans for Chelsea Barracks, provoked the architect to dub his conduct 'unconstitutional'. But the royal resentment caused by that chapter of my book was as nothing to the panic in the Palace prompted by my remarks about Charles's marriage – all too predictably spiced by sycophantic outrage from the fawning British press – four years before Diana's own protests via Andrew Morton proved me right.

I was careful in what I said about the prince's continuing relationship with Camilla Parker Bowles; both were married to other people at the time, and I had no wish for the prince to sue me in his mother's courts. But I did write of Diana that Charles 'no longer understands her – nor even, it seems, much likes her', while noting that 'most of the time, it is clear, she is bored with him.' I also observed that, for a couple with two young sons, Charles spent 'unnatural' amounts of time away from his wife and their children.

This prompted a direct public response from the Palace on the same Sunday, the day before Charles's 40th birthday, that the *Sunday Times* printed the fourth and final instalment of its serial. 'PRINCE'S IRE AT BIRTHDAY TITTLE-TATTLE' was the front-page splash of the paper's main rival, my previous employers *The Observer*, where I knew everyone involved in quoting a senior royal aide, Tom Shebbeare, as calling my book 'fiction from beginning to end', continuing the royal complaints inside under the headline 'A DISTORTED PORTRAIT OF THE PRINCE'. Neither the bylined reporter, Nicholas Wapshott, previously on my team at *The Times*, nor the editor, Donald Trelford, had phoned me for a response, as would only have been professional; in a subsequent letter of apology the news editor, John Shirley, told me he had wanted to, but been overruled. With my ITV documentary going out that evening, I issued a statement that, far from having 'no inside knowledge' (as Shebbeare put it in the prince's name), I had interviewed countless people close to the prince – *including Shebbeare himself*, as viewers could see for themselves that same evening.

And it wasn't as if we had made the film that day, I added for comic effect – a jest which, surprisingly enough, seemed lost on the tabloids.

What was the proudly liberal, republican-leaning *Observer* doing, anyway, leading its weekly agenda with self-confessed royal 'tittle-tattle' worthy of a downmarket tabloid gossip column, not least for its wanton inaccuracy? Was Trelford still harbouring a grudge about my return to his old rival Evans? What had I done to alienate Wapshott?

The next few weeks inevitably amounted to relentless trial by tabloid, as sundry big-name columnists – alias, for me, the usual suspects – roundly trashed me for my impertinent *lèse-majesté*. I had failed to name my Palace sources, they protested, while proceeding to do just that themselves. 'The prince despises the former *Sunday Times* journalist,' announced the *Daily Mail*'s omniscient diarist Nigel Dempster. 'Friends now tell me he has loathed him for eight years.' This intriguingly precise if unsourced disclosure was rendered all the more authoritative by Dempster's charge that my insolence was especially unfeeling because of the 'fact' that 'Holden was at Cambridge at the same time as Charles' – whose unequivocal 'message' to the world, on Dempster's exclusive authority, was an otherwise unsourced: 'Don't buy this garbage'. It was a compliment I could have returned with deadly accuracy. But I deemed Dempster unworthy of a letter pointing out that I had actually been to Oxford.

To the *Express*'s then version of Dempster, Ross Benson, I was 'the most reviled man in Britain', who had 'earned himself the "hatred" – and I use the word authoritatively – of the prince'. The same paper's columnist Jean Rook – the self-styled 'First Lady of Fleet Street' – led the general charge that Holden was no more than a 'rat' who should be 'locked away in the Tower of London'.

To the *Sunday Express*'s editor-cum-columnist John Junor, I was fit only to be 'pimping in Pimlico' or 'shovelling sewage in Shoreditch'; when it came to my qualities as a journalist, I was 'frankly, in footballing terms, towards the bottom of the second division'. Luckily, I had a chance to point out elsewhere that this same sniffy editor, only five years before, had commissioned this same lower-second-class hack to write double-page profiles of all three major party leaders (Margaret Thatcher, Michael Foot and Roy Jenkins) during the 1983 general election campaign.

The climax came the following Saturday, when *The Sun* (before re-serialising the book the following week) led its front page on MURDER THREATS TO ROYAL AUTHOR, citing three anonymous phone calls to my ex-directory number from an 'aristocratic, almost plummy voice' saying: 'Watch out – you've got it coming,' adding sinister mentions of a 'gun' and a 'shooting'. The *Daily Mail*'s front page meanwhile trailed a double-page spread by Geoffrey Levy with my face superimposed on the book's jacket-picture of Charles in tweed cap and country gear. 'The Prince and the Pretender' painted a vivid portrait of an impecunious shop-keeper's son from Southport who had thrown away a glittering academic future for wine, women and song. This cocky northern boy had left a classy pianist from a posh Belgravia family for a blonde American bimbo (in fact, as the *Mail* well knew, a political science graduate of New York's Columbia University) to live in a magnificent house beside the Thames (pictured). Far from saying that I could barely afford the rent, let alone the freehold, the *Mail*'s imaginative version was that I now had to peddle bestselling lies about the heir to the throne to pay off my gambling debts.

To lend authority to this hatchet-job, the *Mail* had pursued my godmother in Southport, my Oundle teacher John Harrison, and my Oxford tutor John Jones, not to mention numerous unnamed 'friends' and 'colleagues' making far from friendly or collegiate remarks. Apart, in the end, from Levy himself (not unknown personally to his victim), who would undermine two pages of venom with a final paragraph all but amounting to a public apology: 'One thing, however, must be said. Holden is a highly likeable man of considerable energy, courage and talent, and the future could still belong to Anthony Holden.'

That same weekend, in the *Sunday Times*, I wrote that friends on the international poker circuit had been surprised to see me in Malta; they had read in the previous weekend's *Sunday Express* that I had 'fled to America' until after publication. 'And if Holden has any sense,' added Graham Lord, 'he will stay there for good'. This was doubly surprising as I had in fact spent the previous weekend in London with my children, before nipping off to Malta for a few days' poker, as my answering machine clearly spelt out to interested parties.

Two weeks earlier – when, according to the *Express*, even my publishers did not know where I was – the *Sunday Mirror* managed to get hold of me at a radio station in New York, where I was on tour for the US publication of *Olivier*. Its reporter asked me, just before I went on air, about the death threats I had received while writing the Charles book. Were they from a member of the royal family – perhaps even the prince himself? 'No!' I replied. 'Emphatically not' – which did not save me a sleepless night after he rang back to double-check.

By the following Wednesday – while I was still in America, according to the *Express* – the *Mirror* had managed to track me down to Malta, where they conducted a telephone interview about the TV documentary. According to Graham Lord in the *Express*, however, I had gone into hiding. No one knew where I was. Could he actually have been trying to talk to me? If so, I was at the end of my own phone, as a piece under my name in the following day's *Sunday Times* testified – before a ten-day publicity tour all over the UK, during which, again, apparently even my own publishers (who had, of course, organised my schedule) did not know where I was.

What I told no one at the time, to avoid re-booting the tabloids, was that Cindy and I had been burgled while I was writing the book. More than once. My car was broken into overnight several times, which did not help with the school run, and we returned from a weekend away to discover that my study had been ransacked. All my files about Charles, plus floppy disks, VHS tapes with his name on and suchlike, had been taken. Nothing else was gone – the TV and other such valuables were all still there – apart from a rare self-portrait by my painter friend and neighbour Julian Trevelyan. When we called the police, the local constabulary looked round carefully before declaring that this was out of their league; they could do nothing more. In other words, as indeed they spelt out in so many words, it looked to them like the expert work of intelligence operatives.

Other royal biographers have testified that they too have suffered similar break-ins, even hacking in this age of computers. No, I am not suggesting that the Prince of Wales personally broke into my house, having seen helpful photos of it in the *Daily Mail*. I am simply rephrasing the words of one of his forebears, *à propos* of Thomas à Becket: 'Who will rid me of this turbulent biographer?'

En passant, just to redress the balance, the respected royal historian Hugo Vickers wrote in *The Times* of my second portrait of Charles: 'I am willingly convinced that this is as near the truth as we are ever likely to get.' In his *Telegraph* Christmas round-up, the monarchist Hugh Montgomery-Massingberd opined that 'Holden writes infinitely more intelligently and incisively than all the other authors in this Christmas crop.' In *The Independent*, Mark Lawson amusingly mused that 'Holden is a major shareholder in the Charles industry, but the kind who raises intelligent questions at the AGM . . . although Holden is part of the royal ratpack, he is at least the thinking man's rat.'

Of the TV film, Lawson wrote that it 'did much to compensate for the "gawd bless you, Sir!" royal journalism in which ITV has so long specialised, courtesy of Alastair [later Sir Alastair] Burnet.' The *Telegraph* considered it 'a deeply serious examination of the Prince's life so far'. My mind went straight back to our first meeting about the film with the prince's private secretary, Sir John Riddell. 'I suppose that to you this is a bit like dealing with the Kremlin?' asked Riddell. 'Well, to us, it feels like having rats nibbling at your private parts.'

Later that November, at the height of my joyride as 'the most reviled man in Britain', Godfrey Smith's column in the *Sunday Times* reported that he had printed 'the very first article' by a young man who had coached his daughter in Latin to the point where she actually said she *liked* Latin. He had gone on to become a family friend. 'His name was Anthony Holden, and I don't care who knows it. I wasn't expecting anything in the New Year honours list, anyway.'

Even better, the London *Evening Standard* ran a profile of me quoting a letter from a Kensington Palace 'insider' to the effect that my book was 'spot on in so many ways' about the state of the royal marriage. 'If the world knew the real behind-the-scenes drama, they would be gasping in amazement.'

Best of all, the following March saw Nigel Dempster leading his Sunday column in the *Mail* with the Prince of Wales's 'revenge', gleefully reporting that I had been blackballed from the Garrick Club, of which the prince had recently become an honorary member. The ensuing furore propelled my book straight back to the top of the bestseller list.

At the time, I was so indignant that I went to consult Britain's leading libel lawyer, Peter Carter-Ruck, in front of whom I spread out a whole table-load of tabloid cuttings that had taken their cue from Shebbeare's remark, in the prince's name, denouncing my book in *The Observer* as 'fiction from beginning to end'.

'I earn my living writing non-fiction,' I told him solemnly. 'So I want to sue the Prince of Wales for libel.'

Carter-Ruck went white. As I sat and watched, he spent a good half-hour reading through the original *Observer* interview, and all the red-top ranting it had provoked. Eventually, he looked up at me and solemnly pronounced: 'Mr Holden, you have a *prima facie* case against the Prince of Wales for defamation.'

My face lit up.

'But I would strongly advise you not to pursue the matter.'

My face fell again.

'Why?'

'For two main reasons. One, you may well think you would put up a decent show in the witness box. But a good barrister would make mincemeat of you with questions like 'Were you under the bed, Mr Holden, that night Mrs Parker Bowles came visiting?'

'And secondly: whatever the rights and wrongs of the matter, no jury in the land is going take your side against the Prince of Wales.'

This last remark I now like to think of as a period piece; it may have been true at the time, but public esteem for the prince has since sunk so low, not least because of his treatment of Diana while talking more fondly to his plants, that I or any other mere mortal might actually stand a chance against him, even in his mother's courts, soon to be his own.

At the time, dejected as I was, I had no alternative but to bow to Carter-Ruck's expertise. 'Well,' said I, 'I am very grateful for your advice. And of course I must accept it. Perhaps the best I can hope for is to put all this in my memoirs one day?' He smiled his assent.

So I am more than pleased, thirty-plus years later, at last to oblige.

AN EARFUL OF CIDER

Weekends do not exist in the Holden household. For a writer, work is work is work, whenever it may summon you, to an imminent deadline or not. And, yes, it may be sedentary; but, boy, it *is* work.

For some thirty years, all but half my adult life, Wednesday was my Sunday, i.e. my day off. Tuesday night being the still point of my turning world, as the designated dateline for my weekly poker game, the following day usually found me in meditative mode. The combination of dog-tiredness (we often played past dawn, till de boids woz singin'), too much booze and too little sleep had me in ruminative, almost philosophical mode, unwontedly quiet and thoughtful, prone to the odd *bon mot* as warranted. I remember an all-day feeling of benevolent bonhomie – especially if I had come home a winner.

Our Tuesday night game cumulatively acquired such a reputation around London poker circles, and beyond, that it featured in various TV programmes, even a learned Open University documentary about chance and probability. The founder members were predominantly arty types, mostly scribblers, and by now the game had even fathered two seminal books about poker, *Total Poker* by David Spanier (1977) and *The Biggest Game in Town* by Al Alvarez (1983).

It was surely time for me too to write a poker book, but how to come up with a distinctive formula for doing it? The summer of 1988 was to answer that question.

By May 1988, one way and another, I had been coming to Las Vegas every summer for a decade and more, since first covering the World Series of Poker (WSOP) as the *Sunday Times*'s Atticus in 1977. In those days the marathon event was staged at Binion's Horseshoe Casino in downtown Glitter Gulch – 'where the real gamblers go', went its slogan, as opposed to those tourists who favoured the florid fleshpots of the Vegas Strip. During the 1980 US election campaign I had used the Nevada primary as an obvious excuse to return for *The Observer*; as a freelancer, I had since secured commissions from every publication willing to pay my way. Once in Vegas, my room and meals were all 'comped' by the Binion family, complete with free entry into the press tournament on the eve of the world championship; but not, alas, the $10,000 entry fee (then as now) for the supreme tilt at the million-dollar world crown.

So I had always been there as a reporter or 'railbird', i.e. a spectator rather than a participant, never having had that kind of money to spare. Until, that is, 1988, when Eric Drache, then the WSOP's tournament director, came up with the bright idea of the 'satellite', where ten players would put up $1,000 each and play till one of them had won the lot, thus securing entry into the world championship for a mere thou.

In those days the 'main event' coincided with my birthday in late May, so the trip soon became an annual outing for most of the Tuesday Night boys. We would often find ourselves sitting at the same low-stakes table in the Horseshoe, despite Alvarez's mantra that 'We didn't come all this way to take money off *each other!*' and it was at one such that I found myself bored witless one evening, not to mention jet-lagged and well-wined – three out of three conditions in which one should *not* play poker in Las Vegas. I was finally trying to persuade myself to go upstairs and pass out when the loudspeaker announced one empty seat in the last $1,000 satellite. No one was more surprised than me when I put up my hand – and a grand – to grab it.

Well, I had exactly that much in my pocket, having just won it at blackjack, and figured I might as well find a more interesting way to lose it. Which became even more interesting when a passing friend persuaded me that I could be kept awake by a line of cocaine. To my own surprise, I accepted – the only time in my life that, apart from the odd joint at Oxford, I have taken a recreational drug. Needless to say, the following few hours passed in the most vivid of blurs, which later had to be reconstructed by tracking down the other players; when they turned out to include my Irish poker pal Donnacha O'Dea, he remembered that I had been 'walking on water' that night. Suffice to say: Reader, I won.

The next day I found myself sitting down amid some 200 starters with a shot at the $1 million first prize. To say I was 'playing for Britain' in poker's world championships is only technically stretching the truth, as I was the sole Brit to make it into the 'main event' finals that year. These days, since poker has taken off on TV and online, the prize money has risen into the tens of millions, and whole planeloads make the pilgrimage to Vegas each summer in hope of one of the richest sporting prizes on earth.

I found myself drawn at the same table as two-time world champ Stu 'the Kid' Ungar and my fellow amateur Telly Savalas – yes, Kojak himself. To my amazement, I beat Ungar out of a big pot early on, and even managed to outlast him in the tournament, achieving my first target by surviving into the second day – when all too soon I ran into a fatal flush.

Ninetieth in the world didn't sound that great until someone pointed out that it was then a higher ranking than any UK tennis player – as I proceeded to boast all year. And, of course, I could call myself the British No. 1.

Back home, I found myself restless and grumpy. All I wanted to do was play poker.

It was Cindy who came up with the idea. Why not turn pro for a year, to see if I could earn my living at the game, not least the entry fee for the following year's world championship, and write a chronicle of my adventures? Her reward was to become my 'moll' in the thrilling twelve-month whirl of high jinks that ensued all over the world. Like golf or tennis, poker has a tournament circuit, on which I proceeded to spend one of the most enjoyable years of my life. From the European championships in Malta, to the Moroccan Open, to a Caribbean poker cruise and an illegal tournament in Louisiana, where we were all thrillingly run out of town by the law, I had found a way of earning a living that was a lot easier – and far more fun – than writing. Poker, as the sage old saying goes, is 'a tough way to make an easy living.'

One early mistake I made, schooled by the high-living Eric Drache, was to assume that all professional poker players fly first class; in truth, of course, the savvy ones sit in the back to preserve their funds for the baize. So on one of my regular trips from London to Vegas I treated myself to a seat on Concorde to New York, where I had fundraising business, and was relishing the delights of the Concorde lounge at Heathrow as I made a fond farewell-for-now call to the moll. When I hung up, so did the guy beside me, and our eyes unavoidably met. It was Rupert Murdoch. 'What are *you* doing here?' he asked menacingly, as if Concorde were his private plane.

'I'm going to New York,' I said limply, feeling obliged to add, 'en route to Las Vegas, to play in the World Series of Poker.'

Murdoch's face brightened.

'Poker, huh?' said he. 'Come and have a drink!'

So I followed him to join his then wife Anna at a corner table. I was still wondering what, if anything, to say about *l'affaire* Evans just a few years earlier when Murdoch solemnly pronounced: 'You know, of all the people involved in that squalid episode, you were the only one to emerge with any trace of honour and integrity.'

'I think you mean that I was the only one not to take any of your money with me . . .'

'That is,' he mused, 'a factor in my judgement.'

As the talk turned to poker, I told him that Robert Maxwell had boasted to me that he had once 'beaten the pants off' Murdoch in a poker game.

'That's a lie!' he stormed. 'I never played poker with that jerk!'

As he calmed down Anna chipped in that, even when playing poker with their children, Rupert was so desperate to win that now they wouldn't play with him. And when challenging them to a race in the swimming pool, he would send them to the diving board while himself taking a running jump to get ahead of them. He swiftly moved the conversation back to *The Times*. 'Best thing that ever happened to you!' he smiled as the flight was finally called. And I have to confess that, in view of the thrilling year on which I was then embarking, I occasionally caught myself wondering if he had a point.

Upon arrival at JFK I again found myself standing beside Murdoch at the baggage carousel as we waited for our luggage. For the first and only time in my life, my suitcase was the first to emerge. So I gave him a cheery wave as I made my exit, leaving him as solitary and forlorn-looking as he had been that evening with the Queen at the Authors of the Year party. The airport baggage carousel, I mused, must be the only place in the world where such global titans are left alone and desolate, with no lackeys to perform life's menial chores for them.

At dinner in Manhattan that night with Harry Evans and Tina Brown, I found myself sitting next to Ahmet Ertegun, founder and president of Atlantic Records. When I told him my Murdoch story, he smiled and said, 'Yes, the baggage carousel is a great leveller.'

As is poker, at its best a form of psychological warfare. The road from average amateur to putative professional would involve frequent pit-stops for self-examination and overhaul. 'Whether he likes it or not,' I wrote, 'a man's character is stripped bare at the poker table. If the other players read him better than he reads himself, he has only himself to blame. Unless he is both able and prepared to see himself as others do, flaws and all, he will be a loser in cards as in life.' Three decades on, this homespun homily still bounces pleasingly around sundry social media sites.

As does another of my Las Vegan intimations of mortality, baldly stating poker's case to be the ultimate card game, distilling all the vicissitudes of everyday life:

> In every deck there are 2,598,960 possible five-card poker hands. The bad news is you are going to be dealt only one of them. The good news, however, is that you don't have to hold the best hand to win. The one dimension unique to poker, which sets it above and apart from any other game ever invented, is the element of bluff. By betting *as if* you are holding the best hand, by 'representing' strength, you can frighten every other player out of the pot and take their money without even having to show your cards. This is true of no other game but life, with which poker has a great deal in common. Most human beings conduct their lives as a series of risks, some more calculated than others. They may not care to admit it, especially to themselves, but they bluff their way through life's complexities, both professional and personal, every day.

This proved, as intended, the theme that caught the attention of reviewers and so readers: poker as the ultimate test of character, as a paradigm for life. 'The best players are those who can turn indifferent hands into winners, through psychological mastery of their opponents.' Poker, in other words, is not just a game of cards played by people, but a game of people played with cards. A few million hands later, this remains for me a truth worthy of inscription upon a Grecian urn.

The unique mechanics of everyday life in Las Vegas offered a salutary boost to the narrative: the absence of clocks or windows around a casino, to help you lose all sense of time; the sparse amenities in your hotel bedroom, to ensure you spend more time in the gaming areas; the oxygen pumped through the ventilators, to keep you fresh through the longest of days (and nights); the free liquor on offer in the gaming areas, to loosen your few remaining inhibitions.

In search of a palatable way to spell out Freud's thinking on gambling – or, should I say, an addiction to highly calculated risks – I came up with the idea of taking my reckless self off to a shrink (also, in truth, a family friend) to explore quite why I was so enthusiastically embarking on an adventure so risk-laden. After I had spelt out all the basics, to spice up my narrative, he came to the conclusion that I was on a Hamlet-like mission to avenge my father's hard-luck story, specifically the mean hand he was dealt in life by the fates.

Yes, my work in-progress had literary pretensions. A devout fan of Damon Runyon, and that inimitable musical based on one of his stories, *Guys and Dolls,* I wanted to call the book *An Earful of Cider,* as in the immortal mantra of Sky Masterson's father:

> Son, no matter how far you travel, or how smart you get, always remember this: Someday, somewhere, a guy is going to come to you and show you a nice brand-new deck of cards on which the seal is never broken, and this guy is going to offer to bet you that the jack of spades will jump out of this deck and squirt cider in your ear. But, son, do not bet him, for as sure as you do you are going to get an ear full of cider.

I used this quote from Runyon's *The Idyll of Miss Sarah Brown* both on the epigraph page and again in the narrative when introducing my hero Titanic Thompson, the supreme master of the proposition bet, and the original of Runyon's Sky Masterson. In his very friendly review for the *Times Literary Supplement*, Salman Rushdie pointed out with a hint of sarcasm that the author is so fond of this quote as to use it twice.

Touché, Salman. *Big Deal* has far outsold any other book I've written. My yearning to call it *An Earful of Cider* was outvoted by the moll and indeed the publishers. It is a particular pleasure to rectify that loss with the title of this chapter.

At the end of my twelve-month adventure, after deducting five-figure expenses, not least the $10,000 entry for the next World Series 'main event', I had made a profit of $12,300 – not to be sniffed at, but far from enough to live on. So back it was to the blank screen.

In the process, however, I had learned a lot about myself, which has since served me well at the green baize of life. Evidently I had infected others, too, as I began to meet people who had read the book and given up their own jobs to turn pro, some more successfully than others. The thought that my book could alter people's lives, perhaps ruin them, was not one I had anticipated, nor one I live with comfortably to this day.

But *Big Deal* is my own favourite of my books, by far the most personal, and certainly the only one to enjoy multiple reissues over thirty-plus years. In essence, it is really a David v Goliath adventure story enhanced by the most exotic of settings. I tried to ensure that it could be enjoyed as much by those with no knowledge of poker as by hardened enthusiasts. It turned out, as I have often been told, that if you don't know how to play the game when you pick it up, you will by the end. Up to a point, that is; there is a fundamental truth in the old adage that poker 'takes a moment to learn, but a lifetime to master'.

When punters in Vegas learned that back home in London I played in the same game as *Total Poker* Spanier and *Biggest Game in Town* Alvarez, they invariably asked: 'How the hell did those three great poker books emerge from that dipshit little London home-game?' There's no answer to that. But *Big Deal* has been going strong ever since. Its patron saint has been its original publisher, Ursula Mackenzie, who took it with her through several imprints before her eventual retirement.

When it was first published in 1990, Ursula enlisted the help of Eric Drache to organise a launch party, including a tournament, at the Mirage Casino-Hotel in Vegas, where the American Booksellers Association happened to be holding its annual convention. With Michael Lewis, whose *Liar's Poker* was also published that year, I was persuaded to run a blackjack table in the Convention Center, where I can never forget the announcement of regret that the ABA would not be holding its annual tour of children's bookshops in that year's host city as there were none to be found in Las Vegas.

Back in Blighty, I shared the stage at a literary luncheon with the sometime Chancellor of the Exchequer, Denis Healey, who had just published his autobiography, and was pleasantly amused when I announced that I was going to address a subject close to his heart: the redistribution of wealth.

In those days, when literary lunches were the order of the day, I spoke at many all over the country, including one in Norwich hosted by Malcolm Bradbury, then running his celebrated creative writing course at the University of East Anglia. The other speakers were the historian Philip Ziegler, who had just published the official biography of King Edward VIII, and the comedian Ernie Wise, promoting his memoirs. When we met up before the lunch, it was Bradbury's suggestion that Wise should speak first, followed by Ziegler, and then me. Just before we all sat down I nipped off to the gents, where I found Ernie Wise hiding away looking very upset, almost on the verge of tears. 'What's wrong?' I asked him. 'I'm sorry,' he wailed, 'but I'm used to closing the show!' So I naturally went back to have a quiet word with Malcolm, and made sure that showbiz justice was done.

My dedication to poker rescued my undoubtedly addictive personality from a lifelong penchant for the horses and other more overt forms of gambling – even, eventually, blackjack. Amid all the compliments about my book came a complaint from the multiple world snooker champion Steve Davis, himself also a poker player, that this whole paean to poker would never have happened without that blackjack win which financed its opening. He had a point. I began to wish I had left out that particular detail.

Only in Vegas could Frank Sinatra have made a second appearance in my life. 'Ol' Blue Eyes' was playing the showroom atop the Golden Nugget on my birthday, when Eric Drache handed over two front-row seats as a present from himself and Steve Wynn, then owner of the Nugget. Cindy not being along on this particular trip, it was with some difficulty that I persuaded Al Alvarez to quit his Hold'em game in the Nugget's card room and come with me as my date. In the middle of his gig, Sinatra paused on a cocktail stool as the band took a break, and began with a surly 'I guess this is the moment I have to talk to you people . . .' For years afterwards Al loved to tell the tale of my 'white-knuckle moment', grabbing his arm when Sinatra went on to announce: 'We have a birthday to celebrate here tonight!' My God, I thought, Steve Wynn has had a word with him; Frank Sinatra is about to wish me happy birthday, maybe even lead the crowd in singing it . . . If my friends could see me now! 'Yes,' he went on, 'today is the birthday of, er, my little granddaughter, er . . .' From the back a member of the audience helpfully yelled out her name. 'That's right,' he said, 'that's the one! Let's sing her "Happy Birthday"!' I slumped in my seat.

Later that summer, back in London, poker was also the backdrop for Alvarez's own sixtieth birthday, for which his beloved wife Anne had organised a surprise party. My role in the conspiracy was to get Al out of the house by 6 p.m. – a bit early to head to our poker club in central London, but easily enough done; the problem was going to be getting him back home again as early as 8. The plot required Cindy to call him at the club at 7.30-ish with news urgent enough to drag him home again, which we found impossible to think up; and when she did call, it happened to be Al's once-a-round turn to deal, so the phone was passed to me, which was no help at all.

Whatever crisis I came up with, Al was mighty put out to have his poker interrupted, and spent most of the trip home wondering what could have happened to interrupt his birthday treat. So when his front door was thrown open to reveal sixty unexpected revellers, from his friends and neighbours David Cornwell, a.k.a. the novelist John le Carré, to the pianist Alfred Brendel, he was at first aghast, then naturally delighted. When it fell to me to propose a toast, I brazenly declared: 'Ladies and gentlemen, we all know that our dear friend Al hates surprises, almost as much as he hates parties, but Anne has gone to a lot of trouble tonight, so: ladies and gentlemen, I give you: "Fuck Al!"'

To which all sixty guests raised their glasses and roared in unison 'Fuck Al!', much to the delight of the beaming birthday boy himself – who wound up dedicating the novel he was writing at the time, *Day of Atonement*, to me and Cindy.

In the autumn of 1990, when *Big Deal* first appeared, *GQ* magazine organised a writers' game at a London nightclub to promote the book, paying David Mamet, Martin Amis, Al Alvarez and myself, plus the *GQ* writer John Graham, £500 each to play with, and then write an account of the game. Modesty naturally forbids me to tell you who won, so I shall quote Amis: 'Anthony Holden was the big winner (well over £1,000); David Mamet doubled his money; Al Alvarez lost, and John Graham lost heavily, as they say; I came out with £200 of the magazine's money. But then I had to write the piece. Holden, in effect, was paid £2 a word for his contribution; I was paid 25p.'

Prior to that, Martin had written: 'It was Anthony Holden who appeared to me to possess the most dangerous mixture of froth and flair. Tony is toney; he has his Vegas mannerisms: the exaggerated slouch, the languidly scornful flickaway of the dead cards. When the pot gets high, the hour late, and you need to see what he has in the hole, then the lounge lizard melds into a loanshark . . . Holden writes whole books about hold'em. He is the Imam of hold'em. He is practically *called* Holdem.' David Mamet, meanwhile, was generous enough to dub *Big Deal* 'an important addition to the literature of gambling'.

Another unexpected bonus came when I received a late-night call in London from another Vegas friend, Erik Seidel. Runner-up to Johnny Chan in the 1988 World Series, and still a respected professional, Erik was then working on a new (but short-lived) magazine called *Poker World*. Seidel had just seen Microsoft's founder Bill Gates, he told me, playing poker in the card room of the Mirage. So he had gone over and said, 'Excuse me, Mr Gates, I didn't know you played poker.'

'I don't,' said Gates. 'I play bridge. But I've just read this great new book about poker and I thought I'd give it a try.'

'That wouldn't be *Big Deal*, by Anthony Holden?' Erik asked him.

'Yes,' replied Gates. 'That's the one.'

'Well, Tony is a friend of mine,' ventured Erik.

'Sounds like a nice guy,' said Gates.

'If I could get him out here to Vegas from London, would you play a game of poker with him for *Poker World*?'

'Sure,' said Gates, which was why Erik was calling me in the middle of the night. Nothing ever came of it, of course, even though I mentioned it during a brief meeting with a friendly Gates years later at the 2001 World Economic Forum in Davos. Ever since, however, I have derived some solace, in darker moments, from knowing that one of the world's richest men seems to think I'm a nice guy.

Big Deal even made a cameo appearance in the opening scene of one of the few really good films about poker to have graced the silver screen. At the beginning of *Rounders* (1998), as Matt Damon slides out of bed with his girlfriend to sneak off to a nocturnal poker game with John Malkovich, the camera pans across the bookshelf beside his bed to reveal a paperback of *Big Deal*. I was later told by the film's writer, Brian Koppelman, that he's such a fan of the book he wanted to make sure it was somehow in his script.

For some years, at the time, I received a handsome annual

payment for the film rights to *Big Deal*, which went through many a script agonising whether its hero should win the million-dollar tournament or get the girl; the rom-com boom of the moment dictated that he couldn't do both. When several papers mentioned that Hugh Grant had been cast as me, opposite Julia Roberts as the girl whom I did or didn't get, I told interested parties that I'd rather be Robert De Niro.

The producer in question was Christian Colson, whom I had first met in the poker room of London's Victoria Casino with our mutual friend Patrick Marber, before both became members of the umpteenth incarnation of my Tuesday night game, from which Colson disappeared for months in 2007–8 to make some film in the slums of Mumbai. You're mad, we all told him; who the hell is going to want to watch *that*? We were obliged to eat our words when *Slumdog Millionaire* won Christian the Oscar for Best Picture at the 2009 Academy Awards. Having stayed up all night to see my friend's moment of triumph, I sent him an email headed 'Slumdog Poker Player', saying, apart from congratulations, 'I've got it!' and that (as in *Slumdog*), 'He wins the million-dollar tournament *and* he gets the girl!'

Despite the frenzy of his big Hollywood moment, Christian even replied. But no movie version of *Big Deal* ever, alas, materialised. In more than thirty years now, however, the book has never gone out of print, been through countless editions and sold close to a million copies.

So much for royal biographies!

13

THE LAST PARAGRAPH

In March 1989, while I was whupping the likes of Johnny 'The Man' Moss at the poker tables of Las Vegas, I received an unexpected call from Tina Brown, by now well established as editor-in-chief of *Vanity Fair*. She was in Los Angeles, for the Academy Awards. Hubby Harry was stuck back home in New York. Would I like to squire her to sundry star-studded Oscar nights out?

You bet I would. When a man is winning in Vegas, the best thing that can come his way is an excuse to leave town, to quit while ahead – let alone an excuse so tantalising. I told Tina I'd be there the next day.

That week turned into a procession of private dinners at the homes of the rich and famous, many of them nominated for an Academy Award and drumming up support. There was an especial emphasis that year, we soon learned, against brazen lobbying for votes; under the Academy's unwritten rules, in the era before publicists developed all their pricey dark arts, only the ubiquitous 'For Your Consideration' adverts were strictly permitted, along with the relatively new idea of mailing video cassettes to all 6,000 Academy voters.

Tina and I were still musing on such nuances as we climbed into the back of her limo one evening after another sumptuous night out with the stars. 'You know,' she said, 'there's a book in all this.'

'Sure is,' said I. 'Bestseller, too. You should write it.'

'No, no,' she replied. 'I'm far too busy with *Vanity Fair*. I meant that *you* should write it.'

In those long-lost pre-internet, pre-Amazon days, my immediate thought was that someone must surely have done so already. Who would know? The next day I called Michael Korda in New York, doubly appropriate as editorial director of Simon & Schuster and, as I knew from *Olivier* onwards, a committed cineaste.

I told Michael about some of the conversations we'd been involved in that week, dropping numerous blue-chip names in the process, and tried to capture the febrile atmosphere of the run-up to the annual Oscar ceremony. Had anyone, I wondered, ever written a critical, anecdote-packed history of Hollywood's Academy Awards?

His immediate reply was: 'I'll give you $300K right now.'

I was gradually becoming accustomed to six-figure advances – but this, for US rights only, raised the bar to a whole new level. And I hadn't even asked Michael for an offer, merely called to tap into his expertise. For some years now, six-figure advances would remain the sustaining subtext of my increasingly expensive life. But this – for what was, as yet, a mere whim – was something else.

I hadn't even consulted my literary agent, as protocol required. I had barely started writing – even if I had nearly finished living – *Big Deal*. Did I really want to spend as much of the next couple of years on the west coast of the United States as I had the last couple?

Of course I did. My three growing sons were all movie fans, and would love a trip to behind-the-scenes Hollywood. Besides, I'd still be in the heartland of American poker, with clubs like the Bicycle in nearby Gardenia, and Vegas itself only an hour away. So that was my next few years sorted. First, I had to write *Big Deal* pretty damn fast; then it was to be a privileged entreé to LA's fast lane.

Yes, I had to admit it, even to myself: right after my year

masquerading as a pro, this latest project was really a flimsy excuse to spend more time in that poker-sodden part of the world. On closer examination, it was actually a pretty garish idea for a book, as Anjelica Huston made clear when I was introduced to her at some party as that guy who was writing a history of the Oscars. 'Why on earth would you want to do *that*?' she asked witheringly.

'It's an alternative history of the movies,' I pleaded, having failed to convince even myself of such wishful thinking.

'Yeah, right,' she replied scornfully (in a definitive usage of what I have since learned to be – and relish as – the 'Morgenbesser conceit').

But the research would prove more than enough fun to make it all worthwhile. The Academy's president at the time was one of my cinematic heroes, Karl Malden, who couldn't have been more charming or more helpful. Thanks to him, I was to be furnished with a pass to the next three annual awards ceremonies, and given free run of the Academy's comprehensive archive, as well as introductions to a host of galactical names. Within a year I would be installed in a suite at the Hollywood Roosevelt Hotel, where the very first Academy Awards ceremony had been held in 1929, hosted by Douglas Fairbanks, and lasting all of fifteen minutes. My job would now be to chronicle that evening and the rather longer ones that had since flowed therefrom.

First, however, I had to play in the 1989 World Series of Poker in Vegas – with, it transpired, as little success as the year before – then head home long enough to move with Cindy into a new house in west London large enough to house all five of our children. There it was in mid-November 1989 that I received a phone call from Harry Evans with the devastating news that my bosom buddy David Blundy had been shot dead in El Salvador. Just forty-four years old, David had recently become chief American correspondent, based in Washington, of his third successive Sunday broadsheet. Typically, he had already filed his piece on a Friday evening, at the end of a week that had seen the public slaughter of six Jesuit priests, then gone out again on the Saturday morning for 'one last look', for 'one last paragraph'. He was huddled among a group of foreign journalists at a crossroads in Mejicanos, a seedy *barrio* of northern San Salvador, observing crossfire between government troops and rebel guerrillas, when a stray sniper's bullet felled him.

David was buried in London's Highgate Cemetery, within nodding distance of Karl Marx, and celebrated in a memorial service at St Martin-in-the-Fields. There followed a booze-up at, of all places, the stately Reform Club in Pall Mall – where the perennially scruffy Blundy, went the consensus, would never have been allowed in.

David left two daughters, nineteen-year-old Anna and two-year-old Charlotte, but little if any money. So they were naturally named the beneficiaries of a collection of his journalism I edited under the title *The Last Paragraph*. 'Any journalist drawn, like him, to scenes of conflict, to the chronicling of violent death, lives with the permanent knowledge that he could be next,' I mused in my agonised introduction, one of the most difficult pieces I have ever had to write. This was not about some macho brand of courage – in Beirut as in Belfast, Blundy had confessed to being 'shit-scared' – so much as a willingness to sublimate fear in pursuit of adventure or a good story, preferably both. David's problem was that he was chronically reluctant to write about anything he hadn't seen for himself. 'Veterans of conflict like him, hooked on scenes of violence for reasons even they can rarely explain, are by definition those who choose to put their lives at risk most often. David was killed, in effect, by the law of averages.'

He was also, meanwhile, the consummate reporter, as dedicated to duty as he appeared not to be. If one last look for one last paragraph cost David Blundy his life, it was also very much the measure of it.

David's perennially disheveled appearance, his unpredicta-
bility, his chaotic working methods – he would often need to
borrow pencil and paper from interviewees – all concealed one
of the most conscientious and dedicated reporters of his time.
He of all journalists was the one who would tease and worry
his copy through the typewriter, pouring an excess of agony
into the eternal problem – never as simple as it might seem – of
getting the right words in the right order.

© News Licensing

The following summer, after three years of co-habitation, Cindy
and I were married at her family's summer home on Cape Cod.
Harry Evans flew up from New York, and Eric Drache east from
Las Vegas, to be incongruously joint best men at this distinctly
Anglo-American occasion. Ten days later, the happy couple jetted
off for a Caribbean honeymoon at a resort in the British Virgin
Islands called Little Dix Bay. Yes, you can imagine the newlywed
jokes that greeted our return.

Life back in Blighty was also brightened by some of the friends we were making in the small square in Hammersmith, west London, into which we were settling. One was the eminent tenor Robert Tear, whose neighbour was a rather different kind of singer in Billy Bragg. Over the next few years, I would be delighted to work with Billy on his radical ideas for constitutional reform, not least the super-smart evidence he gave a few years later to John Wakeham's inquiry into the future of the upper house.

At the time, however, it was back to the States for me, to continue my research on the Oscars while savouring the warm reception over there accorded *Big Deal*, which was soon responsible for a momentous encounter back in Hollywood. Most days saw me meeting another of my movie heroes, but few could outrank the inimitable Walter Matthau, guest of honour at the annual awards lunch of the Publicists' Guild, one of countless such bean-feasts in the run-up to the awards show. The host being my Vegas pal Henri Bollinger, public relations man for Benny Binion and the World Series of Poker as well as that year's Guild president, I managed to secure an introduction to the great man.

Knowing that Matthau's Friday night poker game in LA and my Tuesday night game in London had a particular player in common, the restaurateur Michael Chow, I mentioned the connection and asked Matthau: 'So who's the sucker in your game?'

'If you can't spot the sucker in your first half-hour at the table,' Matthau replied, 'it's you!' – adding that he has just discovered this great line in a 'terrific' new book about poker.

'What's it called?' I asked coyly.

Matthau could not remember.

'It's not called, er, *Big Deal*, by any chance?' I ventured. 'By a Brit called Anthony Holden?'

'That's it!' he exclaimed. 'That's the one!'

'Well, um, that's, er, me.'

Matthau did not believe me. How could this limey in a suit and tie, with a spruce new haircut, be the guy who had written a sassy poker book like *Big Deal*? Our busy host Henri Bollinger was himself summoned to assure Matthau that I was indeed Holden, at which point he asked when the book was due out in paperback, and whether a quote from him might help? Soon, I replied, and you betcha. So Matthau summoned pencil and paper, and sat alone in the corner of the room for quite some time, mostly crossing things out and screwing up sheet after sheet. By the time the luncheon had begun, and he was needed at the top table, the best he could come up with was: 'Reading *Big Deal* is a helluva lot better than losing at poker.'

Seeing my face fall, Matthau conceded, 'You're right. It's not great, is it?' – and told me to come and see him again after the meal. Throughout which he sat furiously scribbling away ... what turned out to be his post-prandial speech, when presenting a lifetime achievement award to his old pal Howard Koch, screenwriter of many memorable movies including the immortal *Casablanca*.

When the lunch finally ended, I hung around for a while as Matthau was mobbed by admirers and thought, *Well, it was a thrill just to meet him, I shouldn't push my luck here.* As I was slinking off, without wishing to bother the great man any further, that unmistakable voice yelled after me: 'Hey, Holden, where d'you think you're going? I got something for you.'

Matthau came towards me with his place card, which he handed over to me, saying, 'Will *this* do?' On the back of it, he had written: '*Big Deal* is the best book about poker I've ever read.'

I thanked him profusely, of course, and the quote duly appeared on the front cover of the American paperback, alongside: 'Precise, provocative and enlightening. A "must" for every poker player's library' – Telly Savalas. Yes, I seemed to be on a roll.

While spending so much time in that part of the world, it was easy enough to nip over to Vegas to front a TV documentary about poker, including extensive footage from the 1991 World Series. For some time now I had been on a personal mission to persuade TV bosses that poker could be as big on television as snooker had proved; after countless tut-tuts and blank looks, I finally got a commission from Alan Yentob, then controller of BBC2, to make a pilot for a series entitled *Anthony Holden on Poker*.

Playing for the cameras in the 1991 main event, I again found myself up against Savalas, who gave me a very charming on-camera interview. To the persistent mantra of the pros – that the world title meant everything, and the prize money was irrelevant – he echoed my own feelings: 'A million dollars is *never* irrelevant!' After I was knocked out, he was even filmed chasing me to the casino exit and pulling me back in an attempt to stop me leaving – 'No, Tony, don't go, don't go' – which inexplicably wound up on the cutting-room floor when the film was finally broadcast – the pilot, as it turned out, for a series that never materialised.

Back in Hollywood for the 1992 Oscars, I also found myself pulled out from behind the rope keeping the press at bay by a beaming Anthony Hopkins, a Best Actor nominee (and indeed winner) that year for his Hannibal Lecter in *The Silence of the*

Lambs, who remembered me from our Olivier encounters. So thrilled was he to have a studio limo that he took me for a ride along the freeway, asking the driver to stop so we could goggle at a giant roadside hoarding bearing his face fifty feet high. 'Look at that!' he said to me, awestruck. 'I've got to savour this moment. It's not going to last, you know . . .'

So what did the roll-call of Hollywood's winners and losers tell us about the history of the movies, about the development of the major art form to have emerged from the United States in the twentieth century?

In the end, I concluded, not a great deal. By my reckoning, the Academy Awards amounted to Hollywood's annual general meeting, a televised promotion of its values, which were about power, intrigue, the fickleness of fame and, above all, money. The Oscars were a high-stakes game orchestrated by the studios to advertise their wares and swell their profits; the films and performers honoured by the Academy tended to be those reflecting the American dream invented and nurtured by Hollywood. It was thus only logical that the Awards bore the same relationship to artistic standards as did that dream to the everyday lives of most Americans. If film is an edited version of life, the Oscars are generally given to those who interpret life as Academy members would like to see it – not necessarily as the rest of us would like to see it, and least of all as it actually is.

That was the solemn bit. The book's success – and it did indeed prove another bestseller – was fuelled by name-dropping anecdotes, to the point where the *Los Angeles Times* lauded its 750 pages for 'more fun facts than you can shake a stick at'.

THE TARNISHED TIARA

Queen Elizabeth II may have suffered an 'annus horribilis' in 1992, with the demise of three of her four children's marriages capped by the taxpayers' refusal to pay for the fire damage at Windsor Castle, casting doubt on the whole absurd institution of monarchy, as chronicled in my wilfully subversive book *The Tarnished Crown*. But my own personal horizons were broadening happily despite the onset of middle age.

Apart from my translations of Greek poetry and Italian operas, I had so far written biographies of a poisoner, a prince, an actor, a poker player (myself) and . . . what next? How best to continue enjoying my work while reflecting my absurdly wide range of interests and enthusiasms? A writer? A painter? A sportsman? A musician?

I was busy pondering this pleasant problem when one of my publishers happened to mention that 1993 would mark the centenary of the death of Tchaikovsky. Ever since my grandfather's gift of his first piano concerto while I was at Oxford, I had been an ardent admirer of the Russian composer's work, not just his familiar concerti and symphonies, but also some exquisite, if much less well-known songs and chamber music. All too often derided as *too* popular a composer, his work dismissed as chocolate-box kitsch, Tchaikovsky was to my mind one of the greatest of all melodists and certainly the most accomplished of orchestrators. There was also the tantalising mystery of his death at the age of only fifty-three, in disputed circumstances. Throw in the chance to spend some time exploring Russia, and this seemed an irresistible opportunity.

In recent years my work had been taking me away from Cindy too much, far more than either of us would have wished, so she joined me on an exploratory trip to Boris Yeltsin's Russia in the summer of 1992.

After visiting Tchaikovsky's home at Klin, 50 miles north of Moscow, we were strolling along the ramparts of the Kremlin one day when we bumped into – of all people – Eddy Shah, who was as surprised to see us there as were we to see him, and invited us back to his hotel for a drink.

Researching the local landscape for a novel he had in mind, Eddy had that morning bumped into the historian David Irving, who was staying in the same hotel; they were meeting up for dinner that evening. What did we know of him? We told Eddy to sup with a very long spoon.

That same evening we ourselves had arranged to have dinner with Peter Pringle, then based in Moscow for *The Independent*. Enterprising to a fault, as always, Pringle used our inside info to track down Irving and shadow him around Moscow. Between us, we managed to establish that Irving was in hot pursuit of the recently discovered diaries of Hitler's propaganda minister, Joseph Goebbels. He had a six-figure deal to pass hitherto unseen extracts to the *Sunday Times* for publication later that year. All of this Pringle revealed in *The Independent* later that week, reporting that Irving had been seen trawling through the complete Goebbels diaries in the Moscow Archives, where they had lain unnoticed since the war. All of which led to a serious falling-out between Irving and the *Sunday Times*.

Back in Blighty, I travelled to Hampshire to consult a global authority on Tchaikovsky, Professor David Brown, who had written a four-volume musical biography of the composer, and was handily available at Southampton University. This genial scholar was warmly welcoming to a populist scribe invading his specialist patch, especially when it came to my new theory about Tchaikovsky's death.

The received wisdom, dating from the first biography by his brother Modest, was that the composer had died of cholera after drinking a glass of untreated water during an outbreak of the disease in St Petersburg. But fresh information had recently been brought to the west by a Russian musicologist named Alexandra Orlova. She had new evidence, which she passed on to me at her home in New Jersey, that Tchaikovsky had been condemned to death by a 'court of honour' convened by his contemporaries at St Petersburg's School of Jurisprudence, the Eton of Russia.

Although tortured by his homosexuality – to the point of trying to disguise it by making a disastrous marriage to an infatuated former student, which soon had him vainly attempting suicide in the River Neva – the composer had recently embarked on an affair with the nephew of a nobleman, a kinsman to the Tsar. At a secret trial three days after he had conducted the first performance of his sixth symphony, the *Pathétique*, he was given an ultimatum by his school contemporaries: either he was dead within a week, or they would report his secret to the Tsar. Six days later, on 6 November 1893, Tchaikovsky lay dead by his own hand. Arsenic-like rat poison accurately enough simulated the symptoms of cholera.

One thing I must always do when writing these biographies is visit the landscapes in which they are set, the places where my subjects lived their lives – right down, metaphorically, to smelling the very grass they trod. So when the BBC invited me to make a documentary about Tchaikovsky for its arts series *Omnibus*, I mentioned this to Professor Brown, and he immediately asked with a modest smile: 'Could I please be your research assistant?'

'Er,' said I, puzzled. 'I fear I'm my own researcher, actually. Why would you ask that?'

'I've always wanted to go to Klin,' he replied forlornly.

'You've never been to Klin?' I asked him in stark disbelief.

'I've never been to Russia,' replied the biographer of Glinka and Mussorgsky as well as those four volumes on Tchaikovsky.

Stunned as I was by this revelation, it was in its way yet another reminder that my school of biography was really that of the overgrown journalist. I could not oblige him, alas, as I then spent several months in Moscow and St Petersburg at the BBC's expense, often travelling on the overnight train between the two in the company of my ebullient director, John Purdie (who had also directed my poker documentary in Las Vegas), and a superb crew from the Russian studio, Mosfilm.

Over boozy dinners on the train, in characteristically Russian style, they would propose many a toast in vodka, to the point where I was rendered all but insensible. 'Right,' said Purdie towards the end of one such evening, to the astonishment of all, 'now we're going to do some work.' Thus did the film acquire its opening scene, in which I am tossing and turning in the bed of my compartment, suffering 'a biographer's nightmare' – as in trying to solve the riddle of Tchaikovsky's death. Ever since I have been able to boast of appearing topless on BBC television.

The annual summer festival of the 'White Nights' in St Petersburg, when the sun still burns bright at midnight, meant that we could film pretty much all night as well as all day – to Purdie's delight, if not my own. As well as wearing me out, this award-winning veteran had another bright idea – that my voiceover could do all the work in this unfolding pictorial story, which he would make distinctive with a complete lack of the usual pieces-to-camera. When we got back home the BBC executive newly in charge of *Omnibus*, Nigel Williams, told Purdie he was mad even to think of such a thing. So we were obliged to embark on a crash course of shots known in the trade as 'cheats'. The viewer would never know it, but the River Neva into which I gazed over a lengthy soliloquy, was in fact the Thames at Richmond; the Russian Orthodox Church around which I wandered, thinking aloud, was the Greek Orthodox Church in

Bayswater, and the silver birch trees in Tchaikovsky's garden at Klin, where I spoke to the camera about a biographer's agonies, were in truth a hundred yards from the front door of my own home in Ravenscourt Park, Hammersmith.

That year the Edinburgh Festival laid on a celebration of Tchaikovsky's centenary, for which I was obliged to return home early from our summer vacation at Cape Cod, thus missing Cindy's fortieth birthday. I made amends, I very much hoped, by renting a plane to write 'Happy Birthday' plus her name in the azure sky in my absence. This also happened to be the August day on which a British tabloid started yet another royal scandal by printing a picture of Sarah, Duchess of York, having her toes sucked by her 'financial adviser'. For me, it was the day I was required to give a lecture on Tchaikovsky in Edinburgh's Queen's Hall, where I noticed my old friend Magnus Linklater, by then editor of *The Scotsman*, sitting in the front row. Afterwards, when we went for a drink, Magnus began – in the feigned Scottish accent which usually heralds some witticism: 'Mr Holden, that was an extremely fascinating talk about the great Russian composer Pyotr Ilyich Tchaikovsky . . . .' Pause. 'But what I really wanted to ask you is what the Queen said to Fer-r-r-r-gie over breakfast at Balmoral this morning . . .'

Touchingly, Magnus was representing the spirit of our mutual friend David Blundy, who would have teased me mercilessly about the very thought of writing a life of Tchaikovsky. Just as incongruously, meanwhile, Harold Evans was talking to Madonna in New York about myself and Tchaikovsky; as the new president and publisher of Random House, where he was publishing a book by her at the same time as my own, Harry was characteristically trying to pioneer the logical art of tucking a CD inside the dust jacket of a book with a musical theme. Reporting that he had sat there with Madonna, blithely co-inspecting naked pictures of her, he asked me to come up with some ideas for such a CD; so I made him a tape of selected Tchaikovsky extracts, which he said he much enjoyed as he drove from Manhattan to his weekend house on Long Island. But in the end, alas, nothing came of Harry's bright idea.

My new theory about Tchaikovsky's death – elaborating on the information given me by Orlova, and approved by Professor Brown, in my BBC film as well as my book – caused quite a stir among (mostly expat) Russian scholars. One of them, Alexander Poznansky, debated the issue with me at a special conference in Tübingen, Germany, and eventually wrote a whole book attacking mine. Another, Richard Taruskin, was still taking me to task more than twenty years later in the correspondence columns of the *Times Literary Supplement*.

While filming my BBC documentary in Tchaikovsky's home at Klin, I was refused entry into the official archive by its curator, Polina Vaidman, whose lips also remained sealed about the composer's sexuality. All of twenty-five years later in mid-2018, her successors finally sanctioned publication of letters long stored therein which revealed not just Tchaikovsky's homosexuality, but the extent of the agonies it caused him. Said their Russian-born editor Marina Kostalevsky, associate professor of Russian at Bard College, New York: '*The Tchaikovsky Papers* offers the reader a personal tour through the private quarters of Tchaikovsky to his most informal and intimate zone. The book keeps open the door unlocked only recently by the keepers of the house-museum in Klin.'

Following the revelation that the princess herself had been the source for Andrew Morton's book *Diana: Her True Story*, Prince Charles broke with royal tradition by authorising a biography in an attempt to salvage his damaged reputation. It was to be written by Jonathan Dimbleby, son of the veteran BBC broadcaster Richard, whose unctuous tones had become synonymous with grand royal occasions even before those of his older son, David. When the *Sunday Times* rang to ask what I thought about this, I said off the top of my head: 'It just goes to show that monarchy isn't the only hereditary job in this country.' Which swiftly found its way into sundry Quotes of the Week columns, so infuriating Jonathan that he stopped speaking to me for several years.

Having left behind my more reckless gambling habits since discovering the favourable odds offered by poker, I found myself sorely tempted by the arrival in the mid-1990s of the fiendish new thrills of sports 'spread betting', which adapted the fine arts of buying and selling shares on the stock market to the more colourful world of sport. Having watched with close interest for some time without actually taking the plunge, I finally succumbed in April 1994 when one of the pioneers of this new art form, Sporting Index, predicted that the West Indian batsman Brian Lara would score a total of 80 in the forthcoming Test match against England in Antigua. If you thought Lara would score less than that, you would 'sell' him for, say, £10 a run, netting £800 if he were out for a duck; if more, you would 'buy' him and hope for the best. My researches revealed Lara's average for the series so far to be 75, so 80 for both innings seemed a gross underestimate. So I 'bought' Lara for £10 a run. The most I could lose, in the unlikely event that he were out for a duck, was £800. Once he reached 80, however, I would start to make a profit at £10 a run.

This turned out be the momentous occasion Lara broke the world record, taking all of three days to score 375. Once he had passed 80, every run was worth £10, every boundary £40 and the occasional six £60. All weekend we entertained friends with champagne to watch the match with us and enjoy our good fortune with every boundary, my winnings mounting with every run. Throw in the fact that I had 'sold' some of the England bowlers, to back my hunch about the batsman, and I wound up making a profit of more than £4,000.

It turned out to be the biggest win in the history of the new art of sports spread betting, as noted in sundry newspaper diary columns. A few days later I received a phone call from the finance director of Sporting Index, inviting me to be the company's guest in its box at Lord's for the next county match; I should come even if rain stopped play, he said, as there was going to be an expert lecture about the fine art of spread betting on sports. I'd love to, said I, and I'll look forward to the talk. 'That's good,' he replied, 'because you're giving it!'

After a few more such sorties into this hazardous world, with largely positive results, I could not resist such witty innovations as the 'magic sponge' bet in a football match, i.e. buying or selling by the minute whether the club physio – the man with the sponge – would come on to the pitch before or after, say, 20 minutes. After more highly fortuitous success in this field, I was eventually invited to lunch by the man who had pioneered the whole idea, Jonathan Sparke, chairman of Sporting's main rival, City Index – with whom I had fun venturing beyond sport to such zany ideas as the 'Charles–Diana divorce index', in which the punter would buy or sell by so much per month whether or not this recently separated couple would finally do the unprecedented (for the heir to the throne) thing by filing for divorce. Before long, Jonathan hired me as a consultant to develop more such ideas – for a, dare I say, princely four figures a month. On top of my book royalties and newspaper work, that sure beat gambling!

1995 saw the release of *The Young Poisoner's Handbook*, a film version of my 1974 book about the serial poisoner Graham Young, with Young played by an Irish newcomer called Hugh O'Conor, and Antony Sher as the well-meaning but reckless psychiatrist who secured him early release from Broadmoor.

Ten years later, in November 2005, it was reported that a sixteen-year-old Japanese schoolgirl was arrested for poisoning her mother with thallium after seeing the film. She had kept a diary, recording dosages and their effects – just like Young, by whom she was said to be obsessed. This made me feel uneasy enough; but I then read that investigators had also found a copy of my book in her room, which had me feeling as guilty as if I had poisoned her mother myself.

In November 1995 Princess Diana gave her jaw-dropping interview to Martin Bashir of the BBC's *Panorama*. I was invited into the *Newsnight* studio to watch it with Margaret Jay, who had become friends with Diana through their work on AIDS, and Nicholas Soames, a close friend of Charles, before commenting on live TV immediately after it finished. 'Don't worry,' I reassured an anxious Margaret as it began, 'I can't believe she's going to say anything too outspoken.'

We then watched aghast as Diana's forlorn portrait of 'three people in this marriage' steadily and sensationally unfolded, climaxing with her opinion that Charles was not up to 'the top job'. I was the only member of the panel, of course, who volubly agreed with all this and indeed everything else she said, to the point where Soames, who had dismissed her onscreen as paranoid, asked me why I had 'deserted' his prince. 'He deserted me,' I replied – in a suave adaptation, to my mind, of the defiant words of Shakespeare's Coriolanus to his fellow Romans – which was entirely lost, of course, on Soames.

Above my desk hangs, as it has for some thirty years, a quote from one of my long-time heroes, the political activist and philosopher Thomas Paine: 'I have always considered monarchy to be a silly, contemptible thing. I compare it to something kept behind a curtain, about which there is a great deal of bustle and fuss, and a wonderful air of seeming solemnity, but when, by any accident, the curtain happens to open, and the company see what it is, they burst into laughter.'

In the mid-1990s I co-founded a pressure group called Common Sense, after Paine's 1776 pamphlet urging America's founding fathers to declare independence from Britain. Our primary objective, in accordance with our motto 'Votes, not genes', was to replace the hereditary monarchy with a democratically elected head of state. Other founder members included the public relations guru Brian Basham, the journalists Roy Greenslade, Jonathan Freedland, Simon Fanshawe and the hon. sec. and president of the campaign group Republic; before long we had also co-opted the lawyers Geoffrey Robertson and Michael Mansfield. Resigned to charges of champagne socialism, we met once a month in the private dining room upstairs at the chic L'Etoile restaurant in Charlotte Street, for a dinner to which each member would bring a guest in a position to influence public opinion: politicians, newspaper editors, broadcasters, columnists, lawyers.

We did succeed in persuading some editors to run republican sentiments in their editorials, such as *The Guardian*, *The Independent* and *The Economist*. On one occasion I brought along the American biographer Kitty Kelley, thus earning an honourable mention in her 1997 book *The Royals* – which I chose as my Book of the Year in *The Observer* not least because it was not published in the UK.

At the time I contemplated writing a biography of Paine, but 1995 saw the publication of a comprehensive one by the Australian academic John Keane. With other members of Common Sense, however, I did get involved in a campaign to erect a statue of Paine across the road from the House of Commons. We were much aided in this endeavour by Richard Attenborough, who had long wanted to make a Gandhi-style epic about Paine, which already had a script by Trevor Griffiths and awaited only the return of his chosen star, Daniel Day-Lewis, from a mysteriously prolonged absence from the screen. One memorable evening in west London we hosted a fundraising event at which the speakers included the Labour leader Michael Foot, and Kenneth Griffith showed his BBC documentary film about Paine, unambiguously entitled *The Most Valuable Englishman Ever*.

Around this time I was invited to speak at the annual general meeting of Republic. When I accepted, I had no idea that I would be required to follow one of the great public speakers of the moment, Tony Benn – only because he had to hurry off to another engagement. I sat alongside Benn while he marshalled an argument of his customary elegance, and then stood to begin my speech as he was leaving the hall.

'I naturally agree with every word we have just heard from the ever eloquent Mr Benn,' I began. 'There is only one policy of his with which I have always disagreed . . .' To my alarm, I saw Benn pause en route to the exit to hear what I might be about to say. With no choice but to carry on, I continued: 'He is an Antony who has spent his entire life trying to become a Tony, while I am an Anthony, who has fought a long, hard battle *not* to become a Tony – largely, alas, in vain.'

Laughter, in Hansard's perennial phrase, ensued – except from the sometime Viscount Stansgate, who proceeded on his way unamused.

At much the same time, I was working on a radical Channel 4 documentary with my old friend Christopher Hird and his colleague Dan Chambers about Britain being declared a republic. Christo was capitalising on the success of his Channel 4 film *The Unruly House of Windsor* – in which I had talked, post-the 'Camillagate' tapes, about the urgent need for Charles to 'Tippex the Tampax'. This time Jon Snow agreed to present the programme as a quasi-Channel 4 news bulletin announcing who had been elected the first president of the British republic, with a starry cast getting up to such high jinks as the *Standard* art critic Brian Sewell chairing a *salon des refusés* to sift out the best of the royal art collection for display in museums converted from palaces under the stewardship of Melvyn Bragg. This was to be part of the multi-faceted build-up to the election of a president popular enough to prove that he or she does not have to be, as then so often argued, a clapped-out politician. A deliberately odd assortment of candidates ranged from the Labour peer Helena Kennedy and Virgin boss Richard Branson to ex-hostage Terry Waite and champion boxer Frank Bruno; but we were still debating who should win when Channel 4, for reasons best known to themselves, got cold feet and pulled out of the project.

In those days, before the men in suits tightened their hold over British newspapers, most editors hated the freelance contracts selectively handed out by their executives. They came with a guaranteed minimum annual income, which the contributor so rarely seemed to earn. While I'd been freelancing for (among others) the *Daily Mail*, I was guaranteed a handsome five-figure minimum per annum. Over the previous three years, thanks largely to the long-running Wars of the Waleses, I had in fact been earning more than twice that much a year from this source alone.

When the time came for the annual renewal, I received a phone call from the *Mail*'s features editor, Richard Addis. He was about to go into the editor, he told me, to see if he could up my annual guarantee to the higher figure. Was this all right with me? You bet it was.

An hour or so later, Richard rang again. 'Have you,' he asked, 'been attacking the monarchy on some TV programme?' He well knew, I replied, of my republican convictions; and, yes, I continued to appear on television to maintain my street cred in this and other areas to do with whatever book I was writing.

'Well, I'm sorry, Tony, but the editor saw you on some such show the other night, and he wasn't at all pleased. So I'm afraid I couldn't get you that higher number we were after – or, actually, even a renewal of the usual one. In fact, I'm frightfully sorry and all that, old chap, but you're fired.'

This was, to say the least, a monumental setback to the Holden household's domestic budget. I was still brooding about it a few weeks later when he rang again. 'Hi, it's Richard. I don't know whether you've heard, but I've just been made editor of the *Express*. I'd like to offer you a weekly column . . . for, yes, that figure the *Mail* wouldn't pay you!' This, he told me, was the first call he had made since sitting down at his editorial desk. 'Oh,' he continued, 'and you'd better come in and discuss it over lunch as soon as possible – in fact, can you make it tomorrow? – as I suspect the new proprietor is about to close down the editorial dining room.' As indeed did Lord (Clive) Hollick when his United Media group bought the *Express* soon after. My Monday musings were soon embellished by the heading 'Anthony Holden – The Man In The Know', which of course caused much merriment at sundry inquisitive dinner tables.

At the same time my old pal Brian MacArthur had become travel editor of *The Times*, which was to prove the source of countless first-class (literally) freebies for the next few years. The first was a trip for two on the Orient Express to Cindy's and my beloved Venice, complete with a suite at the Cipriani which had recently hosted Jimmy Carter for a summit with Giscard d'Estaing. There followed an African safari and sundry wonderful journeys from the South Sea Islands to Australia (where I could visit my son Sam on his gap year), Fiji (where I contemplated a lurid history of cannibalism, another bright idea never fulfilled), Western Samoa, the Cook Islands, Bali and Lombok, not to mention several trips to the Caribbean with Cindy which we both relished so much as to give me an especially bright idea.

Over one of my regular lunches with MacArthur, I told him I had a suggestion which would make him insanely jealous, but he would not be able to turn me down. It would even make that rarity for travel journalism, a four-page pull-out. 'What on earth can that be?' he asked in bewilderment. 'Diana's guide to the Caribbean,' I told him with a grotesquely smug grin. Since her separation from Charles, the princess had been all over the Caribbean, to half a dozen different versions of paradise around its sun-drenched beaches – all, naturally, of the very highest quality, beyond the reach of the paparazzi. Poor Brian was lost for words; he could see what an irresistible notion this was for his travel section, and admitted he had no alternative but to give me carte blanche. He would fix up all the necessary trips for me via the relevant tourist boards and airlines. When I came back to him with the comprehensive list, we realised that it would take us three separate trips, each with ten days at two different destinations, from the K Club in Barbuda to Richard Branson's Necker Island.

About to embark on one of these trips, I happened to spy a

comic actor I much admired waiting for the same flight. Once aboard, John Fortune and his wife Emma turned out to be sitting next to us. Looking for an excuse to start a conversation, I noticed that he seemed extremely nervous, gripping the armrests of his seat as if his life depended on it. 'You all right?' I enquired gently after take-off.

'Not at all,' he replied. 'I hate flying. It's just like going into hospital. You don't want to go in the first place, but they herd you in and strap you down . . . then, after a while, they come down the aisle with a trolley laden with things to make you feel better.' At which point, he started helping himself to miniature bottles of vodka from the trolley which had just arrived to prove his point. The camp BA steward looked at him quizzically and said: 'No, don't tell me . . . you're on telly, aren't you? And you're funny . . .'

'I *try* to be,' replied John solemnly.

Looking at me beside him, the steward asked, 'Are you the other one?' Amused though I was to be mistaken for John Bird, I ignored the question and simply helped myself to some miniature bottles of gin. There ensued a nine-hour flight to Antigua so fuelled by booze and laughter that I said to Cindy on arrival: 'That was a really wonderful holiday. Can we go home again now?'

And so began another enduring friendship, with a supremely smart and witty man who turned out to be a neighbour in west London. Not until a dozen years later, and John's funeral in Hampshire after his sadly premature demise, did I get the chance to tell John Bird that I'd been mistaken for him a mile high, or indeed their TV partner Rory Bremner of the curious consolation afforded by throwing a shovelful of soil onto a friend's coffin just after it has been lowered into the grave.

In 1993 I appeared on Radio 4's *Start the Week* with Melvyn Bragg. I was in the middle of my now familiar mantra that a grown-up democracy should elect its head of state when, of all people, John Mortimer protested, saying that he rather liked the monarchy, as it added to the gaiety of the nation; and besides, we would only get some clapped-out politician living in Buckingham Palace as the elected president of a republican Britain.

'Not at all, John,' I replied genially. 'You're a distinguished lawyer as well as a writer, a proud Brit, and you wouldn't charge us eight quid a head to visit a palace that belongs to us. So what about President Mortimer?'

'Oh, d'you really think so?' he replied with a bashful grin. 'Okay, you've converted me!'

Having improvised this crafty tactic entirely by chance, I began to use it unsparingly, and always with the required result. David Frost was taking me to task on one of his TV panel shows, for instance, to the effect that I wasn't just the guy who wanted to sink the royal yacht, but also to install a clapped-out politician in Buckingham Palace as Britain's elected president.

'Not at all,' I replied without hesitation, 'what about President Frost?'

'Ooh,' said he, preening himself, 'do you really think so?'

Case made. Again and again – to the point where one of the monarchy's most vociferous champions, Norman St John Stevas, had heard me make it once too often when we appeared on opposite sides of a TV debate chaired by Jeremy Paxman. I was flanked by Tony Banks MP and Mike Mansfield, he by Bernard Ingham and David Starkey. When we reached the issue of clapped-out politicians, I said for the umpteenth time: 'No, Norman, what about President Stevas?'

By now he was ready for me. This time he replied with a mischievous grin: 'Well, thank you, Anthony, but actually I'd rather be monarch!'

'Perhaps so, Norman,' said his colleague Starkey. 'But would you be King or would you be Queen?'

Given the turbulence through which the monarchy struggled in the early 1990s, there was no escape from my reluctant role as a royal commentator. While chronicling it all for, among others, the *Daily Mail*, I had become good friends with its royal specialist

Richard Kay, who was well known to be the favourite journalist of Diana, Princess of Wales.

Naturally, like all journalists, we indulged in regular expense-account lunches. In February 1993 Richard invited me to meet him for one such at San Lorenzo, the fashionable restaurant off Knightsbridge, known to be a favourite of Diana's, at the curiously precise time of 12.50 p.m. I noticed that the large table to our right, with places laid for six, was the only one in the entire restaurant adorned with a vase of flowers. On the stroke of 1 p.m., the whole joint paused to gasp as in she walked: yes, Diana herself, with her two small sons and her close friend Lucia Flecha de Lima, wife of the Brazilian ambassador to London. With a shriek of delighted surprise that would have deceived any onlooker – and I had noticed one or two familiar faces around the room – she headed straight over to our corner table and said: 'What are you two boys doing here? What a coincidence! Why don't you come and join us?' Thus were all six seats at her own nearby table suddenly filled.

Diana, it turned out, wanted to thank me for my sympathetic cover story about her which had just appeared in the US magazine *Vanity Fair*. I told her that she would be getting a chapter to herself in a caustic post-'annus horribilis' book I was busy finishing, to be called *The Tarnished Crown*.

'Perhaps', she laughed, 'it should be called *The Tarnished Tiara*!'

On the contrary, I replied, I was going to christen her 'the People's Princess'. As indeed I did in the title of the chapter devoted to her in that book, long before Tony Blair hijacked the phrase in the aftermath of her death four years later.

I complimented Diana on letting her young boys run happily around the restaurant, in and out between the tables, like any other high-spirited children, which no other royal would ever have allowed. The conversation floated merrily along until, as the happy party broke up, Lucia handed each of the young princes a £50 note. 'Oh look, boys,' cooed their mother, 'pink grannies!'

This turned out to be the first in a series of such lunches with Diana around her favourite London restaurants, where it was clear that she was prepared to trust Richard's and my judgement as to whether we wound up publishing any tit-bits in our respective columns. One day, for instance, she turned up to announce that she had just had a phone call from Kevin Costner, a 'ghastly' man who said he was looking for a public figure willing to co-star with him in a sequel to *The Bodyguard*, the hit film he had just made with the singer Whitney Houston. And he had come up with the 'preposterous' idea that she, Diana, might be interested. 'Pass it on to Fergie!' we both suggested.

On another occasion, she turned up with her mother, Frances Shand-Kydd, with whom the tabloids were saying that she wasn't on speaking terms. Diana had just heard that she herself had won the award for the Best Teeth in the World. She joined in our laughter at the absurdity of it all, handing the credit to her mother, with a gleeful cry of 'Show 'em your gnashers, Mum!'

Not a word of these lunches ever appeared in any gossip column, or I suspect they would have been promptly discontinued. Until the day the diary column of the London *Evening Standard* reported that I had been seen lunching with the princess at Kensington Place, the chic eatery near the *Standard*'s offices. My blonde and beautiful (if marginally older) literary agent, Gill Coleridge, was duly flattered.

The Tarnished Crown was published in the States by Random House, where Harry Evans was determined to be a trailblazing boss. He tried hard to dissuade me from advocating the abolition of the royal train, pleading that his father had once been its driver; as touching as I found this, I could only demur. At which point he called in his marketing team and told them: 'We are going to take out a full-page advert for this book in the *New York Times*, saying that if it doesn't tell you everything you always wanted to know about the British royal family, you can have your money back.' There were horrified gasps from his underlings, over whose protests Harry insisted on his bright idea – and, long after the advert had indeed appeared, reassured me that no one had applied for a refund.

All my life I have loved playing cricket, taking pride in such skills as a wicketkeeper as I first developed in my schooldays. In the 1970s I had kept wicket for the *Sunday Times* team which played regular matches on Mondays, our day off, against other Sunday newspapers, who often had stellar ex-professionals as their cricket correspondents. Playing against the *Sunday Express*, for instance, I was once thrilled to catch out Denis Compton, and against the *Sunday Telegraph* I managed to stump the former England captain Tony Lewis.

By the mid-1990s, as I approached the age of fifty, I was also playing for teams put together by my accountants and indeed by a classical musical agency. One Saturday in the summer of 1996 I was representing the latter in a match in Munich played, appropriately enough, in the Englischer Garten against a team calling itself the M.C.C. – as in Munich Cricket Club, run by Peter Jonas, then artistic director of the city's Bavarian State Opera, whom I had first got to know as manager of English National Opera. J Morley naturally turned up to watch his old friend's dexterity at the crease, only to wait for some time before seeing me out first ball while attempting a reckless leg sweep. Keeping wicket thereafter to erratic bowling from middle-aged men left me with sundry aches and pains, not to mention a severe backache – which lasted long enough for me to decide with the greatest reluctance that this was finally the time to hang up my gloves.

At much the same time, my devotion to Arsenal FC was broadening out into yet another social indulgence. For years a few of us had met for lunch before home games in a restaurant inside the club, then still based at Highbury Stadium, where part of the entertainment was an array of comedians, who were often the highlight of the day – until one Saturday in the mid-1990s, this went seriously wrong. My guest that day was a member of my Tuesday night poker game, a Chelsea fan called Rudi Nassauer who always took me to Stamford Bridge when we were playing there, so I annually returned the compliment. He just happened to be Jewish, and on this occasion the comic inexplicably launched into a string of anti-Semitic jokes. Appalled, I led a hasty exit amid profuse apologies. Rudi responded very graciously, even telling me the best Jewish joke I have ever heard (which I won't risk repeating here) by way of making amends.

All the same, I decided it was time to stop eating at the club's restaurant, and move elsewhere. Between us, we found a welcoming Italian trattoria, conveniently midway between Highbury and the new Emirates Stadium to which Arsenal moved in 2006, called San Daniele del Friuli (to us, 'San Dan'). Here we hijacked the long table at the back of the room, large enough to seat a dozen of us. For more than twenty years, until the restaurant's eventual closure, half a dozen Gooner friends including Melvyn Bragg, Alan Samson, myself and others brought along guests, ranging from our sons to head-turning celebrities to the point where San Dan was filled with Arsenal supporters at lunches before every home game – and even the manager, Arsène Wenger, with some members of the team after midweek evening matches.

During these 'Rave Square' years, as they became known, my sons were advancing through their teens, and I would often arrive home of an evening to the sight of my offspring and their friends lounging around the dining table smoking, drinking and playing poker. This would have me on the verge of an auto-parental 'How many times have I told you not to . . .' before realising that I didn't have a leg to stand on, and so changing my tune, with a shrug, to: 'Hey, deal me in!'

Always an earlier riser than me, Cindy would have written half a chapter of a novel before joining me for the black coffee that constituted my breakfast. One such morning – while discussing, as usual, what the day ahead held – I replied gloomily, 'Oh, some boring lunch I'd rather get out of . . . can't remember who with . . . You?'

'Same thing,' she replied. So we both disappeared to our respective studies to check our diaries, only to return with the news that we were apparently due to lunch with each other. It was our wedding anniversary, and we had both forgotten.

Later that day, after returning from a laughter-fuelled lunch with my beloved wife, I thought, 'My God, I've got the perfect marriage!'

'SHOW US YOU CARE'

In the autumn of 1996 – nine months, as it was to prove, before her death – I received a phone call from Diana, Princess of Wales. I was due to lunch with her a couple of days later; she was most dreadfully sorry, but could she possibly postpone? She'd been invited by her friend Dr Magdi Yacoub to watch him performing a heart operation. If she was going to help heart patients in recovery, as was her intent, she should really see what they've been through, shouldn't she? She was sure I would understand.

As, of course, I did – not least because the lunch was rescheduled for the following week. And this time it would not be, as usual, with others in a public restaurant; it would be just the two of us, in her apartment at Kensington Palace. Her divorce was finalised; her £17 million settlement was safely in the bank; now she could entertain whomever she liked – even public enemies (in the eyes of her ex-husband and his family) such as myself – without fear of reprisals.

As the big day approached, I had my sole suit dry-cleaned, and Cindy was thoughtful enough to present me with a new tie for the occasion. I also borrowed the new car I had recently bought her – much smarter than my battered old banger – and drove the few miles to the palace. Having passed the entrance exam at the security lodge, and negotiated the longish drive, I was scrunching the gravel outside Diana's front door when I realised I had no idea how to work the car's new-fangled security system. It required a PIN number I did not know. I was still faffing around with all this, trying to lock the thing before my big date, when a voice behind me said: 'I don't think you need to worry too much about that, sir. I think you'll find your car will be perfectly safe here.' He nodded towards sundry policemen lurking in the trees.

This was Paul Burrell, the butler who became known as Diana's 'rock', later put on trial at the Old Bailey for allegedly stealing her property before the Queen suddenly remembered, just as the defence evidence was starting to turn ugly, that he'd told her he had some of the late princess's possessions for safekeeping. Was this the only trial in British legal history to be abandoned, and the case dismissed, on the word of a witness who didn't even bother to come to court? Well, they are Her Majesty's courts, after all . . .

As Burrell showed me up the imposing staircase to Diana's private quarters, I could hear a Mozart piano concerto tinkling in the background. In response to the faintest upward twitch of my eyebrow, Burrell said, 'Yes, sir, she loves music, especially classical music.' When I was shown into the presence – and offered a respectful bow, as the royals had stripped her of her HRH and so of the *obligation* to bow to her – I checked this out by presenting her with a copy of my Tchaikovsky biography and asking if she liked his music. 'Oh yes,' she replied, 'especially the symphonies.' I was soon to discover that this meant not just, as in my case, the celebrated 4, 5 and 6; the princess could actually tell apart, more readily than the composer's biographer, his much less well-known 1, 2 and 3.

It was Diana's height, as much as her beauty, that lent her such a luminous presence. And it was her mischievous humour that added such charm. Immaculately groomed, as always, she motioned me to a chair and sat down, still clutching my book. 'Oh, you don't have to read it, ma'am.' I volunteered. 'Just leave it lying around on your coffee table for your visitors to see.'

'I *will* read it,' she said. 'No doubt with great pleasure.'

There followed, on both sides, the usual enquiries about

children and so on, with no mention as yet of her ex, before we went through to the adjacent dining room and, once the staff had departed, started talking in earnest. She was later to say to a mutual friend: 'Boy, he really doesn't like Charles, does he?' But she was equally candid about the family into which she had married. This was the occasion on which she described the Queen Mother as 'the chief leper in the leper colony' – one of the few details that, with her agreement, I later revealed.

I told her, not for the first time, that I thought she was unwise to have dispensed with her 'Palace guard' – the detail of royal security officers which followed her every move before she dismissed them after her celebrated 'time and space' speech, semi-retiring from public life. 'But I just want to live an ordinary private life, as an ordinary private person,' she protested. That, I advised her, would never now be possible. As for her thoughts of going to live in the States, I painted an unhappy picture of her swiftly becoming a latter-day Greta Garbo, lurking in Manhattan doorways to avoid the pursuit of the paparazzi.

There was more in this vein, as a dominant topic developed from my suggestion that she should set up a Diana Foundation to co-ordinate the charity work she was intent on continuing. It was something we had discussed before, and now was the time to do it, now she was free of the royals and all their works. 'Oh, but . . .' she protested. She was just back from a visit to the Clinton White House, during which she had spoken to . . . 'If you'll forgive me dropping a name?' Who the heck could that be? We'd already talked about her dealings with the Queen, the Pope, the President and First Lady of the United States, major rock stars, Hollywood A-listers. I waited, nodding absurdly. 'Well, I was talking to Colin Powell last week, and he really advised against it.'

So the former chairman of the US Joint Chiefs of Staff, not even yet secretary of state, let alone a potential presidential candidate, was Diana's idea of a name-drop? I barely listened to her explanation, broadly to do with onerous legal obligations, as I pondered this striking detail. She had obviously warmed to Powell. The other more celebrated names on our lips were just part of her daily routine. He had, moreover, given her advice she did not necessarily want to hear – for her, unusual.

An adjacent bedroom was partly visible through a half-open door. But this time Diana wasn't flirtatious, as she had been in company, in the safety of public places. No, she asked sweetly after Cindy, whom she had met with their mutual friend Rosa Monckton. I told her of the Caribbean jaunts we were enjoying, thanks to my taking her name in vain, and she promised with a laugh to look out for us over Christmas at the K Club in Barbuda. And so we prattled happily on.

A week or so later, a handwritten letter arrived from the princess, complimenting me on my life of Tchaikovsky, saying that she felt especial sympathy with my account of his unhappy childhood. 'It brought tears to my eyes,' Diana wrote, having suffered a wretched childhood herself. She went on to ask if I had a video of the BBC programme I had recently made about him; could she possibly borrow it? The following day I took my only copy round to the palace, with a note asking for it back at her convenience – highly presumptuous of me with any royal but this one. A few days later a liveried flunkey arrived at our front door to return it with her fulsome thanks.

Was I being exploited, as many of my own close friends charged with only the mildest hint of jealousy? It certainly didn't feel that way to me. I was only too grateful to accept the hand of friendship extended by a delightful woman who had in my view been most cruelly and all too publicly wronged. For all the love she longed to lavish on him, Charles never gave their marriage the slightest chance, blithely continuing his affair with Camilla Parker Bowles before, during and after his few years with Diana – thus bringing on the bulimia and other ailments blamed for their estrangement. By simply shaking hands with an AIDS patient, meanwhile, at a time of woeful public ignorance, Diana had proved herself way ahead of the rest of the Windsors in the crucial art of royal symbolism. She asked nothing of me – though my public sympathy for her suffering was not, I assume, unwelcome.

The following summer she was suddenly no more, to the disbelief of an openly moved and grieving British public, whose emotional outpourings offended some po-faced pundits, but which I found profoundly affecting. Commentating for American television on a platform opposite Buckingham Palace, I explained disapprovingly why there was no flag flying over the Palace, let alone one at half-mast, in the monarch's absence. Meanwhile, my written coverage of events, bemoaning this amid the Queen's apparently heedless absence in Scotland, appeared under the front-page headline 'Show us you care'.

A few days later, a Union Jack suddenly appeared at half-mast above the Palace. Several publications complimented me as the man behind this change of royal protocol. Even the archly royalist *Spectator* spoke of 'the growing outrage, bravely voiced in the first instance by the biographer Anthony Holden, at the apparent lack of emotion being shown by the royal family, particularly the matter of the flag remaining absent at Buckingham Palace'. Within days, 'the flag was present, lowered respectfully, and the poignant scenes of Princes Charles, William and Harry personally talking with public mourners marked a turning-point which is proving crucial for the future of the monarchy'.

For the first time in living memory, the British royals had found themselves on the wrong side of public opinion. Had Tony Blair not come to their rescue, finally persuading them back to London from Balmoral to join the outpouring of public grief, the damage could well have been much worse; the very institution might even have foundered. As it was, the Queen herself bowed her head as Diana's coffin passed, and conversed with mourners handing over flowers – not, for once, for her. But her display of grief was much more manifest some months later as the royal yacht was decommissioned by a Labour government otherwise unwilling, alas, to seize this seminal moment to allow the out-of-touch, out-of-date, out-of-synch monarchy to self-destruct.

At the time I was also faced with the problem of what to write next to complete a three-book contract negotiated for me by Hilary Rubinstein before his retirement. Now, said the publishers, was the perfect moment for a third Charles biography, another decade on; in the circumstances, the demand was irresistible. Having already received the relevant payment, I had no option but to comply, if with the greatest reluctance.

But first, at the suggestion of Harry Evans, I dashed off a short but handsome coffee-table tribute to Diana, lavishly illustrated by the royal photographer Kent Gavin. I declined to accept any payment for this; all UK proceeds went to one of Diana's favourite causes, the Children's Hospital in Great Ormond Street. Around Europe, likewise, the revenue was donated to hospitals specialising in child sickness.

Then it was off to South Africa, to gather fresh material for yet another portrait of Charles, who was there on his first overseas visit since Diana's death, taking along thirteen-year-old Prince Harry to ensure a sympathetic reception. Despite my accreditation for a national paper, Charles's press secretary went to some lengths to prevent me joining the trip, and was as obstructive as possible while we were there, excluding me from the chartered aircraft on which the prince chatted with the press for the first time in a decade. It was during this trip that Charles rounded a bush in some urban park to find me lurking behind it, and reprised the first words he had ever said to me in Canada twenty years earlier: 'What are *you* doing here?'

Despite the context, I was so fascinated to be in South Africa during Nelson Mandela's historic presidency that following Charles around became an irritating distraction. I travelled as widely as possible – Capetown, Johannesburg and Durban, of course, but also humbler townships such as Soweto – to relish the heady post-apartheid atmosphere. At the president's official residence I was honoured to shake the hand of Mandela himself, whom I have long considered one of the noblest figures of the twentieth century. But I then found myself appalled to see the photoshoot hijacked by the Spice Girls, whom Charles and his staff had apparently invited along to sprinkle some surrogate stardust over the dullard prince, and who then proceeded to humiliate South Africa's president by having the nerve to put their arms around him, even kiss him with jejune giggles – which he, of course, had to pretend to enjoy.

On the penultimate evening of the visit, as was its wont, the royal press corps went out for a collective dinner before the main event of the trip, on its last night: a Spice Girls concert in Johannesburg, in the presence of Mandela, Charles and Harry (making his first public appearance since his mother's funeral). Despite my own intermittent membership of this fun-loving group, I was informally elected its doyen in the absence of the late, great James Whitaker of the *Mirror*, who customarily made a florid speech on these occasions. Required to fill in for him, I eventually intoned: 'The future of the British monarchy depends on what Prince Harry wears to the Spice Girls concert tomorrow evening.'

This well-informed, hard-working group looked at me in quizzical wonder. What the blank was Holden talking about? When they asked as much, I continued: 'If Harry wears a T-shirt and jeans, as he used to when attending concerts with his mother, it will mean that the spirit of Diana lives on. If he wears a suit and tie, as his father undoubtedly will, it will mean that the Windsors have won – and Diana's memory is already being expunged.'

The following evening, Harry duly materialised at the concert in a suit and tie. My point was not lost in the subsequent coverage of the event, or indeed in the development of the Windsor story – so turbulent while Diana was still alive, so tranquil after her death until the Harry–Meghan and Andrew–Epstein furores of more than twenty years later.

And so I grimly proceeded to churn out my third biography of the Prince of Wales in as many decades, 'a bizarre and relentless punctuation to both our lives', as I wrote in its Preface. Written to mark his thirtieth, fortieth and fiftieth birthdays, hard on the heels of my own, this dogged trilogy now consisted of three different books about three completely different men. The first was a lonely, confused bachelor, still living at home with his parents as he entered his thirties; the second was a driven but troubled husband, the father of two sons, two-timing a wife he had never loved. The third was a divorced widower, suddenly looking older than his years, and facing a stark choice between his children, the love of his life and the throne – or, by trying to have all three, threatening the very future of the institution that gave his tortured life any meaning.

'It is customary in books like this', I wrote, 'to thank the Prince of Wales's office for its courteous co-operation etc., as I myself have done in the past. On this occasion, alas, it is not appropriate.' *The Guardian* reported Mark Bolland, the prince's then spin-doctor, as having told reporters two months earlier, while on tour in Canada: 'We are always polite when someone approaches us with a book project. Except for Tony Holden. We don't bother being polite to him.' *The Guardian* translated this as 'Sod off', a fair paraphrase of a letter I had received from Bolland declining my invitation to lunch on the grounds that it would be a waste of my time. 'I come with no axes to grind,' he wrote, 'but we do not start from the best of wickets.' Mark and I laughed about this after he too fell out with the prince, and we became firm friends.

Anyone who cared about me knew how little I had wanted to write this book, and what a personal ordeal it had been, so I dedicated it to the Arsenal manager, Arsène Wenger, 'a true prince among men', and the 1997–8 Cup- and League-winning squad, 'whose double kept me going through my treble'. Wenger being an unknown quantity in the States, he was replaced in the American edition by my late editor at Random House, Joe Fox, who would never allow his authors to thank him in their acknowledgements or indeed mention his name at all. I was especially pleased by this chance to make posthumous amends.

The combination of Diana's death in still disputed circumstances and my unprecedented (in print) criticism of Charles inevitably saw me return to television with a vengeance, both in interviews and documentaries, to the point where it had all become an acute embarrassment to me. Even I was sick of the sight of my face on TV. So I took a vow never again to write or speak publicly about the royals.

To which, I am pleased to say, I have since largely stuck. Despite the consequent loss of income, especially in an era replete with yet more royal weddings, babies and indeed scandals, I have been much the happier person for it, proudly parading my republican convictions with a renewed sense of self-respect.

16

BUGGER BIOGRAPHERS

I had a particular challenge in mind when I met my long-time publisher Alan Samson one day in the early 1990s for one of our regular lunches at our favourite London restaurant. I had known Alan since the week my mother died in our house in 1985 – all of which he lived through with us while visiting each day to edit a short book I was writing (and would now rather forget). We were both diehard Arsenal fans, and started going to matches together, as we have ever since. Subsequently, through various incarnations, he had published several of my books at sundry different imprints.

When Alan arrived and sat down, ten minutes late as usual, I told him without any preamble: 'I've got one word to say to you.'

He looked a bit alarmed. 'What's that?'

'Shakespeare.'

Without missing a beat, he replied: 'The book you were born to write.'

Yes, Alan knew me that well. For some years I had been nourishing a quiet ambition to write a life of Shakespeare, a popular and accessible but academically respectable account of the man and his work. But even Hilary Rubinstein had said I was mad to think about so recondite a project; I should keep the bucks rolling in by writing yet another royal biography. Now Hilary had retired, and I had been lucky enough to find his perfect successor in Gill Coleridge of Rogers, Coleridge & White.

In retrospect, I can't quite believe my own chutzpah in even contemplating so formidable a challenge as the immortal if elusive

Bard of Avon. In this particular instance, as I was presumptuous enough to point out in my Preface, I wrote a down-to-earth life of Shakespeare primarily because I wanted to read one.

In previous attempts I had read, mostly by academics, the Bard himself slopes off as his story gets bogged down in rural disputes about the digging of ditches and the mending of fences, non-payment of fines and tithes, the construction and logistics of Elizabethan theatres, even how his contemporaries brushed their teeth, right down to the décor of the guest bedroom of an Oxford tavern where he may or may not have bedded the landlord's wife. Throw in the perennial Fair Youths and Dark Ladies, and the man himself is too often allowed to slip away and watch from the wings, no doubt with a smirk, for whole chapters at a time. I strived to keep him squarely in sight, pin him firmly to the page, no matter how hard he struggled to escape. It was fatal, I soon found, to look away even for a moment. He was gone again, vanished to one of his vividly imaginary horizons.

I could date my passion for Shakespeare right back to my parents' silver wedding anniversary in 1965, when my seventeen-year-old self – relishing compassionate leave from school to join them for a long weekend in London – somewhat upset the happy couple by slipping away early from the celebratory lunch atop the Park Lane Hilton to the impossibly upscale Academy cinema in Oxford Street. I just had to see the new Russian film of *Hamlet*, starring Innokenty Smoktunovsky, which had been favourably compared with Olivier's.

Thirty years on, I also now had the perfect companion to share my obsession, not least because he was then at work on a rather different book about the same writer. The first time I met the eminent critic Frank Kermode, in the mid-1980s, I had launched into a light-hearted anecdote about Shakespeare, specifically *The Winter's Tale*, and my tutor John Jones. Frank listened patiently, then responded with a smile: 'Very amusing. But I'm off duty tonight.'

It wasn't the light-heartedness that bothered Frank, I soon learned, so much as the assumption that on first encounter with anyone he would wish to discuss literature, specifically Shakespeare. As a genial rapport between us grew, and we began to spend more time together, I realised that he had long since grown weary of awestruck interlocutors assuming he would wish to address literary matters at all times. This was naturally true much of the time, but he was equally passionate about a vast range of topics, from music to sport, theatre to cricket, snooker to sex, human frailty and beyond. So I soon learned simply to be myself – which swiftly led to the richest and happiest friendship of my fifties and sixties.

Many a visit was made to Cambridge, where Frank was still living despite his premature resignation as Professor of English Literature in 1982 after an acrimonious dispute within the faculty. And many evenings were spent together at productions of Shakespeare plays, where the discussion afterwards – usually over a well-wined meal – would constitute a major advance in my copious research. After driving him to Stratford-upon-Avon, for instance, for a matinee of *Timon of Athens*, I wondered aloud: 'What on earth happened to Shakespeare in 1607–8, between *Timon* and *Coriolanus*?' While acknowledging what lay behind my question, Frank replied with a knowing grin: 'Well, of course, E. K. Chambers thought he had a nervous breakdown . . .'

Another six months' research saved. But the reason for the knowing grin was that Frank disapproved of the very concept of Shakespeare biography, declaring with characteristic precision that 'the only interest in William Shakespeare lies in the works attaching to that name'. On another occasion I was driving him to Cheltenham, to deliver its literary festival's annual Shakespeare lecture, when we stopped for lunch at a wayside inn. During the meal I had the nerve to question one of his observations about the Sonnets, based on the date of their publication. 'Oh, dammit,' he snapped. 'Bugger biographers!'

Later described by the American scholar James Shapiro as 'the best living reader of Shakespeare anywhere, hands down', Frank was simultaneously writing his own magisterial *Shakespeare's Language*, so there were occasional moments when our very different projects could happily converge. It meant a great deal to me, for instance, that he described as an 'important insight' my meditation on the word 'beautified', as in Polonius' dismissal of it as a 'vile phrase' in Hamlet's love letter to his daughter Ophelia; this was conscious revenge, I suggested, for the celebrated insult of 1592 when the London playwright Robert Greene called Shakespeare 'an upstart crow, beautified by our feathers'. A few years later Frank further surprised me in a monograph entitled *The Age of Shakespeare* (2003) by publicly approving my suggestion that the French court in *Love's Labour's Lost*, as exemplified by a self-portrait in Berowne, stood for the 'cultured and playful household' of his friend the Earl of Southampton.

For all our radical differences of approach, we would wind up dedicating our respective books to each other when they were published all but simultaneously at the turn of this century.

My boldest contribution to Shakespeare studies was to suggest that the so-called 'missing' or 'lost years' – specifically, the periods between 1579–82 and 1585 to that first mention of him in London in 1592 – were spent in Lancashire, as a recusant Catholic tutor-turned-actor in a succession of aristocractic households. Shakespeare's connections with Lancashire, and several of its noble families, could be dated back to 1579, when he turned fifteen, then the standard school-leaving age.

With some passion and more evidence I argued that the teenage Shakespeare first came to Lancashire in the household of Alexander Hoghton of Lea, via whose will he passed two years later into the employment of Hoghton's friend (and fellow recusant) Sir Thomas Hesketh of nearby Rufford. Having supplied as much authentication for all this as I could muster, I felt free to indulge in a very personal confession:

> As you read of young Will passing in his teens from the Hoghton family to the Hesketh household, you may or may not care to know that my late father was a shopkeeper in Hoghton Street, Southport, some twenty miles from the scene of these sixteenth-century events, and that one of the first young women on whom I looked with all Silvius' hopeless ardour for Phoebe was a Hesketh, direct descendant of the local toffs who took in the young actor-playwright in the 1580s.

It is especially gratifying that my theory of the Catholic Shakespeare – in my own native Lancashire – has since been endorsed by transatlantic scholars to the point where it has now passed, as it were, into the canon.

In 1999 I spoke at a Shakespeare conference at Hoghton Tower in Lancashire, scene of these earlier events, and still the home of the de Hoghton family. The Lancashire Shakespeare attracted enough national attention for me to argue the case in a debate on BBC *Newsnight* with Professor Stanley Wells, representing the stubborn Stratfordians. With the event's organiser, Richard Wilson of Lancaster University, I helped form a Trust planning to build a Shakespeare theatre there to form the northern corner of a triangle with the Globe in London and the Memorial Theatre in Stratford-upon-Avon. Over time this northern outpost gradually shifted – as had Shakespeare's – to the Liverpool suburb of Knowsley, where the young actor-playwright arrived at Knowsley Hall in 1587 as a member of the players of Ferdinando Stanley, Lord Strange. When Stanley became the 5th Earl of Derby in 1593, the company's name changed to Lord Derby's Men.

The 19th Earl of Derby, Edward Stanley, still lives at Knowsley Hall, where in 2016 he hosted a conference at which I was again invited to speak. I found myself staying overnight in the room once occupied by Edward Lear, in which he wrote *The Owl and the Pussycat* while a retainer in the Derby household in the 1830s. Two hundred and fifty years earlier, another Derby retainer had acted in his own plays at the indoor playhouse in the nearby town of Prescot, a parish within the Liverpool borough of Knowsley – which, by the second decade of the twenty-first century, had become one of the most deprived boroughs in the entire United Kingdom.

So where better for the Shakespeare North Trust to build a replica theatre, based by the architect Nick Helm on Inigo Jones' design for his Cockpit-at-Court? Knowsley's economy would surely be revitalised by so distinctive a northern tourist destination. In 2007 we applied for a grant from the National Lottery Fund – in vain, alas, which so surprised the prime minister, Gordon Brown, that he invited the trustees to Downing Street for a meeting at which he suggested we make the theatre the heart of a 'University of Shakespeare', at which students from all over the world could pay to study the theatrical arts. With Liverpool's John Moores University eager for a partnership, Knowsley Council came up with £12 million as well as student accommodation. Liverpool City council donated £10 million, and the Northern Powerhouse another £5 million towards the budget of £30 million, and private donations started pouring in, along with celebrity patrons from Vanessa Redgrave and Judi Dench to such noted Liverpudlians as Ken Dodd and Paul McCartney.

Early in 2020, some twenty years after we had first conceived the idea, a crane on the site in Prescot finally signalled that construction had begun on the 350-seat theatre, complete with outdoor performance garden, exhibition and visitor centre. It was announced that the first production there would be *A Midsummer Night's Dream*, in tribute to the Derby family, in mid-2022.

Frank Kermode was an absurdly modest man, bemused by his own eminence, habitually seeing himself as 'not belonging', as being a 'displaced' person who had never spent more than eight years in any job, not least because he had never really felt at home anywhere. This wilful self-deprecation reached its elegant nadir in his 1995 memoir, *Not Entitled*, which chronicled his impoverished childhood in the Isle of Man, his wartime service in the navy (where his 'mad captains' supervised him in two years spent vainly trying to build a boom across an Icelandic fjord), and his editorship of the erudite literary magazine *Encounter* in succession to its founder, Stephen Spender, only to resign upon discovering that it was covertly funded by the CIA. There followed an unassuming account of his apprenticeship in academe, on which he had embarked only as a novelist manqué. So tortuous did he find the process of writing this book that he couldn't bear to read the proofs – far too personal, he said – and asked me to read them for him.

'So I can adjust the punctuation, can I?' I asked jocularly, after a lengthy debate about so-and-so's use of the semi-colon. 'Certainly not!' he replied. 'Just keep your eye out for typos.' His prose was perfect, of course, but I was very pleased with myself for finding one spelling mistake. Even I was surprised to know – something to do with my lowbrow childhood – that the surname of the 1930s British bandleader Jack Hylton was spelt with a 'y'. Frank had spelt it with an 'i', like the hotel chain. 'Very impressive,' he mused, startled to have been caught out in such a mistake. 'I am very much in your debt.'

The book's ending took me completely by surprise, describing the garden of the house where he then lived in Cambridge; it had long needed, he wrote, 'a deity to command the perspective, to appear each morning out of the mist, and invite me to feel, as it were, presided over: a household god or goddess to assure me that I was at home.' He had sometimes said to visitors, by way of 'idle' conversation, that the little grove at the end of his garden needed some statue, perhaps of a nymph.

> To my delight some generous friends listened to this chatter and sensed that it was, in its way, serious. By their kindness, Diana now stands there, an arrow in one hand, a bow in the other, and over her shoulder a quiver. Though a virgin, she has left discreetly bared her left breast . . .
> I am inclined to begin my day by drawing the curtains and looking at her. On some winter mornings she has a diadem of frost. Henceforth she will preside over this garden and the commonplace house in it, and as long as she belongs there, I will belong there also, or be as close to belonging as I am entitled to be, for as long as I am entitled to be.

I felt ambushed by this charming coda because it so happened that Cindy and I were the friends who had taken his 'idle chatter' seriously, and presented Frank in the early 1990s with this gift which, I like to think, thus found its own little niche in literary history. He took Diana with him across town to the 'retirement' flat where he spent his final years – and she now stands in the Cambridge garden of his last inamorata, the academic and author Heather Glen.

I had been reading Frank Kermode's magisterial literary studies since I was an Oxford student of Eng. Lit.; little could I have imagined that I would one day co-edit a book with him. But in the late 1990s, while both working on our different versions of Shakespeare, Frank and I were also secretly co-editing a surprise book of tributes – less a *Festschrift* than a *Liber Amicorum*, as he insisted on calling it – for the seventieth birthday of our mutual friend Al Alvarez. We enjoyed a trip that summer to the northern Italian hill town of Barga, where the Alvarezes had a house they dubbed Paradiso, to make the surprise presentation on Al's birthday. After changes in both our domestic arrangements, we also began to spend Christmas and New Year together.

While we were working on that Alvarez book, little did Frank know that at the same time, in conditions of equally solemn secrecy, I was also co-editing with his then consort Ursula Owen, editor of *Index on Censorship*, a *Liber Amicorum* (he'd already had a *Festschrift*, of course) for his own eightieth birthday later that same year – eventually entitled, in a phrase from the contribution by the novelist David Lodge, *There Are Kermodians*. Having commissioned myself to write about the offstage Frank – the Frank (as it were) beyond literature, the Frank with whom I also shared a love of music, sport, snooker, travel, eating, drinking, and generally having fun – mostly to a playful hail of apposite quotes from Shakespeare – I took the risk of opting to write a sonnet.

These are the lines I crafted – with considerable trepidation, given the connoisseur to whom they were addressed – in one of the verse forms we both treasured.

> *Where once you were a name on spines of books*
> *Read, marked and learned in duly franker mode,*
> *Of late you are a friend with knowing looks,*
> *Warm heart, wise counsel, welcoming abode.*
> *Together we have stalked the Stratford bard,*
> *Hip-flasked at Highbury, chalked the Savile baize,*
> *Wept at the opera, watched Lara taking guard,*
> *Set towns from Yale to Barga all ablaze.*
> *Your students know the learned, measured sage,*
> *Your readers the insightful polyglot,*
> *I the chimes-at-midnight chum, sans age*
> *And for all time – whose wingèd chariot,*

Refusing to believe you're just four score,
Is posting flight-plans for a good few more.

High among my feelings ten years later in 2010, as I paid tribute to Frank's long and immensely rich life at his memorial service in King's College Chapel, Cambridge, were relief and delight that those last lines turned out to be true. He was to enjoy another decade and more of vigorous life on all fronts, producing no fewer than ten more books, including *Shakespeare's Language*.

He would even publish *two* books on his ninetieth birthday. Amid this seemingly effortless flow of Olympian thoughts and words, he and I continued to enjoy frequent outings to cricket at Lord's, snooker at his London Club (the Savile – purely for snooker purposes), football at Arsenal. To mark his eightieth birthday I secured him not just a Manx Bible – a fitting gift, I thought, for the Douglas-born co-author of *The Literary Guide to the Bible* – but a mention in the match programme at Arsenal, along with a half-time announcement proclaiming him 'a passionate Gooner these 60 years'. This, he smiled, gave him even more pleasure than the tributes in the *Liber Amicorum*.

Frank also derived much pleasure from an unlikely meeting, including a few frames of snooker, with another new friend whom Shakespeare brought my way.

One evening in the midst of my work Kenneth Griffith invited me for a drink with a lifelong pal of his who happened to be a keen Shakespeare buff. When I arrived, naturally wondering who it could be, our companion for the evening turned out to be none other than Peter O'Toole.

'So what *exactly* are you up to?' O'Toole asked me earnestly, with a mischievous look in his eye. However I spelt out my intentions, they seemed to satisfy him enough to suggest a trip to a nearby restaurant, where an earnest debate continued, with Griffith acting as genial referee while many of my assertions were met with cries from O'Toole of 'Disputed!', punctuated by the occasional 'Bollocks!', which gradually softened to a 'Yes, hmmm, in-ter-est-ing . . . Have you read . . .?'

This veteran Bardolater, it turned out, really knew his stuff. Towards the end of hours of debate, O'Toole spoke movingly of his late friend Moelwyn Merchant, the Welsh-born Shakespeare scholar. Was I, too, lucky enough to have such a mentor? Well, actually, yes, for more than a decade now I had been close to the esteemed critic Sir Frank Kermode. 'Now there's an interesting man,' said O'Toole. 'God, I'd like to dispute a few of his foot-notes. Do you think you could introduce me?'

And so it came to pass that, a few weeks later, I midwifed a meeting between Kermode and O'Toole over lunch and snooker at Frank's club. Amid the occasional double-figure break – of these three fiercely competitive snooker players, O'Toole emerged the winner – the finer points of Caliban and Sycorax vied for attention with plants into the corner pocket, mutual memories of the navy and fond recollections of Diana Wynyard, Gertrude to 26-year-old O'Toole's 'Angry Young' Hamlet at Bristol and one of Frank's lasting pin-ups.

A Shakespeare scholar to be reckoned with, O'Toole kindly offered to read and review my first draft, which soon involved regular visits to his modest home in west London. The frequent cries of 'Bollocks!' in the margins reached a climax one day when I quoted the only recorded contemporary witness of Shakespeare the actor to the effect that the Ghost in Hamlet was 'the top of his performance', thus concluding that the Bard was a considerably better writer than actor. 'Bollocks!' boomed O'Toole, with a flourish of his Gitanes-laden cigarette-holder. 'He was one of life's Mercutios! Can't you just see him?' He left the room so he could make a suitably dramatic re-entrance, and there followed, for my solitary delight, a brief vignette of O'Toole playing Shakespeare playing Mercutio.

Frank and I subsequently went to see O'Toole at the Old Vic in Keith Waterhouse's one-man show *Jeffrey Bernard is Unwell*.

Over a drink in his dressing room afterwards, he talked intensely about how hard it was to get through an entire evening onstage alone, without any cues to respond to. 'No wonder our friend Shakespeare didn't write any one-man plays – he was an *act-or!*'

Some years later, I found myself sitting next to Ian McKellen during a performance on Broadway of *The Merchant of Venice* with Al Pacino as Shylock. Come the interval, when I hoped to engage him in conversation, McKellen leapt up and made a hasty exit before the lights had come up again. As I headed after him, I saw he had dropped his wallet in the aisle – so I naturally picked it up, to the horror of the startled Saturday night audience. 'Hey,' I could hear them thinking, 'wasn't that Gandalf? And who's that schmuck picking up his wallet?'

Outside, where I found him on the sidewalk enjoying a cig-arette, I approached him with a casual, 'Sir Ian, you might be needing this . . .' Wallet duly restored to its grateful owner, we fell to discussing the production, and I ventured my theory that Shakespeare did not realise quite what an outstanding part he had written in Shylock; he doesn't appear in the fifth act, and doesn't even get much of an exit-line in the fourth. When I had said this to O'Toole, I told McKellen, he again left the room to make an entrance and pronounce emphatically, right into my face, 'I am *con-tent!*'

Towards the end of that evening's production, after the court scene in which Shylock is told his money is forfeit and he must convert to Christianity, Pacino mumbled 'I am content' and shuffled off the back of the stage. There followed a scene not in Shakespeare: a bathtub was carried on and filled with water, before Pacino was dragged back onstage, weeping and wailing, to be baptised before our very eyes, finally making the noisiest of exits. 'I think', McKellen whispered to me, 'Mr Pacino agrees with you that Shakespeare did not provide him with an adequate exit line!'

I was in mid-Shakespeare when my fiftieth birthday in May

1997 came with the very welcome bonus of a free trip with Cindy to a Jamaican resort hotel where we were treated to ten days in one of their most luxurious villas, complete with infinity pool.

Later that summer my republican friend Brian Basham invited me to a match at Fulham FC, where he was an adviser to its new owner, Mohamed al-Fayed. Before and after spending half-time chatting beside the Thames with Fayed, whose son Dodi was then romancing Diana, ex-Princess of Wales, I watched the match from the directors' box, where he stationed security guards to survey the crowd with their backs to the game, as if one of us were going to assassinate him. Among them was Trevor Rees-Jones, who later that summer turned out to be the only survivor of the Paris tunnel car crash that killed Diana and Dodi.

Frank looked on with sympathy as an unavoidable burst of royal punditry brought a temporary halt to all things Shakespeare. Once back in harness, however, I realised that (apart from Frank himself, of course, who indeed did not demur) actors and directors were for me much more useful interviewees than scholars and academics. More than one Laertes, for instance, pointed out that 'Oh, where?' is scarcely a natural reaction to the news that your sister has drowned; it is all too clearly a cue to set up Gertrude's elaborate speech about Warwickshire flora and fauna, 'There is a willow grows aslant a brook . . .'

Trevor Nunn told me the tale of a Player King from a Stratford production of *Hamlet* taking a walk one day through the Warwickshire countryside. When he came across two labourers trimming a hedge on the same side of the road, he asked them why did they not each trim opposite sides? 'Ah well, you see, sir,' came the rustic reply, 'I rough-hews them and he shapes their ends . . .'

The first Shakespeare play to which I took my three young sons was *Hamlet*, with Daniel Day-Lewis in the title role, at the National Theatre in 1989. As it turned out, we were lucky to see Day-Lewis, because he didn't last long in the part; all too early in the run he collapsed onstage at the entry of the Ghost of Hamlet's father, saying that he had seen the ghost of his own late father, the poet Cecil Day-Lewis. It was, he mused, less of a metaphor than a hallucination: 'If you're working in a play like *Hamlet*, you explore everything through your own experience.' Day-Lewis has never since appeared onstage.

I was anxious lest my sons — then aged only ten, twelve and thirteen — disturb other members of the audience with too much fidgeting; but in fact they were gripped throughout, demonstrating to me more clearly than anything else the universal appeal of Shakespeare, that his work is as theatrical as poetic, as visually action-packed as linguistically elevated. It proved the first of many more Shakespeare plays to which I enjoyed taking them until they were old enough to take themselves, each having read English Literature at university.

A decade later I finally put the finishing touches to my *Shakespeare: His Life and Work* on my fifty-second birthday in 1999, for which Cindy had organised a celebratory dinner party. For some reason I had been feeling under intense pressure to complete my work by that date; only later did I realise that Shakespeare died on his fifty-second birthday, and I was subconsciously fearing the same fate might befall me before I had finished the task into which I had put so much time, thought and effort.

All that remained was to seek Frank's leave to dedicate my book to him, as felt appropriate with so scrupulous a literary figure. I had finally found what I thought the perfect epigraph, in Hamlet's words to Horatio: 'Give me that man That is not passion's slave, And I will wear him in my heart's core, aye, in my heart of hearts.'

'Oh no, that won't do,' said Frank, turning away to hide a moist eye, then swinging back to me with an emotional half-smile: 'I *am* passion's slave!'

So instead I chose a phrase from the 38th Sonnet:

If my slight muse do please these curious days,
The pain be mine, but thine shall be the praise.

For me, it aptly summed up just how much I had learned from this wonderfully wise and warm-hearted man, and not just about Shakespeare. In my copy of his *Shakespeare's Language*, beside the inscription bearing my name, Frank in his turn has written: 'To Tony, who deserves so much more than a dedication.'

17

A VIEW WITH A ROOM

Post-Shakespeare, as my financial responsibilities began to erode, I made the seemingly grown-up decision to spend my fifties writing less commercial biographies of more obscure figures who led truly distinctive lives. My initial list of candidates included Francis Barber, the Jamaican-born slave who went on to become Samuel Johnson's manservant; Richard Burbage, the leading actor in Shakespeare's company and so the first to play Hamlet, Macbeth, Othello, Lear and other such peerless roles; and Leigh Hunt, the Regency poet, critic and editor who befriended Keats and Shelley, becoming the first to publish their work as well as that of Browning, Tennyson and others.

Hunt had already endeared himself to me as the journalist who continued to edit his paper, *The Examiner*, from jail after being imprisoned for two years in 1813 for denouncing the Prince of Wales, then prince regent, in print as 'a violator of his word, a despiser of domestic ties, a man who has just closed half a century without one single claim on the gratitude of his country or the respect of posterity'. I had quoted this, for obvious reasons, in my third and last, post-Diana biography of Charles.

At the time, fortuitously enough, Frank Kermode noticed an advertisement in an academic journal inviting applications to the New York Public Library for Fellowships at its newly founded venture, an in-house Center for Scholars and Writers. The sole criterion was that the applicant's project should draw upon the Library's many and varied literary archives – one of which, the

Carl H. Pforzheimer collection of Shelley and His Circle, just
happened to be the world's main repository of documents con-
cerning, among others, Leigh Hunt. The applicant required two
references, one of which Frank offered to give me himself. When
I mentioned my plan to Christopher Hitchens, by then long based
in Washington DC, he said, 'Oh, they love me at the NYPL!' and
volunteered to give me the second. Between them, the combination of this unlikely duo and my crafty choice of project managed
to secure me this privileged position.

To be paid to research a book! And in, of all places, my beloved
New York City! This was the first quasi-academic recognition my
work had ever received. It would mean living apart from Cindy
for an academic year, but we would each travel back and forth regularly – and, besides, with all four of our boys now at university,
it would be a welcome chance for her to enjoy some time alone
with her daughter in our usually male-dominated home.

My arrival in New York in September 1999 appeared auspi-
cious. The Library had unwittingly found me an apartment on
the very same block as Harry Evans and Tina Brown. Many was
the evening I would stroll down East 57th Street for a drink and
a chat, or to one of their famously star-studded parties.

Meanwhile, I settled swiftly and contentedly into daily life at
the Library. A brand new $12 million venture, endowed by the
investment banker Lewis B. Cullman and his wife Dorothy, the
Center for Scholars and Writers offered fifteen individual offices
for academics and authors engaged on a remarkably wide variety of projects. The inaugural director was Peter Gay, former
Professor of History at Yale, biographer of Freud and historian of
the bourgeois.

Ranged around an elegant space on the Library's 42nd Street
frontage, with a large table in the middle for catered luncheons,
the Center's individual offices offered as much chance to forge
intriguing new friendships as to hide yourself away, buried in your
own work. The fifteen inaugural Fellows ranged from the cultural

historian Andrew Delbanco, working on a study of Herman Melville, via the novelists Allen Kurzweil and Francine Prose to Harvey Sachs, biographer of Toscanini, and Kathleen Neal Cleaver, widow of the Black Panther leader Eldridge Cleaver, now a lawyer working on her memoirs. Peter Gay helped this unlikely assortment to become firm friends over learned lunchtime symposia.

Each of our offices, needless to say, was equipped with a high-powered new computer, so much of my year was spent discovering the wonders of this brave new world called the internet. At the same time, I seized the opportunity to found an unusually select reading group. Leigh Hunt being the original of Harold Skimpole in Charles Dickens' *Bleak House,* I was eager to re-read this classic in expert company. Peter Gay himself, along with Kurzweil, Delbanco, Prose and others, helped me thoroughly re-explore it, with an especial emphasis on why this apparent innocent turns so ugly as the novel progresses, ultimately betraying his great benefactor, John Jarndyce.

Over a life spanning two seminal eras of English literary history, Hunt had been a poet, playwright and novelist, editor and critic during the Romantic movement, the intimate of Keats and Shelley, friend of Byron, Hazlitt and Lamb, who lived on to become an elder statesman of Victorian letters, companion and champion of Carlyle and Tennyson, Browning and indeed Dickens. What could have made Dickens, whose reputation he had helped to forge, malign him to the point of turning this child-like innocent into an outright villain?

Elsewhere in the Library, as my reading group explored *Bleak House,* I was studying the correspondence between Hunt and Dickens, who in 1846–47 had nobly led an amateur theatrical troupe around the country to raise money for his ever indigent supporter. Within a year, however, Dickens was distinctly displeased to receive a begging letter from Hunt seeking another £500. And so it continued until, in March 1852, *Bleak House* began to appear in twenty monthly instalments.

The second, that April, saw the first appearance of Harold Skimpole as a child-like freeloader at Bleak House, persuading its occupants that he's doing them a favour by constantly borrowing money. 'You ought to be grateful to me for giving you the luxury of generosity,' he purrs, 'I know you like it.' Skimpole soon finds himself arrested for debt, as was only too familiar to Hunt.

Dickens' close friend and eventual biographer, John Forster, was not the only mutual friend to protest strenuously, as he read the proofs, that the likeness to Hunt was too painfully obvious. Dickens relented to some extent, 'toning down' a few passages and changing Skimpole's first name from Leonard to Harold (or, in effect, from Leigh to Hunt). He also ensured that Hablot K. Browne, alias the cartoonist 'Phiz', made Skimpole look quite unlike 'the great original', rendering him a short, tubby figure where Hunt was tall and slender.

Dickens had betrayed himself in a self-satisfied letter to a close friend, saying of Skimpole: 'I suppose he is the most exact portrait that was ever painted in words! . . . It is an absolute reproduction of a real man.' Thereafter the character of Harold Skimpole grew steadily darker; even Hunt's 'sickly large wife' and 'strange, gipsy-looking children' were not spared, with the door of his house answered by a 'slatternly' maid, before a letter from Hunt asking for pre-publication payment for some essays he had written for Dickens' magazine saw Skimpole degenerate into an arrant villain.

There followed more private financial and editorial disagreements between Hunt and Dickens while he was writing the final double instalment of *Bleak House* in which Skimpole, who has died heavily in debt to John Jarndyce, is posthumously revealed to have denounced his great benefactor, the genial character at the heart of the novel, as the 'incarnation of selfishness'.

Five years later, revising his autobiography in the penultimate year of his life, Hunt finally told how he still had not read the book – it was the first of Dickens' he had not read in serial, as his son Vincent had lain dying as it started appearing – when a stranger repeated the rumour that he was the original of Harold Skimpole. A friend of whom he thought highly also believed the chatter to be 'well-founded'. So Leigh Hunt finally read *Bleak House* and met Harold Skimpole.

'I began to consider,' he recalled, 'in what possible way I could have offended the friend who thus unaccountably assailed me . . . I had never supposed him petulant, suspicious, apt to take offence, or given to any other weakness not common to a genius like his. What was it? He could not be jealous of any little attention shewn me in great quarters, for he possessed heaps of it. Envy was out of the question from a man prosperous like himself towards one in a state of adversity. I was old and he young; sick, and he healthy; in sorrow, and he happy. What could it be?'

I attempted to address this question in a public lecture I gave at the end of my year at the Library, the only tithe required by the terms of the Fellowship. Under the title 'The Novelist as Thug', I broadened the subject into a general discussion of the rights and wrongs of novelists basing their characters on real people, whether friends or not. I also examined other, more recent examples, from the Beat Generation writer Neal Cassady as Dean Moriarty in Jack Kerouac's *On the Road* (the manuscript of which, in scroll form, is among the Library's treasures) to Claire Bloom as Eve Frame, the protagonist's nemesis in Philip Roth's latest novel *I Married a Communist*, his all-too-obvious revenge on his ex-wife for her remarks about him in her 1996 post-divorce memoirs, *Leaving A Doll's House*. Roth's book was less a novel, argued one reviewer, than 'an angry, bitter, resentful mess by a man who might have taken another course'. I attempted to argue as much about Dickens, who had allowed Hunt to die without the apology, or even disclaimer, for which he had begged on his deathbed.

Hunt's obituaries inevitably mentioned the Skimpole connection, which saw Dickens denounced on all sides for his 'heartless calumny'. After dismissing the attacks as 'contemptible trash',

Dickens found himself condemned for his 'inexcusable' silence to Hunt – to the point where, four months after Hunt's death, he finally felt compelled to address the matter via a warm review in his magazine *All Year Round* of Thornton Hunt's posthumous edition of his father's autobiography. As 'one who knew Leigh Hunt well', Dickens testified that Hunt's life was 'of the most amiable and domestic kind', condemning his imprisonment during the Regency as a 'national disgrace'. But Dickens' protestations of innocence have not convinced posterity any more than they did his contemporaries. By 1927, to the literary historian Arthur Quiller-Couch, 'Nothing, least of all its verisimilitude, can excuse the outrage perpetrated upon Hunt in the mask of Skimpole.' The wound 'went deep'; Dickens was 'guilty, and he knew it . . . Hunt had been wounded in the house of his friend.'

En passant I had naturally quoted the protest of Martin Amis in his memoir *Experience* that 'only a semiliterate would say that Harold Skimpole is Leigh Hunt . . . even the most precisely recreated character is nonetheless recreated, transfigured; autobiographical fiction is still fiction – an autonomous construct.' None of which stopped the Irish novelist Colm Tóibín, one of the Center's newly arrived second-year Fellows, standing up as I sat down to declare impishly that my protestations had moved him, for the first time in his life, to summon up some grudging admiration for Dickens.

Off-duty, meanwhile, my regular visits to the Evans–Brown townhouse included the door being answered with a grinning 'Good evening – I'm Tina Brown's butler' by none other than Harvey Weinstein, then known solely as an Oscar-winning movie producer. At the time, post-*Vanity Fair* and the *New Yorker*, Tina was embarking on a joint venture financed by Weinstein which included the launch of *Talk* magazine and Talk Miramax Books. Weinstein was a loud, self-satisfied boor, and rarely let you forget it, but there was as yet no discernible hint of the darker side that would prove his undoing some twenty years later.

The same was true of Kevin Spacey, whom I met there in the year of *American Beauty*, for which he too was to win the Academy Award. Given his growing involvement with the Old Vic theatre in London, I told Spacey of my recent encounters with O'Toole, and my visit to see him as Jeffrey Bernard. By way of reply, as he launched into an anecdote, this supreme actor offered more than merely an impersonation of O'Toole; he *turned into* O'Toole.

Then there was the night I found myself sitting next to Henry Kissinger, as he mounted an impassioned protest at the prospect of Augusto Pinochet being sent back to Spain for trial (eventually blocked by the then home secretary, Jack Straw). 'What exactly has Pinochet done?' rasped Kissinger. 'They accuse him of torture and crimes against humanity and genocide. But the most he killed was about 6,000 people over two years. That's 3,000 a year. That's 250 a month. That's sixty a week. It's not even ten a day. I don't call that genocide.'

I owe the exactitude of this detail to the diary of Denis MacShane, then MP for Rotherham, with whom Cindy and I dined at the House of Commons on one of my regular trips home. According to Denis, I did an 'excellent imitation' of Kissinger, but he was appalled that 'no one had the guts to empty a glass of wine over his head or tax him with the many more scores of thousands of deaths of Asian peasants in Cambodia that he was directly responsible for'.

At the urging of Peter Gay, I easily persuaded both Al Alvarez and Frank Kermode to come over to New York to give lectures in the Center. Al's series became a book entitled *The Writer's Voice* and Frank's an updated edition, specifically for the turn of the new millennium, of his most celebrated work *The Sense of an Ending*.

While in town, Frank also took the chance to promote *Shakespeare's Language* in a debate with Harold Bloom, who had recently published his own grandiose *Shakespeare: The Invention of the Human*. There was little to trouble their moderator, the poet John Hollander, until the time came for questions, which the self-important Bloom insisted John vet to ensure they were worth his trouble; evidently he approved of mine, for he soon called my name, so I stood up to enquire saucily if there was a biography of Shakespeare that either professor would recommend. I had begun the Preface to my own book with the portentous quote from Bloom that there are no great biographies of Shakespeare, 'not because we do not know enough, but because there is not enough to know'. Well aware what I was up to, Frank smiled at me indulgently, clearly about to offer me an unavoidable public endorsement, before finding himself silenced as Bloom abruptly stood up and strutted off the stage, thus bringing a premature end to the proceedings.

'I'm sorry the prof pulled the plug on your plug!' Frank said to me afterwards over drinks with Hollander. I myself remained dismayed, to say the least, by what had happened immediately after the debate, when Kermode and Bloom sat down to sign their books. The line for Frank's autograph being longer than Bloom's, his fellow critic stood up and walked out again without a word, not even a farewell to a transatlantic colleague of some fifty years. They might never see each other again, I thought — and indeed said — at the time. As of course they never did.

The offer of free flights back and forth from New York enabled me to accept an invitation to chair the biography panel of that year's Whitbread [now Costa] Book Awards. The worthy winner was the second volume of David Cairns' magisterial biography of Berlioz — which thus went forward, along with the winners of the various other categories, to the final meeting to choose the Book of the Year. That year, for the first time, the rules had been changed to make the Children's Book of the Year eligible to win the overall award — in a clear attempt by Whitbread, it seemed to me, to ensure a victory for *Harry Potter* after three straight years of worthy Faber poets.

Under the chairmanship of the provost of Eton, Eric Anderson, the various chairs including Robert Harris and Ann Widdecombe were joined for this final session by two 'celebrity' judges, Jerry Hall and Imogen Stubbs. As Anderson went round the table canvassing views, I got the distinct impression that he was trying to steer things Potter's way, perhaps under instructions from Whitbread. So I braced myself for when he reached me.

I had first met Anderson years before, when I interviewed him for my first Charles biography – he had taught the prince at Gordonstoun – and I had long savoured the unique distinction that he had directed the young Charles as Macbeth as well as the young Tony Blair as Mark Antony (at Fettes). But I had later crossed swords with him as rector of Lincoln College, Oxford, whence he had threatened to send down my son Joe for 'ignoring' his academic work during the one term he was editor (like his proud father before him) of a student magazine. Summoned to see Anderson in Oxford, I told him in no uncertain terms that if Joe were captain of the college rowing team, he would have had his name inscribed in gold letters on an honours board in the college dining room. On that occasion I won the day, and got him to back down; but this time I feared I might be fighting a lost cause.

So when he reached me, three-quarters of the way round the table, I voted for Seamus Heaney's translation of *Beowulf*. 'But you're chairman of biography,' Robert Harris rebuked me across the table. 'You should be voting for Cairns.'

'You've been a political reporter, Robert,' I replied. 'You should know what I'm doing. It's called "tactical voting"!' To which Ann Widdecombe piped up: 'Have you ever thought of going into politics?'

Both 'celebrity' judges were meanwhile trilling how much they enjoyed reading *Harry Potter* to their children. 'You should try reading them Heaney's *Beowulf*!' I snapped. 'It's about much the same thing – fighting dragons and all that – but written in far more eloquent language!'

I could sense Anderson getting anxious. The dinner at which the result would be announced, live on TV, was due to begin before long. As he went round the table for the last time, I again voted Heaney, announcing that I would resign publicly if Potter were to win. It would amount to 'a national humiliation', I intoned. 'Like the monarchy and the Millennium Dome, it would send another signal to the world that Britain is a Ruritarian theme-park of a country which refuses to grow up and take itself seriously.' Later, when this was quoted on live television, Harris would dub me a 'pompous prat'. At the time, miraculously, it ensured a single-vote victory for Heaney over Potter.

A televised fuss of this order carried over into the next few days' newspapers, with the nation apparently on the verge of a nervous breakdown over whether it was a Beowulf Britain or a Potter Britain. Clearly out for blood, a tabloid rang me with various obscure questions about the text of *Beowulf* – all of which, to its dismay, I got right, less because I had studied it at Oxford thirty years earlier than because I had re-read it in Heaney's elegant version several times in the previous few months. Thus was the paper deprived of its brutal demolition job on the pompous prat; in fact, his words wound up travelling the world in countless 'quotes of the week', even an analysis in the *New York Times*, to the point where I got a letter from a professor of literature at an American university, telling me they were proudly establishing a Pompous Prats Society, and inviting me to become its life president.

Whenever I have since bumped into Robert Harris, invariably in eminent company, we have had a good laugh about all that.

In the summer of 2000, after deciding to stay on in New York once my year at the Library was up, I moved west across Manhattan to a 48th-floor apartment in a stylish block on the corner of East 29th Street and Fifth Avenue. Its balcony commanded a breathtaking view north, taking in both rivers and eyeballing the Empire State building, to the point where I called the place 'a view with a room'. Cindy and I had long talked about leading transatlantic lives together, with a home on each side, and this was to be our US base.

At the end of each day in the Library, meanwhile, I was embarked on an urgent and unexpected, if worrying, task. My life of Shakespeare had sold so well – eventually, to my delighted surprise, it would more than earn its six-figure advance – that Alan Samson was planning a lavishly illustrated version, requiring me to halve the length of my text, which had taken me five years to write. Only one other of his authors had enjoyed such a privilege: Nelson Mandela. Awestruck to find myself in such company, I set nervously to work on the task, which in fact proved embarrassingly easy. With lavish illustrations laid on by Alan's design department, a slimmer but elegant volume entitled *Shakespeare: An Illustrated Biography* would duly appear in 2002.

Both before and after my move across town, Christopher Hitchens would stay with me each Monday evening after coming up from Washington to teach at Manhattan's New School on Tuesday mornings. Just like Princess Margaret, I teased my fellow republican, he sent advance instructions as to which brand of whisky I should get in stock. After a jolly dinner together at some local hostelry, plus a nightcap or three, I would close the window for him before we retired. 'No, no,' he would protest. 'Leave it open! I can't sleep without the traffic noise . . .'

One week he turned up with news of our mutual friend Ian McEwan, whom he had just seen at some conference on the West Coast. They had talked about me long enough, said Christopher, to agree that one Shakespeare was enough for them both finally to forgive me for three Charleses.

As we each retired for the night much the worse for wear, with his shots of Scotch continuing the next morning, I would occasionally worry about what sort of shape Christopher would be in when he turned up to give his morning lecture at the New School. But my mind would then go back to the Amanda years, when Hitchens would stay with us overnight in Highbury, sitting down last thing at night to write some book review, whisky a-plenty beside him, with a request that I fax it to the *Sunday*

Times the next morning as he had an early flight to Prague or wherever. I would naturally descend the stairs next day expecting the worst, only to find immaculate prose beside the empty whisky bottle.

Hitchens was among the guests at a galactical party given at their Manhattan townhouse for me and my Shakespeare book by Tina Brown and Harry Evans. Also there were several of my colleagues from the NYPL's Center for Scholars and Writers, not least Peter Gay, which proved helpful when I prepared in advance a response to the generous speech I expected Harry to be making in my honour – as indeed he did. So I was able to reply, appropriately enough, with a pseudo-Shakespearean Sonnet, which opened with a salute to our hostess:

> *Shall I compare thee to a Doris Day?*
> *Thou art more lovely and more erudite,*
> *A Venus with the brains of Peter Gay,*
> *The dream hostess on this midsummer night . . .*

After a first half addressed to Tina, my focus switched halfway through to Harry, who had recently published *The American Century*, his magisterial volume of recent US history, so he became:

> *Caesar to her Cleopatra,*
> *De Tocqueville with the voice of Frank Sinatra.*

Later in the evening, settled together in a corner, Hitchens and I were delighted to overhear an eminent New Yorker saying, 'Damn these Brits. Why are they so much better than us at after-dinner speeches?

Tina had given my middle son Joe a job at *Talk* straight out of Oxford. At first an intern, he was lucky enough to attend the magazine's lavish launch party at the Statue of Liberty before becoming a fully-fledged *Talk* fact-checker and occasional interviewer. Myself she named a contributing editor, with a hand-some salary in return for the occasional contribution.

I was also writing regularly for *The Observer*, reviewing Broadway openings and interviewing the occasional local lumi-nary. My favourite memory, as a devout fan of the American TV sit-com *Frasier*, was a long lunch with the genial Kelsey Grammer, who was about to take a major risk by coming to Broadway in the title role of *Macbeth*, directed by the RSC's Terry Hands. After nipping up to Boston to see a preview, which received dire reviews, I mustered the nerve to tell Hands what I really thought, as he had asked of me. The intelligent, classically trained Grammer made a noble Thane, I said; Laurence Olivier he wasn't, more Kenneth Branagh, thoroughly convincing in parts without leaving much etched on your soul. But there were some manner-isms, especially his walk, that really needed sorting out. Those sub-Groucho Marx splayed feet were fine for Frasier, loping across the room to tackle some passing crisis, but less appropriate when his Macbeth is required to stride off one side of the stage while, in true RSC fashion, the next scene is already under way on the other. But you can't do much about that, I told Hands down the phone to Wales, where he was taking a post-Boston break to deal with some crisis at his Clwyd Theatr Cymru. 'Oh yes, I can,' he replied. 'What else?' So I wondered aloud about the bouncing eyebrows. To my surprise (and horror), Hands relayed all this to Grammer, who apparently 'cracked up' when he quoted me as calling the production 'too RSC'.

Now, when Hands returned to Broadway for the re-opening, I found myself involved in the last-minute re-rehearsals, sitting with him in the stalls and pointing out those Frasier mannerisms in urgent need of amendment. I really felt for Grammer himself, then the most successful star in the history of US television, enjoying an unrivalled eighteenth year in the Top Ten ratings, and said to earn seven figures per half-hour episode. During *Frasier*'s summer break, he could have been forgiven for lolling beside his

LA pool like any other megastar, idly counting his money in the sun. Instead, he had chosen to take this chance on Broadway, braving one of the stage's ultimate challenges. Why was he putting himself through this? 'I know, we never learn, do we?' he shrugged with a wan grin. 'It may sound corny, but the stage is my first love. It's where I started out. In television, you lose that intimate contact with the audience. If I don't go back to live theatre every few years, I begin to feel . . . rusted.'

Whatever the public thought, alas, the New York critics agreed with Boston's. The show barely lasted a fortnight. As a headline in one of the New York tabloids put it, 'Tomorrow and tomorrow and tomorrow . . . and that's it!'

It proved a vintage season for Broadway. With Gyles Brandreth and his wife Michèle, I went backstage to visit a Barry Humphries intent on winning Dame Edna Everage the same laurels in the States as elsewhere around the world; with my son Joe I relished the stage version of Mel Brooks' immortal musical *The Producers*, with Nathan Lane and Matthew Broderick better replacements than expected for the inimitable Zero Mostel and Gene Wilder.

My growing New York circle ranged from the Evans–Brown coterie and the Library's other Fellows via long-time friends from Everett Fahy (now of the Frick Collection) to my old pal Peter Pringle and his wife Eleanor Randolph, then on the editorial board of the *New York Times*. Many was the Sunday lunch enjoyed chez Pringle in the company of canny writers and journalists such as Nicholas von Hoffman and the publisher Alice Mayhew. They also introduced me to a lasting new friend in Catherine Williams, director of a lively cultural forum called the Center for Communications, where she soon had me making regular appearances.

By now I also had three regular Manhattan poker schools to compensate for the loss of my thirty-year-old seat in London's Tuesday game. And my beloved Arsenal FC were available at the Gooners' Manhattan headquarters, McCormack's Bar on 3rd Avenue.

In Greenwich Village I enjoyed a drink with my fellow Lancastrian Michael Atherton, captain of the England cricket team which had suffered the indignity of watching Brian Lara score his record-breaking 375 in Antigua in 1994. Yes, he told me to my surprise, he was all too aware of my own record-breaking bet on Lara with Sporting Index. Atherton was about to embark on a tour of Pakistan – the only cricketing country, he observed ruefully, where he had never yet scored a century. My money, I boldly predicted, was on his doing so this time round – and again I was proved right, I'm delighted to say, when he notched up 125 in an England victory at Karachi in July 2000. Back in England five years later Atherton consulted me on a book he was writing under the title *Gambling: A Story of Triumph and Disaster*, for which I took him to play poker at a London casino.

Unknown to Atherton, while he was scoring that century in Karachi, I had been in Cardiff to play in the first 'celebrity' edition of Channel 4's *Late Night Poker*. We were each paid £1,000 in chips, winner take all. I was up against Al Alvarez, Martin Amis and Patrick Marber along with Victoria Coren, Stephen Fry and Ricky Gervais. I remember little of the action before it came down to a heads-up between myself and Alvarez – which, despite decades of friendship, I was determined to win – and did. All 7K. If you're going to play poker on television, became my mantra, be sure to win.

[left to right] Patrick Marber, Al Alvarez, Ricky Gervais,
Stephen Fry, A.H., Victoria Coren, Martin Amis

Amid all the fun I was otherwise having in one of the world's most fun-filled cities, I was still coming back home for regular fortnights – including each Christmas, which we were now spending with Frank Kermode and the Alvarez family, in alternating homes. The millennial New Year's Day 2000 I spent with Cindy and her family in Boston, dismayed that she was not interested in coming with me for a day trip to their house at Cape Cod, where I took supreme if solitary pleasure in signing the visitors' book with that especially resonant date.

Six months later, on 1 July 2000 – the date will always be etched on my heart – I came back to London for one of my regular visits. Cindy met me in at Heathrow, then drove us to our local pub for lunch. After half an hour or so of inconsequential catch-up chatter, she told me that she wanted a separation.

The youngest of five children, she said she felt she had never lived life to her own agenda. After two marriages to Englishmen with agendas of their own, she no longer enjoyed being part of a couple, and now wanted to live alone. 'Might we get back together one day?' I pleaded. 'I would hope so,' was all she would say. I was devastated.

After ten uneasy days in London in what had been our house – now, suddenly, hers, and Manhattan solely mine – I flew back to New York alone and broken-hearted, with no idea what my future held.

Diagnosed as clinically depressed, I took myself off for pricey sessions with the aforementioned shrink, who was only too uncomfortably aware from the stench of alcohol and smoke on me by mid-afternoon that he was not helping me at all. Over the musical accompaniment to meals at another of my regular restaurants, the Redeye Grill across Seventh Avenue from Carnegie Hall, I ruefully realised that the most affecting songs were the break-up ones, with such devastating lyrics as 'You took the part that once was my heart, So why not take all of me?'

Yes, I was in serious danger of disappearing into my desultory, post-Cindy self. Every time I came up to my 48th floor in the elevator, I expected her to be standing there, confessing that she had made a giant mistake. But slowly I forced myself to accept that this was never going to happen. I was less acutely unhappy in New York than I would have been in London, so I decided that this was where I was now going to stay. If in London, I would only be yearning for Cindy; in Manhattan, and indeed the rest of her native United States, such pointless longings would only seem more so. It may not rid me of them, but it would certainly make life more tolerable, to leave the UK for good, maybe even take out US citizenship. It was what I had always wanted to do with her, so why not do it without her? When I told Roger Alton that I was renouncing Blighty and all its works, he thought this was a decision momentous enough to merit an *Observer* Review Front.

Headlined 'I'LL TAKE MANHATTAN', beneath a photo of my resolute self forthrightly facing an American future from my New York balcony, the piece was billed: 'Sick of living in a nation he believes is ruled by philistines and in thrall to its own past, Anthony Holden is moving to the land of the free. From a 48th-floor apartment in Manhattan, he waves goodbye to his homeland.' Beneath it was a list of other Brits who had also made the transatlantic leap, from Auden and Hitchcock to Harry Evans and Tina Brown, Christopher Hitchens and Salman Rushdie.

'I hold these truths,' I wrote, 'to be self-evident.'

As long as Britain retains a hereditary head of state, a government formed in the name of that monarch rather than of the electorate, an established but irrelevant Church, not to mention such class-drenched fripperies as an honours system adding antique handles to lists of autopilot names, it cannot truly call itself a popular democracy. As long as its people remain subjects rather than citizens, with no written rights, it is not a country in which any self-respecting democrat can comfortably hang his or her hat . . .

Like his Government, Tony Blair is Her Majesty's Prime Minister, not ours; we are defended by the Royal Navy and the Royal Air Force, not our own; it is illegal even to post a letter without a stamp bearing the monarch's head. 'You can tell a lot about a country,' as William Cobbett put it, 'which refers to the Royal Mint and the national debt.'

Ironically, in view of the referendum result sixteen years later, I lamented a Britain 'still dithering xenophobically about Europe (for me, its only hope of any future as even a wannabe world power)' while 'keeping 92 hereditary peers, for pity's sake, not to mention that pantomime-horse of a monarchy' and 'grumbling nationalistically about immigrants when they are the pulsating lifeblood of my adopted homeland, its raison d'être.' For me, the intellectual, cultural and literary life of America's eastern seaboard was 'more alive, more alert, much feistier than the primping and preening of London's cosy circle of back-patting glitterati'. Viewed from my Manhattan balcony, the old country seemed 'more than ever like some overgrown, nose-in-air, single-sex Pall Mall club, whose pettifogging rules it is so rejuvenating to escape'.

Relishing the rage my piece provoked, I settled into a *vita semi-nuova* of book reviews here and there, but otherwise retreated back into myself. So absent did I become from my usually hectic social scene that Manhattan friends became concerned. Tina Brown thoughtfully tried to help me find myself again by sending me off to Davos to make what I would for *Talk* of the World Economic Forum. There I met up again with Stryker McGuire of *Newsweek*, a sympathetic companion who tried to help me out with a light-hearted 'good-bad-ok-bad' index of my mood over numerous Swiss meals.

Back in New York, my mood was not improved by a sour review of my *Shakespeare* in the *New York Times* by its waspish critic, Michiko Kakutani; one of her kinder remarks was that it was 'perhaps best read not as a work of biography, but as a historical novel starring a playwright as its conquering hero'. There was consolation in spades that very night at my weekly poker game, hosted by the former editor of the *New York Times* Sunday Book Review, Charlie Simmons, and featuring such other long-standing contributors as the critic Walter Goodman. 'Well, if Kakutani doesn't like it,' they all declared, 'it must be good!'

That autumn saw the too-close-to-call, as it turned out, presidential election between Al Gore and George W. Bush. On election night, Tina Brown was co-hosting a party at Elaine's, the fashionable watering hole on the Upper East Side, with Weinstein and Michael Bloomberg. As I arrived on the block, there were police barriers yelling DO NOT CROSS, which led me to suspect that even more than the usual crop of A-list celebrities lay in store. As the party went on, it did indeed gradually become apparent that the president and senator (as she became that night) Clinton were expected to join the throng.

The hour was growing late by the time a Tannoy announcement

apologised that the Clintons had not materialised; the results being so close, the president was still 'working the phones' to the West Coast, where the polls were still open. But they would welcome a small group of guests at their nearby hotel suite. I was about to head home when I found my arm grabbed by Tina, who ushered me towards some stretch limos which had suddenly materialised outside.

So I was one of a handful of guests, including the film stars Uma Thurman and Ben Affleck (who just happens to be Cindy's cousin), driven to the Four Seasons Hotel and admitted via airport-style security to the Clintons' suite. The outgoing president was hypnotic, moving from one TV screen to the next explaining each contest in detail, and fretting about how close the overall result seemed to be.

We were all much amused when the result in Missouri showed that John Ashcroft – the man Bush would later appoint his attorney general – had lost to a dead man. But the race for president remained perilously close, and there was much trashing of Ralph Nader, whose run for the Green Party had evidently cost Clinton's vice-president crucial votes. By the time it was well into the wee small hours, and quite clear there was going to be no result that night, we all gathered round as Clinton shaped up to make a farewell speech.

'No journalists here, are there?' he said with a wry smile, knowing full well that most of us were just that.

'So,' he went on, raising his glass to propose a toast, 'fuck Ralph Nader!' We all repeated the phrase in a farewell refrain, which turned out to be prophetic as months of 'hanging' chads eventually led to the Supreme Court ruling that saw George W. Bush dubbed president.

The following year, long after she'd thrown me out, I was still trying to persuade Cindy to take me back, with the freak result that the week of 9/11 was the only week all year that I spent in London. Pre-summit with Cindy that very day, I was lunching with Gill Coleridge when our waiter told us that a plane had flown into the Empire State Building in New York, devastating the area, with thousands dead. I spent the afternoon at Cindy's learning what had really happened, naturally unable to address my heartfelt agenda. The smell of death was still floating past my window after I finally got back to Manhattan, whence Roger Alton commissioned me to write a weekly New York Diary for *The Observer* on the city's slow recovery from this unique trauma.

When our time at the Library was finally up, Peter Gay hosted a farewell luncheon in the Center for Scholars and Writers at which I was delegated to speak on behalf of the inaugural Fellows. I chose to do so in verse – beginning, with due apologies to Coleridge:

> On 42 did Dorothy a stately pleasure-dome decree
> Where Gay, the sacred scholar, ran
> A Center measureless to man
> Catered from A to Zee . . .

I missed daily life at the Center, but continued to pop into the Library's collection of Shelley and His Circle while still working on my life of Leigh Hunt. Life in Manhattan meanwhile remained a series of adventures which were slowly managing to raise my spirits. It was time for me to make a move. After only a 'virtual' tour online, I bought – rather bravely, I thought at the time – an apartment in a converted school in Hackney, east London. Time to admit defeat and head home.

The *Daily Mail*, in the pseudonymous shape of the ever charitable Ephraim Hardcastle, naturally reminded readers of my recent pledge to quit Britain before quoting unnamed 'friends' of mine as saying 'he'll use the events of September 11 to explain his return'. I didn't. I blamed a broken heart, and the need to see more of my beloved sons – all, by now, contentedly living their own lives.

But Martin Amis would later rub salt in my wounds, albeit inadvertently, by writing of his own father Kingsley's break-up with his second wife, Elizabeth Jane Howard: 'A man who abandons his first wife and is then himself abandoned by her successor loses everything: He becomes an amatory zero.'

Yes, Mart, that was me. I slunk home a forlorn, self-pitying amatory zero.

18

AMNICOLIST

Back in London from New York in mid-2002, unwontedly single and unemployed, I asked Roger Alton if he could give me any work on *The Observer*. Throughout the 1990s, I reminded him over lunch, I had stood in for several of his critics – theatre, music, even restaurants – during the six weeks of the year each went on holiday. What if I now stood in for *all* his critics during the six weeks per annum they were off duty? Throw in film, art, TV, maybe even dance, plus the occasional Review Front, and that would surely be worth a full-time annual salary?

'Nice try,' replied Roger, 'but I need a new music critic.' His existing one, he explained, had just defected to another paper.

'But I can't even read music,' I protested.

'Maybe not,' said he, 'but you've written a book about Tchaikovsky. And you've translated some operas. And you've done it before for us just fine!'

And so, for what turned out to be most of the decade, I became *The Observer*'s classical music critic. And a very pleasant assignment it was, too, with free tickets to all the major operas and concerts in London and throughout the country, occasionally abroad.

I had long been a lover of classical music, even before my first marriage broadened my musical horizons. As early as my school-days, my unlikely initiation had come via a study-mate's copy of *The Rite of Spring*; I can still hear Stravinsky's voice intoning, 'I did not write *Le Sacre*; I was the vessel through which *Le Sacre* passed.' Revision at Oxford was soothed by the strains of Mozart,

Beethoven and Brahms, not to mention the Tchaikovsky my grandfather had given me. Marriage to Amanda had expanded my knowledge of the piano repertoire, as well as introducing me to the songs of Schubert, Schumann and others, plus of course the operatic canon to which she was so devoted. I also loved Ray Charles, Leonard Cohen and the jeux d'esprit of Randy Newman. But 'classical' music – for all the awkwardness of the name – seemed to me beyond challenge for pleasure and at times, yes, pain.

I sympathised with the wisecrack of the American comedian Martin Mull: 'Writing about music is like dancing about architecture'. Perhaps it *helped* that I was musically illiterate? What are critics for, after all? Most take themselves pretty seriously, quite as seriously as the artists they review, growing indignant at any suggestion that they are merely consumer guides, recommending outings that offer the best value for money. In many cases, like concerts, the occasion has been a one-off, so it is more a question of re-evaluating a soloist, orchestra or conductor than recommending an event the reader has already missed; with theatre and opera, it is indeed a chance to suggest whether or not a performance is worth the price of absurdly expensive tickets.

Having been one of the few to have essayed both, I can testify that theatre critics have a strict rule against discussing a performance in the interval, turning away if you offer any kind of comment on the proceedings so far, while music critics pile out into the bar saying, 'Is this as bad as I think it is?' One opera critic of my acquaintance cares only about voice – to the point of taking singers out to dinner after a performance, to advise where his or her career should go from here – while most assess all aspects of a production, including of course staging and design. Me, I attempted no more than to represent the relatively well-informed music-lover, relishing my good fortune in spending my evenings so enjoyably – and being paid for it!

On first returning to London, I had been pleasantly surprised by how much I liked the quiet new bachelor flat in a converted east London school which I had purchased after seeing it only online. But it was bereft, of course, of all the necessary devices, not least telephones. So I went out and bought one, plugged it in and . . . immediately it rang.

'Hello,' said a familiar voice, 'is that Anthony Holden?' Yes. 'This is Simon Russell Beale.'

To which I replied in astonishment: 'You mean the actor?'

'That's right,' he replied with some diffidence.

'Good heavens,' I exclaimed, adding instinctively: 'I saw your Hamlet on both sides of the Atlantic . . . you were wonderful!'

'How kind of you,' said he. 'Appropriate, too, in a way. I'm calling to say how much I'm enjoying your book about Shakespeare. I see you're talking about him at the Bath Festival on Sunday morning. It so happens that I'll be there, too – I'm giving a talk that afternoon – so I wondered if I might buy you lunch?'

Accepting his offer with surprised delight, I naturally wondered how he knew my phone number. In fact, come to think of it, what *was* my phone number? I suddenly realised that even I didn't know it. So, rather than being rude enough to ask my distinguished caller how he had got hold of my number, I asked him instead to be kind enough to tell me what it was.

There followed a happy lunch together in Bath that weekend, after he had attended the talk I gave that morning in the Ustinov Theatre. My sons later told me that Simon did a wonderful impersonation of me, waving my arms around as I rabbited on. Yes, I am delighted to say that this proved the birth of another lasting and precious friendship.

Easter Saturday 2002 saw the death of Queen Elizabeth the Queen Mother at the age of 101. For all his self-imposed vow never again to write about the royals, *The Observer*'s music critic found himself, at the editor's insistence, penning a hasty obituary. At least I managed to turn my farewell to the last British Empress into an assault on those she left behind, especially her eldest grandson.

'The Queen Mother is dead; long live the Queen,' I began, arguing that the demise of the 'grand old matriarch' deprived the monarchy of its last link with its glory days – let alone, given the recent spate of royal divorces, the 'family' image which has so long sustained it through the twentieth century. A new urgency would now attend the long-running debate about the pros and cons of King Charles III, 'that curious amalgam of dedication and decadence, ever his own worst enemy at the court of public opinion.' Not to mention Queen Camilla. 'In fact, monarchists would rather you didn't; these days they fret that this dread prospect alone could bring down the whole crumbling edifice.' At the time of his grandmother's death, the would-be monarch and supreme governor of the Church was a self-confessed adulterer living in sin with another man's ex-wife.

Twenty years earlier, I had sampled the Clarence House gin with her private secretary after being persuaded to write a brief biography of the Queen Mother, later reissued by publishers eager to capitalise on her ever-advancing years. He did not demur when I ventured that his boss was an excellent advertisement for the preservative powers of gin.

Now I could walk into my bank and remark to my manager that it was no wonder their flag outside was at half-mast; they had lost their greatest asset. When he expressed mild surprise at my *lèse-majesté*, I could but quote the Queen herself (ever responsible for her mother's debts) when the Queen Mother's overdraft reached all of £4 million: 'Coutts would have folded long ago but for Mummy's overdraft.'

For all her profligacy, no one has since served more effectively to disarm criticism of her increasingly troubled family, and thus of the antiquated institution in their care. The multi-million-pound overdraft of the state-sponsored Queen Mum was shrugged off as the harmless self-indulgence of a popular old pearly queen with an endearing weakness for gin and the gee-gees.

Three months later, to mark Elizabeth II's Golden Jubilee,

I recalled in *The Guardian* how, in the summer of 1953, like countless six-year-old schoolchildren around the land, I had been 'scrubbed up and shoved into clean short trousers to stand for hours waiting for a distant view of the newly-crowned Queen waving from a provincial town-hall balcony.' In the ensuing half-century, 'The more I studied the workings of the House of Windsor, the more of a republican I became.'

Having recently returned from my second three-year stint in the States, I found that someone had built a giant Ferris wheel across the river from Parliament – 'as if we actually wanted to be perceived as an overgrown baby of a nation,' I concluded, 'with a deeply inbred reluctance to grow up.'

'We *like* the Eye, Anthony,' I was gently admonished by the new chairman of the South Bank Arts Centre, (Lord) Clive Hollick, while inviting me to join its board of governors. Originally built as a temporary attraction, with only a five-year lease, the Eye had since been granted permanent status, and the South Bank was charging it considerable rent – since it stood, just, on its land.

When I accepted Hollick's invitation, Roger Alton raised no objection to what might appear to be a potential conflict of interest. I was highly relieved, for I would much enjoy being a governor during Clive's ambitious renovation of the Festival Hall and indeed the entire South Bank complex; and, of course, I often reviewed concerts there without the slightest compunction to speak my mind.

A fellow republican, Milord Hollick led the governors in renaming the royal box in the Festival Hall as the governors' box; sharing it one night with sundry like-minded friends, we were delighted to find ourselves looking down on the Duke of Kent, the royal patron of that evening's orchestra, sitting in the front stalls like a mere pleb.

Given the tens of millions we were raising to spruce up the concert halls and breathe new life into the whole South Bank complex, I thought that I would try to do my bit by organising an evening in 2005 in which prominent people not known to be musicians came onstage and surprised a packed Purcell Room. Entitled *For One Night Only*, and hosted by Clive James, it featured such highlights as the editor of *The Guardian*, Alan Rusbridger, playing a Chopin étude and the Channel 4 News presenter Jon Snow tearing up the stage with 'Do Wah Diddy Diddy', while Alfred Brendel walked on to glare witheringly at the piano before reciting one of his own quirky poems. Most acts were accompanied from the side of the stage by Ken Follett's band Damn Right I Got the Blues – who that night played for, among others, the children's TV presenter Floella Benjamin, who later became not merely a baroness but the Follett Big Band's resident vocalist.

Delayed by my domestic upheavals, my life of Leigh Hunt finally appeared in 2005 under the title *The Wit in the Dungeon*, the nickname bestowed on him by Byron in a poem inviting their mutual friend Thomas Moore to join him on a visit to Hunt in his prison cell, which had become something of a literary salon.

Not for the first time in my writing career, I discovered that someone else had also been at work at the same time on the same subject: an academic by the name of Nicholas Roe, who rather saucily sub-titled his own work *Fiery Heart: The First Life of Leigh Hunt*, as if my own didn't exist. When I challenged him on this – having agreed to make a joint appearance in Hampstead, under the auspices of the Keats-Shelley Association – he explained that he did not mean that his was the first life of Leigh Hunt, but that his book covered only the first half of his life; and it does indeed end with the death of his friend Shelley, when my own 430-page biography still has 244 to go.

Unlike Roe, I made no great claims for Hunt's poetry, arguing more that he was a shrewd critic and influential champion of other writers; Roe, meanwhile, spoke up for Hunt's qualities as a poet, which I myself considered rather modest. The event being in Hampstead, where the Alvarezes lived, Al and Anne came along with Frank Kermode, and we all went out to dinner afterwards in a nearby restaurant. Teasingly, I leaned across the table to Frank, and asked him with a very straight face: 'So, Sir Frank, 'you're an authority on these matters. Did you learn anything this evening about Leigh Hunt that you didn't already know?'

'Yes' replied Frank without hesitation, and with an equally straight face. 'I learned that Leigh Hunt was a great poet.'

By now I was busy with another long-planned project equally close to my heart. While we had been translating *Don Giovanni* some twenty years earlier, Amanda had given me a copy of the memoirs of Lorenzo Da Ponte, librettist of many operas including Mozart's supreme trio, *The Marriage of Figaro*, *Don Giovanni* and *Così fan tutte*. Highly entertaining but absurdly vainglorious, his memories climaxed with the laughably self-important boast: 'I can never remember without satisfaction and joy that Europe and the whole world owe the exquisite vocal music of this remarkable genius to my own perseverance and determination.' Now, at last, I achieved a long-standing ambition by using this risible claim as the epigraph for a biography of Mozart's gamesome chameleon of a librettist. His was a story so remarkable that the book, for once, all but wrote itself.

Born Emanuele Conegliano in 1749 in the Venetian hill-town of Ceneda (now the 'old town' of Vittorio Veneto), this uneducated, illiterate Jewish boy ran wild until he was fourteen, when his widowed father's wish to marry a teenage Christian girl saw his family received into the Catholic Church. According to custom, the eldest son assumed the name of the bishop who baptised him, Lorenzo Da Ponte.

With the bishop as his sponsor, he received a classical education, and was ordained a Catholic priest. But he soon sought out a new life in decadent Venice, where he became close friends with Casanova, and indulged in numerous affairs with married women, to the point where he found himself banished by the doge. Wandering west, he arrived in Vienna with a letter of introduction to the court composer, Antonio Salieri, who persuaded the Emperor Joseph II to appoint Da Ponte his theatre-poet. Here he made his name writing libretti for Salieri and other leading composers of the day. In 1783, at a party given by Mozart's landlord, the young, unemployed composer from Salzburg was thrilled to meet the eminent abbé. Desperate to abandon the German tradition for Italian opera, Mozart wrote to his father: 'The best thing is when a good composer, who understands the stage enough to make sound suggestions, meets an able poet, that true phoenix.'

In Da Ponte, Mozart had met his 'true phoenix'. The three works they wrote together have stood the test of time as oper-atic masterpieces, to which Da Ponte's poetic skill and theatrical instincts made a vital contribution. It was with these works that opera came of age. When Da Ponte was born, Handel reigned supreme; four years after his death, Wagner made his debut. Da Ponte and Mozart were the twin pillars of that transition, transforming opera into an art form exploring everyday human issues in a potent, accessible but above all realistic manner, via characters with whom the audience could identify.

After Joseph's death, Da Ponte's jealous rivals soon conspired to have him banished from Vienna, as he had been from Venice ten years earlier. There followed adventures in London, where he was frequently imprisoned for debt, and finally the nascent United States, where he made a false start as a grocer before finding work as a teacher of Italian, taking up the Professorship of Italian at Columbia University which still bears his name. Three years later, as he neared eighty, he brought the first Italian opera company to America, not least for a performance of 'his' *Don Giovanni*. In his final decade he built and ran America's first opera house, in Greenwich Village.

Da Ponte died in 1838, in his ninetieth year, and lies buried in the Catholic Cemetery in Queens, the world's largest, beneath the roar of the jets descending into JFK airport. This proud if hedonistic aesthete would be as surprised as dismayed to know that those few pilgrims who come to pay their respects do so solely because of his collaboration with Mozart, whom he had known for just seven of his ninety years.

A major bonus ensued when Melvyn Bragg thought Da Ponte's colourful life was worth a *South Bank Show* documentary. Always a generous supporter of my work, Melvyn had twice before laid ingenious plans to make TV films based on my books. He had been fascinated by the statistic in my life of Shakespeare that, before he could afford a horse, it would take the Bard four days to walk from Stratford-upon-Avon to London; Melvyn thought it would be fun for me to make the same journey over four episodes on camera, meeting relevant Shakespeareans en route (such as Al 'Looking for Richard' Pacino). Again, after the attention accorded *Big Deal*, he had laid plans for me to demonstrate the global appeal of poker in a film called *Around the World with 80K*. Neither had come to pass, alas, but this time I found myself taking photographs in Ceneda as stills for a film that actually did get made. Some of these snaps even wound up in my life of Da Ponte – the only time any book of mine has contained the credit 'Photograph by author', of which I was absurdly proud.

I naturally took the chance to make as many such research trips as possible to Venice, incongruously up there with Manhattan as my favourite places on earth. When I told Frank Kermode that I was also planning to visit Vienna for further research, he asked if he could join me. So I duly devised a Mozart walk around Vienna, on which I had difficulty keeping up with Frank, by then in his mid-eighties. We went to *Le Nozze di Figaro* at the State Opera, but his vertigo kept him resolutely earthbound while I made my own pilgrimage on Orson Welles' *Third Man* Ferris wheel.

During my absence in New York, my Tuesday night poker game had finally ceased to exist, due to some sadly early deaths as well as a few emigrations. The handful of surviving players welcomed me to a new game, also on Tuesday nights, hosted above an Italian restaurant off Knightsbridge by the advertising guru-turned-art connoisseur Charles Saatchi. All afternoon, Saatchi would have been playing Scrabble in the same room for four-figure sums.

It was around this time that poker was really taking off online and on TV – to the point where I finally agreed, fifteen years on, to the request of *Big Deal*'s original publisher and long-time champion, Ursula Mackenzie of Little, Brown, that I write a sequel. Despite my fears (entirely justified, as it turned out) that it wouldn't be able to muster the same spring in its step, I repeated the same formula, winning my way at minimal cost to myself into the $10,000 'main event' at the 2005 and 2006 World Series of Poker in Vegas – with a special emphasis on playing with all those fresh faces who had qualified online and so never before played poker at the same table as actual human beings staring back into the all too revealing whites of their wide eyes.

Bigger Deal, as I called the book, made its point most effectively with the startling effect of online poker on the sheer numbers involved in its world championship. Since the World Series of Poker began with seven players at Binion's Horseshoe in 1970, it had grown to forty-two starters and a first prize of $210,000 when I first covered it for the *Sunday Times* in 1978. By the time I myself first played in it in 1988, at the beginning of what turned out to be *Big Deal*, I was one of 167 starters playing for a first prize of $700,000. In 2006, at the end of *Bigger Deal*, I was but one of almost 9,000 starters competing for a first prize of $12 million, the richest in all sport. That year's World Series, staged over seven weeks in July and August, amounted to the biggest sporting event in the history of the planet. No fewer than 44,500 players took part in at least one of its forty-five events for a prize pool of more than $150 million.

Inevitably, I could not continue my duties as *The Observer*'s music critic while so extensively travelling the poker world; anxious not to forfeit the job, I simply negotiated some extra time off. So music inevitably weaves its way in and out of the plot. One night I reviewed the first night of a new Royal Opera production of Puccini's opera *La fanciulla del West*, in which Minnie, the sole female character in the only opera set in the Wild West, is being pursued by both the bandit and the sheriff who is out to get him. The wounded desperado, Dick Johnson, is hiding in the rafters of Minnie's log cabin when the sheriff, name of Rance, arrives to collar him. Our heroine is just protesting that she has no idea where Johnson is when drops of his blood fall from above on Rance, who promptly drags him out of his hiding place.

In desperation, Minnie makes a bold suggestion: that they sort it all out over a game of poker (*'Una partita a poker!'*). If Rance wins, he gets Minnie but lets Johnson go; if Minnie wins, she gets Johnson and they go free. The crafty girl knows that the sheriff is a bit of a gambler; so Rance agrees to this – foolishly, it transpires, for Minnie pretends to feel faint when she loses the first hand, then fixes the deck while Rance fetches her a brandy. The rest is inevitable – apart from the fact that Minnie and Johnson go free, making her one of the few of his heroines Puccini does not kill off for the sake of a multi-Kleenex climax.

Gambling had been immortalised earlier, of course, in such operas as Verdi's *La Traviata* and Tchaikovsky's *The Queen of Spades*; but in mid-*Bigger Deal* I enjoyed being ambushed by that very word 'poker'. Thinking it would be fun to write it into the book, I made enquiries among expert colleagues and was assured that *La fanciulla* was the only time in all opera that the word 'poker' is specifically mentioned. Six months later, as I prepared to return to Vegas, I was amused to prove the experts wrong while reviewing a revival of John Adams' opera *Nixon in China*. In the last act, a summit-scarred Nixon is reminiscing gloomily with his wife Pat about his wartime service in the South Pacific. As her husband tells her things she has never heard before, Pat tries to console him with the words: 'But you won at poker?'

'I sure did,' sings Nixon. 'Five-card stud taught me a lot about mankind . . .'

In 2007, two years after *Bigger Deal*, I spent the year of my sixtieth birthday writing not, for the first time in four decades, yet
another round-figure birthday biography of Prince Charles, but
the latest volume in my new cottage industry of poker, proprie-
torially entitled *Holden on Hold'em*. While in Barcelona to play for
England in the 2006 World Cup of Poker, I discussed this latest
idea for a manual with the marketing director of the world's
biggest poker website, PokerStars.com. I was looking for some
way to breathe fresh life into a project that might otherwise just
dwindle into another unreadable poker manual. We agreed that
one way of gathering entertaining material would be for me to
play on the European Poker Tour, which was run by PokerStars,
for whom I would now become a sponsored player. So that meant
my entry fee and expenses would be paid for half a dozen EPT
events all over Europe that year, as well as the 2007–08 World
Series of Poker in Las Vegas.

To be paid to play poker, win or lose! Along with free travel
and hotels, this was dreamland. As I donned my stylish PokerStars
shirt, my friends in the Tuesday game were beside themselves
with envy. *Bigger Deal* soon spawned an eponymous website, also
sponsored by PokerStars, on which I was one of a dozen or so
poker writers who contributed regular blogs, and hosted a weekly
online tournament in which anyone could take us on.

While writing *Bigger Deal*, I naturally wanted to meet an online
poker player expert enough – unlike me – to play simultaneous
games on several screens at once. Via my son Ben I met just such
a punter, who had earned his living as an online poker player in
his twenties. His name was Oliver Chubb, and he was to prove
an invaluable adviser to me on both books.

When *Bigger Deal* finally appeared in 2006, I was thrilled to find that the publishers had persuaded Gerald Scarfe to draw a group of surly-looking poker players for the dust jacket. Given that Ralph Steadman had drawn the cover for the paperback of *Big Deal*, this made an unusually distinctive duo, neither of whom usually stooped to illustrating dust jackets. I guess it helped that I had worked with them both at Harry Evans's *Sunday Times*.

So it was yet another bonus the following year when Harry and Tina generously threw another of their inimitable parties to mark the US publication of *Bigger Deal*. And who should invite himself but yet another of my cinematic heroes, Steve Martin, who asked to sit next to me at dinner because he wanted some poker tips. Why? Because he was due to play poker that week against, of all people, Warren Buffett. My God, said I, what sort of stakes do you play for against Warren Buffett?

'Have you heard', he asked me, 'of Netmiles?' No.

'They're what you use to pay for private jets!'

With characteristic style, Harry had set up a poker table, complete with green baize, chips and cards, for half a dozen of us to play poker after dinner. A true masterclass for Steve Martin. But I never did hear how he got on against Buffett.

At the World Series in Vegas that summer, my poker player-writer friend Peter Alson, author of *Take Me to the River*, introduced me over dinner to another player-writer I much admired, James McManus, who had reached the final table of the main event in 2000 and written a wonderful book about it called *Positively Fifth Street*. McManus had been asking me over dinner about Martin Amis when, on our way out of the restaurant, we found – of all people – Christopher Hitchens sitting smoking at the bar. 'I knew I'd find you here somewhere, Buster,' said he with a grin. 'You've just missed little Keith.'

'Little Keith' was what Hitchens called our friend Amis, as if he were a character in one of his own novels. He too was in Vegas to play in the World Series and write about it for the *Sunday Times*. So a couple of nights later we found ourselves having dinner together on the eve of the 'main event', as immortalised in Amis's piece, republished in his 2006 anthology *The Rub of Time*, where he calls McManus and myself 'two of the top writer-players in pokerdom'. After some delicate negotiation with both parties, this ended up as Martin dubbing me 'the top writer in pokerdom' on the jacket of *Bigger Deal*.

While I was in Vegas that summer my youngest son Ben would come over to see me from Hollywood, where he was serving his apprenticeship in the movie business, with his lovely girlfriend Salome Leventis, whom he would marry – with, romantically enough, only a judge and a photographer for company – on an oceanside clifftop in Carmel, California, later that year.

That evening I spent in a London restaurant with my oldest son Sam and his own new girlfriend, Ursula McGeoch; at 8 p.m. sharp – 12 noon West Coast time – we raised a glass to toast the happy couple as they tied the distant knot. The romance of it all seemed to give Sam and Ursula ideas, for before long they too were married at her parents' home in Rhode Island. Given my lifelong love affair with the US, and my own second marriage at Cape Cod, it seemed to me as romantic as unlikely that both my sons had chosen to marry in the States.

That very week, meanwhile, I also became something I had always wanted to be: an amnicolist. Having grown up by the seaside, I have always felt an elemental need to live near water, which is why I looked back so fondly at those all-too-brief eighteen months in that bachelor pad by the river in Chiswick Mall. While living in Hackney, I had rarely bothered even to open the school-room shutters, so little was there to see through the windows in that particular part of London.

For some months, I had been walking along the south bank of the Thames, looking for possible river-view dwellings all the way from Vauxhall via Shakespeare's Globe at Bankside to the many con-verted wharves around London Bridge, Tower Bridge and beyond. Eventually I found the pad of my dreams: an apartment directly on the Thames in Rotherhithe, with a fifth-floor view across the river to Limehouse and Canary Wharf. Unusually for that part of town, it was in an elegant Victorian building; venture out on the roof, and the only Victorian buildings in sight, indeed the only pre-war buildings, were this, the one I was standing on, and The Grapes, the pub across the river at Limehouse, once frequented by Dickens (and now owned by Ian McKellen). Everything else in sight was post-war; this had been the epicentre of the Blitz.

Among my housewarming presents was Peter Ackroyd's book *Sacred River*, his recently published history of the Thames. This, I swiftly realised, was a book I would very much like to have writ-ten myself, in my own way. As I explored the area and its history, however, an even better idea began to take shape in my mind. Given how much of British history had centred on this area — from the Roman and Anglo-Saxon eras to the docks, slavery and the Blitz — you could argue that a large part of British history had pivoted around this maritime square mile, with the Isle of Dogs becoming Canary Wharf as a symbol of Thatcher's Britain and the

Millennium Dome (now the O2) on the Greenwich Peninsula as a symbol of Blair's. So I hatched a plan for a book called *Docklands: A History of Britain* — even drafted a synopsis for my agent, plus a screenplay for a vivid Melvyn Bragg TV series — but got distracted, as so often before, by other pursuits.

Amid my investigations of Rotherhithe's literary pedigree, I found that the stretch of the river beneath my window was the setting for the opening scenes of Dickens' *Our Mutual Friend*, a particular quote from which I wanted solemnly inscribed above my front door: 'The wheels rolled on, and rolled down by the Monument and by the Tower, and by the Docks; down by Ratcliffe, and by Rotherhithe; down by where accumulated scum of humanity seemed to be washed from higher grounds, like so much moral sewage, and to be pausing until its own weight forced it over the bank and sunk it into the river.'

Rotherhithe, in short, where the scum of humanity is washed down into the river by the weight of its own moral sewage . . . J Morley shared my delight in this with such relish as to present me with a family heirloom, a signed photo of Dickens, which hangs on my riverside wall framed alongside the quote.

By this time, I'm pleased to report, my own love life had long since begun to look up again, at last refreshing, nay rejuvenating, my *amour propre*. All this time I had still been reviewing operas and concerts for *The Observer*; a pair of free tickets for such coveted nights out, followed by a stylish West End dinner, proved the perfect formula for the serious, post-Cindy wooing of other women for the first time in quite a while. My self-esteem was soon refurbished by a succession of romances which finally began to restore me to my true self.

As indeed did becoming a grandfather. Just as *Bigger Deal* had been dedicated to the newlywed Ben and Salome, so two years later *Holden on Hold'em* was dedicated to their newborn twins, George and Ione, with a little ditty from 'Grantonio':

> *Let drums be rolled, corks popped and flags unfurl'd;*
> *George and Ione, welcome to the world.*

Thrilled to make my debut as a grandfather at sixty, I was curiously surprised – and often upset – to discover others, some of them older than me, bemoaning the fact that they weren't, and by now presumably never would be. Among them was Frank Kermode, who rather surprised me with so sentimental a confession.

A great music-lover, as well-informed as he was passionate, Frank also had a perverse aversion to French music, which he considered 'sissy'. From the Edinburgh Festival that summer, I sent him a saucy clerihew:

> *I do not care*
> *For La Mer.*
> *Methinks Debussy*
> *Needed some pussy.*

To which he promptly replied:

> *Ravel*
> *Is hell.*

Give me David Bowie
Over Daphnis and Chloe

During 2008 the Queen paid a visit to declare open the newly renovated South Bank Centre. Down the steps to that entrance we were all lined up to greet her, as Clive Hollick told me with a grin that he'd be keeping a close eye on whether or not I bowed. When the big moment came, I found that the steps had me towering above HM. She is so short that, as politely as I could, I shook the royal hand, straining not to bend down towards her beneath Hollick's beady eye. It must have made a strange sight to see the monarch reaching an arm up beyond eye-level to greet this particular host. The occasion is now commemorated by a plaque in the Festival Hall's Waterloo entrance.

As a music critic, I was able to combine my twin passions with a programme note about card games in opera for a production of Tchaikovsky's *The Queen of Spades*, and a Proms interval talk on Radio 3 before Stravinsky's *Jeu de cartes*. Other broadcasts heard me enthusing about personal favourites from Tchaikovsky's sixth symphony, the *Pathétique*, to Antonio Caldara's sublime oratorio *Maddalena ai piedi di Cristo*. On finally calling it a day at the end of 2008, I confessed forlornly: 'After some 1,000 musical nights out, and as many CD reviews, I find I have finally run out of adjectives.'

A few months before, as well as my weekly music review, I had two further, rather different pieces in one Sunday's edition of *The Observer*, each flowing from other perennial passions.

The previous year I had been invited up to Stratford-upon-Avon by friends in the cast of a marathon eight-play Shakespeare history cycle to take part in an RSC poker tournament. When the shows came to the Roundhouse in London, therefore, I felt honour-bound to go and see them all again: eight plays adding up to more than twenty-four hours (excluding intervals), spread over two evenings plus two whole days, each starting at 10.30 in the morning and finishing more than twelve hours later. It was one of the supreme experiences of my long theatre-going lifetime. 'Forget Wagner's Ring cycle, a mere 16 hours of opera spread over four long evenings,' I wrote. 'This is the ultimate cultural marathon.' At post-show parties in the Roundhouse bar, an exhausted if uplifted audience celebrated thirty-four actors playing 264 parts between them.

In the same issue, in the run-up to that year's US presidential election, I revealed the little-known fact that the Democratic candidate against John McCain, Senator Barack Obama, considered himself 'a pretty good poker player' (as he had hinted to the Press Association when asked to name a 'hidden talent'). Subsequent investigations were hampered by a shutdown on the subject from his media minders. But it was already on the record that in 1997, when he first took his seat in the Illinois senate, Obama won over colleagues of all parties with his charm and expertise at the poker table.

Personally, of course, I thoroughly approved. Expertise at poker was once an unwritten job requirement for all US presidents, ranging from Andrew Jackson, Ulysses S. Grant, Theodore Roosevelt and Warren Harding to FDR, Truman, Eisenhower, LBJ and Nixon. Harry Truman had played the game with the White House press corps while pondering whether to drop the first atomic bomb on Japan; Nixon financed his first political race on his wartime poker winnings in the navy; Johnson used his poker know-how to forge political alliances in Texas. In recent years, however, this noble tradition seemed to have fallen out of fashion: Ford, Carter, Reagan, Bush Sr, Clinton, Bush Jr – not a poker player among them.

My inside knowledge of Obama the poker player was due to Jim McManus, a Chicago resident who knew the candidate personally. It was then reported that McCain was a craps addict, whose staff had to dissuade him from playing openly in the casino during a campaign stop in Las Vegas. Urged by Obama's minders to cease and desist, I was thus unable to ask the obvious question: which would you rather have as US president – a poker player who takes carefully calculated risks, or a craps addict who entrusts his (and so the nation's) luck to wild throws of a dice?

In November 2009 George Weidenfeld, who had himself just turned ninety, threw Frank Kermode a stylish ninetieth birthday party. It was followed by a smaller, select dinner party at the Chelsea Arts Club where we also saluted the two books Frank had just published. He was still reviewing for the *London* and *New York Review of Books* while giving lectures in Cambridge and at the British Museum. He had also crafted a libretto from *King Lear* for an opera by his friend Alexander Goehr, performed at the Royal Opera's Linbury Studio under the title *Promised End*.

One Saturday in mid-August 2010 I went to Cambridge, as most weekends, to hang out with Frank. All that Sunday afternoon we sat outside on his balcony in the sun, having a long, unusually emotional talk in which he reminisced more than was his wont, and kept saying, 'I've been so lucky.' That evening, as we parted with our usual hug, he gave me a knowing look and kissed me on the lips.

He died thirty-six hours later.

19

BIGGEST DEAL

In the late summer of 2008 I came home from a holiday in Italy to a spate of messages on my answering machine from someone I had never heard of with the Irish-sounding name of Patrick Nally.

A quick check online revealed Nally to be a sports entrepreneur much my own age, prone to making the grandiose claim that he was 'the founding father of sports marketing'. As a young man he had co-founded a public relations company whose main purpose was the sale of sponsorship rights to sporting events for obscene amounts of money from blue-chip companies.

What on earth could this Nally want with me? When I eventually agreed to meet him, his first question was whether I regarded poker as a game or a sport. Idly wondering what response he might be expecting, I replied jokily that poker featured on the American sports channel ESPN, so it must be a sport.

He took me seriously – and this turned out to be the answer he wanted to hear. But to what purpose?

Nally had been given my name by a friend of his called Gary Bowman, a sometime poker player who had apparently liked *Big Deal*. Born in Rochdale of Ukrainian parentage, then raised in Canada, Bowman had made millions of dollars from a wire-transfer service for American punters. Now he was willing to provide start-up finance for Nally's plan to found an international sports federation for, of all things, poker. So Nally was looking for a nominal figure-head, well-connected within the game, to lead it. Namely, me.

Well, I was newly unemployed, had nothing better to do, and to my surprise rather welcomed the thought of not writing another book for a while. I had only the vaguest notion what a sports federation was, but now I found myself agreeing to head one up. Nally, after all, would be doing all the work. It was immediately clear that he was a supreme control freak. Fine by me.

My first task was to find a No. 2, a smart and industrious young poker-savvy person for the role of executive director. That was a no-brainer. My new friend Oliver Chubb had a good job at an international insurance broker, calculating ferociously complex odds for and against the success of global marketing campaigns for big-name companies like Coca-Cola. Would he be willing to give it up for an adventure into the unknown? 'It may not work out,' I told him, as he later reminded me, continuing with equally uncanny prescience: 'But at least we will have a few years travelling the world in high style, with a bit of poker thrown in!' These could have been the words of a clairvoyant.

I got off on the wrong foot with Bowman, who wanted to become better acquainted over a few days at a spa in his native Ukraine. Like most poker players, I have never been much of an early riser – so, to be on the safe side, I booked a hotel room at Heathrow before travelling with him to Kyiv on an early-morning flight in November 2008. But the hotel alarm call I had ordered failed to materialise; to my horror I woke up only half an hour before the scheduled take-off time. All I could do was phone Bowman, who was waiting in the Departure Lounge, and lodge the feeblest of excuses.

'Not a good start,' was all he muttered before hanging up and harrumphing off without me. He had arranged a TV press conference in Kyiv the next morning, in which I was supposed to take a leading role. All I could do was frantically fix another flight there later that same day, which turned into a nightmare of delays and nearly missed connections. Although himself the constitutional opposite of me, prone to vanishing to his bed by mid-evening, Bowman was patiently waiting at Kyiv airport when I finally arrived at 1 a.m. – and turned out to be the most genial and generous of hosts. We spent a happy few days there with his Russian friend Dmitry Lisnoy, a historian of card games, who had already founded a national poker federation in Russia, as had Bowman himself in Ukraine.

To launch an international sports federation, you need only a handful of member countries. Thanks to Nally's and Bowman's connections as much as my own, we had all of seven by April 2009, including a hastily assembled UK Federation also under my intrepid leadership. So Nally started as he meant to go on by staging a lavish inaugural Congress at a luxury hotel in Lausanne, legal home of the International Olympic Committee as well as most sporting federations. A solemn all-afternoon session saw me formally elected the first president of the International Federation of Poker, and Oliver Chubb appointed its executive director. My presidential speech at the evening banquet was followed by a poker game with the attendant press, for which we belatedly realised that we had cards but no chips. No problem: the hotel obliged by laying on foil-wrapped mini-chocolates. When the Federation's newly appointed media adviser, Des Wilson, turned out to be the winner, I told him it would mean instant dismissal if he ever told anyone that the IFP's first tournament had been played for chockies.

On the *Bigger Deal* website, my farewell dispatch announced rather grandly that

> The chance to lead poker's first governing body, and to work towards poker's international recognition as a skilled 'mind-sport' rather than just another form of gambling, was an offer I couldn't refuse. The consequences for the game we all love, and so for its players and administrators, are potentially monumental . . . IFP will be working to demonstrate that poker is a 'mind-sport' of strategic skill, not a mere game of chance, and so to win it exemption from gambling legislation throughout the world, and place it on a level of respectability and acceptance alongside bridge, chess etc.

Which is exactly what we began to do. Before long, to my own amazement, many sybaritic trips to its headquarters in Paris resulted in the International Mind Sports Association (IMSA), whose other members include bridge, chess, draughts and Go, accepting poker as a provisional member.

Nally himself had originally taken some persuading that poker could form the nucleus of a sports federation; whenever you mentioned the word 'gambling', he would cross his wrists in the Dracula sign, as if fending off evil spirits. Then his Swiss lawyer in Lausanne had convinced him that it was a perfectly viable – and potentially very lucrative – option, offering his legal services to help achieve their goals. So our next objective, after acceptance by IMSA, became membership of SportAccord, the international association of sports federations – and eventually, yes, winning poker the status of an Olympic sport.

During that year the Royal Shakespeare Company asked me to write a programme note for their forthcoming production of *The Merchant of Venice*, directed by Rupert Goold, with Patrick Stewart as Shylock. Goold, they added, had read my book and particularly asked for me. Naturally I agreed, and asked if there was anything in particular I should know about the production. Yes, came the reply, he's setting it in Las Vegas. 'Oh, *that* book!' I exclaimed – and set to work with a smile. At least I could now add 'President of the International Federation of Poker' to the credits at the foot of my piece.

To become president of anything in your early sixties is very good for morale. To have a handsomely paid job which involves little more than recruiting relevant pals to ancillary jobs, while attending the occasional meeting and making the odd speech, is even better. But if we were an international sports federation, even I thought, shouldn't we be staging some sort of tournament, perhaps annually? Amid our constant travels all over the world, mostly to attend grand international conferences, Nally too seemed to think this a good wheeze.

Despite mutterings about past differences with them, Nally soon formed an alliance with the Japanese sports marketing firm Dentsu, one of the world's largest, in the shape of a well-financed joint venture called Mind Sports Partners. With money apparently no object, I made more than fifty trips abroad in IFP's first three years, including a dozen to Germany, seven to Paris, four to Austria, three to Ukraine, three each to New York and Las Vegas, two to Lausanne, and one each to Prague, Madrid, Copenhagen, Dublin, Monte Carlo, Brussels, Philadelphia, Washington DC and Dubai, not to mention the Isle of Man. I found myself dancing with Romanian gypsies high in the Carpathian Mountains, after far too much vodka; looking down on the troubled Middle East from the world's tallest building, Dubai's Burj Khalifa; and spending many happy weeks in Vegas, making yet more vain attempts to win the title of world poker champion (now formally declared unofficial, to the irritation of its multi-millionaire winners, by none other than my amateur self). Was this a sensible schedule, I wondered, for a less-than-fit sexagenarian?

Poker, I had always argued, is a game of skill more than luck; while writing *Big Deal* I had come up with a provocative statistic: 80 per cent skill, 20 per cent luck. Now I grew fond of quoting the words of the golfer Gary Player, who was once called a 'lucky bastard' by a spectator when he sank a chip from a bunker to win some major tournament. 'You know,' Player pointedly told the heckler as he passed him on his way to the green, 'the more I practise, the luckier I get!'

But the skill-v-luck argument remained controversial, as did the inescapable fact that poker is generally played for money, often large amounts of the stuff, which inevitably evokes the dread word 'gambling'. So, at Nally's behest, I reluctantly commissioned Oliver to formulate a poker equivalent of duplicate bridge, in which teams seated at separate tables receive the same cards, thus ensuring the supremacy of skill over luck. Once Oliver had managed this with characteristic efficiency, there remained only the problem of what to call this strange new variant of the game; ever fond of alliteration, I favoured 'Parallel Poker', but the damp squib to emerge from a dozen other candidates eventually proved to be 'Match Poker'.

Jim McManus was appointed IFP's ambassador for Match Poker, to spread the gospel around the poker world. This new game required, as does duplicate bridge, spectator-unfriendly partitions, so that the players cannot see what is going on elsewhere as the same hands are simultaneously dealt and played at different tables. So our next problem was how to make this look sexy as well as skilful. Over our umpteenth lunch on expenses, Oliver and I came up with a solution worthy of James Bond himself: why not sit the separate tables in the thirty-two pods of the London Eye? If we also hired next-door County Hall itself, we could hold IFP's first World Championship in 'regular' poker there as well as its annual Congress – in which I could preside on the same majestic throne once occupied by Ken Livingstone and other GLC leaders until Margaret Thatcher closed it down in 1988.

Mind Sports Partners duly came up with the several million dollars required to stage this glamorous debut event, and IFP's first major tournaments were held at County Hall in November 2011, resulting in some spectacular photographs of sky-high poker being played on the London Eye.

© Getty Images

Next day I wound up presenting the first Nations Cup, as we called IFP's Match Poker world trophy, to Germany; and we launched IFP's first individual world championship in the baroque splendour of County Hall's Rotunda. Entry was free, as befitted a non-gambling mind-sports federation event, but half a million dollars were on offer in prize money, for which we had flown in (to their bemused delight) numerous big-name players from all over the world. Even a seasoned American pro like Mike Sexton, co-host of TV's *World Poker Tour*, told me with wide eyes that he had never played poker in such magnificent surroundings.

For publicity purposes, I had also laid on a few poker-playing celebrities of my acquaintance: world snooker champion Steve Davis, the Australian cricketer Shane Warne, the Tory MP Zac Goldsmith. The $250,000 first prize was eventually won by a little-known Spaniard called Raul Mestre. Each of the other seven players to reach the final table – from Brazil, Serbia, Australia, Germany, England and Japan – also received a five-figure cash prize, as well as the chic Perrelet watch which was to be IFP's equivalent of a WSOP bracelet.

For reasons that will soon unfold, this last event has never since been staged again. A few qualifying events for the Nations Cup were held over the next couple of years – with players so delighted at the rare chance to represent their country at poker as to agree to play duplicate poker on mobile phones, to my surprise, with playing cards nowhere in sight, and no money involved. But a decade later Raul Mestre remains the reigning IFP world champion – and presumably always will.

As Oliver and I painstakingly increased IFP's global membership, reaching our initial target of fifty nations within three years, I thought that another statutory function of an international sports federation must be to codify the rules of the game. So I founded an IFP Rules Committee, chaired by David Flusfeder, otherwise renowned as a fine novelist. When his eminent committee's work was done, we founded IFP Books in partnership with Bobby

Nayyar of Limehouse Books to publish the results in a handsome handbook, launched with a lavish party-cum-tournament in a London club.

A few months later I flew to Boston to co-chair a mind-sports conference at Harvard University with its longstanding Professor of Law, Charles Nesson. Renowned for his successful defence in 1973 of Daniel Ellsberg, who had released the classified 'Pentagon Papers' about US conduct of the Vietnam War to the *New York Times*, Nesson had concluded that court-room tactics had much in common with those of poker. Ever since, he had insisted that his pupils – many of whom went on to highly distinguished careers, not least one Barack Obama – learned how to play poker before he would deign to teach them law.

The conference's first day concluded with the first poker tournament ever to be held in Harvard's stately Law Library. In the presence of delegates from the Massachusetts library and educational departments, the second day climaxed in agreement that the equipment necessary for all mind sports, including poker, would be placed in all state public libraries; it had been demonstrated that mind sports could fend off dementia. My campaign to have poker taught in schools, to improve pupils' mathematical and probability skills, was not met with quite such enthusiasm, though I soon heard that poker was being taught in classrooms around New York's Lower East Side. And the *Times* newspaper, despite my combative history with it, even printed a presidential letter from me arguing that poker be taught in UK schools.

But these proved among the last highs of a year in which all matters IFP grew increasingly murky, and relations ever more strained.

By now, Dentsu's London leaders were openly at war with Nally. That autumn, the supremo of Dentsu Sports Global, the same Japanese grandee who had flown over for the MSP signing ceremony eighteen months earlier, again arrived from Tokyo to summon me to the boardroom for a grilling. How had IFP managed to spend \$12 million of Dentsu's money in little more than two years?

'I have no idea,' I could only reply. 'I have never had access to an IFP cheque book, or indeed to the IFP accounts.' This interrogation was to prove symbolic. Dentsu froze IFP's money supply, with the result that Nally paid neither Oliver nor myself our salaries as of November 2012. To my acute embarrassment, others whom I had myself hired were also suddenly left high and dry. As relations with Nally turned ever frostier, I incensed him yet further by presidentially authorising payments to freelances such as McManus, Flusfeder and others via Dentsu's financial director, the only figure apart from Nally with access to MSP funds.

The end began in February 2013, when Nally fired Oliver Chubb, over my strenuous protests. Within weeks, to Nally's consternation, Oliver had been given a plum job by Dentsu Sports Europe – whose leadership, unlike Nally, had recognised his considerable talents; he is still very contentedly employed there, rising through the ranks. I was still owed several months' salary by Nally when I flew to Cyprus the following month for IFP's annual Congress.

My own relations with Nally had by now become untenable; I was intent on a dignified resignation before anything else could go wrong. So I sat in our Paphos hotel drafting a press release with some lavish praise from Nally for my 'distinguished' stewardship of IFP during its crucial first few years, before heading off to the board meeting, where I excited little surprise among Nally's cronies – and, for once, delighted the man himself – by tendering my resignation as IFP president.

In time IFP became IMSP, championing duplicate poker only, and did eventually resume the Nations Cup first won by Germany at County Hall. Fine by me. This was not something with which I would care to be associated. I look back on it all with a rueful smile amid enormous dismay at the failure of a venture so potentially valuable, which could have done great service to the peerless game of poker so beloved of myself and now, in this online era, many millions of others all over the world. Instead, by promoting a spineless variant of poker, it seems to have served simply to keep one venturesome entrepreneur's finances going for a few more buccaneering years.

Besides, it was surely time for me to get back to the keyboard.

2 0

POST-MORTEM

Friday 14 February 2014: today I am a day older than my father lived to be. Why have I let this self-imposed jinx hang such a shadow over these past few years?

Appropriately enough, this particular Valentine's Day finds me driving to Southampton through torrential rain (soon to escalate into south-coast floods) to see John Shrapnel and his son Lex in Caryl Churchill's father-and-son play *A Number* at the Nuffield Theatre. So dire are the driving conditions that more than once I contemplate turning round for home. But the challenge of that momentous anniversary, combined with some stubborn sexagenarian resolve not to admit defeat, keeps me going on a hazardous journey I dedicate – upon safe arrival – to my father's memory. I later drink to him with John and Lex after their superb performance.

The same milestone with my mother followed, of course, a week later. As I raised a glass to her photo, back in my London apartment, my life was a mess which kept luring my thoughts elsewhere.

Since the IFP debacle had ended in Cyprus nine months earlier, I had been unemployed again – at sixty-five, retirement age for most people, while finding myself still in need of gainful employment. Those wasted four years at IFP had seen such seminal moments as the births of my grandchildren and the deaths of sundry indispensable friends, from Frank Kermode at ninety to Christopher Hitchens at just sixty-two. After Frank had died in

2010, it turned out that he had named me in his will as his executor, leaving me a four-figure sum by way of thanks for my services, which I spent on a handsome Picasso lithograph to remember him by. Christopher I had seen less of in recent years, living on opposite sides of the Atlantic; but I visited him in Washington DC in mid-2011 – only a few months, as it transpired, before his death – and wound up staying for a moving six-hour marathon of a conversation, continued the next day. He reminded me that, when he had arrived in DC just as I was leaving, I had introduced him to the likes of Henry Fairlie and Izzy Stone, amid other heady memories of those very happy days. Knowing all too well that he was suffering from terminal cancer, we parted very emotionally.

By the time my own parental dates of doom arrived, I knew I was lucky to have made it this far. I had taken time off from IFP (not least to avoid yet another royal wedding) for a ten-day break in the Maldives. After a week or so, I took my usual late-morning swim, descending the steps from my water-top villa into the balmy Indian Ocean. Never the strongest of swimmers, I was all too aware of notices warning of dangerous riptides, and thus ever mindful of my six-year-old rescue in Aberdovey by Mr Milk Tray. When I reached my usual hundred yards or so out, and turned to start the undemanding stretch home, I soon realised that for once I wasn't making much progress. In fact, I was slowly but relentlessly heading backwards, towards the depths where we had been warned that sharks lurked in waiting. Feebly, I waved an arm towards the one holidaymaker I could make out on his terrace, but it didn't look like he could see me. By now it was lunchtime, and all the other guests had already headed off to the dining room.

So this was it. This is how it all ends, I reflected, surprised by how calmly I processed the shock as I drifted ever more surely out to sea. 'Drowned off the Maldives' did not seem much of an epitaph, though I caught myself hoping it happened before I reached those sharks. As I grew increasingly short of breath, I asked myself if I now regretted all those years of smoking? No, it had helped me relax, think and work. And the lack of exercise? Well, the time had been spent much more productively. Yet again, even in these dire circumstances, I smiled at the words of Peter O'Toole: 'The only exercise I get these days is walking behind the coffins of my friends who take exercise.' As the ocean grew ominously choppier, other such reflections on my chequered life duly followed, in the time-honoured fashion of the drowning man, until suddenly . . .

From amid the bucking waves a human head bobbed up beside me, asking in regional English: 'You all right?'

'Er, no, not really,' was all I could come up with.

'What's your name?' he asked, in a reassuring manner.

'Tony,' I said, thinking it shorter and simpler, in the circs, than Anthony.

'Okay, Terry,' said he, 'put your arms around my shoulders, and hang on tight.'

Clearly, this man was a professional. Slowly but surely, his strong bulk manoeuvred us the long way back to the hotel, heading round the coastal corner towards the shore outside the dining room, where I finally lay beached and gasping for breath as the waiting medics took over. I was golf-carted off to the island infirmary, where I was injected by anxious-looking medical staff with a variety of potions unknown. Told to rest for the afternoon, I was helped back down the jetty to my room, where I found that still among the team looking after my every need was my intrepid rescuer. With what little breath I had left, I asked his name and told him I'd like to buy him a large drink that evening.

A charmed life? I was indeed fortunate, I reflected, still to be around to enjoy the privilege of driving through that terrifying monsoon to Southampton nearly three years later. Many other life-altering events had punctuated those four years in the IFP wilderness. Beyond births, deaths and marriages, I had also made another treasured new friend in Natalie Galustian, an antiquarian book dealer who asked me to write an introduction to a momentous catalogue of historic poker books – and I had discovered some eye-opening new relatives in Yorkshire.

Three months after dodging the aquatic Grim Reaper in the Maldives, I received a message from a woman in Doncaster named Yve (short for Yvonne), saying that she had seen on Wikipedia that I was Ivan Sharpe's grandson. Had I known him well? Unexpected though the question was, and unknown her reason for asking it, I felt impelled to reply: yes, I had known him very well; he had lived with us as I was growing up, and I had loved him very much. All but fifty years after his death, he remained a major figure in my life.

'Oh dear,' came the reply, 'you might not like what I have to tell you.'

'Don't worry,' I reassured her, 'my feelings for Ivan remain indestructible. And I myself am pretty much unshockable.'

'Well,' Yve replied, 'you say that your mother was Ivan's only child. I'm afraid I have evidence suggesting otherwise. My mother Mona was his illegitimate daughter. So Ivan Sharpe was my biological grandfather, too. You may not wish to know more; but, if you do, I'd be pleased to tell you.'

This was irresistible. I was about to make a trip north, anyway, to see a friend in North Wales, then my brother and his wife in Cheshire; so now I added Doncaster to my schedule. After finding the address she had given me, I parked my car in the spacious drive of a handsome detached house, to find the door answered by a beautiful middle-aged black woman. I told her I had come to see Yve.

'I *am* Yve,' she smiled, and ushered me in, introducing me to her sister Jacqui. The three of us sat down to a delicious Caribbean lunch, over which unfolded a jaw-dropping story.

Their mother Mona, born in the village of Harthill near Sheffield in 1925, was the illegitimate daughter of Evelyn Bennett via a liaison with a married man, a Leeds footballer named Ivan Sharpe. Mona had been brought up by her grandparents, with Ivan strictly banned from her life, though apparently he paid secret visits when she took annual trips south to stay with her cousins. Yve had no documentary evidence of all this, but I instinctively believed her.

For all the drama of this ambush, I immediately found myself reverting fondly to my youth, remembering Ivan with nothing but the utmost affection, and so feeling acutely for him how difficult it must have been to keep so monumental a secret all those years. I also began wondering about his marriage to Ada, whom I had never known. Perhaps it had not been a happy one? I could remember no references to her at all during my childhood and youth, when you would have expected occasional remarks like 'Oh, your mother wouldn't have liked that!' between a co-habiting father and his daughter. There had been much merriment in the Holden household each year about Ivan's annual fly-fishing visits to the village of Pandy, in Monmouthshire, where he used to lodge each year with a mysterious Mrs Lovell. Perhaps, I now wondered, this was when he dropped by to see Mona in Nottingham en route?

But there was more, much more, to come that day in Doncaster.

During the war Mona served in the Women's Land Army, where she met and fell in love with a young RAF serviceman from the Caribbean island of Montserrat. When she took him back to Yorkshire to meet her parents in 1945, they were less dismayed that their daughter's intended was a black man than that his name was Ivan – Ivan Browne, later a renowned West Indian musician who would work with Duke Ellington. But soon they were married, and of their six children Yve and Jacqui became the two determined to find out more about Ivan Sharpe and the Holden family. I was only too happy to oblige, convinced (and more than a little relieved) that my own mother had surely departed this world with no knowledge of all this.

In her youth, it transpired, Yve herself had returned to her father's family home of Montserrat, where she became managing director of the AIR (Associated Independent Recording) studios founded by the Beatles producer George Martin. She was there when musicians such as Elton John, Paul McCartney and Eric Clapton, not to mention groups from the Rolling Stones and Pink Floyd to Dire Straits and The Police, came to record albums celebrated to this day.

Though both were married at the time, Yve had an affair with Eric Clapton and bore him a daughter, Ruth, who was now about to be married; a couple of years later Ruth presented Yve and Eric with their first grandchild, Isaac, whom my son Samuel Ivan and I met when we were taken to an Eric Clapton concert at the Albert Hall as one of my 2015 birthday presents. Yve and I have since stayed in regular touch, taking a keen interest in each other's family lives.

Yve, A.H., Jacqui

Amid all this, my own grandchildren were arriving in profusion: after the twins born to Ben and Salome in May 2008, a daughter named Rosemary to Sam and Ursula two years later. I had never had either a sister or a daughter, to the point where by middle age I felt like I'd missed out on a whole arc of life. Now the stubbornly masculine Holden genes had suddenly blessed me with two granddaughters (later to become three).

I had regularly reviewed books for the *Telegraph* in recent years, and still did so for *The Observer*, but the stark slump in my income since forswearing all matters royal had never been more apparent. But there were plenty of other plans to explore. For two years now my son Ben and I had been working together on an idea that had first occurred to me all of twenty years earlier but, like so many other projects, I had never got around to.

In the mid-1990s my Oxford tutor John Jones, with whom I still enjoyed a much-treasured friendship, had called me unexpectedly one afternoon to say that he had suffered a particularly bad day – his wife Jean had been hospitalised – and he was feeling terribly alone, in need of sympathetic company. Cindy and I headed straight up to Hampstead to take him out to dinner. There we listened sympathetically as he poured out his woes, eventually quoting a poem by Thomas Hardy, 'The Darkling Thrush', which ends on a note of hope:

> *So little cause for carolings*
> *Of such ecstatic sound*
> *Was written on terrestrial things*
> *Afar or nigh around,*
> *That I could think there trembled through*
> *His happy good-night air*
> *Some blessed Hope, whereof he knew*
> *And I was unaware.*

Upon reaching those last two lines, John choked up, unable to get the words out. This was understandable; he was still upset by the day's events, and wasn't feeling much hope. We ourselves were much moved. That I knew him to be a lifelong champion of Hardy's poetry as much as his novels rendered the moment even more poignant.

That weekend I was visiting Frank Kermode in Cambridge. Knowing Jones as he too did, Frank was also touched by his Hardy moment. 'Is there any poem *you* can't recite without choking up?' I asked him. Never an emotionally demonstrative man, Frank said immediately, 'Go and get the Larkin.'

In front of his half-dozen guests he then began to read aloud 'Unfinished Poem', about death treading its remorseless way up the stairs, only to turn out to be a pretty young girl with bare feet, moving the stunned narrator to exclaim: 'What summer have you broken from?' It was this startling last line that rendered Frank speechless; with a despairing waft of the hand, he held the book out for someone else to finish the poem.

For the next few weeks I asked every male literary friend I saw to name a poem he couldn't read or recite without breaking up. It was amazing how many immediately said yes, this one, and embarked on its first few lines. With Frank's encouragement, as I reported to him on my regular visits to Cambridge, I began to contemplate an anthology called *Poems That Make Strong Men Cry*.

Not for the first time, I then remembered I had another project to which I was committed and set the idea aside. But it remained a topic of paradoxically happy conversation between Frank and me until his death. I duly steeled myself to read 'Unfinished Poem' at his funeral service in King's College Chapel; and managed it – just – without choking up.

Over Christmas the following year my son Ben suggested reviving the idea; we could co-edit it together, as indeed we proceeded to do over the next couple of years. Under the title *Poems That Make Grown Men Cry* – between them Ben and the publishers persuaded me that our men should really be 'grown' rather than 'strong' – we brought together one hundred disparate figures distinguished in literature and film, science and architecture, theatre and human rights, representing twenty nationalities and ranging in age from their early twenties to their late eighties. One of the secrets of the book's success, I believe, is that we persuaded each to write a few hundred words explaining why they were so moved by the poem of their choice.

Seventy-five per cent of the selected poems were written in the twentieth century, with more than a dozen by women. Their themes ranged from love in its many guises, through mortality and loss, to the beauty and variety of nature. Three contributors had suffered the pain of losing a child; others were moved to tears by the exquisite way a poet captures, in Alexander Pope's famous phrase, 'what oft was thought, but ne'er so well express'd'. From J. J. Abrams to John le Carré, Salman Rushdie to Jonathan Franzen, Daniel Radcliffe to Andrew Motion, Ian McEwan to Stephen Fry, Stanley Tucci to Colin Firth, Seamus Heaney to Benjamin Zephaniah, these widely admired men were offering a private insight into their souls.

Amid a startling amount of publicity, the anthology was voted Poetry Book of the Year and spent all of six weeks in the *Sunday Times* bestseller list. The following year I was invited to deliver that year's A. E. Housman Lecture on the Name and Nature of Poetry at the Hay-on-Wye literary festival.

As we had planned all along, to the disbelief of some cynics, the same exercise soon followed with the opposite sex. *Poems That Make Grown Women Cry* featured an equally stellar parade, from Bianca Jagger and Elena Ferrante to Germaine Greer and Vanessa Redgrave, Chimamanda Ngozi Adichie and Ursula K. Le Guin to Judi Dench and Olivia Colman.

Some of the choices in that volume were almost unbearably intimate: Antonia Fraser and Yoko Ono both chose the last poem their eminent husbands had written for them before their deaths, and Claire Tomalin proudly made public a heart-rending poem by her 22-year-old daughter prefiguring her own death only months later. A pleasant surprise for me was Joan Baez choosing a poem by Leigh Hunt, 'Abou Ben Adhem' – which reminded her of her father, she said, who used to read it to her, and to whom she in turn had read it as he lay dying. The poem's central line, 'Write me as one that loves his fellow men', is the inscription on Hunt's tombstone in Kensal Green cemetery, as I had discovered when tracking it down a dozen years earlier.

Of the many literary festivals at which we paraded our wares, that in Holt, Norfolk, turned out to be a special treat when the summer visitor Julie Christie offered to read some of the poems in the first book, as did the local resident John Hurt, in a session chaired by another local resident, my schoolteacher-turned-lifelong-friend John Harrison. Julie joined us again two years later when we returned with the second volume.

Julie Christie, John Harrison, Ben Holden, A.H., John Hurt

That summer of 2015 — less than a year, ironically, after congratulating my brother and his wife Susan on their golden wedding anniversary — I realised that after my two failed marriages, lasting in all some fifteen years each, I had spent the past fifteen years living alone. I had remained friends with my first wife,

Amanda, not least as the mother of my children, and with my second, Cindy. Indeed, some of our best friends don't seem to realise that Cindy and I have never divorced; all these years we have remained married, and still are to this day. But by now I had finally grown accustomed to living alone. And I had rarely been so content.

For the best part of thirty-five years, my commute had been a daily clamber down a flight of stairs. More than half my life had been lived in the twentieth century, one of the bloodiest and most brutish on record. Yet I was fortunate enough to have been born directly after its very worst years – like all my baby-boomer generation – and so supremely lucky not to have had to fight in a war or even endure national service. We were spared rationing and blessed with the NHS. Thanks to 'the pill', we were just the right age to relish the sexual revolution: if not quite, in my case, sex, drugs and rock'n'roll, then sex, cigarettes and the Beatles in Liverpool's Cavern Club. We enjoyed a free university education, and it was I who bought my parents their first dishwasher rather than the other way around.

I had no job to retire from at sixty-five, and no significant savings, so I just kept on working. Amid the poetry anthologies, Harry Evans asked me to team up with the siblings Jacqui and David Morris on a documentary about the *Sunday Times*'s long fight for justice for the victims of Thalidomide. My role was to broaden the scope of a film on which the Morrises had already begun work, and to amplify and polish the script, for which I wound up being credited as executive producer.

When the finished product was at rough-cut stage, we organised a viewing in London for Harry, who unexpectedly turned up at the Soho screening room with David Puttnam. As we were walking in, Puttnam asked me, 'What's it called?' 'It's explained in the film,' I told him, 'but it's called *Attacking the Devil*.' This was the phrase used by Harry's personal hero, and predecessor as editor of the *Northern Echo*, the campaigning journalist W. T.

Stead, in a letter spelling out the opportunities open to a news-paper editor; as seen in the film, it still hangs framed on the wall of the editor's office. 'Oh, that's terrific!' replied Puttnam. 'You should always have a meaningless title! *Midnight Express*; what does that mean? Or *Chariots of Fire*?' he laughed about two of his greatest hits as a producer.

Thursday 22 May 2014 was my sixty-seventh birthday. I had made it. I had beaten the parental jinx that had been hanging over this year, and indeed my whole life for far too long. And I was still standing. I still had all my marbles to tell the tale. Maybe I was tempting fate – but, frankly, anything after this would be a bonus.

The second poetry anthology and the Harry Evans docu-mentary were about to appear. Meanwhile, I seemed to have developed a new career in film; now, introduced by our mutual friend Lucy Bright, I was working with the American director Michael Almereyda, whose latter-day Manhattan *Hamlet* (with Ethan Hawke in the title role and Bill Murray as Polonius) I had much admired while living there. Now he was making an update of *Cymbeline*, with Hawke again, Ed Harris, Bill Pullman and Dakota Johnson, and asked for my help in compiling a commen-tary for the DVD. We got on so well that he invited me to work with him again on future updates of Shakespeare.

At the same time I was involved in a new website, as well as mulling plans for another biography. I became a contributing editor to a new UK edition of *Newsweek*. At an age when most men are finally putting their feet up, I was glad of the occasional evening at home watching TV. Weekends were also spent work-ing – or, at least once a month, visiting Cambridge and Frank Kermode's friend Heather Glen, who laid on delightful Sunday lunches with a variety of varsity chums.

Afterwards I would pay regular visits to Clive James, who had been bemoaning his terminal illness so publicly for so long that he was engagingly embarrassed still to be alive. On the umpteenth such Sunday I rang his bell, as agreed, at 4 p.m.-ish . . . but there was no reply. Through the window, I could see that the room at the back where we normally sat and talked was empty. After several more attempts I slipped a note through the letter box saying I'd been there at the agreed time and rung the bell several times – to no avail.

Gloomily I drove back to London, half-expecting to hear Clive's demise announced on the radio any minute. Arriving back at my desk ninety minutes later, I found an email from him, saying: 'Hah! Thought I'd died, didn't you? No, I just took my usual pre-Holden nap, which for some reason turned into the deepest of sleeps. Next time, ring my phone as well as my bell!' Which indeed I did, for a few years yet. Clive eventually lived just beyond his eightieth birthday in 2019.

It was around this time that a friend who happens to be a Labour peer sent me the self-nomination form for the House of Lords, encouraging me to apply and adding that he and two (which later became four) other peers of my acquaintance would be more than pleased to give me references. I was flattered, of course, and momentarily tempted; Westminster, after all, is just four stops up the Jubilee line from where I live, and the £300 per day just for turning up would certainly have come in handy. All too soon I recalled that, some twenty years earlier in 1995, it was I who had written the Charter 88 pamphlet calling for the abolition of the Lords in its unelected, still part-hereditary form. Already realising the whole idea was impossible, I went through my mental Rolodex of people who would never speak to me again, not least myself, if I accepted a peerage. With the very slightest of sighs, I threw the form away.

In mid-June 2016 the cocksure David Cameron committed political suicide, taking his country down with him, by holding a referendum on the UK's membership of the European Union. If Cameron had been to a decent school (to steal a good line from Melvyn Bragg), he might have known enough history to remember Attlee's famous dictum of 1945 when turning down Churchill's request for a referendum on prolonging the war-time coalition rather than holding a post-war general election. 'I could not consent to the introduction into our national life of a device so alien to all our traditions as the referendum,' said Attlee, 'which has only too often been the instrument of Nazism and fascism.' Even Margaret Thatcher had remembered this a generation later, when the question of a plebiscite came up again, this time on the UK's membership of what was then the European Economic Community. 'The late Lord Attlee was right,' Thatcher declared, to call the referendum 'a device of dictators and demagogues.'

In an attempt to heal divisions within his own party, Cameron only made them worse while misjudging the sentiments of a naturally xenophobic country – as I had written from Manhattan nearly twenty years before – now further bruised by years of his own personal brand of *de haut en bas* austerity. One way and another, I had shaken the hand of every prime minister before him since Harold Macmillan, but now I would go to some lengths to avoid shaking his, let alone those of the equally medi-ocre, then squalid, Tory successors he bequeathed us.

2016 held many another woe, with the election of Donald Trump in the same November week that saw the death of Leonard Cohen, to whose melancholy last album *You Want It Darker* I had been listening repeatedly amid my Brexit blues, and which seemed to contain my very own poker epitaph in 'I'm leaving the table / I'm out of the game . . .'

Could I possibly defy my lingering parental jinx by making it as far as three-score-years-and-ten? Apart from Brexit, there was another ill omen in mid-June 2016, soon after my sixty-ninth birthday, when I suffered a heavy fall in the street, less than a hundred yards from my home. On a pavement I had walked a thousand times before, I tripped and fell – without, for some reason, stretching out my arms to break my fall, and so landing heavily on my nose, which I was lucky not to break. But my face was so badly damaged that I had to withdraw from society for ten days, my mind filled with thoughts of obituaries opening, 'Following a heavy fall . . .'

Potentially the year of my seventieth birthday, 2017 began badly from my point of view when a parliamentary committee took barely ten minutes to double the royal income from the taxpayer in order to fund the estimated £360 million needed to upgrade Buckingham Palace. I was a tad consoled when a twenty-four-page Ladybird book by HRH Charles entitled *Climate Change* received a one-sentence review: 'If there is anyone who doesn't yet know that "Extreme weather events such as heatwaves, droughts, floods and storms can cause major damage and disruption, with large costs and sometimes loss of life", this is the book for them.' It was perhaps HRH's lowest point since the celebrated 'black spider' letters of 2015 had revealed the full extent of his incessant meddling in political affairs – moving even his biographer, Jonathan Dimbleby, to predict that 'he will go well beyond what any previous constitutional monarch has ever essayed' – if not the 'Camillagate' scandal of 1993, barely a month after his split with Diana, when he was overheard saying on the phone to his married mistress that he wanted to be her tampon.

No royal had ever sunk so low, as I would have said at the time, were I still bothering to comment on such inanities. I would also have reminded him of the phrase his aunt Margaret had used in her 1955 statement announcing her decision not to marry her father's equerry, the divorced Peter Townsend: 'mindful of the Church's teachings that Christian marriage is indissoluble . . .' The would-be supreme governor of the Church of England, I would have suggested, might also bear its teachings in mind when it came to his own marital arrangements.

Some years before, the then archbishop of Canterbury, Robert Runcie, had told me – at the time, of course,

unattributably – that the advent of King Charles III would provoke a constitutional crisis. How so? The Church of England has
never before crowned a divorced man as king, and so supreme
governor of the Church, let alone one who has publicly confessed to adultery – with the relevant woman, also a divorcée,
sitting beside him, expecting (whatever the Palace may say in
the meantime) to become queen consort. This, said Runcie,
would require a revision of the Coronation Oath, which in
turn would require a new statute of Parliament. Given the convention that Parliament does not debate the monarchy without
the monarch's consent – it is his or her government, after all,
not ours – this would require the prime minister of the day to
go and seek the new King Charles III's permission to debate
whether or not it felt able to crown him.

Mercifully, I could now leave Charles to wrestle with his own
demons, and indeed turned down sundry requests to review
the latest in the ceaseless flow of biographies following my own
long-ago triptych. In other departments, my life was as busy as
ever. I was still writing regularly for *The Observer* and my other
favoured publications. There were still regular requests for programme notes from theatres and opera companies. After nearly
thirty years *The Barber of Seville* was still running at ENO, and
now became the latest live production to be broadcast in cine-
mas; when I decided to go and see it yet again, a local came up to
me in the interval and said, without the least idea who I was: 'I
don't normally like Italian operas in English, but this translation
is rather good, don't you think?' The translation, I was pleased
to assure him, was the only reason I was there.

I also took part in yet another TV documentary about the St
Albans poisoner, Graham Young, filmed on location in his home
suburb of Neasden more than fifty years after his criminal career
began there. So regardless of my age (or probably, in truth,
because of it), I seemed to be working as hard as ever. With
various ideas for books at differing stages of development, I was

still a trustee of Shakespeare North as well as, now, of the New Queen's Hall Trust, founded to build London a shoebox-shaped, acoustically-fine concert hall, unlike any it has at present. Amid all this, I still felt unfulfilled, and often failed to sleep well, unless I had done a solid day's writing.

With Natalie Galustian I revived an idea dating back to IFP days and started co-editing an anthology of poker-centric short stories by player-writers such as James McManus, Peter Alson and Michael Craig; by poker players you didn't know could write, from Barny Boatman to Jennifer Tilly; and by writers you didn't know could play poker, such as D. B. C. Pierre and Lucy Porter, with even a poker poem from the poet laureate, Carol Ann Duffy. All were commissioned specially for the book apart from the title story, *He Played for His Wife*, written in 1899 by the New Yorker David Curtis, in which the protagonist does just that – and loses. My own contribution was, I freely admit, a clunky fictional debut by a veteran writer of non-fiction.

In May 2017, a week before my seventieth birthday, I was invited by the president of the Football Writers' Association, Patrick Barclay, to be guest of honour at a dinner at which its co-founder and first president, my grandfather Ivan Sharpe, was immortalised with the award of an annual life fellowship in his name. With the subsequent help of Paddy and his colleague Mike Collett, the FWA's resident historian, I passed on much Ivan memorabilia to the National Football Museum in Manchester, where there is now a permanent exhibition in his memory.

Life was beginning to look up again in so many ways. As all day every day for a decade, I still relished living beside the river. Twice a day, beneath my window, the Thames would rise and fall some ten metres as stately craft came and went, from ocean liners to the river ferries which had become my chosen method of commuting. In winter, the river could bubble up menacingly, especially if there were those perennial floods in the West Country, as if to say 'I could come and get you if I so chose'. In the heat of summer, there were sundry riverbank pleasures to explore.

On one such day, 22 May 2017, my seventieth birthday, I enjoyed an alfresco lunch with my sons directly across the river from the wharf where I lived. So astonished was I to have made it to this age that for the next few weeks, as I went about my daily business, I was continually thinking, *I'm still doing this and I'm still doing that, and I'm seventy years old!* But my parents' fate still spooked me, to the point where I felt relieved simply to wake up each day.

So let's just say that during that year — as productive and contented as any I could remember — for the first time in my adult life I finally realised, as I turned seventy, that I was not seventeen any more.

AN INSULT TO THE BRAIN

On the morning of 10 August 2017, less than three months after my seventieth birthday, I awoke around 7 a.m. in need of a pee. Nothing unusual about that; what did come as a surprise was that, struggle as I might, I could not get out of bed. For some reason my legs and arms didn't seem to be working properly. Eventually I managed to thrash and wriggle my way down to the floor, then somehow round the corner into the bathroom next door, where I fell heavily to my left as soon as I let go of the doorpost; then had my pee and somehow managed to clamber back into bed, where I went straight back to sleep.

On reawakening an hour or so later, however, I knew something really strange was happening when again I could not lift enough of my body to get myself out of bed. After floundering around for a while, I finally managed to fall out onto my right leg, which now seemed to be working okay, and grab the rail of the staircase, get myself downstairs, even make a cup of coffee before collapsing onto the sofa.

It was all decidedly odd. In Melvyn Bragg's Radio 4 *In Our Time* slot, his summer replacement, Peter Hennessy, was talking to Tony Blair about his brilliant career. Well, that could have been a happier choice, but everything else external seemed routine enough, while something I couldn't make out was clearly wrong with me. Remembering that Cindy and I were due at the Alvarezes that evening, I thought I'd better call her. On standing up to cross the room for my phone, I felt my left side giving way and crashed down into the corner table, knocking over a half-drunk bottle of wine. Otherwise unable to move, I crawled across the room to my mobile phone, which I managed to pull down from its perch beside the TV, but then found I couldn't get back to the sofa. So I started rolling myself around while dialling Cindy's number. I was going to say, 'I don't think I can make it to the Als tonight,' but instead found myself saying, 'I think I'm having a stroke.'

Cindy immediately said she'd call 999 and I thought of my classic dilemma — of which I had long been uneasily aware — that my habit of leaving my keys locked in my front door overnight meant that the emergency services would have to break it down to get in. So, with considerable difficulty, I rolled myself through the narrow doorway towards the front door and manoeuvered myself beside it. Raising my right hand to the keys in the lower lock, I managed to unlock it and pull them out. But the latch of the upper lock I could not reach from my helplessly horizontal position. So I grabbed a nearby umbrella and managed to unlatch the door with its tip and then, as it opened, slide the umbrella between the door and the latch, so that the door would not lock itself shut again.

Before too long I could hear the ambulance crew arriving in the corridor outside. And there was I, lying semi-naked on my back, grateful that at least they would not have to break the door down on top of me. But I was blocking the entrance, and so told them to push gently. Between them, they put me in a wheelchair and we went down in the lift to the front entrance, outside which the ambulance stood waiting. Within half an hour we were at King's College Hospital, Camberwell, which just happens to have a specialist stroke unit.

I later learned that the immediate aftermath of a stroke and especially the first three days are the critical time. So this was a sequence of events that proved extremely fortunate. But it would turn out that I had suffered a near-terminal blow which would henceforth divide the rest of my life firmly into pre-seventy and post-seventy, with all the emphasis of BC vs AD.

So much for the self-styled 'lucky' man you met in my opening pages, although the superstitious atheist would fend off any temptation towards self-pity by giving thanks that I am still alive. Before quoting the relevant statistics, I must join my fellow victim Robert McCrum in insisting that 'stroke' is the wrong term for what befell us. It is too gentle a word; you stroke a baby, or a pet, or indeed a lover. Just as a cardiac arrest is called a heart attack, so a stroke should be called a brain attack. In the UK someone suffers one every three and a half minutes – more than 100,000 a year, of whom one-third will die; one-third will be seriously disabled; and some 30,000, the lucky third, will go on to lead fairly normal lives. In 2017 brain attacks turned out to kill 29,855 people, so I was certainly a lucky septuagenarian to find myself in the second category, fortunate indeed to be in full possession of my memory and indeed my cognitive faculties – although, despite initial hopes, I would never walk again.

So intent had I been all this time on making it past my parents to mankind's biblical allotment of three score years and ten, continuing the while to work and play as hard as ever, that I failed to foresee the prospect of a life-altering 'insult to the brain' (as the medical profession terms it with apt drama). The right capsular striatum infarct I had suffered amounts to a haemorrhage on the right side of the brain, which controls the left side of the body. My left leg and arm thus were – and still are – inoperative, which again means that I was lucky to be right-handed, if now a one-fingered typist, with my left arm in a sling to prevent its limp weight dislocating my shoulder.

When a concerned Cindy turned up at the hospital that first morning – feeling obliged, naturally enough, to report the news to my sons – I told her that I did not want the boys to come back from the Greek island where they happened to be on holiday together. But the next day she arrived at the hospital, straight from Heathrow, with Ben and Sam. And of course, despite myself, I was as delighted as I was moved to see them.

On the third day I was transferred to St Thomas' Hospital in central London, where it so happened that Sam used to work in the ward next door to mine — which, rather worryingly, proclaimed 'hyper-acute' over its entrance. The next day Ben came in with Joe, who had also returned from Greece via his home in Berlin. All three sons were truly wonderful that week and beyond, way beyond, at first taking care of the complex logistics of getting the word out; within days they had set up a personalised website to give friends far and wide a daily update on my progress.

Many were the laughs generated by my supposedly 'James Bond'-like approach to the problem of my door and the ambulance crew, to the point where messages came in to and went out from 0070 (a.k.a. double-oh-seventy). From Munich J Morley, who had himself survived several brushes with death, welcomed me 'with open arms to the Club of Miraculous Survivors into which I, as a long-standing member, recommended your adoption. You will be pleased to hear there were no dissenters. The umbrella ruse was genius.'

The agonised internal debate continued for some time as to whether it was stress, diabetes or high blood pressure (neither of which I knew I had), let alone all those years of fags and booze, which precipitated my right hemispheric capsulostriate hyper-acute infarct. Eventually I was told by my own doctor, then by others, that it was most likely hereditary. My father's death in hospital was precipitated by a cerebral embolism when the machine required to carry out some tests on him turned out, for the umpteenth time, to be unavailable.

So there you had it. My lifelong pre-66 fretting, and my wide-eyed post-66 incredulity, were no more to blame for all this — as I had naturally feared — than a lifetime of smoking and drinking. It was going to happen anyway, sooner or later. Preferably, I have to say, later.

From my hospital bed in St Thomas', through the window of my 'hyper-acute' ward, I could see the oh-so-familiar C10 bus from Waterloo which would eventually stop, half an hour later, 50 yards from my front door in Rotherhithe. Against the backdrop of Lambeth Palace, that bus seemed to go by far more frequently than it did when my healthy self was standing waiting for it at the other end.

From my next, now river-view bed, I could see the Thames Clipper ferries cruising gracefully past the Houses of Parliament. Again, towards the eastern end of their run to Greenwich, these used to stop outside my window across the river at Canary Wharf, and hook up with a smaller ferry which crossed the river directly beneath my view.

It was curiously touching to enjoy such a premature view of the familiar world carrying on without you – as in Auden's wonderful poem 'Musée des Beaux Arts', his meditation on Bruegel's painting *Landscape with the Fall of Icarus*, in which a ploughman proceeds heedlessly on his way as Icarus falls out of the sky beside a ship also sailing on regardless.

> About suffering they were never wrong,
> The old Masters: how well they understood
> Its human position: how it takes place
> While someone else is eating or opening a window or just
>   walking dully along . . .

My major initial regrets were three much-anticipated trips I was now obliged to cancel: first to New York, where Harry Evans and Tina Brown had been about to host a seventieth birthday dinner for me. Then I was booked for a trip to Catalonia, just as it was interestingly embattled over independence, to celebrate Stryker McGuire's seventieth birthday. And, finally, I was due to visit Munich to celebrate fifty-plus years of incomparable friendship with J Morley – whom, as it transpired, I would now never see again.

Struggling to bring myself back to some sort of life was proving an arduous if thought-provoking process. Even being hauled out of bed to sit up in an armchair for half an hour was an exhausting exercise for me, unable to hold my head upright for more than ten or fifteen minutes. Among the array of NHS therapists providing expert daily sessions were not just the physiotherapy team, trying to get me back on my feet, but their colleagues testing my speech and cognitive skills, who would have me re-arranging coloured building bricks and making sounds like k-k-k and ga-ga-ga. So just as I was realising I had irrevocably become an old man, my daily life was suddenly like being back at kindergarten. For those first few weeks, the staff also kept asking me if I knew my name and where I was. Throw in the experience of having your children sit watching as a nurse changes your nappy (or hospital 'pad'), and I began to think that Shakespeare had, for once, seriously under-stated his case about second childishness in Jacques' 'Seven Ages of Man' speech.

There is, what's more, an especially vicious circle of hell reserved in hospital for those, like me, who cannot sleep on their backs. Duly so propped up before lights-out, and unable to move thereafter, I endured many a sleepless night and even, at first, the optical illusions apparently common after a brain attack. One night, I could see matchstick men dancing around the curtain-frame above my bed.

As touching get-well cards began to crowd across the window-sill, my sons were soon marshalling a daily stream of visitors, one of the first being Harry Evans from Manhattan. As Joe recorded on the daily Holden blog, 'Just then, a head emerged round the curtain. One of Dad's physiotherapists had come to see if he might be available for another session. Dad explained: "This gentleman has come all the way from New York to see me," to which Harry added, pointing at Dad: "Yes, you see he owes me a lot of money."

"Shall I come back in an hour?" the physio enquired. Without missing a beat, Harry responded: "By all means. By then I'll be gone with all the loot."'

After a couple of weeks I was chosen as the guinea pig for a young actress called Lorna Brown, about to play a speech therapist in a Young Vic revival of Arthur Kopit's 1978 play *Wings*, alongside Juliet Stevenson as the 'stroke' victim with speech problems. After watching my therapist put me through my vocal paces, Lorna seemed pleased that I launched into Hamlet's 'To be or not to be', swapping alternate lines with her until her memory faltered, and I finished it off.

My own therapist seemed pretty struck by that, too. Only the previous day she had been asking me for a list of words beginning with 'f', to which I avoided the obvious expletive while responding with such wilfully flamboyant examples as 'flamingo' and 'fandango'. Likewise, when my GP came visiting, and pointed to his wristwatch, asking me what it was, I pointedly replied 'chronometer'.

Among the many other tests to which I was routinely subjected, a brain scan soon indicated that I had previously suffered a minor 'stroke' some time before this much more serious brain attack. My mind went straight back to that random fall in the street the previous summer. The specialist in charge of me, Professor Anthony Rudd, recommended my getting out of a hospital smock and into my own clothes. I had no idea that was even an option, but he suggested it would be good for morale. So the boys bought in some of my own tops, and helped me into a garish t-shirt emblazoned: 'Southport – where the mud meets the sea.' When this met with the approval of a mildly amused Rudd, I told him about Napoleon III and Baron Haussmann – even getting the dates right – which certainly seemed to impress him.

Because of my swallowing problems, I was put on the hospital's mash-food diet, which I found largely inedible. But thanks to Natalie – who, along with Cindy, Amanda and the boys, was among my most regular visitors – I soon had my own personal supply of smoked salmon pâté and other such refined goodies to keep me going, not to mention a variety of exotic yoghurts that she made sure were personally labelled and stashed in the ward's private fridge.

To be lying helpless in a hospital bed as you are asked a dozen times a day by medical staff, 'How are you?' is to lose faith in the nature of human communication. My first, far from adequate attempt to convey this was 'I've been better', thereafter interspersed with variations from 'Ready to rumble!' to a grouchy 'Not too great'.

A brain attack brings strong feelings to the surface, increasing emotional outbursts as well as irascibility. So I would often, at first, swear at the nurses or doctors, often in foul language, which would immediately have me apologising, and saying with a choke in my voice that I would much rather they said 'Hello', which was what they really meant. When Ben brought in an iPod I also found myself blubbing at personal favourites from *West Side Story* to Mozart's wondrous concerto for flute and harp. After a couple of months, I was blessed with an NHS wheelchair, which meant that my sons could take me outside by the river. It was always a serious downer to return to the ward and have to ask for help getting out of it and back into bed.

My visitors were pleasantly surprised when I had a book published while in hospital that autumn, but I was distraught that I could not make the party-cum-poker tournament Nat had organised at a London casino for *He Played for His Wife*, the book we had so happily co-edited. I had already been more than dismayed to miss launch parties for the latest books by Harold Evans (*Do I Make Myself Clear?*), Ken Follett (*A Column of Fire*) and Tina Brown (*The Vanity Fair Diaries*) – and now I had missed even my own. Just another of the countless frustrations every day seemed to bring, little redeemed by photos of friends inexplicably managing to have a good time without me.

After nearly three months of all this, there followed a series of earnest family meetings with my medical team before I was finally allowed to go home. To thank the countless NHS personnel for the outstanding care they had lavished on me, my family and I sent the team a huge carton of cupcakes, which I had reason to believe would go down well.

Joe stayed on from Berlin for some time to look after me at home with the help of a Southwark-supplied carer. There was also a range of assorted therapists – physio, occupational, speech, anti-smoking, mental health etc. – who visited regularly. So the daily schedule was surprisingly hectic, much more so than I had expected. As a result I was astonishingly tired, all day every day, even to the point of putting off visitors at times, given the acute fatigue which persists in dogging 'stroke' victims – especially (I was advised) after they get back home.

But not for long. The following month I was dispatched to a neuro-rehab centre in Brixton, an outpost of St Thomas', where I spent the next two months including Christmas and New Year. I was able to make a few new friends over each day's communal meals in the canteen, but I confess I skipped the carol service and other such festive celebrations, declaring myself 'not in the mood'.

As at St Thomas', life on the ward could turn contentious, as when one inmate took solo charge of the remote control for the communal television and subjected us all to interminable daily bouts of TV's unspeakable Judge Judy. Others selfishly listened to their chosen TV- or radio-babble at full blast. Luckily, my friend Douglas Kennedy had just brought me the very latest in ergonomic headphones, so I was able to drown it all out with some maximum Mozart.

The centre's main purpose was intensive physiotherapy sessions in what (as at St Thomas') they archly called the 'gym'. From the occupational team there were sessions on dealing with fatigue and even training in regular bowel movements, then keeping a record of them – so, after outgrowing the kindergarten, I now found myself back at Cartwright's dread Trearddur House.

There were also, not for the first time, cognitive ability tests, which could prove tricky. In an institution where every day is tediously the same, it can be quite a problem remembering which day of the week it is, and other such vital pieces of basic data. The dates of the First and Second World Wars proved no problem, and the memory test a breeze when the address I was required to remember was 'Kingsbridge' – as in Ken Follett's cathedral novels as well as a dear friend's home address in west London. At the last of these curiously enjoyable trials, where I took pleasure in turning the tables on my Irish inquisitor by suggesting a bit of a 'ceilidh', she told me I had done very well – in the top 2 per cent – after getting only one question wrong. Which one? I naturally asked. The one, she replied, where you count down from 100, subtracting seven each time. When I asked her to spell it out more precisely, I was able to demonstrate that it was she, not I, who had made the mistake.

Upon my eventual discharge, I gingerly reversed my power-wheelchair down the ramp of the ambulance that had ferried me home, where my sons Joe and Ben were standing outside waiting to greet me. 'Those are two of my sons,' I explained to my Jamaican nurse. 'Ah,' she said sweetly, 'they are so handsome. Just like you.' At which point a group of a dozen or more strapping young men walked by, swarming around us as they passed the front door of my riverside home. 'And these are some more of my sons!' I quipped to the nurse – who seemed to enjoy my little jest. Polite enquiries revealed that the group, on its way out of the next-door Docklands hotel, was in fact the Derby County football team, due to play nearby Millwall that evening. Given that my beloved grandfather Ivan Sharpe had played for Derby County, this bizarre coincidence felt like some sort of omen – as if Ivan himself were welcoming me home, for good now, I earnestly hoped, after my second lengthy stint as a guest of the NHS.

When we got upstairs, a team of Polish builders were converting my bathroom into a disabled-friendly 'wet room' and my next-door study into a downstairs bedroom, complete with NHS bed. The idea, of course, was that my newly wheelchair-bound life be conducted all on one floor, so my desk had been moved into what had been my living room, where it felt great to be back in my beloved riverside home, if with bittersweet pangs as once again I watched helplessly through the window where 'normal' life continued to proceed blithely without me.

After working my way gratefully through half a dozen choice novellas very thoughtfully sent to me by Ian McEwan, I found myself reluctantly obliged to resort for the first time in my life to a Kindle, books now proving too hard to handle with only one functioning set of digits. With my voice coming and going, I lived on one-fingered email, not least a spirited correspondence with J Morley in Munich, a friend close enough to insist on unvarnished candour. While trying to avoid feeling sorry for myself, I embarked on a debate with him about acceptable literary examples of self-pity, dismissing Malvolio as mere slapstick beside Milton's stately sonnet on his blindness, 'When I consider how my light is spent . . .' There were hints from J, as there had been for twenty years and more, that he would not wish to continue living without his beloved Armgard, who was now so infirm in her nineties as to have a buzzer to summon him after yet another fall. But it still came as a mighty blow in February 2018 when the news arrived from her son Wedigo that both were dead. A month after Morley had turned seventy and Armgard at ninety-two had suffered, it seemed, one fall too many, they were found lying peacefully together on her bed, in a long-planned suicide pact. J's last email to me the previous day had contained a link to a serene online version of Pergolesi's *Stabat Mater*, which he knew I loved, and which now came to appear an aptly self-selected requiem.

This would soon prove just one of the many funerals or memorials I would acutely regret being physically unable to attend, with Joe and J's godson Sam travelling to Munich alongside Amanda to represent me.

For those first few weeks back, while the building work continued down below, my new carers had to ferry me upstairs via the lift and hefty fire doors to and from my bedroom – the scene, as it were, of the crime. Thereafter the NHS bed proved so uncomfortable that this up-and-down lift routine continued indefinitely, with carers coming four times a day to help get me meals and medication as well as helping me in and out of bed. As bittersweet as I had found the sight of the ferry beneath my window going back and forth to the alfresco restaurant across the Thames, Ben managed to get me on it in my wheelchair for a birthday lunch with Natalie and Alan Samson, as later did Joe for another reunion with John Shrapnel and his son Lex. In between came the joyful news of the arrival of a fourth grandchild, Aurelia, born to Ursula and Sam two days after my own birthday in 2018.

Then came a series of unhappy mishaps, such as the night (which just happened to be Friday 13th) when I fell out of bed while reaching for an essential nocturnal item inadvertently knocked off my bedside table. I was thus condemned to spend a *very* long, sleepless night flat on my back on my bedroom floor. Mercifully unhurt, but also unable even to think about trying to climb back into bed, I was reminded yet again that there are few things more upsetting than a human frame half of which does not work. So there are in turn few things more depressing than having to give up and resort to pulling the duvet off the bed, in the hope of keeping naked limbs warm while doubling as a pillow.

Naively, if not absurdly, I assumed I might be able get to sleep on the rock-hard floor. Fat chance. For hour after hour my nose was pressed up against the wheelchair and quad stick which I had vainly prayed every night would not be there when I woke up, as if all this had been some prolonged and monstrous nightmare. If you're newly disabled, I learned that night, you don't so much toss and turn as writhe and wriggle, making interminable attempts to find an on-floor position which is as vaguely comfortable as it might be vaguely warm. After two minutes, you try again. Then again. All this time, with no clock visible, the minutes tick by like hours. And hours.

Finally, after what felt like a month or two, I heard the key in the door that signalled the arrival of my Nigerian carer, Emmanuel.

Never, as I told him, had I been so pleased to see him — and that's saying something. I had spent several hours wondering what to do — out of the reach of clocks, phones and indeed my pendant alarm — if for some reason, as once before (not his fault), he failed to show up. Manfully, he helped me back into an upright position, and then into that dread wheelchair, to bring me downstairs in the lift yet again.

There followed a series of falls in the bathroom, when I had to press the pendant alarm round my neck to summon NHS help while nursing painful bruises but luckily no fractures. Then there was a succession of lift failures, where the only way for me to get downstairs was to bump-bump down the stairs on my bum, with my carer's help, to the wheelchair waiting below.

That June Tina Brown gave Harry Evans a dinner party at Cliveden House on the eve of his ninetieth birthday, to which I couldn't, of course, make it; so Harry chose to spend the evening of his birthday itself with me over dinner at the London home of Ben and Salome, with his children Georgie and Izzy and my grand-twins George and Ione. I wrote a sonnet in honour of the occasion, in an attempt to echo 'Shall I compare thee to a Doris Day?' of some twenty years before.

Izzy and Georgie Evans, A.H., Tina Brown, Harold Evans

Ben had to drive right across London to pick me up from Rotherhithe, helping me squeeze precariously out of my wheelchair into his car and back again, then take me home at the end of a memorably happy evening and, too late for my nightly carer, help me into bed. For once the lift was working, praise be, or we'd have been in serious trouble. At last even I was reluctantly persuaded that it was time for a move to somewhere more practical.

In west London, near where he and Salome live, Ben had occasionally noticed a shuttle bus marked with the name of a retirement home not far from them, just south of the river. On further investigation, it turned out to have just the kind of 'assisted living' facilities I would now need for life. We found a cosy apartment there which would suit my needs, given an external carer three times a day as well as wonderful in-house staff. So in September 2018, after ritually editing my worldly goods into a series of skips, decimating my library to signed copies only, and distributing my few heirlooms – including my grandfather's England caps and Olympic gold medal – among my offspring, I bid a very sad but inevitable farewell to my beloved riverside apartment, and embarked on a *vita nuova* as comfortable as my condition would permit seven or eight miles west along the Thames.

As well as an excellent dining room, my latest home boasts a cinema, even gym and swimming pool – beloved of my grandchildren, but no use, alas, to me anymore. But here, in my power-wheelchair, I am able to take myself across the road into the adjacent park, with its spectacular Buddhist pagoda up on the river as well as a Henry Moore and a Barbara Hepworth on either side of a beautiful, duck-adorned lake. I have gradually made some cherished new friends among the resident community, and have a wonderful Pakistani-born external carer named Malik. With his help, I have made rare excursions as far as hospitals and the dentist; and with Ben's, to more exotic treats such as my grand-twins in a rousing school production of *Oliver!*, David Edgar's one-man show at a Clapham theatre and the wedding reception of Melvyn Bragg and his new bride, Gabriel. Later in 2019 Ben also ferried me to Hampstead for, sadly, Al Alvarez's funeral. Only a few months before, on the eve of his ninetieth birthday, my fellow 'stroke' victim Al had been to visit me in my new home – where I teased him, wheelchair to wheelchair, that I had always modelled my life on his.

Thanks to a freak meeting online, I was delighted to find myself back in touch with David Blundy's daughter Anna, now a divorced fifty-year-old mother-of-two living in Italy. But I much regretted not being able to make it to Brian MacArthur's memorial service in the autumn of 2019. Then came the coronavirus pandemic and lockdown of 2020–21, which postponed the memorial scheduled for, among many others, my close friend (via the Folletts), the wise and witty journalist John Clare. How dear Johnny would have relished the bluntness of one remark in his *Times* obituary, reporting (accurately enough) that 'he enjoyed going to the theatre with the writer Anthony Holden. A man of scrupulously high standards, Clare insisted that they walk out of Glenda Jackson's recent *Lear* in the interval.'

A few months later, to my surprise and momentary alarm, *The Times* emailed me to interview me with a view to my own obituary. Given my account in these pages of my year at the paper with Harold Evans, I expect that when the time comes they will see me off, if at all, as Murdoch-mindedly as they did Harry himself in September 2020.

The previous month I had contacted Harry and Tina at their summer house in Long Island, where they were in quarantine during Manhattan's lockdown, to wish them a happy thirty-ninth wedding anniversary. Tina said that I must be sure to get Ben to bring me over for the party they would be giving for their fortieth the following year. In the meantime, she would set up a Zoom call for me to catch up with Harry – which never, alas, materialised.

A fall he suffered in Quogue meant that Tina had to take him for medical attention back in the city, where because of the pandemic he could no longer enjoy the daily swim which all his life had kept him much younger than his years, now ninety-two. As a result, his congestive heart problems had returned, prompting a rapid decline. On 23 September Tina and their daughter Izzy rang me from Manhattan to put the phone to Harry's ear for five minutes so that I could say goodbye to him. He couldn't speak, but squeezed Izzy's hand by way of appreciation. He died just a few hours later.

Even in his nineties, Harry had twice more been over from New York to visit me in Rotherhithe and Battersea. Far too many more of the people you have met in these pages have also now left us. Over my holiday season in the neuro-rehab centre, the Grim Reaper had indulged in a cull of my *Sunday Times* generation: Godfrey Smith, Francis Wyndham, Philip Jacobson, Brian Moynahan. After J Morley and his Armgard, the following year had also deprived us of John Harrison, Brian MacArthur, Norman Stone, Christopher Booker, Johnny Clare, Jonathan Miller, Clive James, John Shrapnel, Bryan Wharton, Stephen Fay and a host of others culminating in Alvarez and Evans.

My old pals Peter Pringle (from New York) and Magnus Linklater (from Edinburgh) were my last visitors for lunch before March 2020 saw the pandemic lockdown, which was otherwise going to make so little difference to my hermit-like life that I contentedly quoted Hamlet's memorable words to Guildenstern: 'I could be bounded in a nutshell and count myself a king of infinite space.'

Hamlet went on: 'Were it not that I have bad dreams', which was not true of me. Unlike other brain attack victims, I still have frequent and very vivid dreams – in none of which am I ever disabled. Skipping around like a spring lamb, if not Superman, I have as much fun as ever with my children and grandchildren, and repeatedly save the world from unspeakable disasters. Who knows what Dr Freud would have made of that? But it does not delude me into thinking that I am not now living in extra time. Enough, in 2020, for Arsenal to cheer me up by winning a record fourteenth FA Cup Final, and Barbados by following other proud Caribbean nations in discarding the British monarch as their absentee head of state. Yes, such mundane matters still mean a lot. And later in lockdown, thanks to the wonders of Zoom and the internet, I even resumed my weekly game of poker with friends old and new.

Words, words, words: they are all I now have at my disposal – and really, on reflection, all I have ever had. So I should speak what I feel, not what I ought to say, just as much as I should concentrate on all that I can still do, rather than what I cannot. I have seen as much, and lived as long, as someone so absurdly fortunate as myself could but dream of. The rest would be silence, were it not for the journalist's perennially optimistic sign-off . . . more follows later.

Poetry
Please!

Poetry Please!

100 Popular Poems from the BBC Radio 4 Programme

Foreword by
Charles Causley

Illustrated by
Meilo So

By arrangement
with the
British Broadcasting
Corporation

PHŒNIX

A PHOENIX PAPERBACK

First published in Great Britain by J. M. Dent in 1985.

This illustrated edition first published in 1999 by Phoenix,
an imprint of Orion Books Ltd,
Orion House, 5 Upper St Martin's Lane
London WC2H 9EA

A CIP catalogue record for this book
is available from the British Library.

ISBN 0 75380 819 6

Printed and bound in Italy.

～ *Contents*

~ *Introduction*

As a popular radio programme, *Poetry Please!* owes its inception
to Brian Patten, a BBC staff producer who was based in Bristol.
Like many an excellent idea it seems, in retrospect, also a
perfectly simple one, and the wonder is that it hadn't been
put into action before. But this is not to allow for Brian Patten's
quite exceptional energy, imaginative sensibility, and 'feel' for
an audience.

Initially planned as a series of eight programmes, the first was
broadcast on Radio 4 from the BBC Network Production Centre
at Bristol in October, 1979. The series was an immediate success.
It returned in 1980 and is still on the air.

The format is simplicity itself: a half-hour programme
featuring poems requested by listeners, and read by professional
performers. The programme is now presented by the writer and
broadcaster Frank Delaney.

From the beginning, response from listeners was considerable.
Thousands of different poems have been asked for, a great
number of them many times over. The following selection of
100 poems most frequently requested has been made by Margaret
Bradley, a former producer of *Poetry Please!* and Peter Shellard
of Messrs. J. M. Dent and Sons.

The Greek origin of the word 'anthology', in the sense that
it is a collection of flowers, reminds us that the conventionally
edited selection is, more often than not, the work of one hand.
In such cases, the poems chosen may declare themselves well
enough, but the choice itself, as with a bunch of flowers,

remains something personally distinctive; often fascinatingly self-revelatory.

The poems aside, to me the most interesting feature of the *Poetry Please!* anthology is the fact that the various choices were made in the first place by a large number of people by no means all connected necessarily with what might be called the poetry business. Of all the literary arts, poetry – aided by the invaluable mnemonics of rhyme, rhythm and musicality – is something most of us carry in the body's luggage from childhood as, among much else, an affirmative of joy and as a spell against the dark. The poems themselves, or such fragments as we remember, may be great, not so great, the lightest of light verse, or mere jingle: but this is unimportant. What must always be remembered is that no poet in his senses ever wrote for the examination syllabus or the academic dissecting-table. A poem is, in essence, a private communication between a poet and single member of his or her audience. What the reader makes of it, just how it is interpreted, the secret nature of its 'meaning', is for the reader alone, and with perfect validity, to resolve in accordance with an individual experience of life and a personal imagination.

Many of the poems following are well known and well loved. Not a few are also often extremely difficult to track down if general collections by their authors are no longer in print. Thomas Hardy once remarked of his own verse that he hoped for a few poems in a good anthology. Such modesty does great credit to Hardy, who as a poet rarely, if ever, faltered in excellence. But it is a fact that out of very large bodies of work, many poets have proved at their best in only a handful of poems. It is often through the work of the anthologist, then, as well as from the active and passionate desire of the individual reader to share

an enthusiasm with others, that such poems are afforded
a well-deserved continuance of light and life in print along
with the work of the poets of consistent and supreme genius.

It was Dickens's Tony Weller, in *The Pickwick Papers*, who
struck a note of anxiety when his son Sam received a Valentine:

'Tain't in poetry, is it?'
'No, no,' replied Sam.
'Wery glad to hear it,' said Mr Weller. 'Poetry's
unnat'ral; no man ever talked poetry 'cept a
beadle on boxin' day, or Warren's blackin', or
Rowland's oil, or some o' them low fellows;
never you let yourself down to talk poetry, my boy ...'

Poetry Please!, whether in print or on the air, gives the lie
to such subversive sentiments. Sadly, Brian Patten did not
live to see the publication of the present collection, though
he was much involved in the early stages of its preparation.
To me, the happiest tribute to the memory of a delightful man
is the appearance of *Poetry Please!*: an anthology of what, by
its very origins, may be described as truly popular verse.

CHARLES CAUSLEY

For Brian Patten,
whose idea *Poetry Please!* was –
a very special BBC producer

Preparations

(early 16th century)

Yet if his majesty, our sovereign Lord,
Should of his own accord
Friendly himself invite,
And say 'I'll be your guest tomorrow night',
How should we stir ourselves, call and command
All hands to work! 'Let no man idle stand!
Set me fine Spanish tables in the hall,
See they be fitted all;
Let there be room to eat
And order taken that there want no meat.
See every sconce and candlestick made bright,
That without tapers they may give a light.
Look to the presence: are the carpets spread,
The awning o'er the head,
The cushions in the chairs,
And all the candles lighted on the stairs?
Perfume the chambers, and in any case
Let each man give attendance in his place.'
Thus, if the King were coming, would we do;
And 'twere good reason too;
For 'tis a duteous thing
To show all honour to an earthly king,
And after all our travail and our cost,
So he be pleased, to think no labour lost . . .

But at the coming of the King of Heaven
All's set at six and seven;
We wallow in our sin.

Christ cannot find a chamber in the inn.
We entertain him always like a stranger,
And as at first still lodge him in the manger.

Indian Prayer

(traditional)

When I am dead
Cry for me a little
Think of me sometimes
But not too much.
Think of me now and again
As I was in life
At some moments it's pleasant to recall
But not for long.
Leave me in peace
And I shall leave you in peace
And while you live
Let your thoughts be with the living.

Pain

The cry of man's anguish went up to God,
'Lord, take away pain!
The shadow that darkens the world Thou hast made;
The close coiling chain
That strangles the heart: the burden that weighs
On the wings that would soar –
Lord, take away pain from the world Thou hast made
That it love Thee the more!'

Then answered the Lord to the cry of the world,
'Shall I take away pain,
And with it the power of the soul to endure,
Made strong by the strain?
Shall I take away pity that knits heart to heart,
And sacrifice high?

Will ye lose all your heroes that lift from the fire
White brows to the sky?
Shall I take away love that redeems with a price,
And smiles with its loss?
Can ye spare from your lives that would cling unto mine
The Christ on his cross?'

from *Miss Thompson Goes Shopping*

In her lone cottage on the downs,
With winds and blizzards and great crowns
Of shining cloud, with wheeling plover
And short grass sweet with the small white clover,
Miss Thompson lived, correct and meek,
A lonely spinster, and every week
On market-day she used to go
Into the little town below,
Tucked in the great downs' hollow bowl,
Like pebbles gathered in a shoal.

So, having washed her plates and cup
And banked the kitchen fire up,
Miss Thompson slipped upstairs and dressed,
Put on her black (her second best),
The bonnet trimmed with rusty plush,
Peeped in the glass with simpering blush,
From camphor-smelling cupboard took
Her thicker jacket off the hook
Because the day might turn to cold.
Then, ready, slipped downstairs and rolled
The hearthrug back; then searched about,
Found her basket, ventured out,
Snecked the door and paused to lock it
And plunged the key in some deep pocket.

Then as she tripped demurely down
The steep descent, the little town
Spread wider till its sprawling street
Enclosed her and her footfalls beat
On hard stone pavement; and she felt
Those throbbing ecstasies that melt
Through heart and mind, as, happy, free,
Her small, prim personality
Merged into the seething strife
Of auction-marts and city life.

The Forsaken Merman

Come, dear children, let us away;
Down and away below!
Now my brothers call from the bay,
Now the great winds shoreward blow,
Now the salt tides seaward flow;
Now the wild white horses play,
Champ and chafe and toss in the spray.
Children dear, let us away!
This way, this way!

Call her once before you go –
Call once yet!
In a voice that she will know:
'Margaret! Margaret!'
Children's voices should be dear
(Call once more) to a mother's ear;
Children's voices, wild with pain –
Surely she will come again!
Call her once and come away;
This way, this way!
'Mother dear, we cannot stay!
The wild white horses foam and fret.'
Margaret! Margaret!

Come, dear children, come away down;
Call no more!
One last look at the white wall'd town,
And the little grey church on the windy shore;
Then come down!

She will not come though you call all day;
Come away, come away!

Children dear, was it yesterday
We heard the sweet bells over the bay?
In the caverns where we lay,
Through the surf and through the swell,
The far-off sound of a silver bell?
Sand-strewn caverns, cool and deep,
Where the winds are all asleep;
Where the spent lights quiver and gleam,
Where the salt weed sways in the stream,
Where the sea-beasts, ranged all round,
Feed in the ooze of their pasture-ground;
Where the sea-snakes coil and twine,
Dry their mail and bask in the brine;
Where great whales come sailing by,
Sail and sail, with unshut eye,
Round the world for ever and aye?
When did music come this way?
Children dear, was it yesterday?

Children dear, was it yesterday
(Call yet once) that she went away?
Once she sate with you and me,
On the red gold throne in the heart of the sea,
And the youngest sate on her knee.
She comb'd its bright hair, and she tended it well,
When down swung the sound of a far-off bell.
She sigh'd, she look'd up through the clear green sea;
She said: 'I must go, for my kinsfolk pray
In the little grey church on the shore to-day.
'Twill be Easter-time in the world – ah me!
And I lose my poor soul, Merman! here with thee.'
I said: 'Go up, dear heart, through the waves;

Say thy prayer, and come back to the kind sea-caves.'
She smiled, she went up through the surf in the bay.
Children dear, was it yesterday?

    Children dear, were we long alone?
'The sea grows stormy, the little ones moan;
Long prayers,' I said, 'in the world they say;
Come!' I said; and we rose through the surf in the bay
We went up the beach, by the sandy down
Where the sea-stocks bloom, to the white-wall'd town
Through the narrow paved streets, where all was still,
To the little grey church on the windy hill.
From the church came a murmur of folk at their prayers
But we stood without in the cold blowing airs.
We climb'd on the graves, on the stones worn with rains
And we gazed up the aisle through the small leaded panes
She sate by the pillar; we saw her clear:
'Margaret, hist! come quick, we are here!
Dear heart,' I said, 'we are long alone;
The sea grows stormy, the little ones moan.'
But, ah, she gave me never a look,
For her eyes were seal'd to the holy book!
Loud prays the priest; shut stands the door.
Come away, children, call no more!
Come away, come down, call no more!

    Down, down, down!
Down to the depths of the sea!
She sits at her wheel in the humming town,
Singing most joyfully.
Hark what she sings: 'O joy, O joy,
For the humming street, and the child with its toy!
For the priest, and the bell, and the holy well;
For the wheel where I spun,
And the blessed light of the sun!'

And so she sings her fill,
Singing most joyfully,
Till the spindle drops from her hand,
And the whizzing wheel stands still.
She steals to the window, and looks at the sand,
And over the sand at the sea;
And her eyes are set in a stare;
And anon there breaks a sigh,
And anon there drops a tear,
From a sorrow-clouded eye,
And a heart sorrow-laden,
A long, long sigh;
For the cold strange eyes of a little Mermaiden
And the gleam of her golden hair.

  Come away, away children;
Come children, come down!
The hoarse wind blows coldly;
Lights shine in the town
She will start from her slumber
When gusts shake the door;
She will hear the winds howling,
Will hear the waves roar.
We shall see, while above us
The waves roar and whirl,
A ceiling of amber,
A pavement of pearl.
Singing: 'Here came a mortal,
But faithless was she!
And alone dwell for ever
The kings of the sea.'

But, children, at midnight,
When soft the winds blow,
When clear falls the moonlight,
When spring-tides are low;
When sweet airs come seaward
From heaths starr'd with broom,
And high rocks throw mildly
On the blanch'd sands a gloom;
Up the still, glistening beaches,
Up the creeks we will hie,
Over banks of bright seaweed
The ebb-tide leaves dry.
We will gaze, from the sand-hills,
At the white, sleeping town;
At the church on the hill-side –
And then come back down.
Singing: 'There dwells a loved one,
But cruel is she!
She left lonely for ever
The kings of the sea.'

If I Could Tell You

Time will say nothing but I told you so,
Time only knows the price we have to pay;
If I could tell you I would let you know.

If we should weep when clowns put on their show,
If we should stumble when musicians play,
Time will say nothing but I told you so.

There are no fortunes to be told, although,
Because I love you more than I can say,
If I could tell you I would let you know.

The winds must come from somewhere when they blow,
There must be reasons why the leaves decay;
Time will say nothing but I told you so.

Perhaps the roses really want to grow,
The vision seriously intends to stay;
If I could tell you I would let you know.

Suppose the lions all get up and go,
And all the brooks and soldiers run away;
Will Time say nothing but I told you so?
If I could tell you I would let you know.

The Geate A-Vallen To

In the sunsheen of our summers
   Wi' the haytime now a-come,
How busy wer we out a-vield
   Wi' vew a-left at hwome,
When waggons rumbled out ov yard
   Red wheeled, wi' body blue,
And back behind 'em loudly slamm'd
   The geate a-vallen to.

Drough day sheen for how many years
   The geate ha' now a-swung,
Behind the veet o'vul-grown men
   And vootsteps of the young
Drough years o' days it swung to us
   Behind each little shoe,
As we tripped lightly on avore
   The geate a-vallen to.

In evenen time o' starry night
   How mother zot at hwome
And kept her blazing vier bright
   Till father should ha' come,
And how she quickened up and smiled,
   And stirred her vier anew,
To hear the trampen hosses' steps
   And geate a-vallen to.

There's moonsheen now in nights o' Fall
   When leaves be brown vrom green,
When to the slammen of the geate
   Our Jenney's ears be keen,
When the wold dog do wag his tail,
   And Jean could tell to who,
As he do come in drough the geate
   The geate a-vallen to.

And oft do come a saddened hour
   When there must goo away
One well-beloved to our heart's core,
   Vor long, perhaps vor aye,
And oh! it is a touchen thing
   The loven heart must rue
To hear behind his last farewell
   The geate a-vallen to.

Going Down Hill on a Bicycle: A Boy's Song

With lifted feet, hands still,
I am poised, and down the hill
Dart, with heedful mind;
The air goes by in a wind.

Swifter and yet more swift,
Till the heart with a mighty lift
Makes the lungs laugh, the throat cry: –
'O bird, see; see, bird, I fly.

'Is this, is this your joy?
O bird, then I, though a boy,
For a golden moment share
Your feathery life in air!'

Say, heart, is there aught like this
In a world that is full of bliss?
'Tis more than skating, bound
Steel-shod to the level ground.

Speed slackens now, I float
Awhile in my airy boat;
Till, when the wheels scarce crawl,
My feet to the treadles fall.

Alas, that the longest hill
Must end in a vale; but still,
Who climbs with toil, wheresoe'er,
Shall find wings waiting there.

Which Shall It Be?

'Which shall it be? Which shall it be?'
I look'd at John – John look'd at me
(Dear, patient John, who loves me yet
As well as though my locks were jet);
And when I found that I must speak,
My voice seemed strangely low and weak:
'Tell me again what Robert said.'
And then I, listening, bent my head.
'This is his letter: "I will give
A house and land while you shall live,
If, in return, from out your seven,
One child to me for aye is given."'
I looked at John's old garments worn,
I thought of all that John had borne
Of poverty and work and care,
Which I, though willing, could not share;
I thought of seven mouths to feed,
Of seven little children's need,
And then of this. 'Come, John,' said I,
'We'll choose among them as they lie
Asleep;' so, walking hand in hand,
Dear John and I surveyed our band.
First to the cradle lightly stepped,
Where the new nameless baby slept.
'Shall it be Baby?' whispered John.
I took his hand, and hurried on
To Lily's crib. Her sleeping grasp
Held her old doll within its clasp;

Her dark curls lay like gold alight,
A glory 'gainst the pillow white.
Softly her father stoop'd to lay
His rough hand down in loving way,
When dream or whisper made her stir,
Then huskily said John, 'Not her, not her!'
We stopp'd beside the trundle bed,
And one long ray of lamplight shed
Athwart the boyish faces there,
In sleep so pitiful and fair;
I saw on Jamie's rough, red cheek
A tear undried. Ere John could speak,
'He's but a baby, too,' said I,
And kiss'd him as we hurried by.
Pale, patient Robbie's angel face
Still in his sleep bore suffering's trace.
'No, for a thousand crowns, not him!'
We whisper'd, while our eyes were dim.
Poor Dick! bad Dick! our wayward son,
Turbulent, reckless, idle one –
Could he be spared? Nay; He who gave
Bids us befriend him to his grave;
Only a mother's heart can be
Patient enough for such as he;
'And so,' said John, 'I would not dare
To send him from her bedside prayer.'
Then stole we softly up above
And knelt by Mary, child of love.
'Perhaps for her 'twould better be,'
I said to John. Quite silently
He lifted up a curl astray
Across her cheek in wilful way,

And shook his head: 'Nay, love; not thee,'
The while my heart beat audibly.
Only one more, our eldest lad,
Trusty and truthful, good and glad –
So like his father. 'No, John, no –
I cannot, will not, let him go.'
And so we wrote, in courteous way,
We could not give one child away;
And afterward toil lighter seemed,
Thinking of that of which we dreamed,
Happy in truth that not one face
We missed from its accustomed place;
Thankful to work for all the seven,
Trusting the rest to One in heaven.

Tarantella

Do you remember an Inn,
Miranda?
Do you remember an Inn?
And the tedding and the spreading
Of the straw for a bedding,
And the fleas that tease in the High Pyrenees,
And the wine that tasted of the tar?
And the cheers and the jeers of the young muleteers
(Under the vine of the dark verandah)?
Do you remember an Inn, Miranda,
Do you remember an Inn?
And the cheers and the jeers of the young muleteers
Who hadn't got a penny,
And who weren't paying any,
And the hammer at the doors and the Din?
And the Hip! Hop! Hap!
Of the clap
Of the hands to the twirl and the swirl
Of the girl gone chancing,
Glancing,
Dancing,
Backing and advancing,
Snapping of a clapper to the spin
Out and in –

And the Ting, Tong, Tang of the Guitar!
Do you remember an Inn,
Miranda?
Do you remember an Inn?

Never more;
Miranda,
Never more.
Only the high peaks hoar:
And Aragon a torrent at the door.
No sound
In the walls of the Halls where falls
The tread
Of the feet of the dead to the ground
No sound:
But the boom
Of the far Waterfall like Doom.

Diary of a Church Mouse

Here among long-discarded cassocks,
Damp stools, and half-split open hassocks,
Here where the Vicar never looks
I nibble through old service books.
Lean and alone I spend my days
Behind this Church of England baize.
I share my dark forgotten room
With two oil-lamps and half a broom.
The cleaner never bothers me,
So here I eat my frugal tea.
My bread is sawdust mixed with straw;
My jam is polish for the floor.

  Christmas and Easter may be feasts
For congregations and for priests,
And so may Whitsun. All the same,
They do not fill my meagre frame.
For me the only feast at all
Is Autumn's Harvest Festival,
When I can satisfy my want
With ears of corn around the font.
I climb the eagle's brazen head
To burrow through a loaf of bread.
I scramble up the pulpit stair
And gnaw the marrows hanging there.

  It is enjoyable to taste
These items ere they go to waste,
But how annoying when one finds
That other mice with pagan minds

Come into church my food to share
Who have no proper business there.
Two field mice who have no desire
To be baptized, invade the choir.
A large and most unfriendly rat
Comes in to see what we are at.
He says he thinks there is no God
And yet he comes . . . it's rather odd.
This year he stole a sheaf of wheat
(It screened our special preacher's seat),
And prosperous mice from fields away
Come in to hear the organ play,
And under cover of its notes
Eat through the altar's sheaf of oats.
A Low Church mouse, who thinks that I
Am too papistical, and High,
Yet somehow doesn't think it wrong
To munch through Harvest Evensong,
While I, who starve the whole year through,
Must share my food with rodents who
Except at this time of the year
Not once inside the church appear.

  Within the human world I know
Such goings-on could not be so,
For human beings only do
What their religion tells them to.
They read the Bible every day
And always, night and morning, pray,
And just like me, the good church mouse,
Worship each week in God's own house,

  But all the same it's strange to me
How very full the church can be
With people I don't see at all
Except at Harvest Festival.

from *The Burning of Leaves*

Now is the time for the burning of the leaves.
They go to the fire; the nostril pricks with smoke
Wandering slowly into a weeping mist.
Brittle and blotched, ragged and rotten sheaves!
A flame seizes the smouldering ruin and bites
On stubborn stalks that crackle as they resist.

The last hollyhock's fallen tower is dust:
All the spices of June are a bitter reek,
All the extravagant riches spent and mean.
All burns! The reddest rose is a ghost;
Sparks whirl up, to expire in the mist: the wild
Fingers of fire are making corruption clean.

Now is the time for stripping the spirit bare,
Time for the burning of days ended and done,
Idle solace of things that have gone before,
Rootless hope and fruitless desire are there:
Let them go to the fire with never a look behind.
The world that was ours is a world that is ours no more.

They will come again, the leaf and the flower, to arise
From squalor of rottenness into the old splendour,
And magical scents to a wondering memory bring:
The same glory, to shine upon different eyes.
Earth cares for her own ruins, naught for ours.
Nothing is certain, only the certain spring.

The Little Black Boy

My mother bore me in the southern wild,
  And I am black, but O! my soul is white!
White as an angel is the English child,
  But I am black, as if bereav'd of light.

My mother taught me underneath a tree,
  And sitting down before the heat of day
She took me on her lap and kissed me,
  And pointing to the east began to say:

'Look on the rising sun: there God does live,
  And gives his light, and gives his heat away,
And flowers and trees and beasts and men receive
  Comfort in morning, joy in the noon day.

'And we are put on earth a little space,
  That we may learn to bear the beams of love;
And these black bodies and this sun-burnt face
  Is but a cloud, and like a shady grove.

'For when our souls have learn'd the heat to bear,
  The clouds will vanish; we shall hear his voice,
Saying: "Come out from the grove, my love & care,
  And round my golden tent like lambs rejoice."'

Thus did my mother say, and kissed me,
  And thus I say to little English boy:
When I from black and he from white cloud free,
  And round the tent of God like lambs we joy,

I'll shade him from the heat, till he can bear
  To lean in joy upon our father's knee;
And then I'll stand and stroke his silver hair,
  And be like him, and he will then love me.

Time and Grief

O time! who know'st a lenient hand to lay
Softest on sorrow's wound, and slowly thence
(Lulling to sad repose the weary sense)
The faint pang stealest unperceived away;
On thee I rest my only hope at last,
And think, when thou hast dried the bitter tear
That flows in vain o'er all my soul held dear,
I may look back on every sorrow past,
And meet life's peaceful evening with a smile:
As some lone bird, at day's departing hour,
Sings in the sunbeam, of the transient shower
Forgetful, though its wings are wet the while: –
　　Yet ah! how much must this poor heart endure,
　　Which hopes from thee, and thee alone, a cure!

Farewell

Farewell to Thee! But not farewell
To all my fondest thoughts of Thee;
Within my heart they still shall dwell
And they shall cheer and comfort me.

Life seems more sweet that Thou didst live
And men more true that Thou wert one;
Nothing is lost that Thou didst give,
Nothing destroyed that Thou hast done.

The Old Vicarage, Grantchester

(Café des Westens, Berlin, May 1912)

Just now the lilac is in bloom,
All before my little room;
And in my flower-beds, I think,
Smile the carnation and the pink;
And down the borders, well I know,
The poppy and the pansy blow . . .
Oh! there the chestnuts, summer through,
Beside the river make for you
A tunnel of green gloom, and sleep
Deeply above; and green and deep
The stream mysterious glides beneath,
Green as a dream and deep as death.
– Oh, damn! I know it! and I know
How the May fields all golden show,
And when the day is young and sweet,
Gild gloriously the bare feet.
That run to bathe . . .

Du lieber Gott!

Here am I, sweating, sick, and hot,
And there the shadowed waters fresh
Lean up to embrace the naked flesh.
Temperamentvoll German Jews
Drink beer around – and *there* the dews
Are soft beneath a morn of gold.
Here tulips bloom as they are told;
Unkempt about those hedges blows
An English unofficial rose;

And there the unregulated sun
Slopes down to rest when day is done,
And wakes a vague unpunctual star,
A slippered Hesper; and there are
Meads towards Haslingfield and Coton
Where *das Betreten*'s not *verboten*.

E'ιθε γενοιμην . . . would I were
In Grantchester, in Grantchester!
Some, it may be, can get in touch
With Nature there, or Earth, or such.
And clever modern men have seen
A Faun a-peeping through the green,
And felt the Classics were not dead,
To glimpse a Naiad's reedy head,
Or hear the Goat-foot piping low: . . .
But these are things I do not know.
I only know that you may lie
Day-long and watch the Cambridge sky,
And, flower-lulled in sleepy grass,
Hear the cool lapse of hours pass,
Until the centuries blend and blur
In Grantchester, in Grantchester. . . .
Still in the dawnlit waters cool
His ghostly Lordship swims his pool,
And tries the strokes, essays the tricks,
Long learnt on Hellespont, or Styx.
Dan Chaucer hears his river still
Chatter beneath a phantom mill.
Tennyson notes, with studious eye,
How Cambridge waters hurry by . . .
And in that garden, black and white,
Creep whispers through the grass all night;

And spectral dance, before the dawn,
A hundred Vicars down the lawn;
Curates, long dust, will come and go
On lissom, clerical, printless toe;
And oft between the boughs is seen
The sly shade of a Rural Dean . . .
Till, at a shiver in the skies,
Vanishing with Satanic cries,
The prim ecclesiastic rout
Leaves but a startled sleeper-out,
Grey heavens, the first bird's drowsy calls,
The falling house that never falls.

God! I will pack, and take a train,
And get me to England once again!
For England's the one land, I know,
Where men with Splendid Hearts may go;
And Cambridgeshire, of all England,
The shire for Men who Understand;
And of *that* district I prefer
The lovely hamlet Grantchester.
For Cambridge people rarely smile,
Being urban, squat, and packed with guile;
And Royston men in the far South
Are black and fierce and strange of mouth;
At Over they fling oaths at one,
And worse than oaths at Trumpington,
And Ditton girls are mean and dirty,
And there's none in Harston under thirty,
And folks in Shelford and those parts
Have twisted lips and twisted hearts,
And Barton men make Cockney rhymes,
And Coton's full of nameless crimes,

And things are done you'd not believe
At Madingley, on Christmas Eve.
Strong men have run for miles and miles,
When one from Cherry Hinton smiles;
Strong men have blanched, and shot their wives,
Rather than send them to St Ives;
Strong men have cried like babes, bydam,
To hear what happened at Babraham.
But Grantchester! ah, Grantchester!
There's peace and holy quiet there,
Great clouds along pacific skies,
And men and women with straight eyes,
Lithe children lovelier than a dream,
A bosky wood, a slumbrous stream,
And little kindly winds that creep
Round twilight corners, half asleep.
In Grantchester their skins are white;
They bathe by day, they bathe by night;
The women there do all they ought;
The men observe the Rules of Thought.
They love the Good; they worship Truth;
They laugh uproariously in youth;
(And when they get to feeling old,
They up and shoot themselves, I'm told) ...

Ah God! to see the branches stir
Across the moon at Grantchester!
To smell the thrilling-sweet and rotten
Unforgettable, unforgotten
River-smell, and hear the breeze
Sobbing in the little trees.
Say, do the elm-clumps greatly stand
Still guardians of that holy land?

The chestnuts shade, in reverend dream,
The yet unacademic stream?
Is dawn a secret shy and cold
Anadyomene, silver-gold?
And sunset still a golden sea
From Haslingfield to Madingley?
And after, ere the night is born,
Do hares come out about the corn?
Oh, is the water sweet and cool,
Gentle and brown, above the pool?
And laughs the immortal river still
Under the mill, under the mill?
Say, is there Beauty yet to find?
And Certainty? and Quiet kind?
Deep meadows yet, for to forget
The lies, and truths, and pain? ... oh! yet
Stands the Church clock at ten to three?
And is there honey still for tea?

Prospice

Fear death? – to feel the fog in my throat,
　　The mist in my face,
When the snows begin, and the blasts denote
　　I am nearing the place,
The power of the night, the press of the storm,
　　The post of the foe;
Where he stands, the Arch Fear in a visible form,
　　Yet the strong man must go:
For the journey is done and the summit attained,
　　And the barriers fall,
Though a battle's to fight ere the guerdon be gained,
　　The reward of it all.
I was ever a fighter, so – one fight more,
　　The best and the last!
I would hate that death bandaged my eyes, and forbore,
　　And bade me creep past.
No! let me taste the whole of it, fare like my peers
　　The heroes of old,
Bear the brunt, in a minute pay glad life's arrears
　　Of pain, darkness and cold.
For sudden the worst turns the best to the brave,
　　The black minute's at end,
And the elements' rage, the fiend-voices that rave,
　　Shall dwindle, shall blend,
Shall change, shall become first a peace out of pain,
　　Then a light, then thy breast,
O thou soul of my soul! I shall clasp thee again,
　　And with God be the rest!

A Song of Living

Because I have loved life, I shall have no sorrow to die.
I have sent up my gladness on wings, to be lost in the blue of the sky.
I have run and leaped with the rain, I have taken the wind to my
    breast.
My cheek like a drowsy child to the face of the earth I have pressed.
Because I have loved life, I shall have no sorrow to die.

I have kissed young Love on the lips, I have heard his song to the end.
I have struck my hand like a seal in the loyal hand of a friend.
I have known the peace of heaven, the comfort of work done well.
I have longed for death in the darkness and risen alive out of hell.
Because I have loved life, I shall have no sorrow to die.

I give a share of my soul to the world where my course is run.
I know that another shall finish the task I must leave undone.
I know that no flower, nor flint was in vain on the path I trod.
As one looks on a face through a window, through life I have looked
    on God.
Because I have loved life, I shall have no sorrow to die.

Lord Ullin's Daughter

A chieftain to the Highlands bound,
Cries 'Boatman, do not tarry!
And I'll give thee a silver pound
To row us o'er the ferry' –

'Now who be ye, would cross Lochgyle
This dark and stormy water?'
'O I'm the chief of Ulva's isle,
And this, Lord Ullin's daughter.

'And fast before her father's men
Three days we've fled together,
For should he find us in the glen,
My blood would stain the heather.

'His horsemen hard behind us ride;
Should they our steps discover,
Then who will cheer my bonny bride
When they have slain her lover?'

Out spoke the hardy Highland wight,
'I'll go, my chief – I'm ready: –
It is not for your silver bright,
But for your winsome lady: –

'And by my word! the bonny bird
In danger shall not tarry;
So though the waves are raging white
I'll row you o'er the ferry.'

By this the storm grew loud apace,
The water-wraith was shrieking;
And in the scowl of Heaven each face
Grew dark as they were speaking.

But still as wilder blew the wind
And as the night grew drearer,
Adown the glen rode armed men,
Their trampling sounded nearer. –

'O haste thee, haste!' the lady cries,
'Though tempests round us gather;
I'll meet the raging of the skies,
But not an angry father' –

The boat has left a stormy land,
A stormy sea before her, –
When, Oh! too strong for human hand
The tempest gather'd o'er her.

And still they row'd amidst the roar
Of waters fast prevailing:
Lord Ullin reach'd that fatal shore,
His wrath was changed to wailing.

For, sore dismay'd, through storm and shade
His child he did discover; –
One lovely hand she stretch'd for aid,
And one was round her lover.

'Come back! come back!' he cried in grief
'Across this stormy water;
And I'll forgive your Highland chief,
My daughter! – Oh my daughter!'

'Twas vain: – the loud waves lash'd the shore,
Return or aid preventing: –
The waters wild went o'er his child,
And he was left lamenting.

Timothy Winters

Timothy Winters comes to school
With eyes as wide as a football-pool,
Ears like bombs and teeth like splinters:
A blitz of a boy is Timothy Winters.

His belly is white, his neck is dark,
And his hair is an exlamation mark.
His clothes are enough to scare a crow
And through his britches the blue winds blow.

When teacher talks he won't hear a word
And he shoots down dead the arithmetic-bird,
He licks the patterns off his plate
And he's not even heard of the Welfare State.

Timothy Winters has bloody feet
And he lives in a house on Suez Street,
He sleeps in a sack on the kitchen floor
And they say there aren't boys like him any more.

Old Man Winters likes his beer
And his missus ran off with a bombardier,
Grandma sits in the grate with a gin
And Timothy's dosed with an aspirin.

The Welfare Worker lies awake
But the law's as tricky as a ten-foot snake,
So Timothy Winters drinks his cup
And slowly goes on growing up.

At Morning Prayers the Master helves
For children less fortunate than ourselves,
And the loudest response in the room is when
Timothy Winters roars 'Amen!'

So come one angel, come on ten:
Timothy Winters says 'Amen
Amen amen amen amen.'
Timothy Winters, Lord.

                      Amen.

Roundabouts and Swings

It was early last September nigh to Framlin'am-on Sea,
An' 'twas Fair-day come to-morrow, an' the time was after tea,
An' I met a painted caravan adown a dusty lane,
A Pharaoh with his waggons comin' jolt an' creak an' strain;
A cheery cove an' sunburnt, bolt o' eye and wrinkled up,
An' beside him on the splashboard sat a brindled terrier pup,
An' a lurcher wise as Solomon an' lean as fiddle-strings
Was joggin' in the dust along 'is roundabouts and swings.

'Goo'-day,' said 'e; 'Goo'-day,' said I; 'an' 'ow d'you find things go,
An' what's the chance o' millions when you runs a travellin'
        show?'
'I find,' said 'e, 'things very much as 'ow I've always found,
For mostly they goes up and down or else goes round and round.'
Said 'e, 'The job's the very spit o' what it always were,
It's bread and bacon mostly when the dog don't
        catch a 'are;
But lookin' at it broad, an' while it ain't no
        merchant king's,
What's lost upon the roundabouts we
        pulls up on the swings!'

'Goo'luck,' said 'e; 'Goo'luck,' said I; 'you've put it past a doubt;
An' keep that lurcher on the road, the gamekeepers is out';
'E thumped upon the footboard an' 'e lumbered on again
To meet a gold-dust sunset down the owl-light in the lane;
An' the moon she climbed the 'azels, while a nightjar seemed to
    spin
That Pharaoh's wisdom o'er again, 'is sooth of lose-and-win;
For 'up an' down an' round,' said 'e, 'goes all appointed things,
An' losses on the roundabouts means profits on the swings!'

Morning

The morning comes, the drops of dew
Hang on the grass and bushes too;
The sheep more eager bite the grass
Whose moisture gleams like drops of glass;
The heifer licks in grass and dew
That make her drink and fodder too.
The little bird his morn-song gives,
His breast wet with the dripping leaves,
Then stops abruptly just to fly
And catch the wakened butterfly,
That goes to sleep behind the flowers
Or backs of leaves from dews and showers.
The yellow-hammer, haply blest,
Sits by the dyke upon her nest;
The long grass hides her from the day,
The water keeps the boys away.
The morning sun is round and red
As crimson curtains round a bed,
The dewdrops hang on barley horns
As beads the necklace thread adorns,
The dewdrops hang wheat-ears upon
Like golden drops against the sun.
Hedge-sparrows in the bush cry 'tweet',
O'er nests larks winnow in the wheat,
Till the sun turns gold and gets more high,
And paths are clean and grass gets dry,
And longest shadows pass away.
And brightness is the blaze of day.

Say Not the Struggle Naught Availeth

Say not the struggle naught availeth,
   The labour and the wounds are vain,
The enemy faints not, nor faileth,
   And as things have been, things remain.

If hopes were dupes, fears may be liars;
   It may be, in yon smoke concealed,
Your comrades chase e'en now the fliers,
   And, but for you, possess the field.

For while the tired waves, vainly breaking,
   Seem here no painful inch to gain,
Far back through creeks and inlets making
   Comes silent, flooding in, the main.

And not by eastern windows only,
   When daylight comes, comes in the light;
In front the sun climbs slow, how slowly,
   But westward, look, the land is bright!

An Old Woman of the Roads

O, to have a little house!
To own the hearth and stool and all!
The heaped-up sods upon the fire,
The pile of turf against the wall!

To have a clock with weights and chains
And pendulum swinging up and down,
A dresser filled with shining delph,
Speckled and white and blue and brown!

I could be busy all the day
Clearing and sweeping hearth and floor,
And fixing on their shelf again
My white and blue and speckled store!

I could be quiet there at night
Beside the fire and by myself,
Sure of a bed and loth to leave
The ticking clock and shining delph!

Och! but I'm weary of mist and dark,
And roads where there's never a house or bush,
And tired I am of bog and road,
And the crying wind and the lonesome hush!

And I am praying to God on high,
And I am praying Him night and day,
For a little house, a house of my own –
Out of the wind's and the rain's way.

The Water Mill

Listen to the water mill,
  Through the livelong day;
How the clicking of the wheel
  Wears the hours away.
Languidly the autumn wind
  Stirs the withered leaves;
On the field the reapers sing,
  Binding up the sheaves;
And a proverb haunts my mind,
  And as a spell is cast,
'The mill will never grind
  With the water that has passed.'

Autumn winds revive no more
  Leaves strewn o'er earth and main.
The sickle never more shall reap
  The yellow, garnered grain;
And the rippling stream flows on
  Tranquil, deep and still,
Never gliding back again
  To the water mill.
Truly speaks the proverb old,
  With a meaning vast:
'The mill will never grind
  With the water that has passed.'

O, the wasted hours of life
 That have swiftly drifted by!
O, the good we might have done!
 Gone, lost without a sigh!
Love that we might once have saved
 By a single kindly word;
Thoughts conceived, but ne'er expressed,
 Perishing unpenned, unheard!
Take the proverb to thy soul!
 Take, and clasp it fast:
'The mill will never grind
 With the water that has passed.'

O, love thy God and fellow man,
 Thyself consider last;
For come it will when thou must scan
 Dark errors of the past.
And when the fight of life is o'er
 And earth recedes from view
And heaven in all its glory shines
 'Midst the good, the pure, the true,
Then you will see more clearly
 The proverb, deep and vast:
'The mill will never grind
 With the water that has passed.'

The Crowning of Dreaming John of Grafton

I

Seven days he travelled
Down the roads of England,
Out of leafy Warwick lanes
Into London Town.
Grey and very wrinkled
Was Dreaming John of Grafton,
But seven days he walked to see
A king put on his crown.

Down the streets of London
He asked the crowded people
Where would be the crowning
And when would it begin.
He said he'd got a shilling,
A shining silver shilling,
But when he came to Westminster
They wouldn't let him in.

Dreaming John of Grafton
Looked upon the people,
Laughed a little laugh, and then
Whistled and was gone.
Out along the long roads,
The twisting roads of England,
Back into the Warwick lanes
Wandered Dreaming John.

II

As twilight touched with her ghostly fingers
All the meadows and mellow hills,
And the great sun swept in his robes of glory –
Woven of petals of daffodils
And jewelled and fringed with leaves of the roses –
Down the plains of the western way,
Among the rows of the scented clover
Dreaming John in his dreaming lay.

Since dawn had folded the stars of heaven
He'd counted a score of miles and five,
And now, with a vagabond heart untroubled
And proud as the properest man alive,
He sat him down with a limber spirit
That all men covet and few may keep,
And he watched the summer draw round her beauty
The shadow that shepherds the world to sleep.

And up from the valleys and shining rivers,
And out of the shadowy wood-ways wild,
And down from the secret hills, and streaming
Out of the shimmering undefiled
Wonder of sky that arched him over,
Came a company shod in gold
And girt in gowns of a thousand blossoms,
Laughing and rainbow-aureoled.

Wrinkled and grey and with eyes a-wonder
And soul beatified, Dreaming John
Watched the marvellous company gather
While over the clover a glory shone;
They bore on their brows the hues of heaven,
Their limbs were sweet with flowers of the fields,
And their feet were bright with the gleaming treasure
That prodigal earth to her children yields.

They stood before him, and John was laughing
As they were laughing; he knew them all,
Spirits of trees and pools and meadows,
Mountain and windy waterfall,
Spirits of clouds and skies and rivers,
Leaves and shadows and rain and sun,
A crowded, jostling, laughing army,
And Dreaming John knew every one.

Among them then was a sound of singing
And chiming music, as one came down
The level rows of the scented clover,
Bearing aloft a flashing crown;
No word of a man's desert was spoken,
Nor any word of a man's unworth,
But there on the wrinkled brow it rested,
And Dreaming John was king of the earth.

III

Dreaming John of Grafton
Went away to London,
Saw the coloured banners fly,
Heard the great bells ring,
But though his tongue was civil
And he had a silver shilling,
They wouldn't let him in to see
The crowning of the King.

So back along the long roads,
The leafy roads of England,
Dreaming John went carolling,
Travelling alone,
And in a summer evening,
Among the scented clover,
He held before a shouting throng
A crowning of his own.

My Mind to Me a Kingdom Is

My mind to me a kingdom is;
   Such present joys therein I find,
That it excels all other bliss
   That world affords or grows by kind.
Though much I want which most would have
Yet still my mind forbids to crave.

No princely pomp, no wealthy store,
   No force to win the victory,
No wily wit to salve a sore,
   No shape to feed a loving eye;
To none of these I yield as thrall,
For why, my mind doth serve for all.

I see how plenty suffers oft,
   And hasty climbers soon do fall;
I see that those which are aloft
   Mishap doth threaten most of all.
They get with toil, they keep with fear;
Such cares my mind could never bear.

Content I live, this is my stay,
   I seek no more than may suffice;
I press to bear no haughty sway;
   Look, what I lack my mind supplies.
Lo! thus I triumph like a king,
Content with that my mind doth bring.

Some have too much, yet still do crave;
    I little have, and seek no more.
They are but poor, though much they have,
    And I am rich with little store.
They poor, I rich; they beg, I give;
They lack, I leave; they pine, I live.

I laugh not at another's loss,
    I grudge not at another's gain;
No worldly waves my mind can toss;
    My state at one doth still remain.
I fear no foe, I fawn no friend;
I loathe not life, nor dread my end.

Some weigh their pleasure by their lust,
    Their wisdom by their rage of will;
Their treasure is their only trust,
    A cloaked craft their store of skill.
But all the pleasure that I find
Is to maintain a quiet mind.

My wealth is health and perfect ease;
    My conscience clear my choice defence;
I neither seek by bribes to please
    Nor by deceit to breed offence.
Thus do I live, thus will I die;
Would all did so as well as I!

Temper in October

He rode at furious speed to Broken Edge,
And he was very angry, very small;
But God was kind, knowing he needed not
A scolding, nor a swift unpleasant fall,
Nor any high reproach of soul at all.
'It matters not,' said Reason and Good Sense;
'Absurd to let a trifle grow immense.'
'It matters very much,' said Busy Brain;
'You cannot be content and calm again,
For you are angry in a righteous cause.'
'Poor, queer old Waxy!' laughed the hips and haws.
'God has a sense of humour,' said a ball
Of orange-gold inside a spindle-berry –
'And "Christ our Lorde is full exceeding merrie."'

He lingered in the lane at Broken Edge,
Bryony berries burned from every hedge;
Snails in the deep wet grass of fairy rings
Told him of unimaginable things.
Love was in all the colours of the sky,
Love in the folded shadows of the high
Blue hills, as quiet as any Easter Eve.
(O fool, O blind and earthbound thus to grieve!)

He turned his horse. Through level sunset-gleams
He saw a sudden little road that curled
And climbed elusive to a sky of dreams.
His anger over Broken Edge was hurled
To scatter into nothing on a gust
Of wind which brought the twilight to the trees.

The drifted leaves, the white October dust
Hiding the beechnuts for the squirrel's store,
Heard the low whisper spoken on his knees: –
'God, You have made a very perfect world,
Don't let me spoil it ever any more.'

Desiderata

'Go placidly amid the noise and the haste, and remember what
peace there may be in silence. As far as possible without surrender
be on good terms with all persons. Speak your truth quietly and
clearly; and listen to others, even the dull and ignorant; they too
have their story. Avoid loud and aggressive persons, they are
vexatious to the spirit. If you compare yourself with others you
may become vain and bitter; for always there will be greater and
lesser persons than yourself. Enjoy your achievements as well as
your plans. Keep interested in your own career, however humble;
it is a real possession in the changing fortunes of time. Exercise
caution in your business affairs; for the world is full of trickery.
But let this not blind you to what virtue there is; many persons
strive for high ideals; and everywhere life is full of heroism.
Be yourself. Especially do not feign affection. Neither be cynical
about love; for in the face of all aridity and disenchantment it
is as perennial as the grass. Take kindly the counsel of the years,
gracefully surrendering the things of youth. Nurture strength
of spirit to shield you in sudden misfortune. But do not distress
yourself with imaginings. Many fears are born of fatigue and
loneliness. Beyond a wholesome discipline, be gentle with
yourself. You are a child of the universe no less than the trees
and the stars; you have a right to be here. And whether or not
it is clear to you, no doubt the universe is unfolding as it should.
Therefore be at peace with God, whatever you conceive Him
to be. And whatever your labors and aspirations, in the noisy
confusion of life keep peace with your soul. With all its sham,
drudgery and broken dreams, it is still a beautiful world.
Be cheerful. Strive to be happy.'

Mrs Malone

Mrs Malone
Lived hard by a wood
All on her lonesome
As nobody should.
With her crust on a plate
And her pot on the coal
And none but herself
To converse with, poor soul.
In a shawl and a hood
She got sticks out-o'door,
On a bit of old sacking
She slept on the floor,
And nobody nobody
Asked how she fared
Or knew how she managed,
For nobody cared.
 Why make a pother
 About an old crone?
 What for should they bother
 With Mrs Malone?

One Monday in winter
With snow on the ground
So thick that a footstep
Fell without sound,
She heard a faint frostbitten
Peck on the pane
And went to the window
To listen again.

There sat a cock-sparrow
Bedraggled and weak,
With half-open eyelid
And ice on his beak.
She threw up the sash
And she took the bird in,
And mumbled and fumbled it
Under her chin.
>'Ye're all of a smother,
>Ye're fair overblown!
>I've room fer another,'
>Said Mrs Malone.

Come Tuesday while eating
Her dry morning slice
With the sparrow a-picking
('Ain't company nice!')
She heard on her doorpost
A curious scratch,
And there was a cat
With its claw on the latch.
It was hungry and thirsty
And thin as a lath,
It mewed and it mowed
On the slithery path.
She threw the door open
And warmed up some pap,
And huddled and cuddled it
In her old lap.
>'There, there, little brother,
>Ye poor skin-an'-bone,
>There's room fer another,'
>Said Mrs Malone.

Come Wednesday while all of them
Crouched on the mat

With a crumb for the sparrow,
A sip for the cat,
There was a wailing and whining
Outside in the wood,
And there sat a vixen
With six of her brood.
She was haggard and ragged
And worn to a shred,
And her half-dozen babies
Were only half-fed,

But Mrs Malone, crying
'My! ain't they sweet!'
Happed them and lapped them
And gave them to eat.
> 'You warm yerself, mother,
> Ye're cold as a stone!
> There's room fer another,'
> Said Mrs Malone.

Come Thursday a donkey
Stepped in off the road
With sores on his withers
From bearing a load.
Come Friday when icicles
Pierced the white air
Down from the mountainside
Lumbered a bear.
For each she had something,
If little, to give –
'Lord knows, the poor critters
Must all of 'em live,'
She gave them her sacking,
Her hood and her shawl,
Her loaf and her teapot –
She gave them her all.
> 'What with one thing and t'other
> Me fambily's grown,
> And there's room fer another,'
> Said Mrs Malone.

Come Saturday evening
When time was to sup
Mrs Malone
Had forgot to sit up.
The cat said meeow,
And the sparrow said peep,

The vixen, she's sleeping,
The bear, let her sleep.
On the back of the donkey
They bore her away,
Through trees and up mountains
Beyond night and day,
Till come Sunday morning
They brought her in state
Through the last cloudbank
As far as the Gate.
      'Who is it,' asked Peter,
      'You have with you there?'
      And donkey and sparrow,
      Cat, vixen, and bear

Exclaimed, 'Do you tell us
Up here she's unknown?
It's our mother, God bless us!
It's Mrs Malone,
Whose havings were few
And whose holding was small
And whose heart was so big
It had room for us all.'
Then Mrs Malone
Of a sudden awoke,
She rubbed her two eyeballs
And anxiously spoke:
'Where am I, to goodness,
And what do I see?
My dear, let's turn back,
This ain't no place fer me!'
But Peter said, 'Mother
Go in to the Throne.
There's room for another
One, Mrs Malone.'

The Owl Critic

'Who stuffed that white owl?' No one spoke in the shop;
The barber was busy, and he couldn't stop;
The customers, waiting their turns, were reading
The Daily, the Herald, the Post, little heeding
The young man who blurted out such a blunt question;
No one raised a head, or even made a suggestion;
   And the barber kept on shaving.

'Don't you see, Mister Brown,'
Cried the youth with a frown,
'How wrong the whole thing is,
How preposterous each wing is,
How flattened the head, how jammed down the neck is –
In short, the whole owl, what an ignorant wreck 'tis!

'I make no apology;
I've learned owleology,
I've passed days and nights in a hundred collections,
And cannot be blinded to any deflections
Arising from unskilful fingers that fail
To stuff a bird right, from his beak to his tail.
Mister Brown, Mister Brown!
Do take that bird down,
Or you'll soon be the laughing stock all over town!'
   And the barber kept on shaving.

'I've studied owls,
And other night fowls,
And I tell you
What I know to be true!

An owl cannot roost
With his limbs so unloosed;
No owl in this world
Ever had his claws curled,
Ever had his legs slanted,
Ever had his bill canted,
Ever had his neck screwed
Into that attitude.
He can't do it, because
'Tis against all bird laws.
Anatomy teaches,
Ornithology preaches,
An owl has a toe
That can't turn out so!
I've made the white owl my study for years,
And to see such a job almost moves me to tears!

'Mister Brown, I'm amazed
You should be so crazed
As to put up a bird
In that posture absurd!
To look at that owl really brings on a dizziness;
The man who stuffed him don't half know his business!'
    And the barber kept on shaving.
'Examine those eyes,
I'm filled with surprise
Taxidermists should pass
Off on you such poor glass;
So unnatural they seem
They'd made Audubon scream,
And John Burroughs laugh
To encounter such chaff.
Do take that bird down;
Have him stuffed again Brown!'
    And the barber kept on shaving.

'With some sawdust and bark
I could stuff in the dark
An owl better than that.
I could make an old bat
Look more like an owl
Than that horrid fowl,
Stuck up there so stiff like a side of coarse leather;
In fact, about him there's not one natural feather.'

Just then with a wink and a sly
    normal lurch,
The owl, very gravely, got
    down from his perch,
Walked round, and regarded
    his fault-finding critic,
(Who thought he was stuffed)
    with a glance analytic,
And then fairly hooted, as if
    he should say:
'Your learning's at fault, this
    time, anyway;
Don't waste it again on a
    live bird, I pray.
I'm an owl; you're another.
    Sir Critic, good-day!'
  And the barber kept on
    shaving.

from *The Rubáiyát of Omar Khayyam of Naishápúr*

Here with a Loaf of Bread beneath the Bough,
A Flask of Wine, a Book of Verse – and Thou
    Beside me singing in the Wilderness –
And Wilderness is Paradise enow.

'How sweet is mortal Sovranty' – think some:
Others – 'How blest the Paradise to come!'
    Ah, take the Cash in hand and waive the Rest;
Oh, the brave Music of a *distant* Drum!

Look to the Rose that blows about us – 'Lo,
Laughing,' she says, 'into the World I blow:
    At once the silken Tassel of my Purse
Tear, and its Treasure on the Garden throw.'

The Worldly Hope men set their Hearts upon
Turns Ashes – or it prospers; and anon,
    Like Snow upon the Desert's dusty Face
Lighting a little Hour or two – is gone.

And those who husbanded the Golden Grain,
And those who flung it to the Winds like Rain,
    Alike to no such aureate Earth are turn'd
As, buried once, Men want dug up again.

Think, in this batter'd Caravanserai
Whose Doorways are alternate Night and Day,
    How Sultan after Sultan with his Pomp
Abode his Hour or two, and went his way.

They say the Lion and the Lizard keep
The Courts where Jamshýd gloried and drank deep;
    And Bahrám, that great Hunter – the Wild Ass
Stamps o'er his Head, and he lies fast asleep.

I sometimes think that never blows so red
The Rose as where some buried Caesar bled;
    That every Hyacinth the Garden wears
Drops in its Lap from some once lovely Head.

And this delightful Herb whose tender Green
Fledges the River's Lip on which we lean –
    Ah, lean upon it lightly! for who knows
From what once lovely Lip it springs unseen!

Ah, my Belovèd, fill the Cup that clears
TO-DAY of past Regrets and future Fears –
    To-morrow? – Why, To-morrow I may be
Myself with Yesterday's Sev'n Thousand Years.

Lo! some we loved, the loveliest and best
That Time and Fate of all their Vintage prest,
    Have drunk their Cup a Round or two before,
And one by one crept silently to Rest.

And we, that now make merry in the Room
They left, and Summer dresses in new Bloom,
    Ourselves must we beneath the Couch of Earth
Descend, ourselves to make a Couch – for whom?

Ah, make the most of what we yet may spend,
Before we too into the Dust descend;
    Dust into Dust, and under Dust, to lie,
Sans Wine, sans Song, sans Singer, and – sans End!

Brumana

Oh shall I never never be home again?
Meadows of England shining in the rain
Spread wide your daisied lawns: your ramparts green
With briar fortify, with blossom screen
Till my far morning – and O streams that slow
And pure and deep through plains and playlands go,
For me your love and all your kingcups store,
And – dark militia of the southern shore,
Old fragrant friends – preserve me the last lines
Of that long saga which you sung me, pines,
When, lonely boy, beneath the chosen tree
I listened, with my eyes upon the sea.

O traitor pines, you sang what life has found
The falsest of fair tales.
Earth blew a far-horn prelude all around,
That native music of her forest home,
While from the sea's blue fields and syren dales
Shadows and light noon-spectres of the foam
Riding the summer gales
On aery viols plucked an idle sound.

Hearing you sing, O trees,
Hearing you murmur, 'There are older seas,
That beat on vaster sands,
Where the wise snailfish move their pearly towers
To carven rocks and sculptured promont'ries,'
Hearing you whisper, 'Lands
Where blaze the unimaginable flowers.'

Beneath me in the valley waves the palm,
Beneath, beyond the valley, breaks the sea;
Beneath me sleep in mist and light and calm
Cities of Lebanon, dream-shadow-dim,
Where Kings of Tyre and Kings of Tyre did rule
In ancient days in endless dynasty.
And all around the snowy mountains swim
Like mighty swans afloat in heaven's pool.

But I will walk upon the wooded hill
Where stands a grove, O pines, of sister pines,
And when the downy twilight droops her wing
And no sea glimmers and no mountain shines
My heart shall listen still.
For pines are gossip pines the wide world through
And full of runic tales to sigh or sing.
'Tis ever sweet through pines to see the sky
Mantling a deeper gold or darker blue.

'Tis ever sweet to lie
On the dry carpet of the needles brown,
And though the fanciful green lizard stir
And windy odours light as thistledown
Breathe from the lavdanon and lavender,
Half to forget the wandering and pain,
Half to remember days that have gone by,
And dream and dream that I am home again!

The Ice Cart

Perched on my city office-stool
I watched with envy while a cool
And lucky carter handled ice . . .
And I was wandering in a trice
Far from the grey and grimy heat
Of that intolerable street

O'er sapphire berg and emerald floe
Beneath the still cold ruby glow
Of everlasting Polar night,
Bewildered by the queer half-light,
Until I stumbled unawares
Upon a creek where big white bears
Plunged headlong down with flourished heels
And floundered after shining seals
Through shivering seas of blinding blue.
And, as I watched them, ere I knew
I'd stripped and I was swimming too
Among the seal-pack, young and hale,
And thrusting on with threshing tail,
With twist and twirl and sudden leap
Through crackling ice and salty deep,
Diving and doubling with my kind,
Until, at last, we left behind
Those big white, blundering bulks of death,
And lay, at length, with panting breath
Upon a far untravelled floe,
Beneath a gentle drift of snow –
Snow drifting gently, fine and white,
Out of the endless Polar night,
Falling and falling evermore
Upon that far untravelled shore,
Till I was buried fathoms deep
Beneath that cold, white drifting sleep –
Sleep drifting deep,
Deep drifting sleep . . .
The carter cracked a sudden whip:
I clutched my stool with startled grip,
Awakening to the grimy heat
Of that intolerable street.

from *The Deserted Village*

Beside yon straggling fence that skirts the way,
With blossomed furze unprofitably gay,
There, in his noisy mansion, skilled to rule,
The village master taught his little school;
A man severe he was, and stern to view;
I knew him well, and every truant knew;
Well had the boding tremblers learned to trace
The day's disasters in his morning face;
Full well they laughed, with counterfeited glee,
At all his jokes, for many a joke had he;
Full well the busy whisper, circling round,
Conveyed the dismal tidings when he frowned;
Yet he was kind, or, if severe in aught,
The love he bore to learning was in fault;
The village all declared how much he knew;
'Twas certain he could write, and cipher too;
Lands he could measure, terms and tides presage,
And e'en the story ran that he could gauge.
In arguing too, the parson owned his skill,
For e'en though vanquished, he could argue still;
While words of learned length and thundering sound
Amazed the gazing rustics ranged around,
And still they gazed, and still the wonder grew,
That one small head could carry all he knew.

Elegy Written in a Country Churchyard

The curfew tolls the knell of parting day,
  The lowing herd wind slowly o'er the lea,
The plowman homeward plods his weary way,
  And leaves the world to darkness and to me.

Now fades the glimmering landscape on the sight,
  And all the air a solemn stillness holds,
Save where the beetle wheels his droning flight,
  And drowsy tinklings lull the distant folds;

Save that from yonder ivy-mantled tower
  The moping owl does to the moon complain
Of such as, wandering near her secret bower,
  Molest her ancient solitary reign.

Beneath those rugged elms, that yew-tree's shade,
  Where heaves the turf in many a mouldering heap,
Each in his narrow cell for ever laid,
  The rude forefathers of the hamlet sleep.

The breezy call of incense-breathing morn,
  The swallow twittering from the straw-built shed,
The cock's shrill clarion, or the echoing horn,
  No more shall rouse them from their lowly bed.

For them no more the blazing hearth shall burn,
  Or busy housewife ply her evening care:
No children run to lisp their sire's return,
  Or climb his knee the envied kiss to share.

Oft did the harvest to their sickle yield,
    Their furrow oft the stubborn glebe has broke:
How jocund did they drive their team afield!
    How bowed the woods beneath their sturdy stroke!

Let not ambition mock their useful toil,
    Their homely joys, and destiny obscure;
Nor grandeur hear with a disdainful smile
    The short and simple annals of the poor.

The boast of heraldry, the pomp of power,
    And all that beauty, all that wealth e'er gave,
Awaits alike the inevitable hour.
    The paths of glory lead but to the grave.

Nor you, ye proud, impute to these the fault,
    If memory o'er their tomb no trophies raise,
Where through the long-drawn aisle and fretted vault
    The pealing anthem swells the note of praise.

Can storied urn or animated bust
    Back to its mansion call the fleeting breath?
Can honour's voice provoke the silent dust,
    Or flattery soothe the dull cold ear of death?

Perhaps in this neglected spot is laid
    Some heart once pregnant with celestial fire;
Hands, that the rod of empire might have swayed,
    Or waked to extasy the living lyre.

But knowledge to their eyes her ample page
    Rich with the spoils of time did ne'er unroll;
Chill penury repressed their noble rage,
    And froze the genial current of the soul.

Full many a gem of purest ray serene,
  The dark unfathomed caves of ocean bear;
Full many a flower is born to blush unseen,
  And waste its sweetness on the desert air.

Some village-Hampden, that with dauntless breast
  The little tyrant of his fields withstood,
Some mute inglorious Milton here may rest,
  Some Cromwell guiltless of his country's blood.

The applause of listening senates to command.
  The threats of pain and ruin to despise,
To scatter plenty o'er a smiling land,
  And read their history in a nation's eyes,

Their lot forbad: nor circumscribed alone
  Their growing virtues, but their crimes confined;
Forbad to wade through slaughter to a throne,
  And shut the gates of mercy on mankind,

The struggling pangs of conscious truth to hide,
  To quench the blushes of ingenuous shame,
Or heap the shrine of luxury and pride
  With incense kindled at the Muse's flame.

Far from the madding crowd's ignoble strife,
  Their sober wishes never learned to stray;
Along the cool sequestered vale of life
  They kept the noiseless tenor of their way.

Yet even these bones from insult to protect
  Some frail memorial still erected nigh,
With uncouth rhymes and shapeless sculpture decked,
  Implores the passing tribute of a sigh.

Their name, their years, spelt by the unlettered Muse,
　　The place of fame and elegy supply:
And many a holy text around she strews,
　　That teach the rustic moralist to die.

For who, to dumb forgetfulness a prey,
　　This pleasing anxious being e'er resigned,
Left the warm precincts of the cheerful day,
　　Nor cast one longing lingering look behind?

On some fond breast the parting soul relies,
　　Some pious drops the closing eye requires;
E'en from the tomb the voice of nature cries,
　　E'en in our ashes live their wonted fires.

For thee, who mindful of the unhonoured dead,
　　Dost in these lines their artless tale relate;
If chance, by lonely contemplation led,
　　Some kindred spirit shall inquire thy fate –

Haply some hoary-headed swain may say,
　　'Oft have we seen him at the peep of dawn
Brushing with hasty steps the dews away
　　To meet the sun upon the upland lawn.

'There at the foot of yonder nodding beech,
　　That wreathes its old fantastic roots so high,
His listless length at noontide would he stretch,
　　And pore upon the brook that babbles by.

'Hard by yon wood, now smiling as in scorn,
　　Muttering his wayward fancies he would rove,
Now drooping, woeful-wan, like one forlorn,
　　Or crazed with care, or crossed in hopeless love.

'One morn I missed him on the customed hill,
  Along the heath, and near his favourite tree;
Another came; nor yet beside the rill,
  Nor up the lawn, nor at the wood was he:

'The next, with dirges due in sad array
  Slow through the church-way path we saw him borne.
Approach and read (for thou can'st read) the lay,
  Graved on the stone beneath yon aged thorn.'

(There scattered oft, the earliest of the year,
  By hands unseen, are showers of violets found:
The redbreast loves to bill and warble there,
  And little footsteps lightly print the ground.)

The Epitaph

Here rests his head upon the lap of Earth
  A Youth, to Fortune and to Fame unknown.
Fair Science frowned not on his humble birth,
  And Melancholy marked him for her own.

Large was his bounty, and his soul sincere,
  Heaven did a recompense as largely send:
He gave to Misery all he had, a tear,
  He gained from Heaven ('twas all he wished) a friend.

No farther seek his merits to disclose,
  Or draw his frailties from their dread abode,
(There they alike in trembling hope repose,)
  The bosom of his Father and his God.

The Darkling Thrush

I leant upon a coppice gate
    When Frost was spectre-gray,
And Winter's dregs made desolate
    The weakening eye of day.
The tangled bine-stems scored the sky
    Like strings of broken lyres,
And all mankind that haunted nigh
    Had sought their household fires.

The land's sharp features seemed to be
    The Century's corpse outleant,
His crypt the cloudy canopy,
    The wind his death-lament.
The ancient pulse of germ and birth
    Was shrunken hard and dry,
And every spirit upon earth
    Seemed fervourless as I.

At once a voice arose among
        The bleak twigs overhead
In a full-hearted evensong
        Of joy illimited;
An aged thrush, frail, gaunt, and small,
        In blast-beruffled plume,
Had chosen thus to fling his soul
        Upon the growing gloom.

So little cause for carolings
        Of such ecstatic sound
Was written on terrestrial things
        Afar or nigh around,
That I could think there trembled through
        His happy good-night air
Some blessed Hope, whereof he knew
        And I was unaware.

Ducks

*(To F.M., Who drew them
in Holzminden Prison)*

I

From troubles of the world
I turn to ducks,
Beautiful comical things
Sleeping or curled
Their heads beneath white wings
By water cool,
Or finding curious things
To eat in various mucks
Beneath the pool,
Tails uppermost, or waddling
Sailor-like on the shores
Of ponds, or paddling
– Left! Right! – with fanlike feet
Which are for steady oars
When they (white galleys) float
Each bird a boat
Rippling at will the sweet
Wide waterway . . .
When night is fallen *you* creep
Upstairs, but drakes and dillies
Nest with pale water-stars,

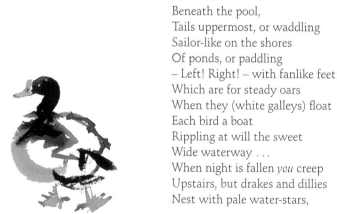

Moonbeams and shadow bars,
And water-lilies:
Fearful too much to sleep
Since they've no locks
To click against the teeth
Of weasel and fox.
And warm beneath
Are eggs of cloudy green
Whence hungry rats and lean
Would stealthily suck
New life, but for the mien,
The bold ferocious mien
Of the mother-duck.

II

Yes, ducks are valiant things
On nests of twigs and straws,
And ducks are soothy things
And lovely on the lake
When that the sunlight draws
Thereon their pictures dim
In colours cool.
And when beneath the pool
They dabble, and when they swim
And make their rippling rings,
O ducks are beautiful things!
But ducks are comical things: –
As comical as you.
Quack!
They waddle round, they do.
They eat all sorts of things,
And then they quack.

By barn and stable and stack
They wander at their will,
But if you go too near
They look at you through black
Small topaz-tinted eyes
And wish you ill.
Triangular and clear
They leave their curious track
In mud at the water's edge,
And there amid the sedge
And slime they gobble and peer
Saying 'Quack! quack!'

III

When God had finished the stars and whirl of coloured suns
He turned His mind from big things to fashion little ones;
Beautiful tiny things (like daisies) He made, and then
He made the comical ones in case the minds of men
    Should stiffen and become
    Dull, humourless and glum,
And so forgetful of their Maker be
As to take even themselves – *quite seriously.*

Caterpillars and cats are lively and excellent puns:
All God's jokes are good – even the practical ones!
And as for the duck, I think God must have smiled a bit
Seeing those bright eyes blink on the day He fashioned it.
And he's probably laughing still at the sound that came out
    of its bill!

The Gate of the Year

And I said to the man who stood at the
    gate of the year:
'Give me a light, that I may tread safely
    into the unknown!'
And he replied:
'Go out into the darkness and put your
    hand into the Hand of God.
That shall be to you better than light
    and safer than a known way.'

So, I went forth, and finding the Hand
    of God, trod gladly into the night
And He led me toward the hills and
    the breaking of day in the lone East.

So, heart, be still!
What need our little life,
Our human life, to know,
If God hath comprehension?
In all the dizzy strife
Of things both high and low
God hideth His intention.

The Enchanted Shirt

Fytte the First: wherein it shall be shown how the Truth is too mighty a Drug for such as he of feeble temper.

The King was sick. His cheek was red
  And his eye was clear and bright;
He ate and drank with a kingly zest,
  And peacefully snored at night.

But he said he was sick, and a king should know,
  And doctors came by the score.
They did not cure him. He cut off their heads
  And sent to the schools for more.

At last two famous doctors came,
  And one was as poor as a rat –
He had passed his life in studious toil,
  And never found time to grow fat.

The other had never looked in a book;
  His patients gave him no trouble –
If they recovered they paid him well,
  If they died their heirs paid double.

Together they looked at the royal tongue,
  As the King on his couch reclined;
In succession they thumped his august chest,
  But no trace of disease could find.

The old sage said, 'You're as sound as a nut.'
  'Hang him up,' roared the King in a gale –
In a ten-knot gale of royal rage;
  The other leech grew a shade pale,

But he pensively rubbed his sagacious nose,
  And thus his prescription ran –
The King will be well, if he sleeps one night
  In the Shirt of a Happy Man.

Fytte the Second: tells of the search for the Shirt and how it was
nigh found but was not, for reasons which are said, or sung.

Wide o'er the realm the couriers rode,
  And fast their horses ran,
And many they saw, and to many they spoke,
  But they found no Happy Man.

They found poor men who would fain be rich,
  And rich who thought they were poor;
And men who twisted their waists in stays,
  And women that short hose wore.

They saw two men by the roadside sit,
  And both bemoaned their lot;
For one had buried his wife, he said,
  And the other one had not.

At last as they came to a village gate –
  A beggar lay whistling there;
He whistled and sang and laughed and rolled
  On the grass in the soft June air.

The weary couriers paused and looked
  At the scamp so blithe and gay;
And one of them said, 'Heaven save you, friend!
  You seem to be happy today.'

'Oh yes, fair sirs,' the rascal laughed
  And his voice rang free and glad;
'An idle man has so much to do
  That he never has time to be sad.'

'This is our man,' the courier said;
   'Our luck has led us aright.
I will give you a hundred ducats, friend,
   For the loan of your shirt to-night.'

The merry blackguard lay back on the grass,
   And laughed till his face was black;
'I would do it, God wot,' and he roared with the fun,
   'But I haven't a shirt to my back.'

Fytte the Third: showing how His Majesty the King came at last
to sleep in a Happy Man his Shirt.

Each day to the King the reports came in
   Of his unsuccessful spies,
And the sad panorama of human woes
   Passed daily under his eyes.

And he grew ashamed of his useless life,
   And his maladies hatched in gloom;
He opened his windows and let the air
   Of the free heaven into his room.

And out he went in the world and toiled
   In his own appointed way;
And the people blessed him, the land was glad,
   And the King was well and gay.

The Green Eye of the Yellow God

There's a one-eyed yellow idol to the north of Khatmandu,
There's a little marble cross below the town;
There's a broken-hearted woman tends the grave of Mad Carew,
And the Yellow God forever gazes down.

He was known as Mad Carew by the subs of Khatmandu,
He was hotter than they felt inclined to tell;
But for all his foolish pranks, he was worshipped in the ranks,
And the Colonel's daughter smiled on him as well.

He had loved her all along, with a passion of the strong,
The fact that she loved him was plain to all.
She was nearly twenty-one and arrangements had begun
To celebrate her birthday with a ball.

He wrote to ask what present she would like from Mad Carew;
They met next day as he dismissed a squad;
And jestingly she told him then that nothing else would do
But the green eye of the little Yellow God.

On the night before the dance, Mad Carew seemed in a trance,
And they chaffed him as they puffed at their cigars;
But for once he failed to smile, and he sat alone awhile,
Then went out into the night beneath the stars.

He returned before the dawn, with his shirt and tunic torn,
And a gash across his temples dripping red;
He was patched up right away, and he slept through all the day,
And the Colonel's daughter watched beside his bed.

He woke at last and asked if they could send his tunic through;
She brought it, and he thanked her with a nod;
He bade her search the pocket, saying, 'That's from Mad Carew',
And she found the little green eye of the god.

She upbraided poor Carew in the way that women do,
Though both her eyes were strangely hot and wet;
But she wouldn't take the stone, and Mad Carew was left alone
With the jewel that he'd chanced his life to get.

When the ball was at its height, on that still and tropic night,
She thought of him and hastened to his room;
As she crossed the barrack square she could hear the dreamy air
Of a waltz tune softly stealing through the gloom.

His door was open wide, with silver moonlight shining through,
The place was wet and slippery where she trod;
An ugly knife lay buried in the heart of Mad Carew,
'Twas the 'Vengeance of the Little Yellow God'.

There's a one-eyed yellow idol to the north of Khatmandu,
There's a little marble cross below the town;
There's a broken-hearted woman tends the grave of Mad Carew,
And the Yellow God forever gazes down.

Invictus

Out of the night that covers me,
  Black as the pit from pole to pole,
I thank whatever gods may be
  For my unconquerable soul.

In the fell clutch of circumstance
  I have not winced nor cried aloud.
Under the bludgeonings of chance
  My head is bloody, but unbowed.

Beyond this place of wrath and tears
  Looms but the Horror of the shade,
And yet the menace of the years
  Finds and shall find me unafraid.

It matters not how strait the gate,
  How charged with punishments the scroll,
I am the master of my fate:
  I am the captain of my soul.

The Pulley

When God at first made man,
Having a glass of blessings standing by;
Let us (said he) pour on him all we can;
Let the world's riches, which dispersed lie,
    Contract into a span.

So strength first made a way;
Then beauty flowed, then wisdom, honour, pleasure;
When almost all was out, God made a stay,
Perceiving that alone of all his treasure,
    Rest in the bottom lay.

For if I should (said he)
Bestow this jewel also on my creature,
He would adore my gifts instead of me,
And rest in nature, not the God of nature:
    So both should losers be.

Yet let him keep the rest,
But keep them with repining restlessness:
Let him be rich and weary, that at least,
If goodness lead him not, yet weariness
    May toss him to my breast.

The Song of the Shirt

With fingers weary and worn,
  With eyelids heavy and red,
A Woman sat, in unwomanly rags,
  Plying her needle and thread –
    Stitch! stitch! stitch!
In poverty, hunger, and dirt,
And still with a voice of dolorous pitch
She sang the 'Song of the Shirt!'

'Work! work! work!
While the cock is crowing aloof!
  And work – work – work,
Till the stars shine through the roof!
It's O! to be a slave
  Along with the barbarous Turk,
Where woman has never a soul to save,
  If this is Christian work!

'Work – work – work
Till the brain begins to swim;
  Work – work – work
Till the eyes are heavy and dim!
Seam, and gusset, and band,
  Band, and gusset, and seam,
Till over the buttons I fall asleep,
  And sew them on in a dream!

'O! Men with Sisters dear!
   O! Men! with Mothers and Wives!
It is not linen you're wearing out,
   But human creatures' lives!
      Stitch – stitch – stitch,
   In poverty, hunger, and dirt,
Sewing at once, with a double thread,
   A Shroud as well as a Shirt.

'But why do I talk of Death?
   That Phantom of grisly bone,
I hardly fear his terrible shape,
   It seems so like my own –
   It seems so like my own,
   Because of the fasts I keep,
Oh! God! that bread should be so dear,
   And flesh and blood so cheap!

'Work – work – work!
   My labour never flags;
And what are its wages? A bed of straw,
   A crust of bread – and rags,
That shattered roof, – and this naked floor –
   A table – a broken chair –
And a wall so blank, my shadow I thank
   For sometimes falling there!

'Work – work – work!
From weary chime to chime,
   Work – work – work –
As prisoners work for crime!
   Band, and gusset, and seam,
   Seam, and gusset, and band,
Till the heart is sick, and the brain benumbed,
   As well as the weary hand.

'Work – work – work,
In the dull December light,
   And work – work – work,
When the weather is warm and bright –
While underneath the eaves
   The brooding swallows cling
As if to show me their sunny backs
   And twit me with the spring.

'Oh! but to breathe the breath
Of the cowslip and primrose sweet –
    With the sky above my head,
And the grass beneath my feet,
For only one short hour
    To feel as I used to feel,
Before I knew the woes of want
    And the walk that costs a meal!

'Oh but for one short hour!
    A respite however brief!
No blessed leisure for Love or Hope,
    But only time for Grief!
A little weeping would ease my heart,
    But in their briny bed
My tears must stop, for every drop
    Hinders needle and thread!'

Seam, and gusset, and band,
Band, and gusset, and seam,
        Work, work, work,
Like the Engine that works by Steam!
A mere machine of iron and wood
        That toils for Mammon's sake –
Without a brain to ponder and craze
        Or a heart to feel – and break!

With fingers weary and worn,
    With eyelids heavy and red,
A Woman sat in unwomanly rags,
    Plying her needle and thread, –
        Stitch! stitch! stitch!
    In poverty, hunger, and dirt,
And still with a voice of dolorous pitch,
Would that its tone could reach the Rich! –
    She sang this 'Song of the Shirt!'

Duty

I slept and dreamed that life was Beauty:
I woke and found that life was Duty:
Was then the dream a shadowy lie?
Toil on, sad heart, courageously,
And thou shalt find thy dream to be
A noonday light and truth to thee.

God's Grandeur

The world is charged with the grandeur of God.
  It will flame out, like shining from shook foil;
  It gathers to a greatness, like the ooze of oil
Crushed. Why do men then now not reck his rod?
Generations have trod, have trod, have trod;
  And all is seared with trade; bleared, smeared with toil;
  And wears man's smudge and shares man's smell: the soil
Is bare now, nor can foot feel, being shod.

And for all this, nature is never spent;
  There lives the dearest freshness deep down things;
And though the last lights off the black West went
  Oh, morning, at the brown brink eastward, springs –
Because the Holy Ghost over the bent
  World broods with warm breast and with ah! bright wings.

Loveliest of Trees, the Cherry Now

Loveliest of trees, the cherry now
Is hung with bloom along the bough,
And stands about the woodland ride
Wearing white for Eastertide.

Now, of my threescore years and ten,
Twenty will not come again,
And take from seventy springs a score,
It only leaves me fifty more.

And since to look at things in bloom
Fifty springs are little room,
About the woodlands I will go
To see the cherry hung with snow.

The Wind in a Frolic

The wind one morning sprung up from sleep,
Saying, 'Now for a frolic! now for a leap!
Now for a mad-cap, galloping chase!
I'll make a commotion in every place!'
So it swept with a bustle right through a great town,
Creaking the signs, and scattering down
Shutters; and whisking, with merciless squalls,
Old women's bonnets and gingerbread stalls.
There never was heard a much lustier shout,
As the apples and oranges trundled about;
And the urchins, that stand with their thievish eyes
For ever on watch, ran off each with a prize.

Then away to the field it went blustering and humming,
And the cattle all wondered whatever was coming;
It plucked by their tails the grave, matronly cows,
And tossed the colts' manes all about their brows,
Till, offended at such a familiar salute,
They all turned their backs, and stood sullenly mute.
So on it went, capering and playing its pranks:
Whistling with reeds on the broad river's banks;
Puffing the birds as they sat on the spray,
Or the traveller grave on the king's highway.
It was not too nice to hustle the bags
Of the beggar, and flutter his dirty rags:
'Twas so bold, that it feared not to play its joke
With the doctor's wig, or the gentleman's cloak.
Through the forest it roared, and cried gaily, 'Now,
You sturdy old oaks, I'll make you bow!'
And it made them bow without more ado,
Or it cracked their great branches through and through.

Then it rushed like a monster on cottage and farm,
Striking their dwellers with sudden alarm;
And they ran out like bees in a midsummer swarm.
There were dames with their 'kerchiefs tied over their caps,
To see if their poultry were free from mishaps;
The turkeys they gobbled, the geese screamed aloud,
And the hens crept to roost in a terrified crowd;
There was rearing of ladders, and logs laying on
Where the thatch from the roof threatened soon to be gone.

(But the wind had passed on, and had met in a lane,
With a schoolboy, who panted and struggled in vain;
For it tossed him, and twirled him, then passed, and he stood,
With his hat in a pool, and his shoe in the mud.)

(There was a poor man, hoary and old,
Cutting the heath on the open wold –
The strokes of his bill were faint and few,
Ere this frolicsome wind upon him blew;
But behind him, before him, about him it came,
And the breath seemed gone from his feeble frame;
So he sat him down with a muttering tone,
Saying, 'Plague on the wind! was the like ever known?
But nowadays every wind that blows
Tells one how weak an old man grows!')

But away went the wind in its holiday glee;
And now it was far on the billowy sea,
And the lordly ships felt its staggering blow,
And the little boats darted to and fro.
But lo! it was night, and it sank to rest,
On the sea-bird's rock, in the gleaming west,
Laughing to think, in its fearful fun,
How little of mischief it had done.

Abou Ben Adhem

Abou Ben Adhem (may his tribe increase!)
Awoke one night from a deep dream of peace,
And saw, within the moonlight in his room,
Making it rich, and like a lily in bloom,
An angel writing in a book of gold:
Exceeding peace had made Ben Adhem bold,
And to the presence in the room he said,
'What writest thou?' The vision raised its head,
And with a look made of all sweet accord,
Answered, 'The names of those who love the Lord.'
'And is mine one?' said Abou. 'Nay, not so,'
Replied the angel. Abou spoke more low,
But cheerly still; and said, 'I pray thee, then,
Write me as one that loves his fellow men.'
The angel wrote, and vanished. The next night
It came again with a great wakening light,
And showed the names whom love of God had blest,
And lo! Ben Adhem's name led all the rest.

The High Tide on the Coast of Lincolnshire, 1571

The old mayor climbed the belfry tower,
    The ringers ran by two, by three;
'Pull, if ye never pulled before;
    Good ringers, pull your best,' quoth he,
'Play uppe, play uppe, O Boston bells!
Play all your changes, all your swells,
        Play uppe "The Brides of Enderby".'

Men say it was a stolen tyde –
    The Lord that sent it, He knows all;
But in myne ears doth still abide
    The message that the bells let fall:
And there was nought of strange, beside
The flights of mews and peewits pied
        By millions crouched on the old sea wall.

I sat and spun within the doore,
    My thread brake off, I raised myne eyes;
The level sun, like ruddy ore,
    Lay sinking in the barren skies;
And dark against day's golden death
She moved where Lindis wandereth,
My sonne's faire wife, Elizabeth.

'Cusha! Cusha! Cusha!' calling,
Ere the early dews were falling,
Farre away I heard her song.
'Cusha! Cusha!' all along;

Where the reedy Lindis floweth,
    Floweth, floweth,
From the meads where melick groweth
Faintly came her milking song –

'Cusha! Cusha! Cusha!' calling,
'For the dews will soone be falling;
Leave your meadow grasses mellow,
    Mellow, mellow;
Quit your cowslips, cowslips yellow;
Come uppe Whitefoot, come uppe Lightfoot;
Quit the stalks of parsley hollow,
    Hollow, hollow;
Come uppe Jetty, rise and follow,
From the clovers lift your head;
Come uppe Whitefoot, come uppe Lightfoot,
Come uppe Jetty, rise and follow,
Jetty, to the milking shed.'

If it be long, ay, long ago,
    When I beginne to think howe long,
Againe I hear the Lindis flow,
    Swift as an arrowe, sharpe and strong;
And all the aire, it seemeth mee,
Bin full of floating bells (sayth shee),
That ring the tune of Enderby.

Alle fresh the level pasture lay,
    And not a shadowe mote be seene,
Save where full fyve good miles away
    The steeple towered from out the greene;
And lo! the great bell farre and wide
Was heard in all the country side
That Saturday at eventide.

The swanherds where their sedges are
   Moved on in sunset's golden breath,
The shepherde lads I heard afarre,
   And my sonne's wife, Elizabeth;
Till floating o'er the grassy sea
Came downe that kyndly message free,
The 'Brides of Mavis Enderby'.

Then some looked uppe into the sky,
   And all along where Lindis flows
To where the goodly vessels lie,
   And where the lordly steeple shows.
They sayde, 'And why should this thing be¿
What danger lowers by land or sea¿
They ring the tune of Enderby!

'For evil news from Mablethorpe,
   Of pyrate galleys warping down;
For shippes ashore beyond the scorpe,
   They have not spared to wake the towne:
But while the west bin red to see,
And storms be none, and pyrates flee,
Why ring "The Brides of Enderby"¿'

I looked without, and lo! my sonne
   Came riding downe with might and main:
He raised a shout as he drew on,
   Till all the welkin rang again,
'Elizabeth! Elizabeth!'
(A sweeter woman ne'er drew breath
Than my sonne's wife, Elizabeth.)

'The olde sea wall (he cried) is downe,
   The rising tide comes on apace,
And boats adrift in yonder towne
   Go sailing uppe the market-place.'

He shook as one that looks on death:
'God save you, mother!' straight he saith;
'Where is my wife, Elizabeth?'

'Good sonne, where Lindis winds away,
    With her two bairns I marked her long;
And ere yon bells beganne to play
    Afar I heard her milking song.'
He looked across the grassy lea,
To right, to left, 'Ho Enderby!'
They rang 'The Brides of Enderby'!

With that he cried and beat his breast;
    For, lo! along the river's bed
A mighty eygre reared his crest,
    And uppe the Lindis raging sped.
It swept with thunderous noises loud;
Shaped like a curling snow-white cloud,
Or like a demon in a shroud.

And rearing Lindis backward pressed
    Shook all her trembling bankes amaine;
Then madly at the eygre's breast
    Flung uppe her weltering walls again.
Then bankes came down with ruin and rout –
Then beaten foam flew round about –
Then all the mighty floods were out.

So farre, so fast the eygre drave,
    The heart had hardly time to beat,
Before a shallow seething wave
    Sobbed in the grasses at oure feet:
The feet had hardly time to flee
Before it brake against the knee,
And all the world was in the sea.

Upon the roofe we sate that night,
    The noise of bells went sweeping by;
I marked the lofty beacon light
    Stream from the church tower, red and high –
A lurid mark and dread to see;
And awesome bells they were to mee,
That in the dark rang 'Enderby'.

They rang the sailor lads to guide
    From roofe to roofe who fearless rowed;
And I – my sonne was at my side,
    And yet the ruddy beacon glowed;
And yet he moaned beneath his breath,
'O come in life, or come in death!
O lost! my love, Elizabeth.'

And dist thou visit him no more?
    Thou didst, thou didst, my daughter deare;
The waters laid thee at his doore,
    Ere yet the early dawn was clear.
Thy pretty bairns in fast embrace,
The lifted sun shone on thy face,
Downe drifted to thy dwelling-place.

That flow strewed wrecks about the grass,
    That ebbe swept out the flocks to sea;
A fatal ebbe and flow, alas!
    To manye more than myne and mee:
But each will mourn his own (she saith).
And sweeter woman ne'er drew breath
Than my sonne's wife, Elizabeth.

I shall never hear her more
By the reedy Lindis shore,
'Cusha! Cusha! Cusha!' calling,
Ere the early dews be falling;

I shall never hear her song,
'Cusha! Cusha!' all along
Where the sunny Lindis floweth,
        Goeth, floweth;
From the meads where melick groweth,
When the water winding down,
Onward floweth to the town.

I shall never see her more
Where the reeds and rushes quiver,
        Shiver, quiver;
Stand beside the sobbing river,
Sobbing, throbbing, in its falling
To the sandy lonesome shore;
I shall never hear her calling,

'Leave your meadow grasses mellow,
        Mellow, mellow;
Quit your cowslips, cowslips yellow;
Come uppe Whitefoot, come uppe Lightfoot;
Quit your pipes of parsley hollow,
        Hollow, hollow;
Come uppe Lightfoot, rise and follow;
        Lightfoot, Whitefoot,
From your clovers lift the head;
Come uppe Jetty, follow, follow,
Jetty, to the milking shed.'

Let Me Not See Old Age

Let me not see old age: Let me not hear
The proffered help, the mumbled sympathy,
The well-meant tactful sophistries that mock
Pathetic husks who once were strong and free,
And in youth's fickle triumph laughed and sang,
Loved, and were foolish; and at the close have seen
The fruits of folly garnered, and that love,
Tamed and encaged, stale into grey routine.
Let me not see old age; I am content
With my few crowded years; laughter and strength
And song have lit the beacon of my life.
Let me not see it fade, but when the long
September shadows steal across the square,
Grant me this wish; they may not find me there.

Warning

When I am an old woman I shall wear purple
With a red hat which doesn't go, and doesn't suit me,
And I shall spend my pension on brandy and summer gloves
And satin sandals, and say we've no money for butter.
I shall sit down on the pavement when I'm tired
And gobble up samples in shops and press alarm bells
And run my stick along the public railings
And make up for the sobriety of my youth.
I shall go out in my slippers in the rain
And pick the flowers in other people's gardens
And learn to spit.

You can wear terrible shirts and grow more fat
And eat three pounds of sausages at a go
Or only bread and pickle for a week
And hoard pens and pencils and beermats and things in boxes.
But now we must have clothes that keep us dry
And pay our rent and not swear in the street
And set a good example for the children.
We will have friends to dinner and read the papers.

But maybe I ought to practise a little now?
So people who know me are not too shocked and surprised
When suddenly I am old and start to wear purple.

Meg Merrilies

Old Meg she was a gipsy,
   And lived upon the moors;
Her bed it was the brown heath turf,
   And her house was out of doors.

Her apples were swart blackberries,
   Her currants, pods o' broom;
Her wine was dew of the wild white rose,
   Her book a churchyard tomb.

Her brothers were the craggy hills,
   Her sisters larchen trees;
Alone with her great family
   She lived as she did please.

No breakfast had she many a morn,
   No dinner many a noon,
And 'stead of supper she would stare
   Full hard against the moon.

But every morn, of woodbine fresh
   She made her garlanding,
And every night the dark glen yew
   She wove, and she would sing.

And with her fingers, old and brown,
   She plaited mats o' rushes,
And gave them to the cottagers
   She met among the bushes.

Old Meg was brave as Margaret Queen
   And tall as Amazon;
An old red blanket cloak she wore,
   A chip hat had she on.
God rest her aged bones somewhere;
   She died full long agone!

from *An Exequy on his Wife*

Sleep on (my Love!) in thy cold bed
Never to be disquieted.
My last Good-night! Thou wilt not wake
Till I Thy Fate shall overtake:
Till age, or grief, or sickness must
Marry my Body to that Dust
It so much loves; and fill the roome
My heart keepes empty in Thy Tomb.
Stay for mee there: I will not faile
To meet Thee in that hollow Vale.
And think not much of my delay;
I am already on the way,
And follow Thee with all the speed
Desire can make, or Sorrowes breed.

Each Minute is a short Degree
And e'ry Howre a stepp towards Thee.
At Night when I betake to rest,
Next Morne I rise neerer my West
Of Life, almost by eight Howres sayle,
Then when Sleep breath'd his drowsy gale.

   Thus from the Sunne my Bottome steares,
And my Daye's Compasse downward beares.
Nor labour I to stemme the Tide,
Through which to Thee I swiftly glide.

   'Tis true; with shame and grief I yield
Thou, like the Vann, first took'st the Field,
And gotten hast the Victory
In thus adventuring to Dy
Before Mee; whose more yeeres might crave
A just præcedence in the Grave.
But hark! My Pulse, like a soft Drum
Beates my Approach, Tells Thee I come;
And, slowe howe're my Marches bee,
I shall at last sitt downe by Thee.

   The thought of this bids mee goe on,
And wait my dissolution
With Hope and Comfort. Deare! (forgive
The Crime) I am content to live
Divided, with but, half a Heart,
Till wee shall Meet and Never part.

Ode to the North-East Wind

Welcome, wild North-easter.
  Shame it is to see
Odes to every zephyr;
  Ne'er a verse to thee.
Welcome, black North-easter!
  O'er the German foam;
O'er the Danish moorlands,
  From thy frozen home.
Tired we are of summer,
  Tired of gaudy glare,
Showers soft and steaming,
  Hot and breathless air.
Tired of listless dreaming,
  Through the lazy day:
Jovial wind of winter,
  Turn us out to play!
Sweep the golden reed-beds;
  Crisp the lazy dyke;
Hunger into madness
  Every plunging pike.
Fill the lake with wild-fowl;
  Fill the marsh with snipe;
While on dreary moorlands
  Lonely curlew pipe.

Through the black fir-forest
  Thunder harsh and dry,
Shattering down the snow-flakes
  Off the curdled sky.
Hark! The brave North-easter!
  Breast-high lies the scent,
On by holt and headland,
  Over heath and bent.

Chime, ye dappled darlings,
    Through the sleet and snow.
Who can over-ride you?
    Let the horses go!
Chime, ye dappled darlings,
    Down the roaring blast;
You shall see a fox die
    Ere an hour be past.
Go! and rest to-morrow,
    Hunting in your dreams,
While our skates are ringing
    O'er the frozen streams.
Let the luscious South-wind
    Breathe in lovers' sighs,
While the lazy gallants
    Bask in ladies' eyes.
What does he but soften
    Heart alike and pen?
'Tis the hard grey weather
    Breeds hard English men.
What's the soft South-wester?
    'Tis the ladies' breeze,
Bringing home their true-loves
    Out of all the seas:
But the black North-easter,
    Through the snowstorm hurled,
Drives our English hearts of oak
    Seaward round the world.
Come, as came our fathers,
    Heralded by thee,
Conquering from the eastward,
    Lords by land and sea.
Come; and strong within us
    Stir the Viking's blood;
Bracing brain and sinew;
    Blow, thou wind of God!

The Glory of the Garden

Our England is a garden that is full of stately views,
Of borders, beds and shrubberies and lawns and avenues,
With statues on the terraces and peacocks strutting by;
But the Glory of the Garden lies in more than meets the eye.

For where the old thick laurels grow, along the thin red wall,
You find the tool- and potting-sheds which are the heart of all;
The cold-frames and the hot-houses, the dungpits and the tanks,
The rollers, carts and drain-pipes, with the barrows and the
    planks.

And there you'll see the gardeners, the men and 'prentice boys
Told off to do as they are bid and do it without noise;
For, except when seeds are planted and we shout to scare the
    birds,
The Glory of the Garden it abideth not in words.

And some can pot begonias and some can bud a rose,
And some are hardly fit to trust with anything that grows;
But they can roll and trim the lawns and sift the sand and loam,
For the Glory of the Garden occupieth all who come.

Our England is a garden, and such gardens are not made
By singing: – 'Oh, how beautiful!' and sitting in the shade,
While better men than we go out and start their working lives
At grubbing weeds from gravel-paths with broken dinner-knives.

There's not a pair of legs so thin, there's not a head so thick,
There's not a hand so weak and white, nor yet a heart so sick,
But it can find some needful job that's crying to be done,
For the Glory of the Garden glorifieth every one.

Then seek your job with thankfulness and work till further orders,
If it's only netting strawberries or killing slugs on borders;
And when your back stops aching and your hands begin to harden,
You will find yourself a partner in the Glory of the Garden.

Oh, Adam was a gardener, and God who made him sees
That half a proper gardener's work is done upon his knees,
So when your work is finished, you can wash your hands and pray
For the Glory of the Garden, that it may not pass away!
And the Glory of the Garden it shall never pass away!

The Meadow Wreath

I made myself a wreath of Adder's Tongue
    And Barnaby and Ramp and Bent and Twitch,
And Weaslesnout and Weld were thereamong,
    And Elbow Out of Joint and Bitter Vetch

And Broomrape and Marsh Lousewort and the flower
    Of Gromwell and the yellow Mellilot
And Butterbur and Dwale and Kitchen Scour,
        There were not many herbs that I forgot.

    I did not cease to gather Stavesacre
        And Leopard's Bane that makes the mole afraid
    And Sauce Alone and Jum and Dittander
        And horrid Jack-in-Hedge that turns the spade:

    And Frogbit that the gentle shepherds love
        And Good King Henry useful for the squint
    And Scammony and Dill and Hangman's Glove
        And Gold of Pleasure and blue Calamint.

    I took the leaves of Water Agrimony
        And Pipsisway and Tutsan and Behen,
    And wove them close with purple Pellitory
        And Whitlow Grass and Brooklime from the fen,

    And tufted Senicle and Feverfew
        And Creeping Charlie and Cow Galingale
    And Adam's Blanket wet with early dew
    And Maiden's Petticoat and Horse's Tail,

Until the thing at last became a bore
    And all the labour of my hands seemed vain.
I did not know what I had done it for:
    I shall not make a meadow wreath again.

Love Songs in Age

She kept her songs, they took so little space,
    The covers pleased her:
One bleached from lying in a sunny place,
One marked in circles by a vase of water,
One mended, when a tidy fit had seized her,
    And coloured, by her daughter –
So they had waited, till in widowhood
She found them, looking for something else, and stood

Relearning how each frank submissive chord
    Had ushered in
Word after sprawling hyphenated word,
And the unfailing sense of being young
Spread out like a spring-woken tree, wherein
    That hidden freshness sung,
That certainty of time laid up in store
As when she played them first. But, even more,

The glare of that much-mentioned brilliance, love,
    Broke out, to show
Its bright incipience sailing above,
Still promising to solve, and satisfy,
And set unchangeably in order. So
    To pile them back, to cry
Was hard, without lamely admitting how
It had not done so then, and could not now.

Snake

A snake came to my water-trough
On a hot, hot day, and I in pyjamas for the heat,
To drink there.
In the deep, strange-scented shade of the great dark carob-tree
I came down the steps with my pitcher
And must wait, must stand and wait, for there he was at the
    trough before me.

He reached down from a fissure in the earth-wall in the gloom
And trailed his yellow-brown slackness soft-bellied down, over the
    edge of the stone trough
And rested his throat upon the stone bottom,
And where the water had dripped from the tap, in a small clearness,
He sipped with his straight mouth,
Softly drank through his straight gums, into his slack long body,
Silently.

Someone was before me at my water trough,
And I, like a second comer, waiting.

He lifted his head from his drinking, as cattle do,
And looked at me vaguely, as drinking cattle do,
And flickered his two-forked tongue from his lips, and mused a
    moment,
And stooped and drank a little more,
Being earth-brown, earth-golden from the burning bowels of the
    earth
On the day of Sicilian July, with Etna smoking.

The voice of my education said to me
He must be killed,
For in Sicily the black, black snakes are innocent, the gold are
    venomous.

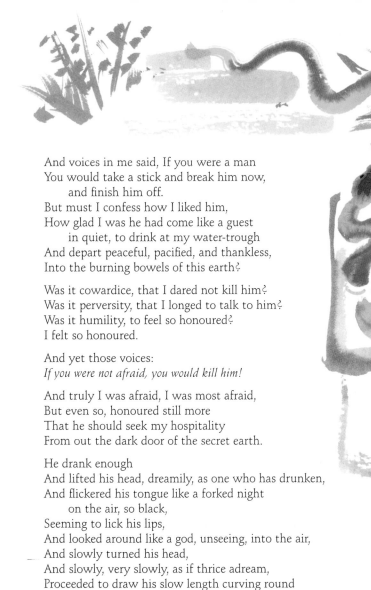

And voices in me said, If you were a man
You would take a stick and break him now,
        and finish him off.
But must I confess how I liked him,
How glad I was he had come like a guest
        in quiet, to drink at my water-trough
And depart peaceful, pacified, and thankless,
Into the burning bowels of this earth?

Was it cowardice, that I dared not kill him?
Was it perversity, that I longed to talk to him?
Was it humility, to feel so honoured?
I felt so honoured.

And yet those voices:
If you were not afraid, you would kill him!

And truly I was afraid, I was most afraid,
But even so, honoured still more
That he should seek my hospitality
From out the dark door of the secret earth.

He drank enough
And lifted his head, dreamily, as one who has drunken,
And flickered his tongue like a forked night
        on the air, so black,
Seeming to lick his lips,
And looked around like a god, unseeing, into the air,
And slowly turned his head,
And slowly, very slowly, as if thrice adream,
Proceeded to draw his slow length curving round
And climb again the broken bank of my wall-face.

And as he put his head into that dreadful hole,
And as he slowly drew up, snake-easing his shoulders, and entered
    farther,
A sort of horror, a sort of protest against his withdrawing into that
    horrid black hole,
Deliberately going into the blackness, and slowly drawing himself
    after,
Overcame me now his back was turned.
I looked round, I put down my pitcher,
I picked up a clumsy log
And threw it at the water trough with a clatter.

I think it did not hit him,
But suddenly that part of him that was left behind convulsed in
    undignified haste,
Writhed like lightning, and was gone
Into the black hole, the earth-lipped fissure in the wall-front,
At which, in the intense still noon, I stared with fascination.

And immediately I regretted it.
I thought how paltry, how vulgar, what a mean act!
I despised myself and the voices of my accursed human education.
And I thought of the albatross,
And I wished he would come back, my snake.

For he seemed to me again like a king,
Like a king in exile, uncrowned in the underworld,
Now due to be crowned again.

And so, I missed my chance with one of the lords
Of life.
And I have something to expiate;
A pettiness.

A Wish

Often I've wished that I'd been born a woman.
It seems the one sure way to be fully human.
Think of the trouble – keeping the children fed,
Keeping your skirt down and your lips red,
Watching the calendar and the last bus home,
Being nice to all the dozens of guests in the room;
Having to change your hairstyle and your name
At least once; learning to take the blame;
Keeping your husband faithful, and your char.
And all the things you're supposed to be grateful for
– Votes and proposals, chocolates and seats in the train –
Or expert with – typewriter, powderpuff, pen,
Diaphragm, needle, chequebook, casserole, bed.
It seems the one sure way to be driven mad.

So why would anyone want to be a woman?
Would you rather be the hero or the victim?
Would you rather win, seduce, and read the paper,
Or be beaten, pregnant, and have to lay the table?
Nothing is free. In order to pay the price
Isn't it simpler, really, to have no choice?
Only ill-health, recurring, inevitable,
Can teach the taste of what it is to be well.

No man has ever felt his daughter tear
The flesh he had earlier torn to plant her there.
Men know the pain of birth by a kind of theory:
No man has been a protagonist in the story,
Lying back bleeding, exhausted and in pain,
Waiting for stitches and sleep and to be alone,
And listened with tender breasts to the hesitant croak
At the bedside growing continuous as you wake.
That is the price. That is what love is worth.
It will go on twisting your heart like an afterbirth.
Whether you choose to or not you will pay and pay
Your whole life long. Nothing on earth is free.

Walking Away

It is eighteen years ago, almost to the day –
A sunny day with the leaves just turning,
The touch-lines new-ruled – since I watched you play
Your first game of football, then, like a satellite
Wrenched from its orbit, go drifting away

Behind a scatter of boys. I can see
You walking away from me towards the school
With the pathos of a half-fledged thing set free
Into a wilderness, the gait of one
Who finds no path where the path should be.

That hesitant figure, eddying away
Like a winged seed loosened from its parent stem,
Has something I never quite grasp to convey
About nature's give-and-take – the small, the scorching
Ordeals which fire one's irresolute clay.

I have had worse partings, but none that so
Gnaws at my mind still. Perhaps it is roughly
Saying what God alone could perfectly show –
How selfhood begins with a walking away,
And love is proved in the letting go.

The Legend Beautiful

from *The Theologian's Tale*

'Hadst thou stayed, I must have fled!'
That is what the Vision said.

In his chamber all alone,
Kneeling on the floor of stone,
Prayed the Monk in deep contrition
For his sins of indecision,
Prayed for greater self-denial
In temptation and in trial;
It was noonday by the dial,
And the Monk was all alone.

Suddenly, as if it lightened,
An unwonted splendour brightened
All within him and without him
In that narrow cell of stone;
And he saw the Blessed Vision
Of our Lord, with light Elysian
Like a vesture wrapped about him,
Like a garment round him thrown.
Not as crucified and slain,
Not in agonies of pain,
Not with bleeding hands and feet,
Did the Monk his Master see;
But as in the village street,
In the house or harvest-field,
Halt and lame and blind he healed,
When he walked in Galilee.

In an attitude imploring,
Hands upon his bosom crossed,

Wondering, worshipping, adoring,
Knelt the Monk in rapture lost.
Lord, he thought, in heaven that reignest,
Who am I, that thus thou deignest
To reveal thyself to me?
Who am I, that from the centre
Of thy glory thou shouldst enter
This poor cell, my guest to be?

Then amid his exaltation,
Loud the convent bell appalling,
From its belfry calling, calling,
Rang through court and corridor
With persistent iteration
He had never heard before.
It was now the appointed hour
When alike in shine or shower,
Winter's cold or summer's heat,
To the convent portals came
All the blind and halt and lame,
All the beggars of the street,
For their daily dole of food
Dealt them by the brotherhood;
And their almoner was he
Who upon his bended knee,
Rapt in silent ecstasy
Of divinest self-surrender,
Saw the Vision and the Splendour.

Deep distress and hesitation
Mingled with his adoration;
Should he go, or should he stay?
Should he leave the poor to wait
Hungry at the convent gate,
Till the Vision passed away?

Should he slight his radiant guest,
Slight this visitant celestial,
For the crowd of ragged, bestial
Beggars at the convent gate?
Would the Vision there remain?
Would the Vision come again?
Then a voice within his breast
Whispered, audible and clear
As if to the outward ear:
'Do thy duty; that is best;
Leave unto thy Lord the rest!'

Straightway to his feet he started,
And with longing look intent
On the Blessed Vision bent,
Slowly from his cell departed,
Slowly on his errand went.
At the gate the poor were waiting,
Looking through the iron grating,
With that terror in the eye
That is only seen in those
Who amid their wants and woes
Hear the sound of doors that close,
And of feet that pass them by;
Grown familiar with disfavour,
Grown familiar with the savour
Of the bread by which men die!
But today, they knew not why,
Like the gate of Paradise
Seemed the convent gate to rise,
Like a sacrament divine,
Seemed to them the bread and wine.
In his heart the Monk was praying,
Thinking of the homeless poor,
What they suffer and endure;

What we see not, what we see;
And the inward voice was saying:
'Whatsoever thing thou doest
To the least of mine and lowest,
That thou doest unto me!'

Unto me! but had the Vision
Come to him in beggar's clothing,
Come a mendicant imploring,
Would he then have knelt adoring,
Or have listened with derision,
And have turned away with loathing?

Thus his conscience put the question,
Full of troublesome suggestion,
As at length, with hurried pace,
Towards his cell he turned his face,
And beheld the convent bright
With a supernatural light,
Like a luminous cloud expanding
Over floor and wall and ceiling.
But he paused with awe-struck feeling
At the threshold of his door,
For the Vision still was standing
As he left it there before,
When the convent bell appalling,
From its belfry calling, calling,
Summoned him to feed the poor.
Through the long hour intervening
It had waited his return,
And he felt his bosom burn,
Comprehending all the meaning,
When the Blessed Vision said,
'Hadst thou stayed, I must have fled!'

Oxford

I see the coloured lilacs flame
In many an ancient Oxford lane
And bright laburnum holds its bloom
Suspended golden in the noon,
The placid lawns I often tread
Are stained and carpeted with red

Where the tall chestnuts cast their flowers
To make the fleeting April hours,
And now the crowded hawthorn yields
Its haunting perfume to the fields
With men and maidens hurrying out
Along Port Meadow to the Trout,
There, by the coruscating stream
To drink and gaze and gaze and dream;
An ageless dame leaves her abode
To caper down the Woodstock Road
And greet a Dean she used to know
A trifling sixty years ago.
Queer tricyles of unknown date
Are pedalled at a frightful rate
Their baskets bulge with borrowed books
Or terriers of uncertain looks.

Perpetual motion in The High
Beneath a blue and primrose sky
And cherry blossom like a cloud
Beside the traffic roaring loud,
While daffodils go dancing gold
In streets where time runs grey and old
And poets, sweating in the throng,
Can sometimes hear a blackbird's song.
All Oxford's spires are tipped with rose
A wind full magic sweetly blows
And suddenly it seems in truth
As if the centuries of youth
Are crowding all the streets and lanes
In April when the lilac flames.

So What Is Love?

So what is love? If thou wouldst know
The heart alone can tell:
Two minds with but a single thought,
Two hearts that beat as one.

And whence comes Love? Like morning bright
Love comes without thy call.
And how dies Love? A spirit bright,
Love never dies at all.

Prayer Before Birth

I am not yet born; O hear me.
Let not the bloodsucking bat or the rat or the stoat or the
 club-footed ghoul come near me.

I am not yet born, console me.
I fear that the human race may with tall walls wall me,
 with strong drugs dope me, with wise lies lure me,
  on black racks rack me, in blood-baths roll me.

I am not yet born; provide me
With water to dandle me, grass to grow for me, trees to talk
 to me, sky to sing to me, birds and a white light
  in the back of my mind to guide me.

I am not yet born; forgive me
For the sins that in me the world shall commit, my words
 when they speak me, my thoughts when they think me,
  my treason engendered by traitors beyond me,
   my life when they murder by means of my
    hands, my death when they live me.

I am not yet born; rehearse me
In the parts I must play and the cues I must take when
 old men lecture me, bureaucrats hector me, mountains
  frown at me, lovers laugh at me, the white
   waves call me to folly and the desert calls
    me to doom and the beggar refuses
     my gift and my children curse me.

I am not yet born; O hear me,
Let not the man who is beast or who thinks he is God
        come near me.

I am not yet born; O fill me
With strength against those who would freeze my
        humanity, would dragoon me into a lethal automaton,
            would make me a cog in a machine, a thing with
                one face, a thing, and against all those
                    who would dissipate my entirety, would
                        blow me like thistledown hither and
                            thither or hither and thither
                                like water held in the
                                    hands would spill me.

Let them not make me a stone and let them not spill me.
Otherwise kill me.

High Flight (An Airman's Ecstasy)

Oh, I have slipped the surly bonds of earth
And danced the skies on laughter-silvered wings;
Sunward I've climbed and joined the tumbling mirth
Of sun-split clouds – and done a hundred things
You have not dreamed of; wheeled and soared and swung
High in the sun-lit silence. Hovering there
I've chased the shouting wind along, and flung
My eager craft through footless halls of air;
Up, up the long, delirious, burning blue
I've topped the wind-swept heights with easy grace,
Where never lark nor even eagle flew;
And while, with silent lifting mind I've trod
The high untrespassed sanctity of space,
Put out my hand, and touched the face of God.

Nicholas Nye

Thistle and darnel and dock grew there,
  And a bush, in the corner, of may,
On the orchard wall I used to sprawl
  In the blazing heat of the day;
Half asleep and half awake,
  While the birds went twittering by,
And nobody there my lone to share
    But Nicholas Nye.

Nicholas Nye was lean and grey,
  Lame of a leg and old,
More than a score of donkey's years
  He had seen since he was foaled;
He munched the thistles, purple and spiked,
  Would sometimes stoop and sigh,
And turn his head, as if he said,
    'Poor Nicholas Nye!'

Alone with his shadow he'd drowse in the meadow,
  Lazily swinging his tail,
At break of day he used to bray, –
  Not much too hearty and hale;
But a wonderful gumption was under his skin,
  And a clear calm light in his eye,
And once in a while he'd smile . . .
    Would Nicholas Nye.

Seem to be smiling at me, he would,
  From his bush in the corner, of may, –
Bony and ownerless, widowed and worn,
  Knobble-kneed, lonely and grey;

And over the grass would seem to pass
    'Neath the deep dark blue of the sky,
Something much better than words between me
    And Nicholas Nye.

But dusk would come in the apple boughs,
    The green of the glow-worm shine,
The birds in the nest would crouch to rest,
    And home I'd trudge to mine;
And there, in the moonlight, dark with dew,
    Asking not wherefore nor why,
Would brood like a ghost, and still as a post,
    Old Nicholas Nye.

The Life That I Have

The life that I have
Is all that I have
And the life that I have
Is yours

The love that I have
Of the life that I have
Is yours and yours and yours

A sleep I shall have
A rest I shall have
Yet death will be but a pause

For the peace of my years
In the long green grass
Will be yours and yours and yours

Sea-Fever

I must down to the seas again, to the lonely sea and the sky,
And all I ask is a tall ship and a star to steer her by,
And the wheel's kick and the wind's song and the white sail's
    shaking,
And a grey mist on the sea's face and a grey dawn breaking.

I must down to the seas again, for the call of the running tide
Is a wild call and a clear call that may not be denied;
And all I ask is a windy day with the white clouds flying,
And the flung spray and the blown spume, and the sea-gulls crying.

I must down to the seas again, to the vagrant gypsy life,
To the gull's way and the whale's way where the wind's like a
    whetted knife;
And all I ask is a merry yarn from a laughing fellow-rover,
And quiet sleep and a sweet dream when the long trick's over.

The Farmer's Bride

Three Summers since I chose a maid,
Too young maybe – but more's to do
At harvest-time than bide and woo.
     When us was wed she turned afraid
Of love and me and all things human;
Like the shut of a winter's day
Her smile went out, and 'twadn't a woman –
     More like a little frightened fay.
     One night, in the Fall, she runned away.

'Out 'mong the sheep, her be,' they said,
'Should properly have been abed';
But sure enough she wadn't there
Lying awake with her wide brown stare.
So over seven-acre field and up-along across the down
We chased her, flying like a hare
Before our lanterns. To Church-Town
     All in a shiver and a scare
We caught her, fetched her home at last
     And turned the key upon her, fast.

She does the work about the house
As well as must, but like a mouse:
     Happy enough to chat and play
     With birds and rabbits and such as they,
     So long as men-folk keep away.

'Not near, not near!' her eyes beseech
When one of us comes within reach.
    The woman say that beasts in stall
    Look round like children at her call.
    I've hardly heard her speak at all.

Shy as a leveret, swift as he,
Straight and slight as a young larch tree,
Sweet as the first wild violets, she,
To her wild self. But what to me?

The short days shorten and the oaks are brown,
    The blue smoke rises to the low grey sky,
One leaf in the still air falls slowly down,
    A magpie's spotted feathers lie
On the black earth spread white with rime,
The berries redden up to Christmas-time.
    What's Christmas-time without there be
    Some other in the house than we!

    She sleeps up in the attic there
    Alone, poor maid, 'Tis but a stair
Betwixt us. Oh! my God! the down,
    The soft young down of her, the brown,
The brown of her – her eyes, her hair, her hair!

Renouncement

I must not think of thee; and, tired yet strong,
I shun the love that lurks in all delight –
   The love of thee – and in the blue heaven's height,
And in the dearest passage of a song.
Oh, just beyond the sweetest thoughts that throng
   This breast, the thought of thee waits hidden yet bright;
But it must never, never come in sight;
I must stop short of thee the whole day long.
But when sleep comes to close each difficult day,
   When night gives pause to the long watch I keep,
And all my bonds I needs must loose apart,
Must doff my will as raiment laid away, –
   With the first dream that comes with the first sleep
I run, I run, I am gathered to thy heart.

Dirge Without Music

I am not resigned to the shutting away of loving hearts in the
   hard ground
So it is, and so it will be, for so it has been, time out of mind:
Into the darkness they go, the wise and the lovely. Crowned
With lilies and with laurel they go: but I am not resigned.

Lovers and thinkers, into the earth with you.
Be one with the dull, the indiscriminate dust.
A fragment of what you felt, of what you knew,
A formula, a phrase remains – but the best is lost.

The answers quick and keen, the honest look, the laughter, the
   love –
They are gone. They have gone to feed the roses. Elegant and
   curled
Is the blossom. Fragrant is the blossom. I know. But I do not
   approve.
More precious was the light in your eyes than all the roses in
   the world.

Down, down, down into the darkness of the grave
Gently they go, the beautiful, the tender, the kind:
Quietly they go, the intelligent, the witty, the brave.
I know. But I do not approve. And I am not resigned.

Overheard on a Saltmarsh

Nymph, nymph, what are your beads?
Green glass, goblin. Why do you stare at them?
Give them me.
No.
Give them me. Give them me.
No.
Then I will howl all night in the reeds,
Lie in the mud and howl for them.
Goblin, why do you love them so?
They are better than stars or water,
Better than voices of winds that sing,
Better than any man's fair daughter,
Your green glass beads on a silver ring.
Hush, I stole them out of the moon.
Give me your beads, I desire them.
No.
I will howl in a deep lagoon
For your green glass beads, I love them so,
Give them me. Give them.
No.

Dunkirk (a ballad)

Will came back from school that day,
And he had little to say.
But he stood a long time looking down
To where the gray-green Channel water
Slapped at the foot of the little town,
And to where his boat, the Sarah P,
Bobbed at the tide on an even keel,
With her one old sail, patched at the leech,
Furled like a slattern down at heel.

He stood for a while above the beach,
He saw how the wind and current caught her;
He looked a long time out to sea.
There was steady wind, and the sky was pale,
And a daze in the east that looked like smoke.

Will went back to the house to dress.
He was half way through, when his sister Bess
Who was near fourteen, and younger than he
By just two years, came home from play.
She asked him, 'Where are you going, Will?'
He said, 'For a good long sail.'
'Can I come along?'

'No, Bess,' he spoke.
'I may be gone for a night and a day.'
Bess looked at him. She kept very still.
She had heard the news of the Flanders rout,
How the English were trapped above Dunkirk,
And the fleet had gone to get them out –
But everyone thought that it wouldn't work.
There was too much fear, there was too much doubt.

She looked at him, and he looked at her.
They were English children, born and bred.
He frowned her down, but she wouldn't stir.
She shook her proud young head.
'You'll need a crew,' she said.

They raised the sail on the Sarah P,
Like a penoncel on a young knight's lance,
And headed the Sarah out to sea,
To bring their soldiers home from France.

There was no command, there was no set plan,
But six hundred boats went out with them
On the gray-green waters, sailing fast,
River excursion and fisherman,
Tug and schooner and racing M,
And the little boats came following last.
From every harbor and town they went
Who had sailed their craft in the sun and rain,
From the South Downs, from the cliffs of Kent,
From the village street, from the country lane.

There are twenty miles of rolling sea
From coast to coast, by the seagull's flight,
But the tides were fair and the wind was free,
And they raised Dunkirk by fall of night.

They raised Dunkirk with its harbor torn
By the blasted stern and the sunken prow;
They had raced for fun on an English tide,
They were English children bred and born,

And whether they lived, or whether they died,
They raced for England now.

Bess was as white as the Sarah's sail,
She set her teeth and smiled at Will.
He held his course for the smoky veil
Where the harbor narrowed thin and long.
The British ships were firing strong.

He took the Sarah into his hands,
He drove her in through fire and death
To the wet men waiting on the sands.
He got his load and he got his breath,
And she came about, and the wind fought her.

He shut his eyes and he tried to pray.
He saw his England where she lay,

The wind's green home, the sea's proud daughter,
Still in the moonlight, dreaming deep,
The English cliffs and the English loam –
He had fourteen men to get away,
And the moon was clear, and the night like day
For planes to see where the white sails creep
Over the black water.

He closed his eyes and he prayed for her;
He prayed to the men who had made her great,
Who had built her land of forest and park,
Who had made the seas an English lake;
He prayed for a fog to bring the dark;
He prayed to get home for England's sake.
And the fog came down on the rolling sea,
And covered the ships with English mist.
The diving planes were baffled and blind.

For Nelson was there in the Victory,
With his one good eye, and his sullen twist,
And guns were out on The Golden Hind,
Their shot flashed over the Sarah P.
He could hear them cheer as he came about.

By burning wharves, by battered slips,
Galleon, frigate, and brigantine,
The old dead Captains fought their ships,
And the great dead Admirals led the line.
It was England's night, it was England's sea.

The fog rolled over the harbor key.
Bess held to the stays, and conned him out.

And all through the dark, while the Sarah's wake
Hissed behind him, and vanished in foam,
There at his side sat Francis Drake,
And held him true, and steered him home.

He Fell Among Thieves

'Ye have robbed,' said he, 'ye have slaughtered and made an end,
    Take your ill-got plunder, and bury the dead:
What will ye more of your guest and sometime friend?'
    'Blood for our blood,' they said.

He laughed: 'If one may settle the score for five,
    I am ready; but let the reckoning stand till day:
I have loved the sunlight as dearly as any alive.'
    'You shall die at dawn,' said they.

He flung his empty revolver down the slope,
    He climbed alone to the Eastward edge of the trees;
All night long in a dream untroubled of hope
    He brooded, clasping his knees.

He did not hear the monotonous roar that fills
    The ravine where the Yassin river sullenly flows;
He did not see the starlight on the Laspur hills,
    Or the far Afghan snows.

He saw the April noon on his books aglow,
    The wistaria trailing in at the window wide;
He heard his father's voice from the terrace below
    Calling him down to ride.

He saw the gray little church across the park,
    The mounds that hide the loved and honoured dead;
The Norman arch, the chancel softly dark,
    The brasses black and red.

He saw the School Close, sunny and green,
    The runner beside him, the stand by the parapet wall,
The distant tape, and the crowd roaring between
    His own name over all.

He saw the dark wainscot and timbered roof,
    The long tables, and the faces merry and keen;
The College Eight and their trainer dining aloof,
    The Dons on the daïs serene.

He watched the liner's stem ploughing the foam,
    He felt her trembling speed and the thrash of her screw;
He heard her passengers' voices talking of home,
    He saw the flag she flew.

And now it was dawn. He rose strong on his feet,
    And strode to his ruined camp below the wood;
He drank the breath of the morning cool and sweet;
    His murderers round him stood.

Light on the Laspur hills was broadening fast,
    The blood-red snow-peaks chilled to a dazzling white:
He turned, and saw the golden circle at last,
    Cut by the Eastern height.

'O glorious Life, Who dwellest in earth and sun,
    I have lived, I praise and adore Thee.'

                                A sword swept.
Over the pass the voices one by one
    Faded, and the hill slept.

An Arab's Farewell to his Steed

My beautiful, my beautiful! that standest meekly by,
With thy proudly-arched and glossy neck, and dark and fiery eye!
Fret not to roam the desert now with all thy winged speed:
I may not mount on thee again! – thou'rt sold, my Arab steed!

Fret not with that impatient hoof, snuff not the breezy wind;
The farther that thou fliest now, so far am I behind!
The stranger hath thy bridle-rein, thy master hath his gold: –
Fleet-limbed and beautiful, farewell; thou'rt sold, my steed,
    thou'rt sold.

Farewell! – Those free untired limbs full many a mile must roam,
To reach the chill and wintry clime that clouds the stranger's
    home;
Some other hand, less kind, must now thy corn and bed prepare;
That silky mane I braided once must be another's care.

The morning sun shall dawn again – but never more with thee
Shall I gallop o'er the desert paths where we were wont to be –
Evening shall darken on the earth: and o'er the sandy plain,
Some other steed, with slower pace, shall bear me home again.

Only in sleep shall I behold that dark eye glancing bright –
Only in sleep shall hear again that step so firm and light;
And when I raise my dreamy arms to check or cheer thy speed,
Then must I startling wake, to feel thou'rt sold! my Arab steed.

Ah, rudely then, unseen by me, some cruel hand may chide,
Till foam-wreaths lie, like crested waves, along thy panting side,
And the rich blood that in thee swells, in thy indignant pain,
Till careless eyes that on thee gaze may count each starting vein!

Will they ill-use thee; – If I thought – but no, – it cannot be;
Thou art too swift, yet easy curbed, so gentle, yet so free; –
And yet, if haply when thou'rt gone, this lonely heart should
     yearn,
Can the hand that casts thee from it now, command thee to
     return!

'Return' – alas! my Arab steed! what will thy master do,
When thou that wast his all of joy, hast vanished from his view!
When the dim distance greets mine eyes, and through the
     gathering tears
Thy bright form for a moment, like the false mirage, appears?

Slow and unmounted will I roam, with wearied foot, alone,
Where with fleet step, and joyous bound, thou oft has borne
     me on;
And sitting down by the green well, I'll pause and sadly think
'Twas here he bowed his glossy neck when last I saw him drink.'

When *last* I saw thee drink! – Away! the fevered dream is o'er!
I could not live a day, and know that we should meet no more;
They tempted me, my beautiful! for hunger's power is strong
They tempted me, my beautiful! but I have loved too long.

Who said that I had given thee up? Who said that thou were sold?
'Tis false! 'tis false, my Arab steed! I fling them back their gold!
Thus – thus, I leap upon thy back, and scour the distant plains!
Away! who overtakes us now shall claim thee for his pains.

The Highwayman

I

The wind was a torrent of darkness among the gusty trees,
The moon was a ghostly galleon tossed upon cloudy seas,
The road was a ribbon of moonlight over the purple moor,
And the highwayman came riding –
      Riding – riding –
The highwayman came riding, up to the old inn-door.

He'd a French cocked-hat on his forehead, a bunch of lace at his chin,
A coat of claret velvet, and breeches of brown doe-skin;
They fitted with never a wrinkle: his boots were up to the thigh!
And he rode with a jewelled twinkle,
      His pistol butts a-twinkle,
His rapier hilt a-twinkle, under the jewelled sky.

Over the cobbles he clattered and clashed in the dark inn-yard,
And he tapped with his whip on the shutters, but all was locked and
    barred;
He whistled a tune to the window, and who should be waiting there
But the landlord's black-eyed daughter,
      Bess, the landlord's daughter,
Plaiting a dark red love-knot into her long black hair.

And dark in the old inn-yard a stable-wicket creaked
Where Tim the ostler listened; his face was white and peaked;
His eyes were hollows of madness, his hair like mouldy hay,
But he loved the landlord's daughter,
      The landlord's red-lipped daughter;
Dumb as a dog he listened, and he heard the robber say –

'One kiss, my bonny sweetheart, I'm after a prize to-night,
But I shall be back with the yellow gold before the morning light;

Yet, if they press me sharply, and harry me through the day,
Then look for me by moonlight,
      Watch for me by moonlight,
I'll come to thee by moonlight, though hell should bar the way.'

He rose upright in the stirrups; he scarce could reach her hand,
But she loosened her hair i' the casement! His face burnt like a brand
As the black cascade of perfume came tumbling over his breast;
And he kissed its waves in the moonlight,
      (Oh, sweet black waves in the moonlight!)
Then he tugged at his rein in the moonlight, and galloped away to
    the west.

   II

He did not come in the dawning; he did not come at noon;
And out o' the tawny sunset, before the rise o' the moon,
When the road was a gipsy's ribbon, looping the purple moor,
A red-coat troop came marching –
      Marching – marching –
King George's men came marching, up to the old inn-door.

They said no word to the landlord, they drank his ale instead,
But they gagged his daughter and bound her to the foot of her
    narrow bed;
Two of them knelt at her casement, with muskets at their side!
There was death at every window;
      And hell at one dark window;
For Bess could see, through her casement, the road that *he* would ride.
They had tied her up to attention, with many a sniggering jest;
They had bound a musket beside her, with the barrel beneath her
    breast!
'Now keep good watch!' and they kissed her.
      She heard the dead man say –
Look for me by moonlight;
      Watch for me by moonlight;
I'll come to thee by moonlight, though hell should bar the way!

She twisted her hands behind her; but all the knots held good!
She writhed her hands till her fingers were wet with sweat or
    blood!
They stretched and strained in the darkness, and the hours
    crawled by like years,
Till, now, on the stroke of midnight,
       Cold, on the stroke of midnight,
The tip of one finger touched it! The trigger at least was hers!

The tip of one finger touched it; she strove no more for the rest!
Up, she stood to attention, with the barrel beneath her breast,
She would not risk their hearing; she would not strive again;
For the road lay bare in the moonlight;
       Blank and bare in the moonlight;
And the blood of her veins in the moonlight throbbed to her
    love's refrain.

Tlot-tlot; tlot-tlot! Had they heard it? The horse-hoofs ringing
    clear;
Tlot-tlot, tlot-tlot, in the distance? Were they deaf that they did
    not hear?
Down the ribbon of moonlight, over the brow of the hill,
The highwayman came riding,
       Riding, riding!
The red-coats looked to their priming! She stood up, straight
    and still!

Tlot-tlot, in the frosty silence! *tlot-tlot*, in the echoing night!
Nearer he came and nearer! Her face was like a light!
Her eyes grew wide for a moment; she drew one last deep breath,
Then her finger moved in the moonlight,
       Her musket shattered the moonlight,
Shattered her breast in the moonlight and warned him – with
    her death.

He turned; he spurred to the westward; he did not know who stood
Bowed, with her head o'er the musket, drenched with her own red
 blood!
Not till the dawn he heard it, and slowly blanched to hear
How Bess, the landlord's daughter,
      The landlord's black-eyed daughter,
Had watched for her love in the moonlight, and died in the darkness
 there.

Back, he spurred like a madman, shrieking a curse to the sky,
With the white road smoking behind him and his rapier brandished
 high!
Blood-red were his spurs i' the golden noon; wine-red was his velvet
 coat;
When they shot him down on the highway,
      Down like a dog on the highway,
And he lay in his blood on the highway, with the bunch of lace at
 his throat.

And still of a winter's night, they say, when the wind is in the trees,
When the moon is a ghostly galleon tossed upon cloudy seas,
When the road is a ribbon of moonlight over the purple moor,
A highwayman comes riding –
      Riding – riding –
A highwayman comes riding, up to the old inn-door.

Over the cobbles he clatters and clangs in the dark inn-yard
And he taps with his whip on the shutters, but all is locked and barred;
He whistles a tune to the window, and who should be waiting there
But the landlord's black-eyed daughter,
      Bess, the landlord's daughter,
Plaiting a dark red love-knot into her long black hair.

Adieu! And Au Revoir

As you love me, let there be
No mourning when I go, –
No tearful eyes,
No hopeless sighs,
No woe, – nor even sadness!
Indeed I would not have you sad,
For I myself shall be full glad,
With the high triumphant gladness
Of a soul made free
Of God's sweet liberty.
– No windows darkened;

For my own
Will be flung wide as ne'er before,
To catch the radiant inpour
Of Love that shall in full atone
For all the ills that I have done;
And the good things left undone;
– No voices hushed;
My own, full flushed
With an immortal hope, will rise
In ecstasies of new-born bliss
And joyful melodies.

Rather, of your sweet courtesy,
Rejoice with me
At my soul's loosing from captivity.
Wish me 'Bon Voyage!'
As you do a friend
Whose joyous visit finds its happy end.

And bid me both 'à Dieu!'
And 'au revoir!'
Since, though I come no more,
I shall be waiting there
        to greet you,
At His Door.

And, as the feet of The
        Bearers tread
The ways I trod,
Think not of me as dead,
But rather –
'Happy, thrice happy, he
        whose course is sped!
He has gone home – to God,
His Father!'

The Toys

(from *The Unknown Eros*)

My little Son, who looked from thoughtful eyes
And moved and spoke in quiet grown-up wise,
Having my law the seventh time disobeyed,
I struck him, and dismissed
With hard words and unkissed,
– His Mother, who was patient, being dead.
Then, fearing lest his grief should hinder sleep,
I visited his bed,
But found him slumbering deep,
With darkened eyelids, and their lashes yet
From his late sobbing wet.
And I, with moan,
Kissing away his tears, left others of my own;
For, on a table drawn beside his head,
He had put, within his reach,
A box of counters and a red-veined stone,
A piece of glass abraded by the beach,
And six or seven shells,
A bottle with bluebells,
And two French copper coins, ranged there with
 careful art,
To comfort his sad heart.

So when that night I prayed
To God, I wept, and said:
'Ah, when at last we lie with
    trancèd breath,
Not vexing Thee in death,
And Thou rememberest of
    what toys
We made our joys,
How weakly understood
Thy great commanded good,
Then, fatherly not less
Than I whom Thou hast moulded
    from the clay,
Thou'lt leave Thy wrath, and say,
"I will be sorry for their childishness."'

from *Goblin Market*

Morning and evening
Maids heard the goblins cry:
'Come buy our orchard fruits,
Come buy, come buy:
Apples and quinces,
Lemons and oranges,
Plump unpecked cherries,
Melons and raspberries,
Bloom-down-cheeked peaches,
Swart-headed mulberries,
Wild free-born cranberries,
Crab-apples, dewberries,
Pine-apples, blackberries,
Apricots, strawberries; –
All ripe together
In summer weather, –
Morns that pass by,
Fair eves that fly;
Come buy, come buy:
Our grapes fresh from the vine,
Pomegranates full and fine,
Dates and sharp bullaces,
Rare pears and greengages,
Damsons and bilberries,
Taste them and try:
Currants and gooseberries,
Bright-fire-like barberries,
Figs to fill your mouth,
Citrons from the South,
Sweet to tongue and sound to eye;
Come buy, come buy.'

from *Canto Sixth (1)*
of *The Lay of the Last Minstrel*

Breathes there the man, with soul so dead,
Who never to himself hath said,
   This is my own, my native land!
Whose heart hath ne'er within him burn'd,
As home his footsteps he hath turn'd,
   From wandering on a foreign strand!
If such there breathe, go, mark him well;
For him no Minstrel raptures swell;
High though his titles, proud his name,
Boundless his wealth as wish can claim;
Despite those titles, power, and pelf,
The wretch, concentred all in self,
Living, shall forfeit fair renown,
And, doubly dying, shall go down
To the vile dust, from whence he sprung,
Unwept, unhonour'd, and unsung.

Shall I Compare Thee to a Summer's Day?

Shall I compare thee to a summer's day?
Thou art more lovely and more temperate:
Rough winds do shake the darling buds of May,
And summer's lease hath all too short a date:
Sometime too hot the eye of heaven shines,
And often is his gold complexion dimmed;
And ever fair from fair sometimes declines,
By chance or nature's changing course untrimmed;
But thy eternal summer shall not fade,
Nor lose possession of that fair thou owest;
Nor shall Death brag thou wander'st in his shade,
When in eternal lines to time thou growest:
  So long as men can breathe, or eyes can see,
  So long lives this, and this gives life to thee.

Not Waving but Drowning

Nobody heard him, the dead man,
But still he lay moaning:
I was much further out than you thought
And not waving but drowning.

Poor chap, he always loved larking
And now he's dead
It must have been too cold for him his heart gave way,
They said.

Oh, no no no, it was too cold always
(Still the dead one lay moaning)
I was much too far out all my life
And not waving but drowning.

The Inchcape Rock

No stir in the air, no stir in the sea,
The ship was still as she could be,
Her sails from heaven received no motion,
Her keel was steady in the ocean.

Without either sign or sound of their shock
The waves flowed over the Inchcape Rock;
So little they rose, so little they fell,
They did not move the Inchcape bell.

The Abbot of Aberbrothok
Had placed that bell on the Inchcape Rock;
On a buoy in the storm it floated and swung,
And over the waves its warning rung.

When the Rock was hid by the surge's swell,
The mariners heard the warning bell:
And then they knew the perilous rock,
And blessed the Abbot of Aberbrothok.

The sun in heaven was shining gay,
All things were joyful on that day;
The sea-birds screamed as they wheeled round,
And there was joyance in their sound.

The buoy of the Inchcape bell was seen
A darker speck on the ocean green;
Sir Ralph the Rover walked his deck,
And he fixed his eye on the darker speck.

He felt the cheering power of spring,
It made him whistle, it made him sing;
His heart was mirthful to excess,
But the Rover's mirth was wickedness.

His eye was on the Inchcape float;
Quoth he, 'My men, put out the boat,
And row me to the Inchcape Rock,
And I'll plague the Abbot of Aberbrothok.'

The boat is lowered, the boatmen row,
And to the Inchcape Rock they go;
Sir Ralph bent over from the boat,
And he cut the bell from the Inchcape float.

Down sunk the bell with a gurgling sound –
The bubbles rose and burst around;
Quoth Sir Ralph, 'The next who comes to the Rock
Won't bless the Abbot of Aberbrothok.'

Sir Ralph the Rover sailed away,
He scoured the seas for many a day;
And now grown rich with plundered store,
He steers his course for Scotland's shore.

So thick a haze o'erspreads the sky
They cannot see the sun on high;
The wind hath blown a gale all day,
At evening it hath died away.

On the deck the Rover takes his stand,
So dark it is they see no land.
Quoth Sir Ralph, 'It will be lighter soon,
For there is the dawn of the rising Moon.'

'Canst hear', said one, 'the breakers roar?
For methinks we should be near the shore.
Now where we are I cannot tell,
But I wish I could hear the Inchcape bell.'

They hear no sound – the swell is strong;
Though the wind hath fallen they drift along.
Till the vessel strikes with a shivering shock, –
'Oh! heavens! it is the Inchcape Rock!'

Sir Ralph the Rover tore his hair;
And curst himself in his despair;
The waves rush in on every side.
The ship is sinking beneath the tide.

But even in his dying fear
One dreadful sound could the Rover hear,
A sound as if, with the Inchcape bell,
The Devil below was ringing his knell.

The Vagabond

To An Air of Schubert

Give to me the life I love,
   Let the lave go by me,
Give the jolly heaven above
   And the byway nigh me.
Bed in the bush with stars to see,
   Bread I dip in the river –
There's the life for a man like me,
   There's the life for ever.

Let the blow fall soon or late,
   Let what will be o'er me;
Give the face of earth around
   And the road before me.
Wealth I seek not, hope nor love,
   Nor a friend to know me;
All I seek, the heaven above
   And the road below me.

Or let autumn fall on me
   Where afield I linger,
Silencing the bird on tree,
   Biting the blue finger.
White as meal the frosty field –
   Warm the fireside haven –
Not to autumn will I yield,
   Not to winter even!

Let the blow fall soon or late,
   Let what will be o'er me;
Give the face of earth around,
   And the road before me.
Wealth I ask not, hope nor love,
   Nor a friend to know me;
All I ask, the heaven above
   And the road below me.

The Seed-Shop

Here in a quiet and dusty room they lie,
  Faded as crumbled stone or shifting sand,
Forlorn as ashes, shrivelled, scentless, dry –
  Meadows and gardens running through my hand.

In this brown husk a dale of hawthorn dreams;
  A cedar in this narrow cell is thrust
That will drink deeply of a century's streams;
  These lilies shall make summer on my dust.

Here in their safe and simple house of death,
  Sealed in their shells, a million roses leap;
Here I can blow a garden with my breath,
  And in my hand a forest lies asleep.

from *The Brook*

I come from haunts of coot and hern,
   I make a sudden sally
And sparkle out among the fern,
   To bicker down a valley.

By thirty hills I hurry down,
   Or slip between the ridges,
By twenty thorps, a little town,
   And half a hundred bridges.

Till last by Philip's farm I flow
   To join the brimming river,
For men may come and men may go,
   But I go on for ever.

I chatter over stony ways,
   In little sharps and trebles,
I bubble into eddying bays,
   I babble on the pebbles.

With many a curve my banks I fret
   By many a field and fallow,
And many a fairy foreland set
   With willow-weed and mallow.

I chatter, chatter, as I flow
   To join the brimming river,
For men may come and men may go,
   But I go on for ever.

I wind about, and in and out,
   With here a blossom sailing,
And here and there a lusty trout,
   And here and there a grayling.

And here and there a foamy flake
   Upon me, as I travel
With many a silvery waterbreak
   Above the golden gravel.

And draw them all along, and flow
   To join the brimming river,
For men may come and men may go,
   But I go on for ever.

I steal by lawns and grassy plots,
   I slide by hazel covers;
I move the sweet forget-me-nots
   That grow for happy lovers.

I slip, I slide, I gloom, I glance,
   Among my skimming swallows;
I make the netted sunbeam dance
   Against my sandy shallows.

I murmur under moon and stars
   In brambly wildernesses;
I linger by my shingly bars;
   I loiter round my cresses;

And out again I curve and flow
   To join the brimming river,
For men may come and men may go,
   But I go on for ever.

Black Monday Lovesong

In love's dances, in love's dances
One retreats and one advances.
One grows warmer and one colder,
One more hesitant, one bolder.
One gives what the other needed
Once, or will need, now unheeded.
One is clenched, compact, ingrowing
While the other's melting, flowing.
One is smiling and concealing
While the other's asking, kneeling.
One is arguing or sleeping
While the other's weeping, weeping.

And the question finds no answer
And the tune misleads the dancer
And the lost look finds no other
And the lost hand finds no brother
And the word is left unspoken
Till the theme and thread are broken.

When shall these divisions alter?
Echo's answer seems to falter:
'Oh the unperplexed, unvexed time
Next time ... one day ... one day ... next time!'

Fern Hill

Now as I was young and easy under the apple boughs
About the lilting house and happy as the grass was green,
    The night above the dingle starry,
      Time let me hail and climb
    Golden in the heydays of his eyes,
And honoured among wagons I was prince of the apple towns
And once below a time I lordly had the trees and leaves
      Trail with daisies and barley
    Down the rivers of the windfall light.

And as I was green and carefree, famous among the barns
About the happy yard and singing as the farm was home,
    In the sun that is young once only,
      Time let me play and be
    Golden in the mercy of his means,
And green and golden I was huntsman and herdsman, the calves
Sang to my horn, the foxes on the hills barked clear and cold,
      And the sabbath rang slowly
    In the pebbles of the holy streams.

All the sun long it was running, it was lovely, the hay
Fields high as the house, the tunes from the chimneys, it was air
    And playing, lovely and watery
      And fire green as grass.
    And nightly under the simple stars
As I rode to sleep the owls were bearing the farm away,
All the moon long I heard, blessed among stables, the night-jars
    Flying with the ricks, and the horses
      Flashing into the dark.

And then to awake, and the farm, like a wanderer white
With the dew, come back, the cock on his shoulder: it was all
    Shining, it was Adam and maiden,
      The sky gathered again
    And the sun grew round that very day,
So it must have been after the birth of the simple light
In the first, spinning place, the spellbound horses walking warm
    Out of the whinnying green stable
      On to the fields of praise.

And honoured among foxes and pheasants by the gay house
Under the new made clouds and happy as the heart was long,
    In the sun born over and over,
      I ran my heedless ways,
    My wishes raced through the house high hay
And nothing I cared, at my sky blue trades, that time allows
In all his tuneful turning so few and such morning songs
    Before the children green and golden
      Follow him out of grace.

Nothing I cared, in the lamb white days, that time would take me
Up to the swallow thronged loft by the shadow of my hand,
    In the moon that is always rising,
      Nor that riding to sleep
    I should hear him fly with the high fields
And wake to the farm forever fled from the childless land.
Oh as I was young and easy in the mercy of his means,
    Time held me green and dying
    Though I sang in my chains like the sea.

Adlestrop

Yes. I remember Adlestrop –
The name, because one afternoon
Of heat the express-train drew up there
Unwontedly. It was late June.

The steam hissed. Some one cleared his throat.
No one left and no one came
On the bare platform. What I saw
Was Adlestrop – only the name

And willows, willow-herb, and grass,
And meadowsweet, and haycocks dry,
No whit less still and lonely fair
Than the high cloudlets in the sky.

And for that minute a blackbird sang
Close by, and round him, mistier,
Farther and farther, all the birds
Of Oxfordshire and Gloucestershire.

Cynddylan on a Tractor

Ah, you should see Cynddylan on a tractor.
Gone the old look that yoked him to the soil;
He's a new man now, part of the machine,
His nerves of metal and his blood oil.
The clutch curses, but the gears obey
His least bidding, and lo, he's away
Out of the farmyard, scattering hens.
Riding to work now as a great man should,
He is the knight at arms breaking the fields'
Mirror of silence, emptying the wood
Of foxes and squirrels and bright jays.
The sun comes over the tall trees
Kindling all the hedges, but not for him
Who runs his engine on a different fuel.
And all the birds are singing, bills wide in vain,
As Cynddylan passes proudly up the lane.

Daisy

Where the thistle lifts a purple crown
    Six foot out of the turf,
And the harebell shakes on the windy hill –
    O the breath of the distant surf! –

The hills look over on the South,
    And southward dreams the sea;
And with the sea-breeze hand in hand
    Came innocence and she.

Where 'mid the gorse the raspberry
    Red for the gatherer springs,
Two children did we stray and talk
    Wise, idle, childish things.

She listened with big-lipped surprise,
    Breast-deep 'mid flower and spine:
Her skin was like a grape, whose veins
    Run snow instead of wine.

She knew not those sweet words she spake,
    Nor knew her own sweet way;
But there's never a bird, so sweet a song
    Thronged in whose throat that day.

Oh, there were flowers in Storrington
    On the turf and on the spray;
But the sweetest flower on Sussex hills
    Was the Daisy-flower that day!

Her beauty smoothed earth's furrowed face!
    She gave me tokens three: –
A look, a word of her winsome mouth,
    And a wild raspberry.

A berry red, a guileless look,
    A still word, – strings of sand!
And yet they made my wild, wild heart
    Fly down to her little hand.

For, standing artless as the air,
    And candid as the skies,
She took the berries with her hand,
    And the love with her sweet eyes.

The fairest things have fleetest end,
    Their scent survives their close:
But the rose's scent is bitterness
    To him that loved the rose.

She looked a little wistfully,
    Then went her sunshine way: –
The sea's eye had a mist on it,
    And the leaves fell from the day.

She went her unremembering way,
    She went and left in me
The pang of all the partings gone,
    And partings yet to be.

She left me marvelling why my soul
    Was sad that she was glad;
At all the sadness in the sweet,
    The sweetness in the sad.

Still, still I seemed to see her, still
    Look up with soft replies,
And take the berries with her hand,
    And the love with her lovely eyes.

Nothing begins, and nothing ends,
    That is not paid with moan;
For we are born in other's pain,
    And perish in our own.

The Curfew Must Not Ring Tonight

Slowly England's sun was setting o'er the hilltops far away,
Filling all the land with beauty at the close of one sad day;
And the last rays kissed the forehead of a man and maiden fair,
He with footsteps slow and weary, she with sunny floating hair;
He with bowed head, sad and thoughtful, she with lips all cold and
    white,
Struggling to keep back the murmur, 'Curfew must not ring tonight!'

'Sexton,' Bessie's white lips faltered, pointing to the prison old,
With its turrets tall and gloomy, with its walls, dark, damp and cold –
'I've a lover in the prison, doomed this very night to die
At the ringing of the curfew, and no early help is nigh.
Cromwell will not come till sunset'; and her face grew strangely white
As she breathed the husky whisper, 'Curfew must not ring tonight!'

'Bessie,' calmly spoke the sexton – and his accents pierced her heart
Like the piercing of an arrow, like a deadly poisoned dart –
'Long, long years I've rung the curfew from that gloomy, shadowed
    tower;
Every evening, just at sunset, it has told the twilight hour;
I have done my duty ever, tried to do it just and right –
Now I'm old I still must do it: Curfew, girl, must ring tonight!'

Wild her eyes and pale her features, stern and white her thoughtful
    brow,
And within her secret bosom Bessie made a solemn vow.
She had listened while the judges read, without a tear or sigh,
'At the ringing of the curfew, Basil Underwood must die.'
And her breath came fast and faster, and her eyes grew large and
    bright,
As in undertone she murmured, 'Curfew must not ring tonight!'

With quick step she bounded forward, sprang within the old church
    door,
Left the old man treading slowly paths he'd often trod before;
Not one moment paused the maiden, but with eye and cheek aglow
Mounted up the gloomy tower, where the bell swung to and fro
As she climbed the dusty ladder, on which fell no ray of light,
Up and up, her white lips saying, 'Curfew shall not ring tonight!'

She has reached the topmost ladder, o'er her hangs the great dark bell;
Awful is the gloom beneath her like the pathway down to hell;
Lo, the ponderous tongue is swinging. 'Tis the hour of curfew now,
And the sight has chilled her bosom, stopped her breath and paled her
    brow;
Shall she let it ring? No, never! Flash her eyes with sudden light,
And she springs and grasps it firmly: 'Curfew shall not ring tonight!'

Out she swung, far out; the city seemed a speck of light below;
She 'twixt heaven and earth suspended as the bell swung to and fro;
And the sexton at the bell rope, old and deaf, heard not the bell,
But he thought it still was ringing fair young Basil's funeral knell.
Still the maiden clung more firmly, and, with trembling lips and white
Said, to hush her heart's wild beating, 'Curfew shall not ring tonight.'

It was o'er; the bell ceased swaying, and the maiden stepped once more
Firmly on the dark old ladder, where for hundred years before
Human foot had not been planted; but the brave deed she had done
Should be told long ages after – often as the setting sun
Should illume the sky with beauty, aged sires, with heads of white,
Long should tell the little children, 'Curfew did not ring that night.'

O'er the distant hills came Cromwell: Bessie sees him, and her brow,
Full of hope and full of gladness, has no anxious traces now.
At his feet she tells her story, shows her hands all bruised and torn;
And her face so sweet and pleading, yet with sorrow pale and worn,
Touched his heart with sudden pity – lit his eye with misty light;
'Go, your lover lives!' said Cromwell; 'Curfew shall not ring tonight!'

Romance

When I was but thirteen or so
   I went into a golden land,
Chimborazo, Cotopaxi
   Took me by the hand.

My father died, my brother too,
   They passed like fleeting dreams.
I stood where Popocatapetl
   In the sunlight gleams.

I dimly heard the master's voice
   And boys far-off at play,
Chimborazo, Cotopaxi
   Had stolen me away.

I walked in a great golden dream
   To and fro from school –
Shining Popocatapetl
   The dusty streets did rule.

I walked home with a gold dark boy
   And never a word I'd say,
Chimborazo, Cotopaxi
   Had taken my speech away:

I gazed entranced upon his face
   Fairer than any flower –
O shining Popocatapetl
   It was thy magic hour:

The houses, people, traffic seemed
   Thin fading dreams by day,
Chimborazo, Cotopaxi
   They had stolen my soul away!

A Ballad of Semmerwater

Deep asleep, deep asleep,
Deep asleep it lies,
The still lake of Semmerwater
Under the still skies.

And many a fathom, many a fathom,
Many a fathom below,
In a king's tower and a queen's bower
The fishes come and go.

Once there stood by Semmerwater
A mickle town and tall;
King's tower and queen's bower,
And wakeman on the wall.

Came a beggar halt and sore:
'I faint for lack of bread.'
King's tower and queen's bower
Cast him forth unfed.

He knocked at the door of her herdman's cot
The herdman's cot in the dale.
They gave him of their oatcake,
They gave him of their ale.

He has cursed aloud that city proud,
He has cursed it in its pride;
He has cursed it into Semmerwater
Down the brant hillside.
He has cursed it into Semmerwater
There to bide.

King's tower and queen's bower,
And a mickle town and tall;
By glimmer of scale and gleam of fir,
Folk have seen them all.
King's tower and queen's bower,
And weed and reed in the gloom;
And a lost city in Semmerwater,
Deep asleep till Doom.

Barbara Frietchie

Up from the meadows rich with corn,
Clear in the cool September morn,

The clustered spires of Frederick stand
Green-walled by the hills of Maryland.

Round about them orchards sweep,
Apple and peach tree fruited deep,

Fair as the garden of the Lord
To the eyes of the famished rebel horde,

On that pleasant morn of the early fall
When Lee marched over the mountain-wall;

Over the mountains winding down,
Horse and foot, into Frederick town.

Forty flags with their silver stars,
Forty flags with their crimson bars,

Flapped in the morning wind: the sun
Of noon looked down, and saw not one.

Up rose old Barbara Frietchie then,
Bowed with her fourscore years and ten;

Bravest of all in Frederick town,
She took up the flag the men hauled down;

In her attic window the staff she set,
To show that one heart was loyal yet.

Up the street came the rebel tread,
Stonewall Jackson riding ahead.

Under his slouched hat left and right
He glanced; the old flag met his sight.

'Halt!' – the dust-brown ranks stood fast.
'Fire!' – out blazed the rifle-blast.

It shivered the window, pane and sash;
It rent the banner with seam and gash.

Quick, as it fell, from the broken staff
Dame Barbara snatched the silken scarf.

She leaned far out on the window-sill,
And shook it forth with a royal will.

'Shoot, if you must, this old gray head,
But spare your country's flag,' she said.

A shade of sadness, a blush of shame,
Over the face of the leader came;

The nobler nature within him stirred
To life at that woman's deed and word;

'Who touches a hair of yon gray head
Dies like a dog! March on!' he said.

All day long through Frederick street
Sounded the tread of marching feet:

All day long that free flag tost
Over the heads of the rebel host.

Ever its torn folds rose and fell
On the loyal winds that loved it well;

And through the hill-gaps sunset light
Shone over it with a warm good-night.

Barbara Frietchie's work is o'er,
And the Rebel rides on his raids no more.

Honor to her! and let a tear
Fall, for her sake, on Stonewall's bier.

Over Barbara Frietchie's grave,
Flag of Freedom and Union, wave!

Peace and order and beauty draw
Round thy symbol of light and law;

And ever the stars above look down
On thy stars below in Frederick town!

Solitude

Laugh, and the world laughs with you,
  Weep, and you weep alone,
For sad old earth must borrow its mirth,
  But has trouble enough of its own.
Sing, and the hills will answer;
  Sigh, it is lost on the air,
The echoes bound to a joyful sound,
  But shrink from voicing care.

Rejoice, and men will seek you;
  Grieve, and they turn and go.
They want full measure of all your pleasure.
  But they do not need your woe.
Be glad, and your friends are many,
  Be sad, and you lose them all;
There are none to decline your nectared wine,
  But alone you must drink life's gall.

Feast, and your halls are crowded,
  Fast, and the world goes by.
Succeed and give – and it helps you live,
  But no man can help you die;
There is room in the halls of pleasure
  For a large and lordly train,
But one by one we must all file on
  Through the narrow aisles of pain.

The Burial of Sir John Moore After Corunna

Not a drum was heard, not a funeral note,
  As his corse to the rampart we hurried;
Not a soldier discharged his farewell shot
  O'er the grave where our hero we buried.

We buried him darkly at dead of night,
  The sods with our bayonets turning,
By the struggling moonbeam's misty light
  And the lantern dimly burning.

No useless coffin enclosed his breast,
  Not in sheet or in shroud we wound him;
But he lay like a warrior taking his rest
  With his martial cloak around him.

Few and short were the prayers we said,
  And we spoke not a word of sorrow;
But we steadfastly gazed on the face that was dead,
  And we bitterly thought of the morrow.

We thought, as we hollowed his narrow bed
   And smoothed down his lonely pillow,
That the foe and the stranger would tread o'er his head,
   And we far away on the billow!

Lightly they'll talk of the spirit that's gone,
   And o'er his cold ashes upbraid him –
But little he'll reck, if they let him sleep on
   In the grave where a Briton has laid him.

But half of our heavy task was done
   When the clock struck the hour for retiring;
And we heard the distant and random gun
   That the foe was sullenly firing.

Slowly and sadly we laid him down,
   From the field of his fame fresh and gory;
We carved not a line, and we raised not a stone,
   But we left him alone with his glory!

Lucy Gray; or, Solitude

Oft I had heard of Lucy Gray:
And, when I crossed the wild,
I chanced to see at break of day
The solitary child.

No mate, no comrade Lucy knew;
She dwelt on a wide moor,
– The sweetest thing that ever grew
Beside a human door!

You yet may spy the fawn at play,
The hare upon the green;
But the sweet face of Lucy Gray
Will never more be seen.

'To-night will be a stormy night –
You to the town must go;
And take a lantern, Child, to light
Your mother through the snow.'

'That, Father! will I gladly do:
'Tis scarcely afternoon –
The minster-clock has just struck two,
And yonder is the moon!'

At this the Father raised his hook,
And snapped a faggot-band;
He plied his work; – and Lucy took
The lantern in her hand.

Not blither is the mountain roe:
With many a wanton stroke
Her feet disperse the powdery snow,
That rises up like smoke.

The storm came on before its time:
She wandered up and down;
And many a hill did Lucy climb:
But never reached the town.

The wretched parents all that night
Went shouting far and wide;
But there was neither sound nor sight
To serve them for a guide.

At day-break on a hill they stood
They overlooked the moor;
And thence they saw the bridge of wood,
A furlong from their door.

They wept – and, turning homeward, cried,
'In heaven we all shall meet;'
– When in the snow the mother spied
The print of Lucy's feet.

Then downwards from the steep hill's edge
They tracked the footmarks small;
And through the broken hawthorn hedge,
And by the long stone-wall;

And then an open field they crossed:
The marks were still the same;
They tracked them on, nor ever lost;
And to the bridge they came.

They followed from the snowy bank
Those footmarks, one by one,
Into the middle of the plank;
And further there were none!

– Yet some maintain that to this day
She is a living child;
That you may see sweet Lucy Gray
Upon the lonesome wild.

O'er rough and smooth she trips along,
And never looks behind;
And sings a solitary song
That whistles in the wind.

The Lake Isle of Innisfree

I will arise and go now, and go to Innisfree,
And a small cabin build there, of clay and wattles made:
Nine bean-rows will I have there, a hive for the honey-bee,
And live alone in the bee-loud glade.
And I shall have some peace there, for peace comes dropping slow,
Dropping from the veils of the morning to where the cricket sings;
There midnight's all a-glimmer, and noon a purple glow,
And evening full of the linnet's wings.

I will rise and go now, for always night and day
I hear lake water lapping with low sounds by the shore;
While I stand on the roadway, or on the pavements grey,
I hear it in the deep heart's core.

~ *Acknowledgements*

The publishers wish to thank the following for permission to use copyright material:

Martin Armstrong, 'Miss Thompson Goes Shopping', by permission of Peters Fraser & Dunlop Group Ltd on behalf of the author ~ W. H. Auden, 'If I Could Tell You' from *Collected Poems*, by permission of Faber & Faber Ltd ~ Hilaire Belloc, 'Tarantella' from *Complete Verse*, Random House UK, by permission of Peters Fraser & Dunlop Group Ltd on behalf of the estate of the author ~ John Betjeman, 'Diary of a Church Mouse' from *Collected Poems*, by permission of John Murray (Publishers) Ltd ~ Laurence Binyon, an extract from 'The Burning of Leaves', by permission of The Society of Authors on behalf of the estate of the author ~ Charles Causley, 'Timothy Winters' from *The Collected Poems of Charles Causley*, Macmillan, by permission of David Higham Associates on behalf of the author ~ Padraic Colum, 'An Old Woman of the Roads', by permission of Schram & Carew, PC on behalf of the New York County Public Administrator of the estate of the author ~ John Drinkwater, 'The Crowning of Dreaming John of Grafton', by permission of Samuel French Ltd on behalf of the estate of the author ~ Max Ehrmann, 'Desiderata' from *The Desiderata of Hope* by Max Ehrmann, Crown Publishing Co. Copyright © 1927 by Max Ehrmann, by permission of Robert L. Bell ~ Eleanor Farjeon, 'Mrs Malone' from *Silver Sand and Snow*, Michael Joseph, by permission of David Higham Associates on behalf of the estate of the author ~ W. W. Gibson, 'The Ice Cart' from *Collected Poems*, by permission of Macmillan ~ A. E. Housman, for 'Loveliest of trees . . .' from 'A Shropshire Lad, II', by permission of The Society of Authors as the literary representative of the estate of the author ~ Jenny Joseph, 'Warning', by permission of John Johnson Ltd on behalf of the author ~ Rudyard Kipling, 'The Glory of the Garden' from *The Definitive Edition of Rudyard Kipling's Verse*, by permission of A. P. Watt Ltd on behalf of The National Trust for Places

~ *Index of first lines*